AF378347

THE CULTURAL DEVOLUTION

BRITISH ART AND VISUAL CULTURE SINCE 1750
New Readings
General Editor: David Peters Corbett, University of York

This series examines the social and cultural history of
British visual culture, including the interpretation of individual
works of art, and perspectives on reception, consumption and display.

In the same series

The Emergence of the Professional Watercolourist
Contentions and Alliances in the Artistic Domain, 1760–1824
Greg Smith

Difficult Subjects
Working Women and Visual Culture, Britain 1880–1914
Kristina Huneault

Memory and Desire
Painting in Britain and Ireland at the Turn of the Twentieth Century
Kenneth McConkey

Art and its Discontents
The Early Life of Adrian Stokes
Richard Read

The Quattro Cento and *Stones of Rimini*
A Different Conception of the Italian Renaissance
Adrian Stokes

British Artists and the Modernist Landscape
Ysanne Holt

The Cultural Devolution

Art in Britain in the Late Twentieth Century

Neil Mulholland

ASHGATE

Published by
Ashgate Publishing Limited
Gower House
Croft Road
Aldershot
Hants GU11 3HR
England

Ashgate Publishing Company
Suite 420
101 Cherry Street
Burlington, VT 05401-4405 USA

Ashgate website: http://www.ashgate.com

British Library Cataloguing in Publication Data
Mulholland, Neil
The Cultural Devolution: Art in Britain in the Late
Twentieth Century. – (British Art and Visual
Culture since 1750: New Readings)
1. Art, British – 20th century. 2. Art criticism –
Great Britain. 3. Art and state – Great Britain.
I. Title
709.4'1'09048

Library of Congress Cataloging-in-Publication Data
Mulholland, Neil.
The Cultural Devolution: Art in Britain in the
Late Twentieth Century / Neil Mulholland.
     p.   cm. – (British Art and Visual Culture
   since 1750: New Readings)
   Includes bibliographical references.
1. Art, British – 20th century. 2. Art and society –
Great Britain – History – 20th century.
I. Title. II. Series.

N6768 .M85 2002
700'.941'09045–dc21

                              2002026138

ISBN 0 7546 0392 X

Typeset in Palatino by Manton Typesetters, Louth, Lincolnshire, UK and printed and bound in Great Britain by Biddles Ltd, Guildford and King's Lynn

Contents

List of figures

297 × 115 × 115 cm. Photo: The Saatchi Gallery, London; © the artist (photo: Hugo Glendinning)

6.4   Stewart Home, *Art Strike Bed* (1993–), any bed endorsed by the artist. Photo courtesy of Stewart Home and the Institute of Contemporary Art, London, 2001

6.5   Jim Medway, installation at The Annual Programme, Manchester (1999). Image courtesy of Martin Vincent and The Annual Programme; © the artist and The Annual Programme

6.6   Ross Sinclair, *The Irascibles* (1991), photograph. Reproduced courtesy of and © the artist

6.7   Douglas Gordon, *Twenty Four Hour Psycho* (1993), Hayward, first shown in 1993 as video installation at Tramway, Glasgow. Courtesy of the artist, Tramway, Glasgow and the Lisson Gallery, London

6.8   David Shrigley, *Ladder Used for Viewing Atrocity* (1996), drawing. Courtesy of the artist; Book Works, London; and Stephen Friedman Gallery, London

6.9   BALTIC, 2000. Photo: Etienne Clement

6.10   Installation view of 'Protest and Survive', Whitechapel Art Gallery, London, 2000. © the artists; reproduced courtesy of the Whitechapel Art Gallery, London

6.11   Invitation card for 'Heart & Soul', London, 1999. © the artists; courtesy of Liam Gillick

6.12   Joanne Tatham & Tom O'Sullivan, *Blow Your Mind* (1998), mixed media installation, Collective Gallery, Edinburgh. Courtesy Tatham and O'Sullivan; photo: Alan Dimmick

6.13   Installation view of Charisma 'How Long Can We Keep This Up?', altered gallery sign (2000), *It May Be a Year of Thirteen Moons but It's Still the Year of Culture*, Transmission, Glasgow, 2000. Reproduced courtesy of the artists and Transmission, Glasgow

Jacket illustration: Keith Farquhar, *Q: What does Woman Want? A: What the Women Want*, tissue paper and pencil on canvas. Courtesy of Lucy McKenzie and the artist; photo: Alan Dimmick

Acknowledgements

Jane Allan, Conrad Atkinson, Terry Atkinson, Frank Auerbach, BALTIC, Kirsten Berkeley, Michael Bracewell, Andrew Brighton, The British Council, Victor Burgin, Cabinet Gallery, John Calcutt, Steven Campbell, Sadie Coles, Collective Gallery, Richard Cork, Terry Dennet, The Very Reverend Ryan Doolan, Keith Farquhar, James Faure Walker, Lyndsay Fielding, Duggie Fields, Simon Ford, Leigh French, Lucien Freud, Douglas Gordon, Paul Graham, Althea Greenan, Jennifer Higgie, Damien Hirst, David Hockney, Stewart Home, Richard Hooker, Dean Hughes, Alexis Hunter, Dick Jewell, Lucinda Lax, Lisson Gallery, London Records, Marlborough Fine Art, Lucy McKenzie, Ray McKenzie, Jim Medway, Malcolm Miles, Letty Mooring, Alice Mulholland, Craig Mulholland, Ian Mulholland, David Musgrave, National Galleries of Scotland, Tom O'Sullivan, Graham Parker, Clive Philpot, Alex Pollard, Anthony Reynolds, Saatchi Gallery, Jon Savage, Peter Saville, The Scottish Arts Council, David Shepherd, David Shrigley, Ross Sinclair, Matthew Slotover, Polly Staple, Linder Sterling, Tate Gallery, Joanne Tatham, Transmission, Rob Tufnell, Cosey Fanni Tutti, Martin Vincent, John A. Walker, Gary Webb, Jack Wendler, Nell Wendler, White Cube, Whitechapel Gallery, Anthony H. Wilson, Elaine Wilson, Women's Slide Library, Peter York.

Introduction

The Cultural Devolution primarily focuses on the indeterminate relationships between institutions and practical/theoretical shifts in the British artworld from 1975 to the end of 2000. These developments are explored in relation to the momentous political upheaval during the last years of the Callaghan administration following the body blow of the 1976 International Monetary Fund crisis, and the revolutionary ultraconservatism of the Thatcher government of 1979–1990.

Significantly, it was during this period that the British fine art establishment found itself under resolute attack from both the left and right for the first time since the Second World War. The IMF crisis led the Labour government to look at ways of 'devolving' high culture, advocating social democracy by making the Arts Council of Great Britain financially and ideologically accountable to 'the public'. Given that the British artworld was, at this time, highly dependent on public subsidy, the art and criticism of the period can only begin to be understood if read in relation to its cultural and economic revolutions. This is especially pertinent given that both the Labour government and the Conservative opposition were making populist claims, the Conservatives demanding that the Arts Council be dismantled so that people could choose their own art (if they could afford it). Callaghan's drastic economic experiments were accelerated under the first Thatcher administration, which cut public subsidy and encouraged private patronage. I demonstrate the ways in which the ideological change from Keynesian culturalism to monetarist populism generated and financed the new art of the era: from proto-Punk performance to postmodernist object sculpture. In part, then, this forms a necessary pre-history to Charles Saatchi's alleged dominance of the British art scene, charting the pedigree of the Young British Artists (yBas) of the late 1980s and early 1990s. This serves as a corrective to accounts of '90s British art which lack an historical basis for assessing it. It also presents a very different account of postmodernist art practice to that found in texts which draw heavily on American examples, particularly the *October* School's interpretation of postmodernism.

This book points to numerous contradictions emerging within the new art and criticism of the 1970s and '80s. In contrast, proponents of the triumphant critical postmodernism of the '70s and '80s (the Semiotic Art, Structuralist Marxism, Feminisms, Poststructuralism and New Art History which are the subject matter of this book) sought to ensure that its powerful and culturally significant reactionary elements were excluded from the official pre-occupations of art history and theory. It is also my contention that critical postmodernist accounts of British art in the '80s suppressed the importance of forms of cultural practice not associated directly with institutionalized art. Furthermore, I understand that the pursuit of theory led critical postmodernists to deny historical contradiction. This critical amnesia allowed untold opportunism in the British artworld as yBas sought to displace critical postmodernism, characterizing it as an irrelevant and outdated academic pursuit, eternally stuck in its golden era of the 1980s. If the theory and art historiography of recent British art are to escape their present aesthetic relativism, a vast number of practices and debates have to be reconsidered.

In the mid-to-late 1970s practice, theory, criticism and art history interlocked around the question of photography and its relation to the 'crisis' in modernism. Among many others, visual and verbal dialogues were established between Mary Kelly, Victor Burgin, T. J. Clark, Griselda Pollock, Art & Language, John Tagg, *Camerawork*, The Hackney Flashers and Jo Spence. Although I do not want to suggest that participants in these debates constituted a school (united in disagreement), operating under the banner of the 'politics of representation', there was commitment to radically revising the history, theory and practice of modernist art and photography along Marxist/feminist lines, but little agreement on the details. While some chose to historicize the politics of representation (Tagg), others suspended it in theory (Burgin).

Great difficulties arise in writing about this. First, contradiction must be maintained in order that some meanings of the period might be reconstructed. However, writing, especially the writing of history, tends to eliminate contradiction since it is a narrative form. Theoretical strategies designed to disrupt narrative, such as deconstruction, tend towards aestheticism in practice. The theoretical desire to demonstrate the impossibility of reading leads to idealism (that is, every text is seen to contain contradiction). Another problem emerges in that much of the work in the period is not merely art history, criticism, theory and practice, but historiography and metacriticism. This suggests that any accounts of the period will in some way be meta-historiographic but with less opportunity for retrospective contemplation and revision than we might expect if writing about an earlier period. Can an interpretative study of this nature lead to any form of enlightenment, or are we destined to repeat trains of thought that are already prevalent? How can we logically separate our writing and that which it discusses, if both are sustained by similar descriptions?

This presents only part of the problem. The late 1970s was also a period in which the 'avant-garde' came under attack from populists *within* the artworld. Ron Kitaj and David Hockney made similar, populist defences of painting while making very different practical efforts to tackle the problem. The 'crisis critics' (Richard Cork, Andrew Brighton and Peter Fuller) proposed that artists should restore to the artworld a sense of social purpose. Related to Cork's and Brighton's pleas was the work of artists such as Conrad Atkinson and various forms of Muralism, while Fuller set the agenda for the conservative defence of the School of London in the 1980s. These events were all in some way inspired by the *Daily Mirror*'s criticisms of the Tate Gallery for purchasing Carl Andre's *Equivalent VIII*, or 'the Tate bricks'. Although such populism has been seen as a reaction to the politics of representation (Mary Kelly's *Post-Partum Document* was called the 'nappy-show' in 1976), in fact it shared many of its concerns. Both camps were anti-modernist, viewer-orientated, overtly sociological and critical of the Arts Council. Ironically, as the aims and ideals of the left and right became increasingly confused, being involved in artworld historiography became *more* of a case of taking sides. 'Not one of us' conservatism became prevalent in the left and the right, obscuring the art practices that arose in the early 1980s. The most interesting practices of the late 1970s – COUM Transmissions, Punk and the New Wave – ridiculed and exploited this situation. In turn, such work became a major target for reprisals in the 1980s when the old critical camps regrouped and began to do battle over the return to painting.

Current British art is the legacy of this competition for power over the production and interpretation of art. What has been lost are the arguments and contradictions that provided the subject matter of Punk and New Wave. Instead, the rise of the New Art History in the early 1970s allowed strong defences to be built around the politics of representation, or what later came to be called 'critical postmodernism', leaving Punk and the New Wave to cultural studies and sociology. Moreover, in dismissing virtually all New Image painting, critical postmodernists failed to recognize the complex post-Punk ethos found in the work of painters such as Steven Campbell. The contradictions that produced such work were elided in favour of transforming the contingencies of 1970s Marxism and feminisms into Research Assessment Exercise-friendly theory. This situation is complicated further by debates over the rise of the yBas in the 1990s which, in many ways, marked a reaction to and remodelling of the dominant critical paradigms of the '80s. It could be argued that the yBas continued a 'British' preoccupation with issues of class and gender, preoccupations which marked a clear division between American and British postmodern art of the '70s and '80s, and American and British Punk and New Wave. This preoccupation with class and gender over semantics is one which can be traced to the end of the twentieth century, to exhibitions which jangle sabres in the name of a wistful class-war.

It must be noted that the subject matter and methodology of this book are equally problematic. What is 'Britain'? How can we produce narratives of 'British art' if these very terms are constantly under dispute? British sovereignty largely ended in the mid-1970s as its economic self-determinism was taken away by international economic forces beyond its control. 'Britishness' has also been deconstructed by Scottish, Irish, English and Welsh republicans and post-colonial theorists. A reaction against Modernist

Internationalism in art and criticism from this period onwards is largely symbolic, signifying the cultural last gasp of a dying national imaginary in the face of totalizing globalization. Yet 'Britishness' was a tag which refused to be buried, cropping up in the reactionary sentiments of neo-conservatives such as Fuller in the '80s and in the more ironic 'Cool Britannia' rhetoric of the yBas and New Labour in the '90s. In each case a nostalgic notion of Britishness (white, male and worried about the work ethic) in art and (sub)culture was rearticulated for political ends. Britishness has had to survive increasing cultural devolution during this period as the Arts Council was forced to recognize its position in a post-culturalist, post-colonial Britain being pulled towards federalism internally and externally. More recently, devolution and ever-expanding global capitalism have fostered economic and political discrepancies across the ideology of Britishness, discrepancies which look set to put an end to the ideology of a national culture. Artists in Britain have readily adapted to such circumstances, organizing their own exhibitions, running their own spaces and creating their own connections with like-minded international artists.

I have taken 'critics' to include artists, anti-artists, art historians, journalists, art critics, anarchists, neo-conservatives, Punks and affronted members of the public, among others. By approaching 'critical texts' as a mesh of different discourses at work within the ideology of 'British' 'art' and 'society', I have sought to write a non-unified history of the late '70s, '80s and '90s. By focusing chapters around specific groups of artists and critics and making extensive use of quotation, I have sought to allow the rehearsal of accounts of the same events from different points of view. Assumptions about cause and effect, or the relationship between theory, practice and reception, differ in each chapter. The timescale of events and the timescale of their description are not the same. Each chapter has a different explanation of events and of the connections between them. This book, therefore, presents a refracted picture of the period in some of its complexity.

1

The British art crisis

Suddenly it was the morning after, with its splitting headache of unemployment, class and racial friction and economic slump. The Seventies, like the Thirties, saw crisis become a daily condition of life.[1]

Harold Wilson once said, 'A week is a long time in politics.' At the moment, it is every bit as long in the visual arts. We are living through one of those famous upheavals which are the stuff of art history books, but which are much harder to understand when you are caught up in them.[2]

On the one hand, by its very nature experimental or alternative art in whatever medium is bound to cause a public stir; on the other hand, from many artists' points of view, funding through the Arts Council of Great Britain was constantly criticised for its conservatism. It began to seem as though the slices of subsidy-cake available were not enough to feed both the artists who defended 'art for art's sake' and those who were asking 'art for whom?': 'rubbish' and 'waste of public money' seemed to win the day.[3]

In 1972 and 1973 the Tate Gallery acquired three works by the American sculptor Carl Andre: a carved wood-timber structure entitled *Last Ladder* (1956); *144 Magnesium Square* (1966), composed from the said number of metal floor tiles; and *Equivalent VIII* (1969), a sculpture (re)constructed from 120 firebricks (Figure 1.1). They were shown without controversy several times during the next few years, until 15 February 1976 when an article entitled 'The Tate Drops a Costly Brick'[4] written by Colin Simpson appeared in *The Sunday Times* in the Business News section. Here Simpson suggested, without evidence, that Treasury eyebrows had been raised at the use of government funds to acquire for the nation works of art which included a stack of 120 firebricks: 'Modern art is alive and well and some of its practitioners are laughing their way to the bank. Some forms of public expenditure, it seems, are still sacred.'[5] The following day the story created an eruption in the popular press which would make Andre's 'Bricks' the best-known work of contemporary art in Britain. On the whole, these comments were predicated on the supposition that artworks ought to be organized around a subject that may be identified by the viewer. In Andre's sculpture, the opposite was true; there was nothing to reveal: 'People expect art to be mystifying. Mine isn't.'[6] If sculpture traditionally required a spectator

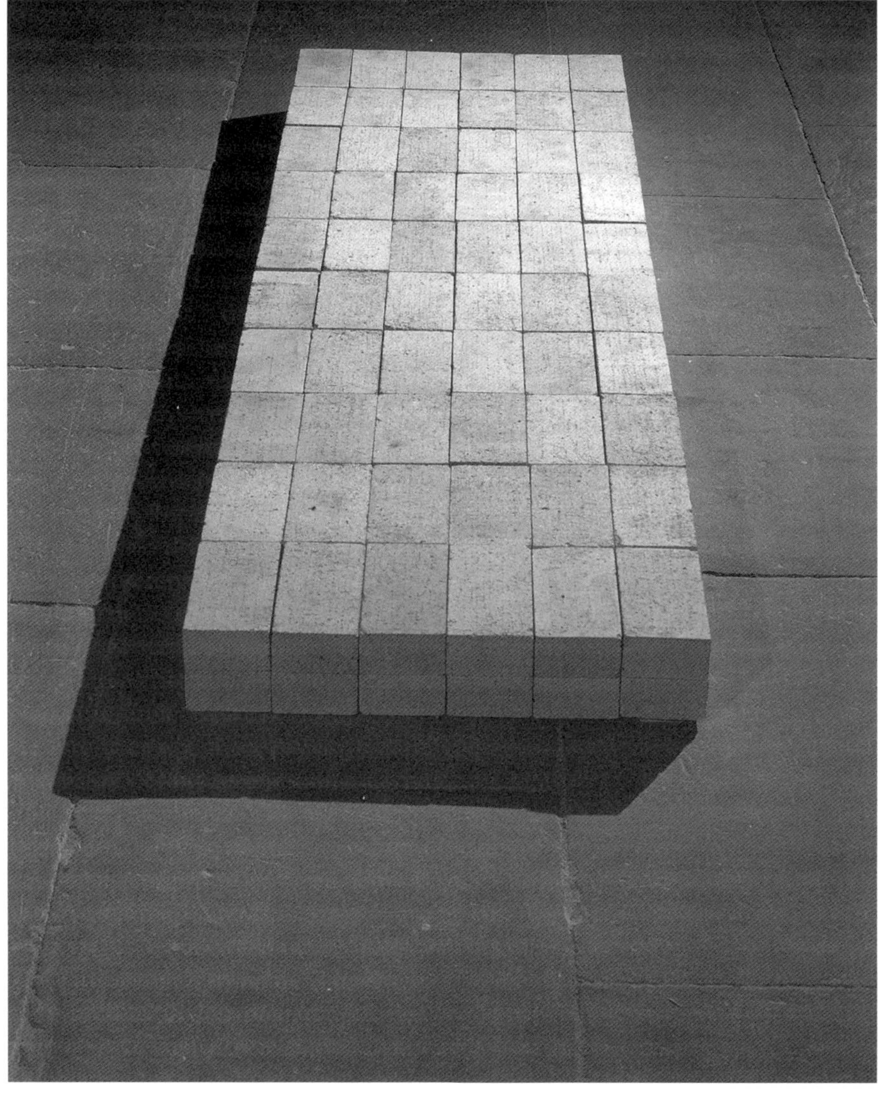

1.1   Carl Andre, Reconstruction of *Equivalent VIII* (1969), 120 firebricks, 12.7 × 68.6 × 229.2 cm, Tate, London, 2001

who was willing to become engaged in an intense viewing activity, Andre again invited the very opposite: his work merely required a glance. This refusal to meet ideological requirements to think in terms of categories – 'completed' works produced in 'definable' materials – generated a certain anxiety in viewers. The expectation of an explanation is that all anxiety will be quelled. No explanation was granted; closure was denied.[7]

The artist and purchasers were thus seen to be guilty of charlatanism and collusion in order to achieve fame and fortune. Following this, a plethora of new offending 'modern' artworks were met with the press's contempt on the grounds that they spoke in the profane language of unsanctioned materials, events or processes. The extent to which the Tate Gallery's relationship with the bricks themselves encouraged this is, however, a matter for concern. The first showing of the *Equivalents Series* was in 1966 at the Tibor de Nagy Gallery in New York. The Tate did not approach Andre until 1972, when it was thought that his work might constitute a 'classic' of Minimalist art fit for Britain's national collection. That the Tate purchased a 1969 're-construction' of *Equivalent VIII*, rather than the installation as a whole, suggests that it viewed the piles of bricks as individual sculptures rather than as inseparable parts of a site-specific whole.[8] The public reaction confirmed that the sculpture did not signify without its *Equivalents*.

The Tate's policy then came under scrutiny in relation to the physical characteristics of the bricks themselves. After initially showing the work, Andre sold the original sandlime bricks back to the manufacturer in order to raise some money, as he was unable to find a buyer:[9]

In Andre's opinion, art is inspired by matter and not by ideas. T.1534 [the Tate's acquisition number for its version of *Equivalent* VIII] in its first (destroyed) form was inspired by one particular brick. Along with other works in the same *Equivalents* series, it was reconstituted three years later using a different brick. It is thus part of the second *Equivalents* series, intimately related to the first but distinct from it. The type of brick employed in T.1534 was no less carefully selected than that employed in its first version, and unless made of this kind of brick, T.1534 does not exist. Thus physically, as well as an idea, it is, in its own right, an important work by Carl Andre.[10]

Hence, when T.1534 was vandalized by being sprayed with blue food colouring on 23 February 1976 by Peter Stowell-Phillips, an amateur painter from London, the firebricks were taken to the Conservation Department rather than simply being replaced, further infuriating taxpaying newspaper readers.[11] This effort to copyright and legitimize Andre's 'sculpture' and therefore gain 'value for the taxpayers' money' backfired.[12] Soon the Tate was reeling under a barrage of trite artworks sent in by members of the public. Significantly, the public echoed the press's utilitarian attack on Andre's sculpture by sending objects which were designed for domestic tasks (vacuum cleaners) or for the workplace (bricks, paper clips, string). The Tate was now forced to consider a plethora of faux-Dada objects and return each of them by post at considerable expense (to the taxpayer).

Significantly, Andre claimed that the only difference between his bricks and ordinary bricks was his 'self-conscious intent to have made it art'.[13] In this, the artist revealed himself to be an exponent of proceduralism, the notion that art is produced according to certain rules and procedures, and defined in relation to social institutions. This may help to explain the generally negative reaction to his work. To some extent, Andre's viewers were required to become connoisseurs given that they needed to be equipped to relate objects being proposed as artworks to an already acknowledged group of art objects by means of a theoretical claim about the nature or value of art.[14] Andre could not simply claim that 'What you see is what you see' since his proceduralism ruled out the 'innocent eye'. As such, it might be argued, contrary to Andre's claims, that his work was not transparent but was, rather, *entirely reliant upon mystification*: 'If there is a radical side to Andre's work, it is not in his vector diagrams which, like so many diagrams drawn by professed artistic radicals, indicate "Art" and "Society" as differing forces and hope for some vague point of divergence in pictorial representation. Rather it must be in exposing the naked economic injustice in Andre's ability to sell metal plates, produced by the appropriation of other men's labour, for a profit margin which verges on the ridiculous ... Art works can only signify social relations as symptoms.'[15] A corollary of Andre's proceduralist view is that anyone with a conception of art, an understanding and application of art theory, might create art, thereby fully democratizing the 'profession' (by eliminating it as an arena of reified competence). This was something that Andre sought to promote, 'analogising his work with shoe-making, talking about being an "art-worker" and professing Marxism'.[16] Yet, as an artisan and mercantile capitalist (selling 'unique' expensive commodities), it was something that he had to prevent, given that it would have destroyed his monopoly in the art market. Likewise, Morphet was more than willing to allow *Andre* to present himself as a 'democratized' artist, thereby ensuring that the Tate would appear to be at the forefront of proceduralist research. However, the Tate was unwilling to allow the full implications of proceduralism to run, since a completely democratized artworld would mean the end of the Tate's ostensible monopoly on deciding what constituted modern art fit for public consumption.[17] Hence, the illusion had to be maintained that the act of conferral of art status is an exercise of authority vested in socially defined roles, in order that the brokers of the artworld could continue to provide explanations of *who* can confer art status on *what* and *when*.

The Tate Bricks scandal primarily served to bolster the power and authority of professional members of the artworld, particularly those who understood its politics and were willing to play power games. The scandal drew attention to a number of Minimalist issues in a novel manner. Indeed, judged against the reception of work by other American Minimalists, Andre's work appears to have been a great success. Ten years earlier in 'Notes on Sculpture: Part II', Robert Morris had written 'Some of the new work has expanded the terms of sculpture by a more emphatic focusing on the very conditions under which certain kinds of objects are seen. The object itself is carefully placed in these new conditions to be but one of the terms.'[18] The idea that Minimalist sculpture might be no more or less important than any other 'term' in a gallery was realized in the debate surrounding Andre's work as the public was tacitly forced to critically interrogate the 'condition of sculpture'. For Andre in 1976, however, the possibility that the bricks debate was of considerably more interest than T.1534 itself was a very real one. Indeed it was precisely this point which was raised by Andre when he produced a homage to his detractors for the first edition of *Art Monthly* (see Figure 1.2).[19] Press claims that this was a case of the emperor's new clothes helped extend the work outside its modernist frame, dragging contemporary British art along for the ride.

In sanctioning 'useless' activities, the Tate Gallery helped to focus the public's attention on then-current debates concerning monetarist economics.

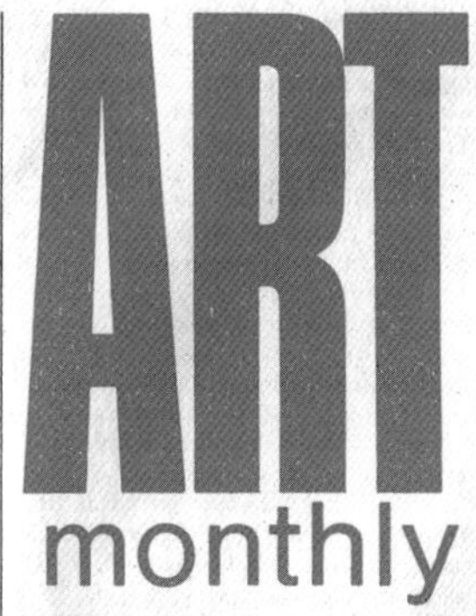

October 1976   40p   No.1

Contents

Editorial note

Starting a magazine in an economic trough may not be the wisest thing to do, but it has the advantage of keeping expectations modest, and Art Monthly has a fairly modest aim. That is, to fill a gap.

There is at present no visual arts magazine which emphasises contemporary British art and its national context. That is the gap this magazine will try to fill, hopefully keeping the price low enough to reach a wide audience, including students, and running its printing schedules tightly enough to allow current news material to be included.

Price obviously conditions the presentation, but not wholly. We have deliberately chosen a cheap paper, fast and cheap printing, and a quality of illustrative reproduction which gives any textual illustrations a symbolic value only, because we feel that a magazine with the aim we have in mind should avoid a glossy look and not be ashamed of its throwaway character.

Having said that, we shall try to provide informed coverage on contemporary art and the issues that surround it — the quality of criticism; standards of art education; aspects of patronage, both public and private; the presentation of 20th-century art; gallery policies; and suchlike.

To do this adequately the magazine will need the co-operation of its readers; it welcomes correspondence, advance information from galleries, propositions for articles, suggestions as to areas or activities which should be written about, and constructive criticism of its own performance.

Why, as an opening shot, run so much material on Scotland? Not only, as it happens, because devolution is bound to alter the structure of the art establishment and will perhaps give artists there more confidence in their surroundings and rather wider access to the world outside, but also because very few people south of the Border ever bother about Scotland's cultural life outside of the Edinburgh Festival, or are ever offered any information about it.

For similar reasons later issues will carry material on Wales and the regions generally, and, in December, a supplement on the visual arts in Eire.

A word about Marcel Broodthaers (see p.3), who died last January, after a long period of ill-health, at the age of 51. He had been given major exhibitions at Oxford's Museum of Modern Art, the Palais des Beaux Arts, Brussels, CNAC in Paris, the National Gallery of Berlin, and the Dusseldorf Kunsthalle. He was also an active film maker; some of his films are to be shows at The Tate later this year.

An insular view of British art magazines

If the principal function of magazines dealing with living art is to facilitate communication within their area of specialization, there seem to be four main overlapping aspects: the communication, first, within the art world itself; second, within specialized sectors of the art world; third, between the art world and the outside world; and fourth, between the art world and other areas of specialization, such as literature, science or music. (By 'art world' I mean professional artists and those representing the secondary support — and/or saprophytic — structures such as the galleries, the media, the academies, etc.)

The first two groups predominate in what follows. The third category is conspicuous by its absence. While *Arts Review* might seem the most likely candidate for the latter, it is so fragmented that it provides little for those with a casual interest to hold on to. *Art & Artists* might be a better bet, even if not on current form. However, at present the role seems to be mostly taken on, with varying degrees of ineffectiveness, by the daily and weekly general press. As for the fourth category, those straddling adjacent specialisms, the few in this country are all specialized small-circulation magazines. To my mind there is a major gap in Britain for a combined forum, for a magazine which would take a serious *equal* interest in progressive art, literature, music, etc., and in the society in which these arts operate.

Content

What might one expect to find in a general art magazine with the art world as its public, or in a spectrum of such magazines? First, current information, one of the principal reasons for their existence. Because of their short gestation period magazines are more up-to-date than books, and often publish information long before it appears in book form. This information may be verbal or visual. While there are dangers in letting reproductions speak for artworks, there is no doubt that illustrations help to make texts about unseen artworks more specific.

A further reason for the existence of any magazine is to carry writing that is not of book length, and which would not otherwise be published. Artists themselves may present work in a conventional literary form, or may be involved through interviews or by contributing visual and/or verbal works designed for the magazine medium.

1.2   Cover of *Art Monthly*, October 1976, No. 1

A key ideological trope of monetarists – such as Alfred Sherman, Director of the Conservative Party's Centre for Policy Studies – was to encourage people to believe that more money was being spent on public services without any noticeable benefits.[20] Although monetarists found their most powerful supporter with the election of Margaret Thatcher as leader of the Conservative Party in 1975, Harold Wilson's Labour government keenly implemented their ideas. In January 1976, the Chancellor Denis Healey, arguing that inflation was an enemy of democratic socialism since it placed a greater burden on the poor, adopted a tough monetary policy against inflation, making a £3.5 billion cut in public expenditure. In February, the month in which Andre's bricks were put back on display, the Treasury decided to devalue sterling, precipitating a crisis. Following the International Monetary Fund crisis in the autumn of 1976, policies now characterized as Thatcherite were fully launched by James Callaghan, who reduced public spending by £2 billion in two years.[21]

It soon became apparent that the monetarist battle against inflation meant abandoning the Keynesian-consensus commitment to full employment and wage increases that had been set out in the Conservative government's 1944 White Paper on employment policy. Given that monetarist policies quickly resulted in huge increases in unemployment, it is hardly surprising to find that art scandals (underlining an area seen to be desperately in need of popular disciplinary cuts) came to play an increasingly important part in tabloid-newspaper politics during 1976. An important part of the success of this tactical manoeuvre by Labour monetarists lay in its capacity to separate any perceived negative effects of monetarist policy (such as rising un-employment) from apparent successes (such as putting a stop to inflation and the public funding of 'rubbish' art). By coincidence, the public artworld provided an ideal scapegoat in relation to this model since it was made up of a quasi-autonomous non-governmental organization (or quango).

Despite the fact that it played *no* role in the purchase of the Tate Bricks (the Tate being funded directly by Whitehall) the Arts Council performed to plan, meeting the confounded objections of the non-artworld with an infuriatingly measured response. Predisposed to feudal patronage, Roy Shaw, head of the Arts Council, sought to defend its role as an 'arts service', much like the National Health Service, voicing his concern to extend what he called 'learning's golden gifts'.[22] In this, Shaw was clearly working within the modernist tradition of the Arts Council of Great Britain (ACGB), an institution greatly indebted to 'culturalism', a tradition that had been fostered by British critics such as Matthew Arnold, T. S. Eliot, F. R. Leavis, Richard Hoggart and Raymond Williams. Distinguishing between the principles of utility and culture, culturalists opted for state education as cultural resistance to materialist civilization. These values were central to the post-war Labour government's consensual vision of a liberal-socialist Britain nurtured by the democratizing of education. The manual industrial economy of low wages and long hours would be replaced with an intellectual post-industrial economy of short hours and high wages. The pre-eminence of democratic socialism appeared to be pre-ordained given that rational *educated* individuals would comprehend that their quality of life was the result of state support for the subsidy of education and the arts.[23]

Having gained secure intellectual employment from state-subsidized opportunity, Shaw was clearly a model 'citizen', a defender of the rationalists' division between the affective and the cognitive and the concomitant high-cultural refusal of the popular pleasures of material civilization: 'All the arts are a source of pleasure but some pleasures are of a higher quality and not simply of greater quantity than others.'[24] For Shaw, as for most democratic socialists, the individual's knowledgeable 'will to form' had to be publicly legitimated and controlled in order to ensure its highly worthwhile social benefits: 'Despite Mrs. Thatcher's belief in "Victorian values", her government's attitude to education and the arts suggests that she is not aware, as William Gladstone was, that "The higher instruments of human cultivation are also the ultimate guarantees of public order".'[25] Such an attitude, it would seem, had become increasingly incompatible with much state-sponsored art in the mid-'70s. Some state-sponsored art nevertheless helped 'guarantee public order' by bestowing justification upon proposed bans on the lower instruments of human depravity.

On 18 October 1976, in the middle of the IMF crisis, COUM Transmission's 'Prostitution' show opened at the Institute of Contemporary Arts (ICA) in London, a retrospective guaranteed to dislocate human cultivation and public order. The infamous exhibition, which featured pornography, used tampons and maggots, most famously met with a furious attack by veteran right-winger Nicholas Fairbairn – a QC and MP for Kinross and West Perthshire – in language somewhat akin to Roy Shaw's defence of 'cultural value': 'It's a sickening outrage, Sadistic, Obscene, Evil … The Arts Council must be scrapped after this … Public money is being wasted here to destroy the morality of our society. These people are the wreckers of civilisation. They want to advance decadence.'[26] That Fairbairn should have mimicked some of the ACGB's rhetoric while criticizing activities it endorsed should come as no surprise. Fairbairn, like the ACGB, clearly endorsed the notion of art as the cultural activity of the educated classes, to which Fairbairn, a quintessential representative of the Tory old guard, felt he belonged. However, even such incongruous work could be defended on Fairbairn's grounds in that it offered the educated modernist cognoscenti a brief, well-charted escapade into anarchism. Indeed, this was precisely the position of the Artistic Director of the ICA: 'The arts in this country are still dominated by middle-class attitudes. This has got to be broken down.'[27]

Confronted with such liberal curatorial practices, it has recently become customary for critical art historians[28] to argue that – unlike the work of modernists such as Manet, Picasso and Pollock – the new art of the mid-1970s did not force a new set of critics to adopt a new way of seeing since it had already been publicly legitimated by educated figures: 'the objections raised by columnists in the popular Press are quite irrelevant, because the critical and curatorial success of [Andre's] work as modern art was achieved quite independently of such reservations (where originally, as in the case of [Manet's] *Olympia*, … a sense of the modern was constructed, to a certain extent, out of the commentaries of the critics)'.[29] While this comprehensive claim might elucidate one possible difference between modernist and postmodernist artworlds, its wider implications remain to be judged against the specific cultural and political contradictions which took place in Britain around the question of cultural and economic paternalism during the 1970s.

Despite (or because of) their leftist sympathies, it might be claimed that many of the late-modernist cognoscenti of the mid-1970s had deliberately effected an exaggeration or reversal of the ACGB's original culturalist aims, using public money with the specific intent of *offending* (as opposed to 'altering') the public sensibility. Such an argument could be countered by the fact that COUM Transmissions had aimed to make art more popular by undermining the mass media's manipulative sensationalism, while seeking more 'direct' forms of experience.[30] Yet the assault on culturalism rapidly became a dead end for the institutionalized avant-garde, who found themselves accepting paternalist support in order to attempt to negate cultural feudalism. One of the few avant-garde groups to recognize this was COUM, who used the opening night of the 'Prostitution' exhibition to finally abandon the artworld, re-launching themselves as an industrial band called Throbbing Gristle.[31]

With the artworld's ideals scarred by the 'failure' of the '70s late avant-garde, art historian T. J. Clark soon proclaimed that when negation becomes too complete the late avant-garde 'erase what they meant to negate, and therefore no negation takes place; they refute their prototypes too effectively and the old dispositions are – sometimes literally – painted out; they "no longer apply"'.[32] Recognizing the vast political potential of this situation were the New Right, who chose to emphasize the manner in which the ACGB's cultural elitism seemed to deliberately denigrate and patronize the consumers of mass culture. The New Right expressed concern that the paternalistic administration of culture was socially divisive; it drove a wedge between culture and society by treating culture as a separate ideal sphere and treating mass-consumer society as witness of a secular decline that was to be deplored from the critical standpoint of elite minority culture. In an ingenious rhetorical ploy, the New Right suggested that the 'culture industry' could be democratized simply by being turned over to the private sector.[33] Such a proposal refuted Thatcher's wish for a return to 'Victorian values'; in breaking down the Victorian distinction between utilitarianism and cultural life, the New Right mimicked Labour's social democratic policies.[34] However, the dissolution of such distinctions was not ultimately to be achieved by an Arnoldian educational emancipation of the labouring classes, but by the triumph of the New Right's 'economic rationalism'. Implicitly endorsing the reduction of objects of cultural preference to the level of commodities for sale in the market place, the New Right's consumption aesthetics owed more to the thematics of powerful business interests and a limited form of calculating possessive individualism than to any inherent theoretical innovation.

In an important sense, then, the New Right was fully exploiting monetarist 'reforms' initiated by the Callaghan government. If proof were needed of the New Right's intention to take advantage of Labour's monetarist epiphany, it need only be stated that the Association for Business Sponsorship of the Arts (ABSA) was launched on 12 February 1976, only three days prior to Colin Simpson's article on the Tate Bricks in *The Sunday Times* Business News.[35]

Behind the New Right's social-democratic cloak lay the more familiar criticism that the Arts Council was overly obsessed with abstract generalities which failed to engage with the vital, responsive, intuitive nature of 'authentic' cultural consumption, and that paternalism restricted the creative (enterprising) nature of the arts. Taking a monetarist line, radical Conservatives argued that the high taxes required for public arts administration left the public with less money to spend on their choice of art. What ought to be of primary importance in cultural life were those aspects which experience had publicly 'endorsed'. What to endorse, therefore, should be decided by 'the public' (taken to mean the sacrosanct rights to/of private assets).[36] Colin Tweedy, ABSA's Director General, wrote that 'the artistic patron is not new – from Maecenas through to the Medicis and Mellon, we have seen that money and art go together. British examples range from the Earl of Southampton to the Tate family to Sir Charles Clore and the Sainsbury family. However, it is to America that we look for development of the business and arts movement which we in Britain now call business sponsorship of the arts.'[37]

Despite the obvious aim of the ABSA to improve the image of big business ('sponsorship of the arts is an important way business can be seen to be helping the community to flourish'),[38] the New Right claimed to be helping browbeaten 'ordinary' people to snip the cultural and economic ties that bound them. This aspect of Thatcherite policy constituted a more totalized assault on the related ideologies of culturalism and Keynesian macroeconomics than the Labour government had envisaged. Monetarist Conservatives understood democracy as a 'market'. As far as the arts were concerned, Labour offered an expensive, yet comprehensive service. What was perhaps unique in the case of the arts, however, was that this service was relatively unpopular with the electoral 'market', who tended to associate state-subsidized culture with wealth and privilege. The Labour government ended citizenship as a viable ideological and economic model with their decision to put the market place at the centre of all political decisions by implementing monetarist 'reforms' in 1976.[39] All that remained was for the New Right to capitalize on Labour's policies by pledging further cuts, designed to obliterate the last cultural vestiges of Keynesianism.[40] Shaw, meanwhile, continued to reject a consumption model of culture – envisaging instead a society peopled not by mere passive consumers but by connoisseurs who interpret, stating that 'uncultivated feelings and the irrationalism which often accompanies them are the stuff on which demagogues and dictators thrive'.[41] In contrast, the Conservatives implicitly rejected the possibility of aesthetic de-familiarization, the claim that art might revitalize our jaded, routine, everyday habits of perception by forcing us to break with those habits and see things radically anew. While the New Right and the ABSA argued that pluralism in arts subsidies would lead to a re-invigorated artworld, the institutionalized avant-garde knew that ending public subsidy would also end their 'critical' activities.

A number of critics, however, went further, arguing that the ACGB, with its powers of assimilation, had effectively neutralized the project of modernity. The possibility that a disintegrating modernism might radically alter or disrupt given structures of meaning was unacceptable since it was by now a comprehensible strategy with its own history. The relationship between an intellectually demanding culture, museums as institutions which legitimized this difficulty and the corresponding industry of explanation was therefore quickly identified by a large number of producers and administrators of British art as *the* matter for practical and critical engagement. For them to remain independent of popular reservations about 'Modern art' was deemed suicidal, as the threat to their secure, intellectual employment now came *from* the (de-regulated) state. Culturalists who feared an end to their privileged status were therefore forced to contrive an impetus for the systematic rejection of modernism in Britain. Significantly, it was during 1976 that the modernist criticism found in the pages of specialist art journals such as *Studio International* started to come under attack from freelance writers troubled by high art's marginality. Unwittingly, the Conservative Party's political aspirations were being aided by these 'crisis critics' who saw their primary task as being to question paternalistic attitudes towards the visual arts.

The seeds of such critiques were sown by Raymond Williams, whose chief concern had been with the culturally disinherited masses. In this, Williams had a great deal in common with the Arts Council's Keynesian origins; indeed he spent three years as a member of the Council. However, Williams eventually came to believe that the possibility of social democracy was severely hampered by the paternalistic nature of Britain's arts administration system. In Britain, debate and control of the arts were entirely the province of whatever body of trustees had power vested in them, and whatever groups of advisers, experts and officials were brought in to assist the regional Arts Councils.[42] Andrew Brighton, one of the most Williamsian of the crisis critics, offered the following explanation of this development:

In Britain there is no tradition of a strong indigenous art world. Unlike the European or American rich the wealthy in this country have not in sufficient numbers affected or accepted the values and evaluations of the traditional intellectuals so far as painting and sculpture are concerned … State patronage has helped to professionalise the British art world by changing the balance of its population; as the amount of state financial support has grown, so too has the number of cultural civil servants.[43]

As Williams pointed out, this quango model served to encourage the depoliticization of art in Britain, an attitude inherent in the ACGB's professional and managerial ethos. The modernist approach to art, in which normative assertions were argued for as if objective, and the Leavisite hierarchical view of culture, which Williams began to reject in the 1950s, were held to be corollaries of this structure. Williams therefore argued that the illusion of an apolitical critical objectivity central to maintaining the 'standards' of British art and International Modernism was in fact merely a method of maintaining the cultural supremacy of the educated classes. Due to the persistence of paternalist attitudes, Williams concluded, culture was being shaped by the dominant classes elevating their culture to *the* culture. In the emerging postmodern climate of the mid-1970s Williams was far from alone in his attack on the modernist consensus.[44] What was peculiarly British about his attack, however, was that it was argued in terms of entrenched class antagonism. In the United States, on the other hand, the turn against modernism had emanated from artists whose primary concern was with examining the semantics of expression.[45] Such semiological art had certainly influenced a number of British Conceptualist-orientated artists practising throughout the 1970s. For a number of influential British art critics, however, the most important issues remained in the writings of Ruskin, Arnold, Leavis and Williams.

Richard Cork spent much of the 1970s 'trying to explain the wrong heap of objects to the wrong bunch of people'.[46] While he was art critic for the London *Evening Standard*, Cork served on the Art Panel of the Arts Council of Great Britain in 1971–1974, a period during which the avant-garde was put under specialized protection. The exhibition 'The New Art' – including the work of Keith Arnatt, Art & Language, Victor Burgin, Hamish Fulton, Gilbert & George, John Hilliard, Richard Long and John Stezaker organized by Anne Seymour at the Hayward in November 1972 – largely inaugurated this policy.[47] In support, for his first 'Critic's Choice' exhibition selected for Arthur Tooth & Sons, London in 1973, Cork included works by Long, Stezaker, Hilliard, Conrad Atkinson, John Latham, David Dye, Gilbert & George, Bob Law, Gerald Newman and the Nice Style Pose Band. The following year he was invited to select 'Beyond Painting and Sculpture', an ACGB touring exhibition which included works by Arnatt, Dye, Newman, Stezaker, Fulton, Burgin, Gilbert & George and David Lamelas: artists united by their 'wish to question the supremacy of a value-system which until recently remained unchallenged except for a few outstanding twentieth century pioneers'.[48] In many ways, however, Cork's selection *was* the prevailing orthodoxy: according to Janet Daley, 'the Panel then has the authority to appoint committees to organise exhibitions and to judge the awards schemes ... Panel members dispense awards one year, only to receive awards in the next from the very people (now serving as panel members) to whom they had presented them.'[49]

This might explain why Cork carried his allegiance to these artists into the editorship of *Studio International* when he replaced Peter Townsend as editor in the summer of 1975, at the suggestion of Michael Spens, an Edinburgh-based architect and the new owner of this international journal of modern art. In March 1976, Cork 'published an issue of *Studio International* on "Art and Social Purpose" and began referring to himself as a "committed socialist"'.[50] Cork was soon at pains to state that the British artworld's lofty modernist ideals were arrogant myths, proposing 'to restore a sense of purpose, to accept that artists cannot afford for a moment longer to operate in a vacuum of specialised discourse without considering their function in wider and more utilitarian terms'.[51] For art critic John Roberts, commentators such as Cork

overtly and idealistically concentrated their criticisms and complaints on the contradictions of distribution. Much of this writing has been framed within liberal debates on distributive rights: that as citizens and consumers all people have a right to the equal share of satisfaction from art. The result has been a general *populist* tone to a large amount of art political writing: that if art can produce the right socially minded themes, accompanied by the right institutional provision, some organic link between art and the working class can be forged.[52]

Roberts' distaste towards Cork's populism is warranted, yet populism was not entirely what Cork had in mind.

Cork seems to have adopted a position similar to the 'cultural materialism' developed by Williams towards the end of the 1970s in the pages of the *New Left Review*, where he had sought to convict Marxists of an *insufficiently* materialist understanding of the superstructures.[53] In *Marxism and Literature*, Williams rejected the concept of 'superstructure' on the grounds that it evaded the question of whether culture is determined or determining.[54] All aspects of the superstructure, he argued, had become so marked by the logic of power that they were now material. Hence it had become impossible to explain culture with reference to the economic base since there was no basis for distinction between the two. A result of this view was that those areas that had hitherto been regarded as superstructures, such as culture, could now be seen to hold immense political power. In the right hands, culture could be as effective a political weapon as economic intervention. Similarly, Cork believed that art could be a harbinger of new class relations rather than a populist representation of the status quo. Art was not social glue; it performed an avant-garde function. The belief that Marxism had hitherto underestimated cultural agency encouraged Cork to use *Studio International* and the *Evening Standard* as platforms to promote 'Art for Social Purpose'. Problems emerged immediately. 'Embedded in the use of this phrase is the negation of the (true) axiom that art always and everywhere has a social and political purpose', wrote art critic Jeffrey Steele.[55] Moreover, there was a risk that 'Art for Social Purpose' might simply be a boost to the bourgeois 'culture industry'.[56] Indeed, as a critical experiment, Cork's interventions caused enormous shockwaves to ripple through the subdued British art press, the impact of his take-over being magnified during 'the national nervous breakdown'.[57]

From the moment he took over *Studio*, Cork virtually banished discussion of painting and sculpture. As a result, in January 1976 painter James Faure Walker and a group of artist friends associated with SPACE studios in Martello Street, Hackney, East London decided to set up *Artscribe*, with a small grant from the Greater London Arts Association.[58] Based around a series of open studio-forums which had taken place in SPACE since 1974, this artist-run typewritten broadsheet was initially intended to make critics redundant, launching itself with an anti-*Studio* editorial endorsing 'the conviction of the primary aesthetic element in human experience'.[59] Faure Walker used *Artscribe* as a platform from which to launch a sustained attack on Cork's critical territory.[60] The semantically based artistic practices being pursued by artists such as Hilliard, Atkinson and the St Martin's Group saw the artist speak 'as a dictator, demanding that artists be put in control of all communications media – artists as an elite corps of super brains, cultural engineers who should take over the TV stations from the mindless technicians that brainwash the masses – the artist as demystifier, the liberator of consciousness ... the artist must not be an artist, so much as an ordinary member of society ... '[61] Faure Walker's attack on Photoconceptualism has much in common with the contemporaneous disdain of Art & Language (A&L) for the movement.[62] Art historian Brandon Taylor, however, claimed that *Artscribe* had a different agenda from A&L given that it was seeking a critical ground for a 'narrowly partisan defence of a highly limited range of painting and sculpture'.[63]

Taylor's characterization of the ill feeling around at the time was subtly different to Faure Walker's. Like Faure Walker, Taylor claimed that *Artscribe* was initially 'dedicated to a modest but interesting programme of disestablishmentarianism. In those early days *Artscribe* was designed to prick the flesh of official indifference to younger artists on the one hand, and to oppose the woolly Marxism of *Studio International* on the other.'[64] Indeed, it is clear that Faure Walker created an eclectic journal rather than a partisan parish magazine: 'My model of a magazine was actually *Transition*. I just wanted a fantastic magazine. I didn't care for all that pseudo-intellectual stuff about art/society, which always rang hollow, which always seemed to come from people who were creatively blocked or mixed up like Peter Fuller.'[65] This model clearly persisted beyond its first year of publication, as was borne out in 1978 when covers featured performance group Theatre of Mistakes as well as William Blake, Duggie Fields, Alexis Hunter and Michael Craig-Martin.

In the first edition of the magazine, Taylor took A&L's journal *Art–Language* to task for being formalist, arguing that analytical conceptualism had a close relationship with the tactics of holistic or non-relational painting: '[In contrast to analytical philosophy] Art & Language were apt to induce nothing much better than a sense of unfocussed inattention, if not of actual somnolence, in which the eye is left to search in and between the lines of text, never discerning more than a vague stringing-together of concepts and barely ever being able to bring into sharp definition what was being positively asserted or denied ... – so the eye is enlisted in a vain search for intelligible detail, just as it did within the open field of an Olitski or a Noland.'[66] Taylor used his newfound editorial power to promote the work of a group of artists, theorists and students meeting at St Martin's School of Art, including Rosetta Brooks, Yve Lomax, Peter Challis, Jonathan Miles, John Stezaker, John A. Walker and Paul Wombell.[67] Using a reproduction of the *Daily Mirror*'s attack on Andre's *Equivalent VIII* to illustrate his point,[68] Taylor argued that high and radical culture were now fused, and as such art could no longer be thought of as a radical force.[69] In recognition of this, Taylor claimed, 'the St. Martin's Group begin from the proposition that the public at large have become reasonably well familiarised with the general range of avant-garde postures and attitudes'.[70] This visual culture discussion group, committed to bringing together staff and students and to fusing theory and practice, did not amount to much in practical terms. According to the collective's *Manifesto* of April

1976, works such as Walker's *Capitalism Works* – a poster of Clint Eastwood as his gun-toting Dirty Harry alter ego – countered 'advertising rhetoric on its own terms, using its own methods, thereby avoiding the avant-garde tag'.[71] This being the case it is difficult to see how the St Martins School of 'Semio-Art' differed from Photoconceptualism generally. Indeed, as Taylor concluded, the 'present attempt by the St. Martin's group to de-structure poster and magazine advertising in a society which neither reveres advertising techniques nor controls their use might therefore ultimately prove to be unstrategical'.[72] From the beginning, then, *Artscribe* was an intoxicating brew. While aping *Studio*'s thematic approach, initial issues were devoted to decidedly anti-*Studio* topics such as 'Sculpture' and 'Painting Now'. However, 'Education', a bumper fourth issue edited by Taylor and supported by a loan from the dealer Leslie Waddington, had much in common with Cork's preoccupations. Cork's critical position was subsequently the topic of one issue.[73] For some this radical phase did not last long: 'conventional trading with art critics by issue seven, marked the diminution of their vanguard stance. (Even the rock column vanished.)'[74] *Studio* and *Art Monthly* writers such as Fuller and Timothy Hyman were recruited as regular contributors, each with yet another set of radically different critical agendas.[75]

Having digested the writings of the New Left, Fuller was able to convince Cork that they were in agreement.[76] Fuller's copy soon became very welcome at *Studio*, wherein he emulated Brighton by claiming that 'capitalism has destroyed the traditions of Fine Art which it created'.[77] In many ways, however, Fuller was experimenting with a more intemperate litigation against the fine art establishment, arguing that the late modernist artworld, now robbed of its social and political functions, had *no* convincing justification for its existence: 'There can be no serious long-term argument for the continuous allocation of Government funds for a middle-class obsessional game; that is why the Tate's present acquisitions policy has been so vigorously opposed from both left and right, and from the entire art world spectrum, from *The Burlington Magazine* to Marxist critics.'[78] Rather than attempting to recombine art and life, Fuller never concluded, as others did, that the artworld should be abandoned for community art or avant-garde provocation. His conservative upbringing told him that a higher order of discriminating authority had to be found, fortuitously safeguarding his future career as Britain's critical helmsman; all that was required was a suitable protégé.

In his introduction to the catalogue of 'The Human Clay' in 1976, Ron Kitaj famously coined the term 'the School of London' for Frank Auerbach, Francis Bacon, Lucien Freud, Howard Hodgkin and Leon Kossoff (see Chapter 4, below). Observing links between their figurative approaches, Kitaj hoped that this group would become a 'potent' force, and would develop into something comparable to Dickens and T. S. Eliot for F. R. Leavis. In 1977, many critics were despondent about the kind of art which Kitaj was promoting. Fuller was typically dismissive, remarking that much of 'The Human Clay' show 'consisted of images by sweaty life-class traditionalists, those who still wear Euston Road spectacles … '.[79] By 1980, however, Fuller was *the* most ardent among an army of critics who held the School of London to be the most accomplished artists in the Western world. The catalysts for this critical shift were numerous. As we have seen, Fuller's close involvement with Brighton and Cork saw him launch comparable attacks on modernism and the controversies concerning the Arts Council's relationship with the political avant-garde. Unlike his fellow crisis critics, however, Fuller was something of a mongrel convert to populism.

During the early 1970s, the influence of John Berger led him to attempt to formulate a series of 'Marxist' theories of expression.[80] Although Fuller claimed to remain congenial towards Marxism during the late '70s, it was during this period that he began to experience a 'growing dissatisfaction with the aridity of much of the current left debate about the visual arts'.[81] Unlike the New Right, Fuller was interested in rescuing the emancipatory view of the aesthetic rather than with finding somewhere to shift the uncomfortable burdens of capitalism.[82] Fuller's peculiarly narrow reading of Herbert Marcuse led him to believe not only that an aesthetic dimension was exempt from the distortions of capitalism, but that it was the potential saviour of oppressed consciousness. In addition, the writings of Williams, Perry Anderson, Edward Thompson and Sebastiano Timpanaro on the subject of Marxism had a particularly strong influence on Fuller's revisionism during this period.[83] Following Timpanaro's *On Materialism* (1975), Fuller came to believe that there were 'enduring representations' in art: 'I have found myself forming the view that a central flaw within classical Marxism was its lack of any adequate conception of man's relationship to nature, indeed of man, not as an ideological entity, but as a specific species, limited by a relatively constant, underlying biological condition, dependent upon natural processes and a natural world he cannot command.'[84] Thoroughly disenchanted with the left's miasmatic touch, Fuller joined with Cork and Brighton in announcing a crisis in art. As early as 1976, however, the career-minded Fuller was sagacious enough to state that his emphasis was distinct from the Marxist principles of the core group of crisis critics; indeed one of his prevalent critical pursuits was soon to become maligning the politicization which critical postmodernist practices and debates had encouraged.[85]

The development of Fuller's ideas in this period has to be seen in the context of changes in the art press. Fuller's views regarding the (public) artworld would never have been heard without the rapid expansion of the (private) art press in Britain that took place in 1976. Controversy sold more art magazines and gave each journal a distinctive marketable agenda. Capitalizing on the hole for expansion in the art press, Fuller launched his bid for critical supremacy in 1978, turning against Cork by writing disparagingly of the '"Social Functionalism" [that] has been infecting the fringes of art institutions, and looks set soon to flood its citadels as well', while declaring his decision to throw himself 'in front of the wheels to impede the bandwagon's progress, rather than to climb on board for what looks like an easy, if at times rather bumpy, ride'.[86] Fuller then went further, manufacturing a crisis in 'crisis criticism':

At a party, not 18 months ago, Cork was said to have surprised his listeners by wondering aloud what would come next after political art. Perhaps, with the change of government this has become *the* urgent question for him. For, in the end, Cork has shown himself to be a critic who floats without direction, according to the ebbing of the mainstream. But even his buoyancy is more like that of a sponge: soaking up an eddying ocean around him, his theory of art is as fluid and vacuous as his theory of politics; he accretes from the writings of others without developing a theoretical spine of his own.[87]

Fuller, of course, had just spent the past two years very publicly 'soaking up' anything which appeared in the *New Left Review*, in highly autobiographical texts. Cork, meanwhile, had at least been busy trying to change the structure of the artworld at a practical level. In 1976, any planned descent into a neo-conservative defence of 'tradition' seemed to hold little promise. *Artscribe* did not remain the sole contender for *Studio*'s mantle for long; Townsend had been working on a project of his own. In October 1976 he launched *Art Monthly* with Jack and Nell Wendler, with the aim of promoting 'British Art in its national context'.[88] The first issue concentrated on the *Equivalent VIII* debate,[89] in addition to the effects that political devolution might have on the Scottish artworld, giving detailed discussion of new arts institutions such as Glasgow's Third Eye Centre, which had opened in May 1975. By circumventing thematics and lengthy academic articles, *Art Monthly* was able to respond quickly to the turmoil of events that would take place in the British artworld during the next few years. The second issue in November was able to devote its front page to a report on COUM's ordeal at the ICA.[90] *Artscribe* quickly followed *Art Monthly*'s lead. Abandoning its initial penchant for theme-based issues, it saw its circulation in the UK, France and the USA spiral beyond *Art Monthly*'s, leading to merger offers from *Artforum* and *Art Monthly*. *Art Monthly*'s provincial (mainly UK) concerns clearly distanced the new journal from the inter-nationalism of *Studio*. The low price, wider distribution, flexibility and frequent and focused coverage of a wide range of issues quickly made both *Artscribe* and *Art Monthly* contenders for *Studio*'s mantle.[91]

As editor of *Studio*, Cork's penchant for thematic, issue-based editions promptly and deliberately provoked the disapproval of its readership, and he stated that dissent from the heart of the art-educational establishment proved that he 'had begun to draw blood'.[92] Following Cork's review of the 1977 Hayward Annual Exhibition in the London *Evening Standard*, a series of heated letters were printed in the *Guardian*, with Peter Blake, leader of the recently formed Brotherhood of Ruralists, leading the critical onslaught.[93] On being asked to devote two columns a month to a round-up of current exhibitions, Cork resigned from the *Evening Standard* in March 1977.[94] The final edition of Cork's *Studio International* followed within a year, consisting simply of an unedited transcript of the conference 'The State of British Art' held at the ICA in London in 1978 – a discussion of his ideas concerning social art organized by Andrew Brighton, Peter Fuller and John Tagg. Having exhausted popular and institutional art journalism, Cork (re)turned his attention to the machinations of contemporary art's primary distribution network: the gallery.

Cork began to encourage a form of art practice analogous to Williams' debate over ethics and aesthetics by organizing a series of gallery exhibitions intended to persuade artists *to forgo* the gallery system in order to make art for 'ordinary people'. Cork's time on the Art Panel of the ACGB, when he had supported the conceptual and performance art he now discredited, had served him well: his 'new' efforts to lend critical and financial support to art for social purpose were given the Council's full backing, thereby ensuring that any dissent was immediately recuperated, assimilated by the establishment. Cork's curatorial stance was widely disseminated in 1978 with 'Art for Whom?', selected by him, at the Serpentine Gallery in London (22 April–14 May). Cork and his artistic associates remained true to Williams' ideals, suggesting that the artworld should be restructured along the lines of a participating democracy.[95] Cork's response to this challenge was to industriously favour artists who produced 'socially responsible' art forms, selecting 'artists whom, with one exception, he had begun to support in articles written during his last year as critic of the *Evening Standard* … The climate of opinion must have changed very rapidly in the four years since he had enjoyed the "unaccustomed luxury" of lavishing public money on just such art as he now decried.'[96]

The social functionalism beloved of Cork was largely prefigured in the practice of Stephen Willats, who began drawing heavily on systems theory in the mid-1960s.[97] During the 1970s, his projects sought to uncover general laws that might allow problems to be solved in any type of system (social, political, scientific).[98] Published in 1976, Willats' *Art and Social Function* contended that, while art was a complex, adaptive, self-regulating system, taking part in this system necessitated preaching to the converted.[99] *Art and Social Function* documented three projects that sought to release art from this predictable social environment, examining art and social intervention in and beyond the gallery: *The West London Social Resource Project* (1972–1973), *The Edinburgh Social Model Construction Project* for the Edinburgh International Festival (August 1974) and *Meta Filter* (1973–), a computerized interactive learning system which allowed gallery visitors to bridge the differences in their perceptions.[100] Documentation of Willats' *From a Coded World* (1975), a project which examined the ways in which the people of the community of Perivale, West London, structured their relationships with each other, was included in Cork's 'Art For Whom?' in 1978.

Willats was committed to reordering the audience's perception of their own behaviour, his role as an artist limited to the function of steersman. Drawing an audience's attention to their conditions of existence, information, control, feedback and communication, Willats emphasized the connectedness of the different components of social systems. The steersman-artist was to simply raise awareness, leaving it up to the participants to change things. While working to abstract concepts common to all systems, he did not seek to divorce observed systems from his observing system. Gallery spaces, in contrast, were characterized by Willats as non-transparent media that do not attempt to include the observer in the description. If, as Willats claimed, social environment is the key determinant of coded meaning, in stepping out of the ritualistic space of the artworld, did he cease to make art? Arthood can be claimed for Willats' practice, given that cybernetics converges practically all disciplines. This interdisciplinary approach became characteristic of postmodernist academia, a fuzzy disdain for specialist knowledge in their preference for dependence on vague, dynamic 'systems'. The effectiveness of this as an intellectual project is questionable, given that the social environment of art continued to exist, largely by embracing such complex systems as new types of socially functional 'art'.

Despite Willats' attempt to abdicate editorial responsibility to the participants in his projects, there remained a sense nonetheless that he *was* in control of the projects documented in *Art and Social Function*, selecting and crudely juxtaposing the images for the 'problems books', fielding the 'problems' and collecting and displaying the responses. The 'life codes' that Willats depicted were predominantly associated with the notion of conformity, the normative drive towards social stability. Lacking agency, people were seen to adopt codes in order to fit into a pre-existing model. Gaining insight into the ritualistic models and contradictions inherent in British cultural politics, Willats believed, would allow people to take control of them. Willats desired to remodel a new objective consensus on social life, a consensus to be brought about by allowing people to vote for their favourite responses to the problems set in his projects. This objectivity was seen to derive from shared agreement about meaning, where information is regarded as an attribute of interaction. However, it could be that ballots simply contributed to the illusion of participation. Willats' model situation sat uncomfortably with an obvious passion for relativism and difference expressed directly by the participants in the West London and Edinburgh projects. Would they ever want to achieve consensus in terms of social coding?[101] What would it mean if they did? Willats' obsession with paperwork may have been partly satirical, an ironic model of a participatory democracy, with its overbearing, alienating and complex bureaucracy. His position remains far from clear. Representationally speaking, Willats seemed to identify with diagrams and models as much as with the people and relationships they express. However, this was tempered by his commitment to the notion that the conceptual games of the artworld and the numerous institutionally based critiques entirely distracted people's attention from the urgent need for action in the 'real' world.

In this, Willats had much in common with Conrad Atkinson, who made use of letters, photography, super 8mm films and video, drawing together 'facts' in the manner of a newspaper reporter and images in the manner of a collagist, to produce a synthesis that would make them understandable to the viewer (see Figure 1.3). Although they could have constituted 'exhibits in a court room prosecution'[102] their information was arranged in such a way as to be entirely overwhelming, to present society as unsustainably divided and decadent, to force viewers into action by nauseating them. In using collage, montage, graphics, photographs and text, Atkinson's work was not scripted by the self-reflexiveness that was beginning to dominate photo-

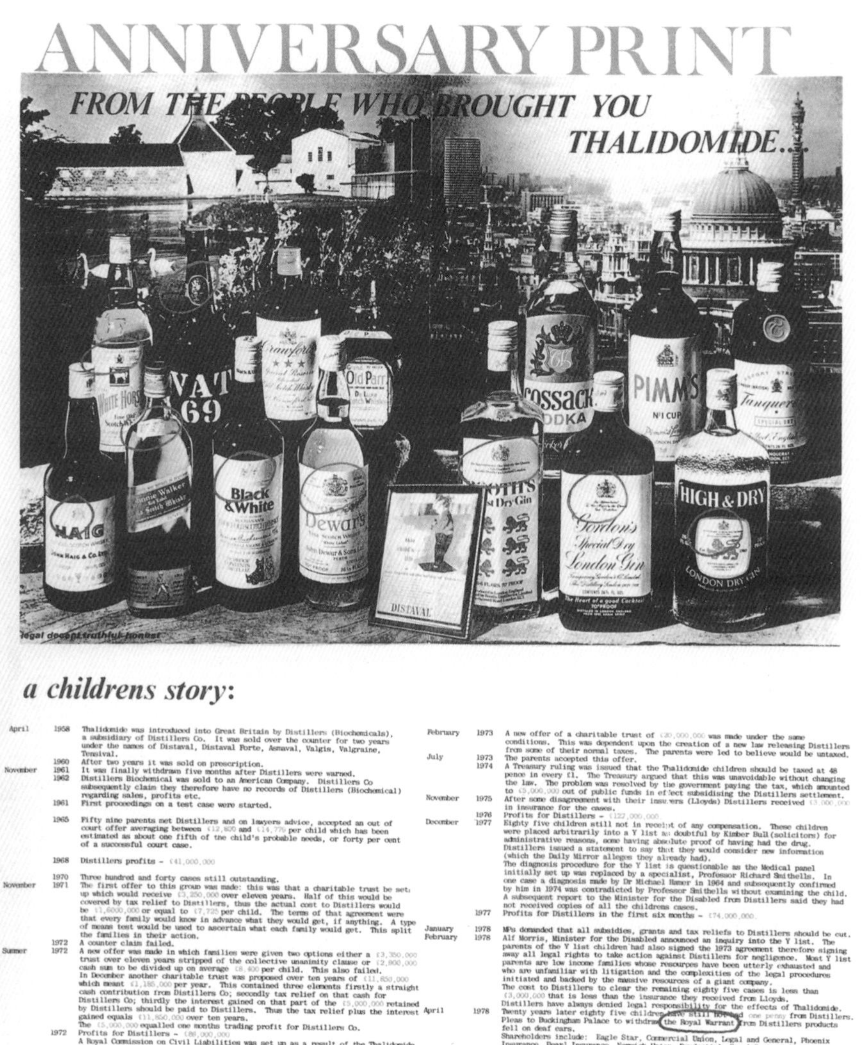

1.3   Conrad Atkinson, *Anniversary Print: From the People Who Brought You Thalidomide, A Children's Story for Her Majesty* (1978), photolithography, silkscreen and watercolours, print presented to the Queen Mother to commemorate the 150th anniversary of University College London in April 1978 (also the 20th anniversary of thalidomide), now in the Arts Council Collection, Hayward Gallery, London

based Conceptualism nor by the cybernetic preoccupations of Willats' practice. On the contrary, Atkinson adopted the stance of a theoretical Luddite: 'It was saying the medium isn't the message, the message is the message.'[103] This was a difficult position to negotiate, as Atkinson was only too aware: 'I've always felt … that it's pointless to imitate the sophisticated polish and the means of capitalism if you are involved in an oppositional culture, so I was not after the smoothness of professional TV.'[104] This speaks of a frustration which was largely warranted. At art college, Atkinson believed he had to toe the line as a figurative painter in order to achieve the social mobility he felt he needed to have his voice heard.[105] Coming from a working-class background, he saw that he had to work through sanctioned channels, reasoning that he could not drop out of a cultural class to which he did not yet belong. Yet Atkinson was involved with the counter-culture. In 1966 he helped to organize the 'Destruction in Art Symposium' at the Dover Street ICA with Gustav Metzger and John Latham, while in 1968 he was involved with debates at the London School of Economics and the student revolt at the Hornsey School of Art against archaic art education, authoritarianism and imperialism. He is remembered also for setting up the Artists' Union, seeking cultural links with the trade union movement while encouraging artists to work in dispute situations.

Following his appointment to a Northern Arts Fellowship towards the end of 1974, Atkinson was invited by the Arts Council of Northern Ireland to present an exhibition relating to life in the province. As a consequence of his belief in the integrity of subject matter, not of formal methods of interpreting a specific object, he concentrated initially on the banner and mural imagery of opposing religious and political groups, spending a couple of months visiting Belfast, Armagh and Londonderry, photographing, collecting information and making videos. Two exhibitions followed: 'A Shade of Green, An Orange Edge', in Belfast in May 1975, and 'Northern Ireland 1968; Mayday 1975', which went on to tour the mainland Midland Group Gallery and Art Net, London, in 1976. Each consisted of hundreds of colour photographs of street murals, sectarian graffiti and propaganda posters. These were supported by a number of documents, newspaper cuttings and public-relations statements by official and unofficial organizations. Although many of the exhibits were set out in groups, visitors were largely left to co-ordinate the untitled documentary photographs and information for themselves.

One of the predicaments of Northern Ireland is that politicians and paramilitary organizations have tended to dictate the dominant cultures. This being the case, the question is 'Did Atkinson help to perpetuate this situation?'[106] It could be argued that Atkinson shared Willats' view of the artist as steersman, that his disinterestedness is not altogether different from the state's indifference. Atkinson neither promoted nor criticized the culture of politics; he merely chose to connote and to encourage active rather than passive engagement with the issues at hand.[107] Atkinson's refusal to accept responsibility for his use of other people's imagery or to precisely define his 'political' position was much maligned,[108] yet it indicates a complexity of attitude: 'The artist is not there to say yes or no, but as a participant in a creative series of debates which may in the end contribute to theory, and whose motivation is not to begin by illustrating a theory.'[109] This suggests that Atkinson, far from being a producer of political culture, wished to defend 'art' as a cultural sphere in which to encourage people to consider once more the basic anomalies.

In other works of this period Atkinson continued to turn his attention towards modern-day political horrors, writing these issues into history via high culture. Major world affairs, such as starvation in the Third World ('Hunger', 1975–1978), were tackled. 'Iron Ore' (1977) documented the case for compensating a number of Cleator Moor iron ore miners while 'Asbestos' (1978) criticized the callousness of multinational industries. For critic Allan Wallach, the central problem of such work revolved around the problematic delineated by Willats' practice and the polemicizing of 'Art for Whom?': 'The gallery space is not a neutral, transparent medium through which one looks at works of art. The space carries an ideological charge of its own ... modern gallery spaces are devoted to a type of ritual activity. That activity might be described as aesthetic contemplation.'[110] The problem of the gallery environment would seem to be related to Atkinson's use of the tableau form, which always risked being the primary interest. Were bourgeois audiences being presented with bodiless victims compatible with their habits of living by proxy, undergoing the catharsis of political edification in a public art gallery?

Against this, Atkinson continued to advocate the theory that dislocating events would give viewers the freedom to recombine and recontextualize information on a critical level. Indeed, would heeding Wallach's demand that political art needed a 'different type of space – a political meeting room, a union hall or meeting room, a workers' club or residence, etc.'[111] not simply have led to preaching to the converted? A more sophisticated critique came from the theory and practice of A&L, for whom the 'repulsive idealisations of *Art for Society*'[112] were 'primitive embarrassments'.[113] A paper was delivered and discussed by Mike Baldwin, Charles Harrison, Philip Pilkington and Mel Ramsden at the Whitechapel Art Gallery in May 1978[114] in which Cork's 'Art for Society' exhibition[115] was criticized for having 'become a rallying point of the self-promotional activities of the soi-disant left (typified by the "socialist artist" Conrad Atkinson's fearless expose of the Queen Mother as an aristocrat)'.[116]

Notwithstanding such misgivings, political art could and did have an impact on the ritual and meaning of the gallery space. Cork's 'Art for Society' ran into a great deal of controversy when a number of artists had their work excluded from the exhibition when it reached Northern Ireland. Over 40 museum attendants intended to take action, and, ironically (given that Atkinson was such a prominent trade unionist), they had official General and Municipal Workers' Union support.[117] The Trustees of the Ulster Museum gave way, stating that it was 'the duty of this institution – a national museum representing all the citizens of Northern Ireland – to be apolitical'.[118] Atkinson's general presentation of the 'troubles', John Pakenham's anti-paramilitary paintings, Hugh Alexander's collage *I Study Violence*, Margaret Harrison's painted collage *Rape* and Alexis Hunter's satirical look at the stereotype of the muscle-bound male were all cited as possible casualties, though they were shown in the end. After the matter had engaged the attention of *The Times* and its letter columns, *Time Out* and other publications, the Ulster Museum and the Arts Council of Northern Ireland decided to present the show in two sections. Atkinson's work in Northern Ireland was, to some extent, successful, the scandal surrounding its censorship drawing people's attention to issues raised.

Atkinson's career was soon to achieve more notoriety. In 1979 Atkinson's *Thalidomide* (see Figure 1.3) series and Tony Rickaby's paintings of right-wing organizations in London were withdrawn from the ACGB's 'Lives: An Exhibition of Artists Whose Work is Based on Other People's Lives' 'because the Council was advised that their display might lead to action in the courts'.[119] Given the nature of its subject matter, it is ironic that the only political controversy generated by the exhibition should have come from the banning of Atkinson and Rickaby's works. Atkinson's *Silver Liberties, a Souvenir of a Wonderful Anniversary Year* (1977) was produced in response to the smokescreen of the 1977 Silver Jubilee celebrations. This opportunity to represent the Arts Council as yet another reactionary Ideological State Apparatus was something of a convenience designed to affirm the continued radicality of Atkinson's work. Naively, the ACGB took the bait, completing Atkinson's web of conspirators by fortuitously implicating itself in the British atrocities of the late 1970s, withdrawing work without consulting the artists or curator. As the correspondence pages of arts magazines were filled once more with letters criticizing the handling of the affair, the issues raised by Atkinson's work were gradually obscured by the 'big question' of the late 1970s: who ran the artworld? Atkinson's analysis of the situation was startlingly prophetic:

the Arts Council of Great Britain is attempting to move into a dominating and decisive role (e.g. 'inescapable editorial responsibility') in the arts in preparation for the eighties. This will, I believe, see a 'tightening up' of the 'problematic' areas of art practice, particularly, though not exclusively, in the visual arts. Thus the work funded will be more populist (towards a visual arts 'Cross-roads'). In my opinion this will affect work in all media but most vulnerable will be documentation, work with socio-political content, performance work and work which is contentious and moves outside the accepted norms.[120]

A move for a more populist approach to art practice was already afoot in the late 1970s in social functionalist circles. On 16 October 1977, two years after it was first conceived, Arthur Latham MP unveiled what was then the largest exterior mural in Britain. Desmond Rochfort's *The Construction Workers* and David Binnington's *Office Work*, painted on adjacent sides of one of the main supporting piers of the Westway Urban Motorway, were intended to offer a 'restorative' to the graffiti-defaced surfaces which form the concrete complex of under- and overpasses adjoining the Harrow Road. As members of the editorial board of *Artery*, a magazine dedicated to providing a platform for class-conscious working-class expression in the arts, Rochfort and Binnington (of the Public Art Workshop) found the critical support of Jeff Sawtell, *Artery*'s editor. Sawtell praised the Workshop in an editorial[121] and in *Artscribe*.[122] In April 1978, Cork welcomed the murals as providing 'an object lesson in how publicly-sighted paintings can gain great resonance from their settings, unlike easel pictures which are so often compromised and abused by the locations in which they are displayed'.[123] Cork evidently wished the new Muralism to retain the critical standpoint of avant-garde art (an avant-garde which he now allegedly deplored). The crucial difference for

Cork, however, lay in the context in which this criticism was received: 'A work of art in a gallery is confined by a whole host of limitations – narrowness of audience, of viewing possibilities, of future as a collector's private possession – which do not affect the street mural at all.'[124] While Cork *may* have been correct to imply that the Muralists differed from gallery artists in taking their inspiration from the public locale in which they worked, the financial history of the paintings reveals that they were just as compromised as gallery works. Hence, in defiance of Cork's declarations, Sarah Kent justly pointed out that murals were just as susceptible to 'establishment pressure'[125] as any other form of art. Yet to Kent the Royal Oak Murals could never have been a paragon of endeavour, since they were 'pathetic'[126] examples of pseudo-Socialist Realism which appeared tawdry in terms of imagination and execution even when compared with the most elementary of gallery modernisms.

In some senses, this was a rather unfair assertion. Neither of the Royal Oak Muralists sought to produce a visual equivalent of music hall. On the one hand, Rochfort's style was particularly influenced by Stanley Spencer, Léger and Giotto; his construction workers 'fall into several groups, with distinct gestures and character which Giotto lends his figures, like a tableau vivant, against the background of cranes and girders'.[127] On the other, Binnington's mural engaged with the ideas of William Morris and Georg Grosz concerning the disaffection of modern workers. Kent missed the obvious fact that both members of the Public Art Workshop were inspired by Mexican Muralists of the 1930s such as David Siqueiros, Diego Rivera and José Orozco.[128] Fuller, recognizing the historical precedents that appeared to escape Kent, was nevertheless as sceptical as ever: 'They are derived primarily in relation to other works of art (especially Siqueiros' hideously rhetorical Stalinist nightmares); they show no discernible attempt to make art through giving plastic expression to lived experience in the world, in its actuality and becoming … The Westway is a montage of art-book clichés, most of which were false when they were first devised, and which are double false when reproduced in west London today.'[129]

Of course, this supports Kent's claim that, in their use of multiple viewpoints, Binnington and Rochfort had simply transplanted Cubo-Futurist space onto a motorway flyover, with less complex results. It was along these lines that Cork's formalist assertions were also flatly rejected in *Artscribe*, in which David Sweet pronounced that 'the new social role tendered to the artist is not that of the artist at all, but that of the illustrator/decorator, and it is against this vision and the spirit of philistinism which pervades it, that the principles of Modernism stand'.[130] Cork had stressed the point that the Royal Oak Murals were not 'simply whimsical decorations brightening up an oppressive locale. [Binnington] chose … to confront a central aspect of city life on its own harsh level. The result, far from applying ornamental bandages to areas that desperately need radical social surgery, appears to grow forcefully out of the dehumanised wasteland so evident all around.'[131]

Did such claims justly hold against all pictorialist mid-'70s mural schemes? The Scottish Arts Council commissioned the Gable End Mural scheme, four murals begun in 1974, as a means of patching up the ends of tenement blocks severed by new motorways running through the heart of Glasgow.[132] Painted in 1975, John Byrne's primitivist 'Patrick' painting, *Boy on Dog Back*, James Torrance's vernacular *Celtic Knot*, Stan Bell's abstract *Hex* in St George Street, George's Cross, and John McColl's colloquial *Klapa II* for Bell Grove, Denniston (see Figure 1.4) (a homage to the enormous horse mussels devoured in the West of Scotland) were blow-ups of gallery art previously exhibited at the Glasgow League of Artists co-operative.[133] The works were an undoubted success in so far as they provided a way of involving communities that had been broken up by the new road schemes, encouraging children to participate in their realization, something that the Public Art Workshop scorned.[134]

According to Cork, its popularity notwithstanding, the Glasgow pilot scheme still failed in that it did not take into account the ways in which Muralism made it possible to stress the integral relationship between the artwork and its surroundings in terms of both structure and subject matter.[135] Certainly, the limits of the picture plane of the east and north walls of the Royal Oak flyover were clearly determining factors of the physical limits of the paintings, while the Glasgow murals were basically enlarged easel pictures. However, Cork's second claim, that Muralism made it possible to stress the integral relationship between the artwork and its surroundings in terms of *subject matter*, is entirely erroneous. Cork described Binnington's east wall mural as a 'remorselessly satirical panorama of office life' designed to be seen by 'people going to their jobs and returning home via Royal Oak tube Station'.[136] At the centre of *Office Work* sits an imperialist eagle with a machine cog for a heart, a symbol of multinational capitalism's technological aggression often used by Siqueiros. Below this, huge thrusting hands grab a number of smaller cogwheels, presumably intended to represent piece-workers, while nearby bosses leer at rows of identical secretaries, executives snore, and automaton-like figures stamp documents. There is little doubt that Binnington intended to foreground issues and problems facing white-collar workers: bureaucracy, sexism, boredom and the illusion of security and material wealth. Despite Rochfort and Binnington's consultation work,[137] the extent to which such issues demanded to be examined on a motorway flyover, and the extent to which their 'audience' examined them, is questionable.[138]

Despite efforts to encourage artists to reject the institutionalized artworld, the major battles over British art at the end of the 1970s continued to be conducted in relation to the official art supported by the Arts Council. Until 1980, Cork continued to champion artists who maintained a critical stance in relation both to conventional notions of popular taste and to the capitalist system as a whole. To critics like Cork, however, Social Art was an experiment. If a work failed to gain public support, it would retain kudos by having been *oppositional*. It is in this sense that the foundations for cultural devolution within the British artworld were tentatively and unwittingly set. At the end of the 1970s, the emphasis of most major practices and debates remained on cultural *revolution*, on replacing the Keynesian centralized arts culture and

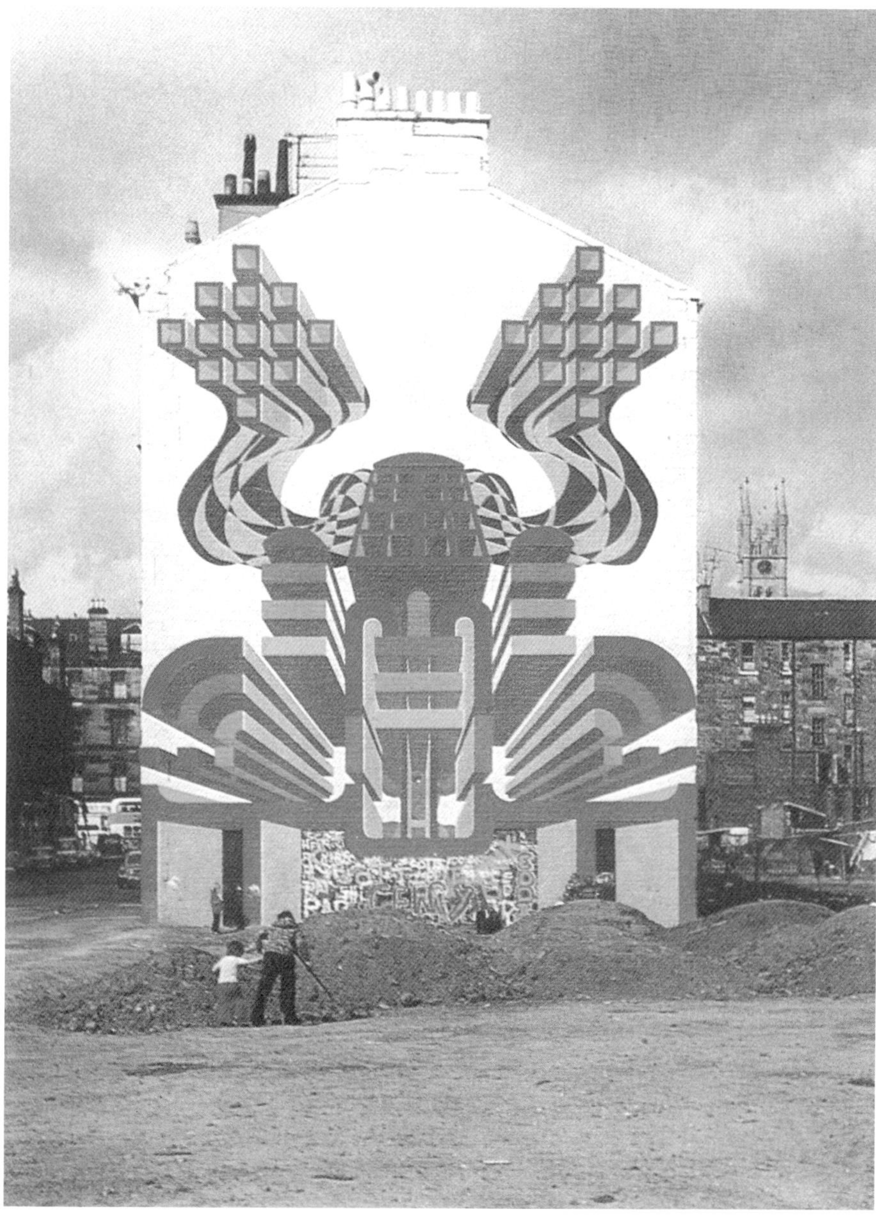

1.4   John McColl, *Klapa II* (1974), wall mural in Glasgow commissioned by the Scottish Arts Council in 1974, dimensions unknown

its humanist, culturalist and modernist supporters in academies and art institutions with new ideological precepts. This was a complex affair. While a substantial body of radical artists and new art historians sought to shake up the cultural cadre from their positions of rank and privilege, freelance critics such as Fuller saw it as their task to continue attacks against *this* newly enfranchised intelligentsia. In this sense, specific arguments against centralizing tendencies which emphasized the cultural and political erosion of peripheral centres only managed to surface by default. Firstly we can see them as resulting from the populist demand for a more audience-centred art. Secondly, devolutionary readings of 'British' art seemed to emerge from nationalist reassessments of the 'British tradition' which followed the alleged collapse of International Modernism. Thirdly, the devolutionary trend can be taken as the product of the increasing radicalization of the academies of art in the UK. Radical academics sought to place great cultural and political emphasis on the margins of British society, seeking to deconstruct ideological constructs such as 'British', 'art' and 'culture'. It is this quest for cultural enfranchisement as the project of a critical postmodernism which I will now turn to.

Radical academicism

From around 1973, a number of erstwhile Conceptualists began to explore captioning and context with regard to photography. For such artists, Cork's support of social functionalism was a clear example of the representation of politics, taking a didactic, propagandistic approach to the problem of art and social purpose. For artists primarily interested in the uses and abuses of language, this was seen as an authoritarian stance. As an alternative, they advocated the politics of representation, analysing and deconstructing the subjective positions from which we experience material reality.

Victor Burgin had grown tired of the modernist perpetual-revolution syndrome that he had been exposed to as a student at the Royal College of Art (from 1962 to 1965) and at Yale (from 1965 to 1967), where he studied under Robert Morris and Donald Judd.[1] In 1971 he began to combine visual images with texts in what he would later term a scripto-visual discourse. During this period, Burgin's growing list of theoretical commitments forced him to avoid, as far as possible, an account of art practice based around single object categories. He later wrote that there was '*another* story of art, a history of *representations* … Art practice was no longer to be defined as an artisanal activity, a process of crafting fine objects within a given medium, it was rather to be seen as a set of operations performed in a *field* of signifying practices, perhaps centred on a medium but certainly not bounded by it.'[2] Like many artists and academics in the 1970s, the rhetorical schema of Marxism, psychoanalysis and poststructuralist linguistics enchanted Burgin, leading him 'to oppose that pervasive and dominating idealism in which "visual art" is held to transcend language and history'.[3] While this had been a primary concern of Burgin's practice throughout the 1960s, the English publication of Louis Althusser's 'Ideology and Ideological State Apparatuses: Notes towards an Investigation' in 1971 sounded a death knell to his overtly Conceptualist aesthetic. For Burgin, 'representation' quickly became *the* site of ideological struggle.

Given the enormous academic growth of Marxist and feminist theory during the 1970s, it is informative to compare Burgin's analytical description of art as a system of 'signifying practices' with T. J. Clark's 'notions of signification'. In Clark's art historical work of the early 1970s, a neo-semiotic form of analysis was part of an attempt to reconstruct a political reading of art history in the wake of poststructuralist theory and the scholarship associated with Althusser, Jacques Lacan and Michel Foucault, scholars who were to be the formative influences on Burgin's theoretical and practical work in the mid-1970s.[4] While there are significant differences among them, such theorists were seen to share similarly pragmatic theories of power and knowledge, each postulating that people are 'written into' subject positions already constructed for them in cultural discourse. For historical materialists such as Clark, the weakness of such a position lay precisely in the absence of a theory of human agency, in the failure to provide a concrete basis for an effective oppositional political movement. This formed the basis for Clark's infamous attack on feminist and deconstructive forms of art history: 'We need *facts* – about patronage, about art dealing, about the status of the artist, the structure of artistic production … '.[5]

By 1973, Marxists such as Clark had come to the conclusion that Barthesian poststructuralists, in reducing meaning to free-play, were particularly guilty of collaborating with the operations of panoptic power. Underlying Clark's historiographic project was the notion that if discourse did mediate reality, as poststructuralists claimed with monotonous frequency, then the meanings it assigned might still be challenged: '[The artwork] may become intelligible only within the context of given and imposed structures of meaning; but in its turn it can alter and at times disrupt those structures.'[6] By concentrating on the complex social construction of individual artists' actions and intentions, Clark's historiographic method powerfully refuted the notion that culture might be hermeticized into a self-sustaining sign system. The emphasis was on the artist as a manipulator rather than as a bearer of signifying practices. In Burgin's post-Althusserian schema, however, the artist was denied access to material struggle: 'The text is not seen as a passage to the presence of the author, but rather as a place of work, a structured space within which the reader deploys what codes he has in order to make sense … The prime locus of meaning is neither "author" nor signifier but the subject.'[7] When used as a guide to reading cultural production, Burgin's definition of art as a 'set of operations performed in a *field of* signifying practices' deprives his work of any communicative capacity since it offers audiences no principle of demarcation: 'In that the substances of their signifiers extensively coincide, an initially *mechanistic* materialism allows the otherwise distinct practices institutionalised as "advertising", "conceptual art" and "photography" to be treated in parallel.'[8]

As Burgin was well aware, *mechanistic* materialism sounds a death knell for the concept of 'fine art' in the West. While his particular materialist model would seem to allow the analysis of our entire visual environment, in practice it in fact denies us even the arbitrary decision of dividing up the endless continuum of 'signifying practices' (culture) into units for analysis. This is not to say that such a definition of art is inaccurate, merely that it was never adequately specific to be put convincingly into practice. For Burgin, however, Clark's considerations missed the urgency of the role that the left could play in the visual arts. Before value judgements might be considered, the left should first examine those codes and practices we know *de facto* to be mass consumed. It is these codes which enshrine the dominating ideology and it is therefore these codes which are to be deconstructed: hence the interest in advertising and photography … in addition to constituting a practical critique of the institutionalised practices of official *Art*, left art practice becomes a matter of practical work in semiotics.[9]

This allowed Burgin to present a critique of advertising imagery, using its own images and conventions to undermine themselves. *Saint Laurent Demands a Whole New Lifestyle* (1976), for example, is a photograph taken by Burgin of an immigrant Asian woman working on an electronics assembly line. The photograph is overlaid with a promotional text for Yves Saint Laurent, which is intended to highlight the gulf between production and consumption in the capitalist world. The ways in which this work relates to the society in which it was produced are made as transparent as possible, the overriding thematic being that, in Western culture, pleasure-images are pervaded by advertising for commodities which require an unrealistic income in order to be possessed. The result is an obscene imbalance of power and profits in favour of a small minority of owners. The captions of such 'lifestyle' advertising, popular in the 1970s, interpellated people to *act*, to pursue and consume lifestyle ideas as though they were religious commandments.[10] Of course, the impression intended by such advertising was of a society in which everyone was free to act in any way they chose, to invent themselves and their culture from scratch. This impression was undermined in the exhibition 'UK '76' as Burgin rendered the exceptional systematic, while exposing the conditions of production hidden behind the mechanisms of advertising's means of seduction.

Shortly after, in 1976, Burgin produced a subvertisement entitled *It's Worth Thinking About … Class Consciousness, Think about It* for the 'Art & Social Purpose' issue of *Studio International*.[11] An enlarged Ben Day dot reproduction of Rodin's *The Thinker* was juxtaposed with a smaller photograph of a bored woman and the following accompanying text, appropriated from Raymond Williams: 'How many supposedly middle-class people really own their houses, or their furniture, or their cars? Most of them are as radically unpropertied as the traditional working class, who are now increasingly involved in the same process of usury.'[12] Burgin's two-page spread directly followed John Stezaker's ten-page image-text piece *The Pursuit*, which reproduced a number of advertisements: 'Freedom', a promotion for Spain showing a figure swimming in an open blue sea; a PanAm advertisement showing a girl walking by a Panamanian beach; and 'You are free', an advertisement for Fiat depicting a car driving through a field. Stezaker accompanied the advertisements with three types of discourse. The first was a conversation concerning freedom between two unnamed individuals. The interviewer asks probing Marxist questions, while the interviewee defends bourgeois notions of freedom and responsibility. The transcription of this interview was subtended on each page by passages quoted from John Stuart Mill and Jeremy Bentham, both advocates of utilitarianism. Finally, the entire project was accompanied by Stezaker's notes, which were 'in analogy with the dialogue of the work or this more specific context concerning the artist's pursuit of social independence (and his social dependence on the concept of the "free floating intellectual") which similarly conceals and perpetuates the economic basis of bourgeois striving, to which the work is addressed'.[13]

As with Burgin's work, then, the emphasis was on deconstructing advertisements as examples of false consciousness, to 'correct society's false picture of its actual conditions of existence'.[14] The ways in which such works related to the intellectual preoccupations of the left, then, were fairly obvious, and not particularly new, visually re-enacting John Berger's juxtapositions of advertising in his *Ways of Seeing*.[15] Both Stezaker's and Burgin's photoworks identified pleasure in the imaginary enjoyment of something as taking place in an imaginary time and place. However, given that such photoworks were, in one sense, forms of dreamscape, they remain striking in their impersonal, factual appearance. For Marxists such as Berger and Althusser, ideology emphasized 'imaginary relationships of individuals', as opposed to structurally and materially defined circumstances. Were Burgin and Stezaker both faithful to the Marxist view that imaginary pleasure is merely a substitute for and an evasion of the life that might really exist during the time of the illusion? Stezaker's notes for *The Pursuit*, lying just outside the border of the 'work', situated the project within such an ideological framework. Its clearly demarcated hierarchies of discourse signalled that there was a 'preferred' way to read the work, and this involved retaining the view that Marxism was a metalanguage, corroborating Althusser's claims that Marxism lay outside ideology. Although 'UK '76' and *Class Consciousness ...* saw Burgin juxtapose (pictorial) 'illusions' with materialist (literary) 'facts', as he had in his earlier work, both works signalled something of a break with his earlier scripto-visual practice.[16] Rather than 'comment on the commentary', as Stezaker continued to do, Burgin left the juxtapositions freer for the viewer to interpret. This was the result of Burgin's reading of Laura Mulvey's psychoanalytic 1975 article in *Screen* 'Visual Pleasure and Narrative Cinema',[17] in which she conceived ideology as a space to which there is neither outside nor end, a space the subject negotiates through transitions that are predominantly unconscious. While an Althusserian hierarchy remained Burgin's practice, there were possibilities that the viewer could read his work in other ways, for example as undermining the epistemological legitimacy of both discourses, capitalist and Marxist.

Despite these apparent differences, Burgin and Stezaker remained similar in that both continued to invalidate the humanist implications of being a *producer* of culture. It was for this reason that they chose simply to intervene in already prevalent modes of iconicity, dismantling codes and recombining them in such a way as to produce different, often contradictory, pictures of the world. Photoconceptualist pictures thus arose through juxtaposition and incongruity rather than through composed humanistic 'inspiration'. While Burgin and Stezaker continued the conceptualist use of non-crafted materials such as reproducible photographs, they did not produce affordable multiples.[18]

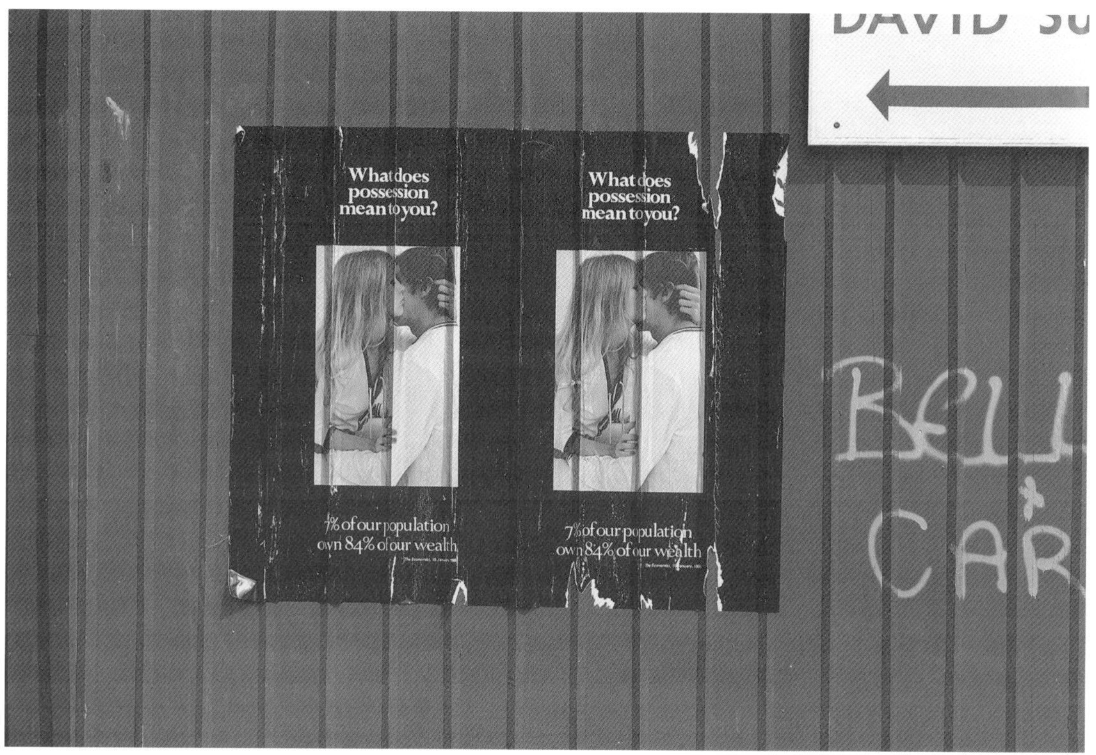

2.1   Victor Burgin, *What Does Possession Mean to You?* (Summer, 1976), edition of 500 photolithographic prints, 124 × 84 cm, posted in the streets in the centre of Newcastle-upon-Tyne

Early in 1976, Burgin was commissioned by the Scottish Arts Council (SAC) to produce a poster to accompany a group exhibition held at Edinburgh's Fruitmarket Gallery.[19] The poster, entitled *Possession*, was seen throughout Scotland, ensuring a wide audience for Burgin's message. However, any suggestion that Burgin might have been looking to circumvent the private gallery network was in turn circumvented that November when the exhibition's selector, the art dealer Robert Self, gave Burgin a solo show at his Covent Garden gallery and commissioned a new edition of the poster without the reference to the Edinburgh exhibition.[20] On 21 June 1976, 500 copies of *What Does Possession Mean to You?* were posted throughout the streets of Newcastle-upon-Tyne (see Figure 2.1). According to Burgin, the new version of *Possession* used a mass-media source to expose its own covert meanings, with the photographs printed on a large scale similar to that of public advertising hoardings. It is significant in this case that Burgin did not take the photograph himself, but rather appropriated a cardinal example of the kind of glamour photography used in advertising at the time. Given that his previous brand of semiotic deconstruction had risked becoming the means for transferring ontological value to a new socially accountable artworld context, Burgin felt it necessary to make it even more difficult to distinguish his work from advertising, thereby collapsing the distinction between art and visual culture, or between object and subject texts. Hence, unlike the exposé of 'UK '76', *Possession* operated like a striptease, promising access to a product (the 'meaning' of the work) but never delivering it. This had much to do with Burgin's realization that semiotics had 'no way of accounting for the emotional force of texts' for 'what are external ("objective") and what are internal ("subjective") areas in a relation of mutual affectivity'.[21] Burgin was slowly moving away from Althusserian Marxism towards theories of sexuality, subjectivity, pleasure and photography as visual fantasy.

On the one hand, Burgin was undoubtedly continuing his practice of pairing photographs of commonplace advertisements with typeset messages that negate or parody their rhetorical language. At the same time, however, his use of a soundbite from *The Economist* on the *Possession* poster made his work purposely complicitous with the fast narrative drive of advertising, with its need to sell quickly and efficiently. This ambiguous device suggests that our desire for critical knowledge is also part of a quest to purchase more and more products, our desire being to uncover and devour meaning. The 'factuality' of the written text is therefore deemed to be as questionable as the image it accompanies. Consequently, *Possession* was most unlike *Saint Laurent Demands a Whole New Lifestyle*, promising to stimulate additional cultural consumption through desire (what *else* does this poster mean?), as opposed to desire through consumption (who/what will Burgin expose next?). This subtle distinction is openly apparent in the photograph chosen by Burgin, which relates to a more direct, base form of consumption than purchasing products from Yves Saint Laurent: sexual desire, the voyeuristic-scopophilic gaze that Mulvey had identified as being crucial to visual pleasure. 'Natural' desires, then, are also commodified; they too are inseparable parts of the network of capitalist relations. Of course, sexuality was a form of desire which advertisers habitually and wantonly exploited in the 1970s, with their routine use of masculine and feminine types. By appropriating such images, *Possession* confirmed that the attraction of such images from the manufacturers' and advertisers' rationalized point of view lay in their efficiency, predictability and calculability. Burgin's subtle manipulation of commercial signifying practices therefore suggested that consumption was not the special lifestyle event it pertained to be. However, while revealing such social structures to be fallacious, Burgin's view of the means of control as a self-supporting sign system meant that he did not leave the viewers with much optimism that something could be done by them to change this system.

This was highlighted in *Studio International* which contained an edited transcript of a series of responses to the posters made by members of the public, and recorded by Radio Newcastle on 7 July.[22] As would later be the case with the Royal Oak Murals, the interviewees were largely unaware of the messages that Burgin was trying to convey, and clearly feared that voicing their opinion would lead to embarrassment. In producing artworks in which 'interlocking levels of practice [i.e. high and low art] coexist in the same text'[23] Burgin had *intended* to cater to the widest interpretative community possible, producing a pluralistic mode of leftist production which would avoid the pitfalls of populism. What he *achieved*, nonetheless, was a practical challenge to the New Art History which appeared to forego its hierarchy of metalanguages. Despite itself, the New Art History attempted to put the critic at a confrontational distance from the world, which would then be seized in order to be known. It therefore indulged in a kind of 'false transcendence'. Although they made no effort to appear omniscient, and insisted on the illusory nature of art, Clark and his followers were being accused of standing outside the frame of events in their texts, thereby invoking metaphysical notions of homogeneous 'reality' as the common referent to serve as an index of truth.[24]

Clearly the meaning of Burgin's work is socially constructed, but the role of his images *as rhetorical statements* about culture necessitates the tacit acknowledgement of their formal hierarchy from their source materials. Were this hierarchical distinction formed purely on an institutional basis, as Burgin implied, viewers of his work would be returned empty-handed to the barren terrain of purposeless fact, and so to a futile inertia which is altogether antithetical to the moral and political imperatives of his work. As Clark put it, 'It may be that we are too eager, now, to point to the illusory quality of that circling back, that closure against the "free play of the signifier". Illusion or not it seems to me the necessary ground on which meanings can be established and maintained: kept in being long enough, and endowed with enough coherence, for the ensuing work of dispersal and contradiction to be seen to matter – to have to matter, in the text, to work against.'[25] Burgin's work in many ways continues the modernist fascination with blocking, refusing and deconstructing 'facile' pleasures such as identification, cleansing our gaze of any involvement or immersion in the subject matter, in the fictional or imaginary world that makes art possible.[26]

Indeed, Burgin's paradigmatic argument that 'left art practice [was] a matter of practical work in semiotics' was fraught with difficulties. For example, the Burginian project of convoking *all* aspects of culture into textual units for analysis *assumed* an analogy between visual representations and verbal language.[27] This is implicit in the concept of 'visual ideology', the view that representations define and construct the 'self'. Although this view is presumably legitimate, it is extremely difficult to clarify the mode in which visual representations interpellate the viewer, for while pictorial systems can have structure, they have no commonly available grammar. As such, it is difficult to explain how specific visual signifiers might determine the meanings of the whole. It is impractical to define visual signifiers since the changing function of representation precludes a universally valid model.[28] There is therefore a sense in which Burgin and his followers were relying on structuralism, not for its claims but for its technicalities which created a powerful illusion of objectivity and critical integrity.[29] It was in this sense that Burginian photography was said to have interpellated *its* audience: '[Burginian photography] takes as its premise the idea that it is up to the intelligentsia to both conceive of and analyse "the world" as "a picture" and then proceed to change "the world" by intervening in *the picture*.'[30] An issue of *Art–Language* published in October 1976 addressed the fashion for such semiological art and 'university art' associated with the American journal *October*. Art & Language (A&L)[31] saw Burgin's form of practice as manifestly illusionary. Burgin *et al.* were in fact *producing* the conditions they intended to resolve, improving a flawed picture of their own conception: 'In his distrust of his own ideological position, the fearless exposer develops (cultural) techniques rather than accept the assertion that production is an historical (complex dialectical) rather than a psychological task. There's no stake in the objective conditions of production since fearful horror-shock is a project for approaching what the fearless Kunstler believes are basic conditions ... his defence or quantification of his "objective conditions".'[32]

By 'exposing' the false forms of exploitation Semio-Artists created a pervasive image, a substitute world full of mythological representations which needed to be unmasked and which would automatically lose their claim to 'nature' once unmasked by reason. Hence, for the Semio-Artists, the world was not only objectified, it was full of myths that only their reason could save us from, revealing a paradise in which everything was finally opaque. Hence, Semio-Art was completely pervaded with this Romantic attitude, transfixed as it was by a culture it imagined it could successfully overmaster simply by unmasking it. Where Romanticism lionized the artist and Formalism focused on the art object, Semio-Art was based on logical operations instead of the intuition of perceptual gestalts. The search for iconic form was abandoned in favour of an aesthetic based on propositional logic. Drawing on parallels between visual representation and language, Semio-Artists turned from the considerations of formal perception to approach culture in self-analytic conceptual terms. A&L's criticism of this approach might appear hypocritical given that they had been instrumental in adapting structural linguistics as a conceptual reference for assessing art's methodological integrity in the late 1960s. A&L were important co-authors of the semiological aesthetics developed from the theories of Saussure, Barthes, Chomsky, Wittgenstein, Lacan and Levi-Strauss (among others). Their realization that the figure of speech had more to do with what could be known than with the subject it addressed prompted a number of artists to abandon philosophical and psychological models for understanding art. The new anti-aesthetic soon created the assumption that art was a form of logic that could be understood through language-based theory. By the early 1970s, a large number of Conceptual artists had become concerned with producing art that established its own context within the dialectics of aesthetic discourse. The intent was to provoke aesthetic sensibilities into the realization of art as a semiotic device.

A&L and Semio-Artists therefore undoubtedly found commonality in their emphasis on language. However, while rejecting what earlier movements took for granted – that art communicates non-discursive ontological knowledge – Semio-Artists failed to explore the possibility of 'knowledge' that logic cannot arrive at, producing what Martin Kemp calls a 'creative tangle of intuitions, perceptions, rationalisations and actions which fire with multi-layered simultaneity ... a bubbling cauldron of cerebral processes'.[33]

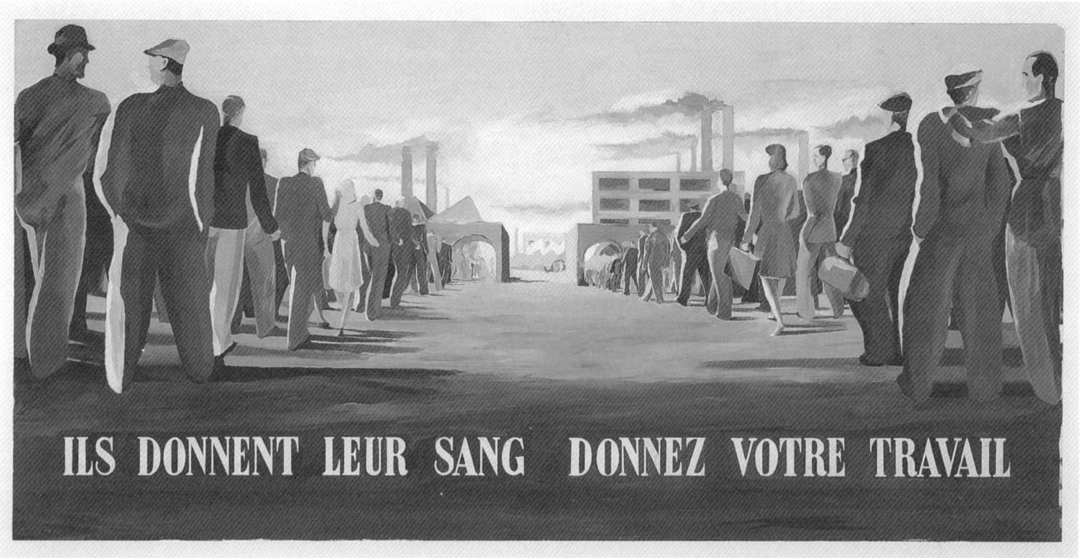

2.2   Art & Language, *Ils Donnent Leur Sang Donnez Votre Travail* (1977), paint on canvas, 127 × 254 cm, also illustration in *Art–Language*, Vol. 3, No. 4 (*Fox 4*)

According to A&L, Semio-Artists had entrenched themselves behind a reductive and arrogant hypothesis that denied the relevance of the numinous art experience. A&L responded appropriately by developing an intentionally ineffective practice: 'Our work has been, is, and will be done, not *made*';[34] 'Ideological material must be located where we can point out its historical modalities. And this means that being wrong (as distinct from fraudulent or stupid, etc.) is an historical product of transitional practice.'[35] Given A&L members Terry Atkinson and Mike Baldwin's debt to Wittgenstein's *Philosophical Investigations*, it could never have been the business of A&L to resolve contradiction, but to make it possible for artists and viewers to get a clear view of the state of affairs *before* the contradiction *might* be resolved.[36] For A&L, as for Clark, art practice needed to tread a thin line between success and failure:

Exhibited works of 1977–78 were travesties of various kinds, designed to dramatise irony and mystification in the conjunction of pictures and texts. These were displays made with dirty hands, forms of 'black propaganda' launched on the supposedly untendentious – 'ideologically proper' – world of semiotic systematicness. The work was resolutely irresponsible.[37]

A good example of such a work was the large oil painting *Ils Donnent Leur Sang Donnez Votre Travail*, painted by Baldwin, Harrison, Pilkington and Ramsden, and exhibited at the Robert Self Gallery, London, December 1977–January 1978. The subject was taken from a poster produced by the Nazis in 1942 to recruit industrial labour in Vichy France. The original poster showed an idealized factory, with workers marching triumphantly through its gates. A soldier lay wounded nearby to remind the workers of the 'cause' for which they were labouring. A&L removed the soldier as a means of making the image ideologically unstable.[38] A connection was thereby suggested between the idealization of the working class expressed in the original and 'those associated with the (possibly left-wing) avant-garde, with art-and-social purpose as its essential services … ' (*Art–Language*, Vol. 4, No. 2, October 1977).[39] In a caustic response to Burgin's *What Does Possession Mean to You?*, a large poster was made of this image and displayed in the Eldon Shopping Centre in Newcastle-upon-Tyne in 1977.

For A&L, further contradictions lay at the heart of Semio-Art in that its advocacy of a conceptual education actually encouraged a mythological split between the semiologist-as-hero and the world. In direct contrast, A&L's *School* project of 1975–1976 advocated breaking up 'the regimentation of structures which makes some people "experts", some "learners" … '.[40] In this, A&L might be said to have aimed to emphasize the directed accumulation of skills and knowledge, including self-knowledge, in everyday life: 'The overall aim of teaching as envisaged within A&L was to enable and assist student self-activity, and positively not to produce acolytes. Students were seen this time not as potential recruits to A&L (though this was not ruled out) but as agents on their own behalf once the grounds for social activity and learning were established.'[41] While A&L's work may have constituted a valid satirical critique of Burgin's practice, it simultaneously mirrored many of its presumed failings.[42] Their aim to redress the 'all-too-automatic virtue of art as "theory"'[43] by reasserting 'the opacity of art'[44] was to be achieved by way of the most philosophically esoteric and linguistically abstruse methods obtainable (for example, 'You can't have fights about vanguard orthodoxy because all decisions have a nomothetic purport subject to the closure of assiduous librarianship').[45] Accompanying a 'refusal to signify' with a 'refusal to clarify'[46] was a deliberately absurd theoretical challenge to Burgin, especially if read as a manneristic or satirical assault on his inflated poststructuralist prose. In another sense, it functioned as part of A&L's long-running analytical critique of the chain of dualisms which rest on the fundamental switch of Aristotle's logic; what remains unclear, however, is how such cryptic rhetorical anomalies could be seen to aid in the dissolution of differences between teachers and students, between the academy and the world. One of Mel Ramsden's more succinct statements of the reasoning behind the 1972 work *Documenta Index* is informative: 'In really old fashioned Situationist International terms, it requests of the consumer to be a participant, in a way. And if the consumer was not a participant, then the work did not mean "bugger off" – it failed to signify.'[47]

A&L were not intentionally philosophical. Despite their intellectual passions, they presented themselves as artists. Their approach was intuitive rather than analytical.[48] For many, however, A&L widened the gap:

Art & Language have no currency whatsoever, if that was ever their intention, outside the artworld; and in fact I don't think it was their intention, I think that they were more like the Surrealists, I think that's how they thought of themselves: as an avant-gardist group making provocations. I think you should see their work mainly as satire, even though I don't think they intended themselves all the time to be satirical.[49]

This effect was magnified by such factors as the high cost of the *Art–Language* journal, A&L's ties to the gallery system and a wilful obscurantism, all of which ensured that the production and reception of their work remained closely tied to a group of cognoscenti conversant with the intricacies of their rhetoric: 'Conceptual art emerged, certainly in our hands, as an attempt to restrict reflective content and didactically to reduce the consumer's contribution, in order to produce an artist's closure on the content of the work.'[50] Indeed, since beginning work as an art historian with the Open University in January 1977, Charles Harrison has sought to guarantee that A&L's practice was *irreversibly* written into the history of art since the late 1960s, much as Clement Greenberg had previously monopolized and institutionalized his favoured brand of formalism.[51]

It was perhaps due to the overwhelming popularity of political 'Semio-Art' in the artworld of the time that A&L's interventions made little institutional impact on it.[52] In the mid-'70s, Burgin and Stezaker were far from alone in their methods and concerns. In 1974 Jo Spence and Terry Dennett established the Photography Workshop in London as an independent education, research, publishing and resource project. Spence and Dennett went on to co-found the journal *Camerawork* in 1976 with the specific purpose of exploring 'The Politics of Photography'.[53] Criticizing the mainstream media's implicitly sexist and racist attitudes, *Camerawork*'s inaugural editorial pointed out the poverty of the current photographic mainstream's obsession with Social Realism and photojournalism: 'Printed in the mass press, or alongside the hi-fi and sherry adverts in the colour supplements, this imagery eventually becomes just another commodity for us to thumb through in our search for distraction or for the "truth".'[54]

Rather than being a platform from which to explore a Burginian 'politics of representation', *Camerawork* initially provided a showcase for photography recording social conditions and inequalities.[55] Formed in 1974, the Hackney Flashers Collective, for example, originally aimed 'to develop an ongoing activity' in the area where they lived and worked, producing 'what has become known as community photography – or rather one of its many varieties'.[56] In keeping with this democratic spirit, community photography exhibitions such as the Hackney Flashers' 'Women and Work in Hackney' (20 September–3 October 1975) were available for hire, allowing photography to function primarily as an educational tool, 'a mirror to show events considered "un-newsworthy" by the national press',[57] such as women working in sweatshops, cleaning and child-minding. In such works the Flashers concentrated on the division of labour within the factory, examining the new problems facing women as industry adjusted to the 1975 Equal Pay Act by cutting wages and reorganizing workforces into double day and evening shifts unsuitable for women. Unlike Burgin's practice, such community photography seemed to form a true alternative to the contaminations of modernist art's distribution network, being exhibited initially at the Hackney Town Hall in conjunction with the women's subcommittee of Hackney Trades Council, before travelling to the Half Moon Theatre. Whether community photography was a critical success remains, nonetheless, debatable.

The propagandist use of *Camerawork* was criticized from the political left and by photographers concerned that the magazine was itself deteriorating into photojournalism,[58] transforming itself into a political vehicle for the latest crisis with themed issues such as 'Lewisham: What are you taking pictures for?'[59] and 'Reporting on Northern Ireland'.[60] It was somewhat ironic that Spence intended *Camerawork* to oppose community photography. A more innovative visual tradition fostered by *Camerawork* was that of montage, the only form which presented a challenge to the Social Realism of the growing number of community photographers. Describing herself as an 'educational photographer', Spence had long been interested in deconstructing standardized forms of representation and subject matter. Although she had exhibited and educated from the late 1960s onwards, working mainly in documentary photography, the establishment of the Photography Workshop and *Camerawork* led to a series of innovative collaborations with social/feminist photographic collectives such as the Faces Group, the Camberwell Beauties and the Hackney Flashers.[61] The first indication of a critical reaction came in July 1978, when the Hackney Flashers' 'Who's Holding the Baby?' opened at Centerprise Community Project in Hackney:

The limitations of documentary photography became apparent with the completion of the *Women and Work in Hackney* exhibition. The photographs assumed a 'window on the world' through the camera and failed to question the notion of reality rooted in appearances. The photographs were positive and promoted self-recognition but could not expose the complex social and economic relationships within which women's subordination is maintained.[62]

Rather than Social Realism, the exhibition consisted of cartoons, collage, montage and graphics with photographs and text. As the Hackney Flashers gradually adopted a Burginian form of montage to 'indicate the contradiction between women's experience and its representation in the media', their work began to appear less politically engaged, in stark contrast to their earlier work which often veered dangerously close to agit-prop. This shift was also met with Burgin's Althusserian approach to the subject, the contention that 'Advertising doesn't present us with a false image of ourselves; it places us in relation to its images in such a way that it thereby defines us.'[63]

This form of practice had grown in popularity over the preceding five years as iconoclasts abandoned text for image. At the Women's Art Conference in 1975, Phil Goodall, a founder member of the Birmingham Women's Art Group, met Kate Walker and the Communist historian and social worker Tricia Davis. Following Goodall's suggestion, this group decided to establish a visual communication exchange by post in order to demonstrate the problems housebound women artists faced, torn between the needs of their families and the needs of their work: 'Each person replies to the art-work she has received by making either an image/object that reflects something of her perspective

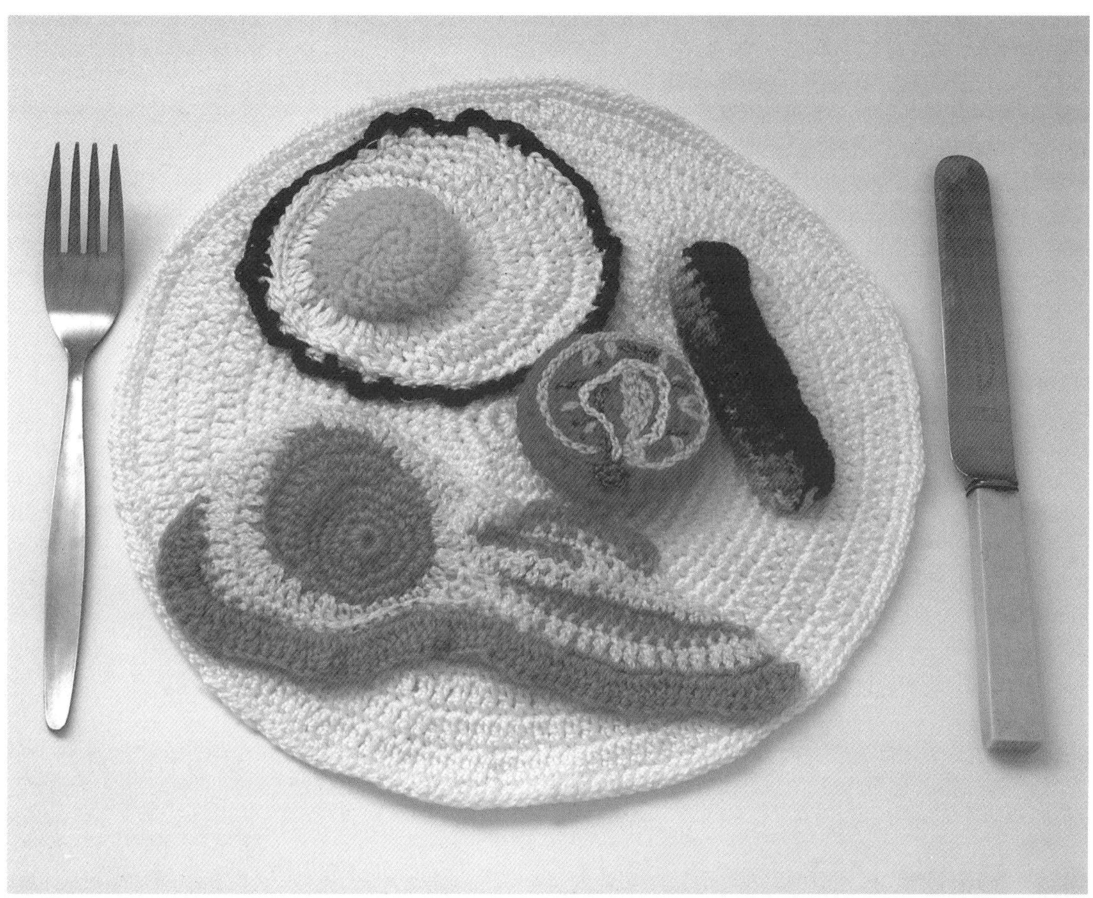

2.3 Su Richardson, *Burnt Breakfast* (1975–1977), knife, fork and wool, dimensions unknown

on life, or that responds directly to the image she has received.'[64] The network, involving women from all over Britain and Germany, became known as Feministo, a pun relating to the male engendering of modern art found in avant-garde manifestos and the generic label given to the practice of *mail* art. The mail art produced by Feministo was based on their experiences as women, artists, mothers and domestic workers. While harbouring the 'home-made' character and small scale of much mail-based activity, a great deal of Feministo's production was allied to the project of Photoconceptualism, utilizing film, photo-collage and installations.[65]

Significantly, Feministo was contaminating the minimal formal concerns of Photoconceptualism by being aligned with what Goodall tacitly referred to as 'female/domestic' skills.[66] (See Figure 2.3.) This helped to incapacitate the hitherto unquestioned Conceptualist penchant for minimal forms and ascetic mediums by associating them with the artisanal and the 'personal', concerns which were anathema to the Conceptualist psyche:

Techniques vary. The show contains a great deal of assemblage, some painting and drawing, but a lot is knitted or sewn. On one level the use of craft validates women's traditional skills and emphasises how much pleasure there is in, for example, crocheting. On another level it draws attention to the way our time and energy has been absorbed by our massive contribution to the domestic economy: knitting, sewing and furnishing the home.[67]

Attempting to negate (male) modernist art's long-standing anti-craft position was mainly intended to weaken its (patriarchal) position of infallibility. The separation between art and craft had functioned to differentiate between the creative activities of the ruling and working classes and, by extension, the 'differences' between men and women.[68] This function was maintained in Photoconceptualism which was decidedly anti-artisanal, adopting an obsessive distaste for fine art values. This, of course, was a style in its own right, cool, detached, super-minimal. Many Feministo artists adopted opposite characteristics, hot, engaged, maximal, emphatically non-technological, non-academic, reflecting their limited resources. It should be stressed that Feministo was not a coherent artists' group; it was more a forum for an exchange of ideas. As such there were many artists associated with the group who mocked the associations between 'femininity' and 'craft', and whose work constituted a continuation of Conceptualism's anti-craft stance. Despite this, Feministo's miscellaneous negations were seen to provide an alternative to patriarchal practices by presenting them with a mirror. The network was maligned by some feminists for confirming women in their role as housewives. There is a strong sense, then, that Feministo's negations partially reinforced various aspects of the status quo; indeed the pre-eminence of Photoconceptualism was necessary for their negation of artworld professionalism to carry meaning.

Like most community photographers, Feministo avoided the conventional distribution network, choosing to show their mailings under the title 'A Portrait of the Artist as Housewife' in Manchester during May 1976, and at Birmingham Central Library, Liverpool and Coventry during 1977. This much, however, suggested that Feministo were unacquainted with the debates that had taken place within the mail-art network. Despite being placed in unusual contexts, the public display of mail art was frowned upon by many mail artists since it encouraged their work to be publicly judged. This trapped Feministo and the Women's Art Group, who were attempting to escape from the artworld, while simultaneously seeking its sympathy for their cause. Feministo exhibitions failed to convey the fact that mail art can *never* remain stable enough to seek public recognition of its existence. Since mail art is created by self-declaration there can be no possibilities for the fixing of rules, no public display and no judgement.

By the time Feministo were given a retrospective at the ICA in London in 1978, diluted and hackneyed concepts of 'image-text' had come to dictate not only the form of individual artists' productions but the concerns of curators and art historians up and down the country. For example, in 1977, the Arts Council invited Rudi Fuchs, Director of the Van Abbemuseum in Eindhoven, to purchase work by British artists. Introducing his travelling exhibition of artists using word and image, Fuchs wrote, 'A photograph of a tree on a hill or a text describing a hill, are somehow closer to the real thing they portray than in a painting – provided the photograph and the text are unadorned and plainly descriptive. The straight photograph and the plain text are almost reality itself.'[69] That Fuchs (and many others) had entirely missed the point of the new photography was a point sorely noted in 1979 when the controversial 'Three Perspectives on Photography: Recent British Photography' exhibition opened at the Hayward Gallery in London.[70] The exhibition, organized by Paul Hill, Angela Kelly and John Tagg, was intended to be the first biennial British photography show. Tagg discredited the

idea – so dear to the left-liberal documentary tradition – that the 'truth' of photographic representation lies somewhere 'outside' or 'behind' the image and the institutional framework within which it is represented. The struggle around 'truth' or the status of 'truth' in photography is not a struggle for something 'outside' or a struggle 'in favour' of 'truth'. It is a battle around the rules, operative in our society, according to which 'true' and 'false' representations are separated. It is a battle around those institutions which are privileged in our society to produce and transmit 'true' discourse.[71]

'Three Perspectives' was certainly one of the most representative and concise presentations of critical photography. It was, however, to be the last: 'The Arts Council officials took one look at the show and the complaints from conservatives and, mysteriously, it never happened again.'[72]

By 1979, Semio-Art had provided the institutional framework for a plethora of cultural analysts as consistent in their aims and methods as the rationalized society to which they were opposed, steering many potential artists towards a 'post-productivist' position.[73] Tagg's contribution to 'Three Perspectives' represented something of a climax of Burgin's 'linguistic turn', a complete shift from the contingencies of practice towards the manipulative and managerial discourse of 'Theory', Burgin's distaste for 'fine art photography' precipitating something of a crisis in art history and in the practice of conceptually based photography. While taking account of the determinations exerted by the means of representation upon that which is represented, Tagg's anti-art historiography led him to adopt a mode of analysis which caused him to ascribe importance to photographs as political and historical texts. This was the logical conclusion of Conceptualist photography. Art was not to become 'practical work in semiotics'. On the contrary, 'art' was to be abandoned entirely by the liberal left, to be replaced predominately by academic.

In such a climate, the emphasis quickly shifted from production to questions of *consumption*: 'What I wanted to suggest was that, if there is a crucial connection between debates about realism and an emergent social order, perhaps the significant debates on realism, on representations claiming the status of the real, do not go on in art criticism alone. Perhaps there are other levels of debate and negotiation which might take you to very different spaces … ', said Tagg.[74] In 1979, Tagg's 'different spaces' were connecting with those explored by cultural analysts such as Hall and Paddy Whannel at the Centre for Contemporary Cultural Studies (cccs) in Birmingham during the early 1970s. Towards the end of the decade, Tagg, like Hall, had moved from an essentially left-Leavisite culturalism toward the news of Althusser and Antonio Gramsci. Like Burgin, Tagg sought to bring these two approaches into critical dialogue with structuralism and poststructuralism, producing a complex and often conflictual historical-critical practice. As with Burgin, depoliticized structuralism imbued Tagg with an indifference to the cultural value of his object, bringing similar philosophical problems.

Tagg was making fast inroads into academia, being appointed as a research fellow at the School of Communication at the Central Polytechnic of London in 1977, and teaching at University College London, Goldsmiths, St Martin's, Leeds University and the University of California at Los Angeles. At the end of the 1970s, Middlesex Polytechnic (incorporating the erstwhile bastion of British student radicalism, Hornsey Art School) set up a number of courses designed to intervene in the discourses dominating the interpretation and validation of 'visual culture'. Following the cataclysmic events of recent years in the British artworld, a need was felt among many radical academics to examine visual culture more broadly. Ways had to be found to accommodate and analyse visual subcultures in the manner in which critical theory had investigated high art. For participants in these academic manoeuvres, this was due to a radical, post-Arnoldian anthropological conception of culture as a 'whole way of life'. For participants in the subcultural trends of 1975–1980, however, this was entirely due to the need of cultural commissars to find new arenas to police following their 'discovery' of the cultural and ethical bankruptcy of high art. The hierarchy operating within Middlesex Poly is clear from Jon Bird's description of the MAs in 'Design History' and 'Visual Culture' as being launched specifically as a means of resisting 'tendencies to reproduce the descriptive and historiographical categories of bourgeois art history'.[75] In 1979, art historians at Middlesex established BLOCK, 'a manifestation of the cultural logic of a newly self-conscious, historicised and politicised initiative in the cultural realm; and simultaneous allergic reaction to the idealism of art history'.[76] Again, while this would seem benevolent, it arose in part from a need to keep up with culture as it is lived, not by living it but by regulating it from a distance.

The idea that Middlesex was embarking upon a brave new path is questionable. As an academic institution, Middlesex Polytechnic was building upon successes elsewhere, most notably at the Birmingham CCCS. Yet, as a department of art history, Middlesex's most obvious predecessor was the Department of Fine Art in Leeds, which had been at the nexus of Tim Clark's call to arms, establishing its MA in 'The Social History of Art' in 1975. By 1980, Clarkian forms of 'New Art History' seemed academically established.[77] The Association of Art Historians' journal *Art History* tapped into the discussion at this moment by adding sections on 'new' historiographical methods. *The Oxford Art Journal*, established in 1978, also began to print an increasing number of materialist articles devoted to the circulation and reception of nineteenth-century art, akin to Clark's project. Confirmation of a shift in the world of academic art history came with the launch of the Open University's 'Modern Art: Practices and Debates' in 1983, a course which remains dominated by the new methodologies of the 1970s and '80s.[78]

The protagonists in these professed *coups d'état* have written much about this methodological revolution.[79] While the numerous internecine dogfights of these punitively radical intellectual manoeuvres were posited on a highly complex, 'fairly loosely formulated set of intentions and objectives',[80] 'there was a sense of a ragged consensuality and coherence of purpose'.[81] Hence, without suggesting that any single line of enquiry had pre-eminence, the fact that BLOCK 'asked John Berger for a contribution demonstrates an intention of furthering the tradition of Marxist art history from Frederick Antal, Arnold Hauser, Max Raphael, Meyer Shapiro, through to the publication in the mid-1970s of the work of T. J. Clark and Nicos Hadjinicolaou'.[82] The first edition of BLOCK included an 'Editorial' emphasizing the need to 'address the problem of the social, economic and ideological dimensions of the arts in societies past and present'[83] and an article by Terry Atkinson discussing the relevance of materialism to the analysis of visual culture.[84] Also included were illustrations of Tony Rickaby's *Fascades* (1979), the controversial paintings which had been banned from the Arts Council's 'Lives' exhibition that year.[85] This much was intended to signify BLOCK's politicized commitment to the present state of the art. Jon Bird's 'The Politics of Representation',[86] printed the following year, however, was more obviously in tune with the interests of artists and critics inspired by *Screen* theory.[87] As such, this marked something of a break not only with the Clarkian tradition of social art history but with the explicitly sociological concerns of the journals *Studio International*, *Camerawork* and *Ten 8*.

Of course, art historians such as Clark and Harrison were known for their work on established art historical categories (Courbet, Manet, Greenbergian Modernism). This remained a bone of contention for *Screen*-influenced critics who thought that such interests undermined the anthropological models of culture found in the writings of Barthes and Hall.[88] The accusation here was that social art history was merely a way of polishing up the tarnished institutions of art, perhaps ensuring not business-as-usual, but that doing business with the hegemony of the traditional canon continued nonetheless. Hence, a second theoretical input into art historical discourse had taken 'analysis away from the realist paradigm towards questioning the epistemological strategies and values of representation itself'.[89]

At the end of the '70s, educational photographers such as Jo Spence had also become particularly drawn to such post-culturalist criticism.[90] Spence, nonetheless, was dissatisfied with purely analytical approaches: 'I'm interested in striking at the same kind of mythologies as the post-structuralists are but coming at it from a completely different direction. So the virgin, the bride, the Madonna, Hollywood, are target areas of mine, but ultimately my work is concerned with saying to people "you can do this unpicking for yourself" ... '[91] In 1979 she enrolled on a BA in Film and Photographic Arts degree at the School of Communication, Central London Polytechnic, where, in addition to being taught by Burgin, she was able to attend Mary Kelly's lectures in women's studies. This gave her a thorough theoretical groundwork from which to proceed with her own talks on 'Images of Women'. Also while at the CLP, Spence teamed up with Charlotte Pembrey, Jane Munro and Ann

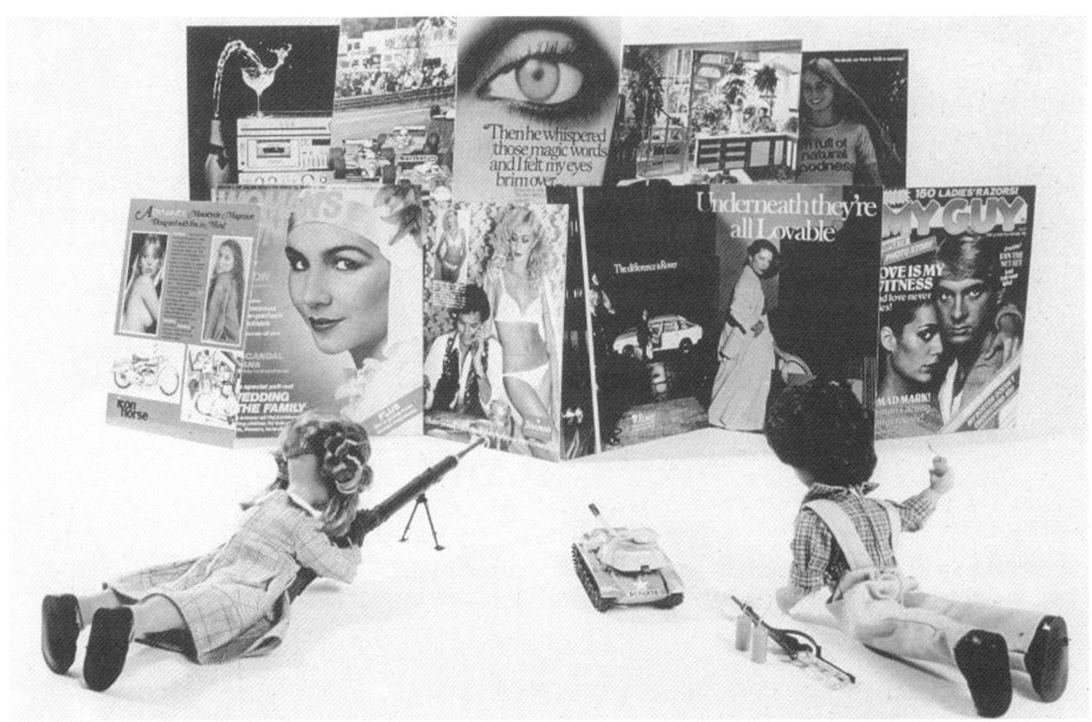

2.4 The Pollysnappers Collective, *Family, Fantasy, Photography* (1979), photographic panel

Kennedy to form the Polysnappers Collective (see Figure 2.4). As Wells wrote, 'The work involves what they term *didactic montage*, employing a variety of representational devices to engage in ways in which "the family" has become viewed as the "natural" way to live. In this work dolls are used in place of people to *avoid the problems of exploiting people as "camera fodder"*.'[92] The use of dummies was one instance in the effort to reform radical photographic practice, avoiding the dangers of appropriating the media's forms.

In 1979, Spence co-edited the inaugural edition of the Photography Workshop's new journal *Politics / Photography*,[93] following her expulsion from *Camerawork* by the Half Moon Gallery for being 'too theoretical'.[94] From this point, Spence's theoretical commitments shifted subtly away from the theoretical reductionism that had afflicted Photoconceptualism since its inception: 'I want to broaden the question of decoding images of woman to take into account not just the symbolic sexual lack, but also the exploitation of woman's labour power under capitalism.'[95] Spence was not regressing to a 'vulgar materialism' but to a particularizing insistence that 'stereotypes are not *universal* but differ markedly depending on the context in which they are used, and the type of (class) audience'.[96] This quest for a particularizing form of practice found expression in Spence's major solo project *Beyond the Family Album* (1978–1979). Spence's reworked *Family Album* revealed the relationship between the poses, images and identities promoted by the 'Kodak regime' and the mass media and those we believe we discover in our snapshots. However, they did not always explicitly question the concept of authenticity by playing out a kind of drama in which the clean lines between the posed and the authentic, the object and the subject, culture and self are deconstructed, opting for a more ideologically ambiguous autobiographical approach.

It was during this period that Spence began to develop the form of practice that she would later term 'photo-therapy', work in which the photographic image is used to explore personal history and conflicts.[97] Spence's work now centred more firmly on 'herself' as a source of explorations, in part obscuring the fact that the phototherapy programme was supposed to be a transferable skill. The problem for Spence, perhaps, was that most critics tended to focus on *her* work rather than on her programme, reading her practice as though it were traditional gallery art. Hence, for Liz Wells, Spence's exploration of the politics of health care tipped 'the emphasis of her work too far into the personal'.[98] In *Property of Jo Spence*, photographed by Terry Dennett, frank depictions of her mutilated body encouraged viewers to merge with the subject matter of her photography (her unsuccessful attempt to reclaim control of her body from both cancer and medics), to understand her work empathetically rather than as a text designed to enlist the spectator in a writerly process of discovery. Although this runs counter to her analytical approach – which was directed against the notion of the artist as bearer of culture – it remains clear that to identify or merge with Spence's photography would be to negate her 'right to refuse', to see 'her' only as *subject*, as opposed to 'the *mediator* as well as the *subject* of the information'.[99] To continue to treat Spence's images analytically as espoused by Wells, however, is equally problematic. Adopting an anti-authorial mode of analysis, viewers might choose to counterpoise the encoding of Spence's body against the presumed sensuousness of the conventional female nude. The problem with this mode of cognition is that it forces us to embrace as granted a pure/impure dichotomy. By confronting one half of the dichotomy with its opposite, Spence contested closure on the fixed category of the 'feminine' body, but did so within the dualistic tradition of Western metaphysics.

An equally concerted attempt to renegotiate the critical bind of radical academicism was made by ex-A&L member Terry Atkinson. After his departure from A&L in 1974 over a dispute concerning *Index 01* (1972), he produced a series of photo-text pieces entitled *The Bridging Works*, combining historical images with satirical renditions of the *Index*. Given that by 1973 the Conceptualist photograph was becoming integrated into the regime of avant-garde Conceptual art, or university art, as A&L called it,[100] Atkinson consequently took up painting harsh, non-aestheticized images, making visible corrections that rendered the surfaces of his paintings tactile, the joins between the different blocks clearly visible. As Tagg pointed out, such deconstructive strategies were by no means significant manoeuvres in the de-aestheticization of post-war painting.[101] If Atkinson was merely attempting to transgress against painterly decorum (if such a thing still existed in the 1970s), he failed to sufficiently differentiate his practice *formally* from that of his peers. What was and remains of interest is the way in which Atkinson's works engaged with then-current debates, and the way in which he provided some groundwork for the critical reception of some performance-based painting of the mid-1980s. Atkinson was instrumental amongst erstwhile British Conceptual artists in closing the gap between the critical possibilities of painting and photography in the wake of the debates around representation, thereby reinvigorating second-order approaches to practice. For Atkinson, the fact that painting required a greater degree of manipulation than text or photography-based forms of practice served only to emphasize these issues.

On a formal level, then, Atkinson's paintings re-introduced an important yet almost entirely neglected component into the image-text work: that the image itself may be manipulated, in ways other than by its framing, by its context or by being accompanied by a written text. Atkinson ensured that these formal concerns were allied to his concern with the ways in which human experience is threatened or governed by the uncontrolled development of technology and the media. In recognition of this, Atkinson's paintings displayed a resistance of their subject matter to an inner ordering, postulating the absence of a foundation for composition, or what has subsequently been inappropriately packaged as 'awkward authenticity'. Atkinson's activity was registered through recognition that it was a form of 'acting':

Terry Actor – suggesting the artist as an agent of (some kind of) action, no matter how historically puny when placed in relation to such an event as Hiroshima. Also perhaps suggesting the artist as a theatrical and decorative figure unable to do very much about the relations of power themselves but highly visible on the ideological stage of those relations.[102]

In addition, there was a Brechtian form of recognition that literalist attempts to 'rectify' ideology failed to produce the required 'alienation effect', since to 'critically think and interrogate the notions of critical thinking and interrogative procedure' cannot be simply achieved as 'this would undermine the structural and a priori assumptions which are critical thinking and interrogative procedure'.[103] Profitable political and cultural 'intervention' had therefore to be considered as a form of theatre.

Painting *had* to be the chosen medium for Atkinson's project precisely because it was so unfashionable with the critical cognoscenti. (See Figure 2.5.) This tactical decision proved to be particularly fortuitous given that the critical and financial foundations were then being laid for 'A New Spirit in Painting', to increasingly hysterical howls of derision from critical postmodernists.[104] Atkinson did not paint with 'vigorous imagination'; indeed his paintings were almost entirely devoid of lyricism, executed in a blunt and crude manner that made Philip Guston's or Julian Schnabel's Bad Painting look virtuoso. Despite apparent visual similarities, Atkinson's practice was promoted by himself and by others by emphasizing that he was resolutely opposed to the kinds of Neo-Expressionist work emerging from mainland Europe and the States in the run-up to the art boom of the early '80s:

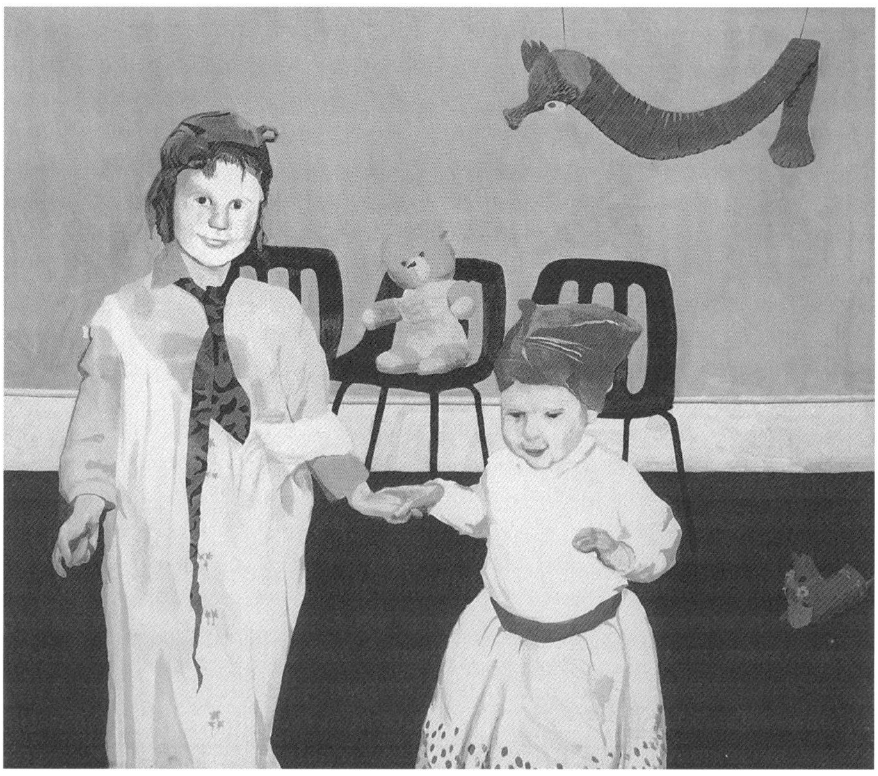

2.5   Terry Atkinson, *Dragon, Teddy, Plastic Chairs, Horse and Ruby and Amber Dressed Up – All Against Cruise, ss20s and All the Poisoning Apparatus* (1983), acrylic on canvas, 120 × 135 cm

The strong moral streak persists among British artists, preventing a wholehearted flight into fantasy – so the imaginative excesses of New Image have not flowered here … survival as a marginalized group – is too insistent to allow the 'suspension of disbelief' necessary to embrace the state of grace conjured up the New Image in rag-bag of reference and symbols. Chia, Clemente, Cucchi, Fetting, Paladino *et al.* offer a vision of universalised 'man', a free spirit at one with wild nature, governed by his passions, fears and animalism.[105]

On a formal level, Atkinson's paintings certainly differed radically from the provocatively frivolous paintings of the Italian Trans-Avantgardia,[106] since they were determinably neglected in a way which made them almost completely undesirable. There was a knowing dilettantism in his treatment of the image, the ways in which the quality and finish of the paint were suppressed. In this, however, it was difficult to see how Atkinson differed from Neo-Expressionist painters such as Schnabel or Anselm Kiefer. Both Kiefer and Schnabel had achieved a significant degree of fame by including incongruous, perishable and unalluring objects in their tableau-style paintings, while painting in as poor a fashion as possible. Schnabel even took to painting on velvet in order to give his oil paint the texture and appearance of excrement. To what extent, it should be asked, did Atkinson's paintings differ from the simplistic reaction of critical postmodernists? By painting ineffectively, Atkinson sought to ridicule what they perceived to be the machismo of Bad Painting and the allegedly spontaneous unconventionality of Expressionist theories of painting. Used in relation to what would soon be termed the New Image, this was the most false of claims. As many involved in the production and promotion of the New Image phenomenon would have freely admitted, New Image painting was deliberately and emphatically *inauthentic*; it was, after all, *Neo*-Expressionist.[107]

Was Atkinson's critique aimed at a straw man? It was thirty years too late for its target. His anti-Expressionism was entirely in keeping with the traditions of Post-Expressionist art which had dominated modernist practices since the late 1950s. Atkinson should perhaps have been critical of supporters of this critical orthodoxy, who loved to continually debunk the artist as 'genius'. Competent critical judges were seen as geniuses themselves: 'Art practice after the death of art seems to require a special talent to invent new games, new manipulations of the social context, perhaps laced with some insight or wit. Post-art cultural practitioners – Duchamp, Warhol, Johns, Beuys, Koons, Richter *et alia* – turn out to be pretty special people after all.'[108] Atkinson's paintings, nonetheless, could be read as meditating on this very problematic, this being that 'the absence of some intention for art, the once avant-gardist idea that "If someone calls it Art, it's art" ("Don Judd's Dictum") leaves the world very much as it was'.[109] In opposition to this game, Atkinson called into his work historical events, the political implications of which have borne a significant impact upon our perceptions about the world: the First World War, the Russian Revolution, Stalinism, Trotsky, the Second World War, the war in Vietnam, Northern Ireland, nuclear warfare and the domestic realm. Atkinson attempted to deconstruct the conventional picture of the historical event as it has been reported by the media and the academic establishment.

While representing a concerted effort to reflect upon the complex inter-relations between power and knowledge operating independently of individual artists, those who suggested in the 1970s that a reactionary conspiracy by the CIA *alone* ensured the success of Abstract Expressionism for purely propagandist ends were vastly oversimplistic. Abstract Expressionism cannot simply be seen as the opposite force to Socialist Realism since 'Socialist Realism did not … constitute a single unvarying doctrine and … never really constituted an exceptionless or monolithic style.'[110] In recognition that such history is negotiable, Atkinson juggled Western European and Soviet definitions of socialism. By presenting mutually incompatible assertions, Atkinson hoped that neither view would be able to predominate, decentring Western institutionalist avant-gardism by placing it in a permanent state of unrest/collusion with Soviet totalitarian art. The bringing together of two ideologically incoherent world-views that was central to Atkinson's paintings provided the way in which A&L would later enter the arena of the pictorial and introduce a *discursive* form of politics and history into their work, aiding the argument that the creation of such contradictions was fundamental to the dialectics of heterogeneous cultural practices. In a way, then, Atkinson's history paintings of the 1970s were inconspicuously symptomatic critiques of the unrecognized sociological posturing of post-Althusserian and feminist art historians who, in their obsession with hegemonic relations of dominance and subordination, could easily become the unwitting producers of similar forms of cultural exclusion.

The radical academic and critical postmodernist artists of the late '70s and early '80s had learned the lessons of the '60s counter-culture perhaps too well, choosing to oppose cultural hegemony from the inside in the belief that the 'outside' never existed in the first place. The bowdlerization of '60s revolutionary idealism was theoretically justified in terms of establishing new grounds of dispute (as Tagg might have put it), of squaring up to the bleak political situation the British left was faced with by 1980 as Thatcher and Reagan were swept to power by the 'silent majority'. Defenders of responsible negation rapidly risked stagnation, having little in common with the carnivalesque tendencies of the '60s counter-culture with which they might once have been associated. However, carnivalesque assaults on high cultural and political hegemony did not simply fade from view; indeed, at the end of the '70s they were to re-emerge across the UK with renewed vigour and were to be discovered in the most unlikely places. In political terms, the quest for a deregulated culture of play was deliberately ambiguous, incorporating hip capitalists, cults with no name, fashion as politics and politics as fashion. As I shall demonstrate in the following chapter, much of this renaissance teetered on the verge of anti-art and non-art. Moreover, many of the cultural practices that did emerge were never intended to be read as art (as they often were in the '90s), for if the hybridized British new wave wanted to achieve anything it was to stop making sense.

3

Dynamic perversity

Looking at the historiographically stable Modernism of the Sixties and early Seventies, the apparent mannerism of today seems causally dependent upon the contradictions in 'mainstream' modernism. Punk-art, artistic Rocking, 'bad painting', right-wing enthusiasm for the 50s' epigones create hiatuses for differentiation and identification. These are frequently vague and fugitive. There is little in the way of stability in interests and conventions to enable a clear differentiation of the *symptoms* of decadence and ruin from critical activity in respect of decadence. It is the cultural material we have to work with.[1]

The art crisis of 1976 also initiated an entirely different approach to the problems identified by the various factions of the mainstream artworld. For those on the far left, the Williamsian materialism adopted by the 'crisis critics' was held to be symptomatic of the class system that it was designed to critique. As English Situationist Ralf Rumney put it, 'The organisers of the Whitechapel show ['Art for Society'] about "political" art are the thought-police of official revolution. They fulfil a very similar role to that of the French Communist Party which collaborated with Pompidou to restore the bourgeois status quo which is the only environment in which Communist *parties* feel at home.'[2] Accordingly, David Hockney and Ron Kitaj also failed their audiences by continuing to operate comfortably within the constricting hierarchies of the artworld, effectively abetting the reactionary onslaught of Fuller and his followers. Despite their reforming zeal, 'radical academic' artists such as Burgin and Spence never achieved an audience other than among the modernist cognoscenti. According to some British artists, what was needed was an art form that would undermine the myth of the omnipotent universal intellectual, reconsidering power as something which circulates, as something never localized in anybody's hands, but exercised through a net-like organization.

The COUM Transmissions performance art ensemble as a group were adept at provoking shock and outrage within the narrow boundaries of the art network. Founding COUM members Genesis P-Orridge and Cosey Fanni Tutti maintained many of the preoccupations of the 1960s underground while gradually moving their activities within the orbit of the artworld. After moving to a SPACE studio in 1973,[3] COUM came fully within the orbit of the institutionalized avant-garde, successfully applying for a grant from the

Arts Council's newly founded Performance Art Committee. Tutti began posing for soft porn magazines as a way of supplementing her income. In March 1974, this attracted the attention of Peter 'Sleazy' Christopherson, who introduced the group to the performance work of Viennese Actionists such as Hermann Nitsch, after which their performances became characterized by a self-destructive violence and a profound cynicism regarding humanity: 'Art must be concerned with death, fear, sex, humiliation. Obsessionally self-destructive we have lost contact with our shamanic selves. How to prove we are alive. Sadism, murder, revelation of our terrors ... Affirmation of existence is art. All is contradiction, to understand is to lie.'[4]

Following Nietzsche, P-Orridge argued that the affirmation of 'identity through action' would awaken a decadent culture anaesthetized by mass mediation. Extending Nietzsche's paradigm further, P-Orridge held that *anything* that affirms existence is art, effectively leaving no means of differentiating art from non-art: 'The simple nomination of an object as art appears sufficient qualification of that nominating agent as an artist, [but] the promiscuous use of this causality on an extensional and intentional level could endanger the historicity and meaningfulness of art. The fact that "artist" is not axiomatically defined is no reason for its not being axiomatically defined.'[5] This very problem was highlighted rather than resolved by COUM, who seemed to revel in the irresponsibility of generating such contradictions. Ritual purification, involving both literal and symbolic elements including bloodletting, defecation, urinary actions and primitive body decoration, were brought into contradiction with a great self-awareness concerning the inherently contrived nature of their actions. Acquiring jurisdiction over the will of death through self-destruction, Cosey would claim that the work was 'not performance (entertainment) but action art'.[6] P-Orridge likewise asserted Tutti's thesis that 'COUM is not "about" entertainment', but concluded with the oxymoronic statement that it was 'concerned with *direct, symbolic* interpretation of actions to realise a uniquely personal perception'.[7] Hence, COUM simultaneously incorporated two antithetical authorial intentions: one anti-aesthetic, anti-theoretical 'direct' strategy designed to subvert the artworld by denying any responsibility for their work, and one 'symbolic' strategy whereby actions were strategically created to achieve acceptance by the artworld.

COUM's ability to manipulate their bodies was, in effect, a manifestation of their ability to fashion reality. The group claimed that they found it 'hard to define between TV image of thee real and thee movies they mirror'.[8] Accordingly, COUM's coded actions were designed to glorify the seemingly magical basis behind the artistic process, a process that remained inaccessible to the audience. Initially, 'the essential process of reflection focused the viewer's awareness, not on the affinities between himself and the performer, but the intrinsic sameness of self and performer'.[9] After a period of 'orderly' behaviour, however, P-Orridge might begin to nonchalantly drink his own urine, leading on to the breaking of as many taboos as possible. 'In Amsterdam we did a performance in the red-light district ... I urinated down Cosey's legs while she stuck a lighted candle up her vagina, so there were flames coming out of her vagina. Just ordinary everyday ways of avoiding the commercials on the television.'[10]

In all, a COUM action would take the audience's 'customary' behaviour and slowly transform it into a series of 'deviant' actions, resulting in a subversion of 'ordinary' behaviour which the audience would be powerless to prevent. Hence, while mimicking the spontaneous, plotless character of a happening, COUM's performances left little or no room for audience participation other than in an experiential capacity, the audience's sense of intimate involvement being enforced only by the fact of their close proximity with the performance. P-Orridge conceived artists to be 'people who are more like magicians or alchemists of a different sort, people who are delving deeper than art problems, art structures and aesthetics and so on as a kind of logical functional activity'.[11] For COUM there were no transparent forms of knowledge innocent of coercion and repression. Given that power is exercised through the production of 'truth', COUM's cabalistic art rituals metaphorically battled against both the mass media and their Semio-Artist demystifiers.

On the one hand, this strategy owed much to the harder edge of the '60s counter-culture from which COUM had emerged: 'If your communication is to result in action, in change of direction, then argument, McLuhans's "hot" information, the communication used by CND, by all political protesters, ostensibly by all politicians, is useless. The advertisers had the people moving their way. What was required was an explosive planted straight into the human subconscious to blow it off course.'[12] Yet COUM also had much in common with the numerous self-mutilation performances of the 1970s, most of which were officially endorsed by the international arts establishment, as opposed to being part of the 'underground'. Such performances indicated a shift back towards the notion of the artist as performer, as the writerly focus and creative source of the action. As P-Orridge remarked in 1975, 'The meaning somehow comes from the repetition or from the personality imbuing meaning into that action – not the action itself.'[13] In this, P-Orridge was also verifying the transformation towards the 'pop-Situationist' interpretation of body art dominant in Punk. Particularly proto-Punk was P-Orridge's debt to the 'active nihilism' of the '60s underground, resuscitating their interest in 'the praxis of deviants – psychotics, the mentally collapsed (it was somewhat hip to have been through a mental asylum) and petty crooks'[14] in order to sell it to an institutionalized artworld that had previously been preoccupied with Minimalist and Conceptualist austerities. The sick art of taboo-breaking was a puritanical form of nihilism, a means of deconstructing the spectacle by amplifying it. Although organic bodily excretions could not escape semiosis, COUM's resistance to reified language was fairly typical of the late 1970s artist's 'recognition' of the corruption and falsity of signification.

For P-Orridge the problem of how to reach outside the insular confines of the artworld remained a pressing one as it had for many British artists in the late 1970s. P-Orridge advocated the use of the mass media, maintaining that 'fame is a medium, not a phenomenon'.[15] Nonetheless, he was aware of the limitations of this position:

> I believe the worst problem art now faces is an industrial one, in two parts SAMENESS, the onward progression toward uniformity … MYSTIFICATION, in keeping a monotonous culture and society under a control process one creates a facade of experts guarding knowledge information. The public at large feel, I am sure, that art is not for them. Artists have deliberately made them feel inferior, excluded through not being trained in understanding of art. De-mystification is our duty.[16]

This presented a major challenge. While COUM's actions were seen to lie somehow within 'Art', it would be relatively easy for the press to extinguish its critique through ridicule. Agitational situations, on the other hand, risked becoming spectacles in their own right. COUM's promotional stickers encapsulated the nature of this problem: *This Sticker Exploits COUM* and *COUM Guarantee Disappointment*.

COUM believed that the answer lay in creating covert actions which were not only sophisticated enough to fool the press but capable of confusing artworld, and non-artworld, audiences: 'Infiltration of mass media and systems is vital. It means subliminal performance reaches an arbitrary, unchosen, unsafe public … Cosey Fanni Tutti models for pin up and porno magazines, in order to get magazines containing her image. The public buy them, see her, do not know her, do not have to know it's her performance art.'[17] Tutti's modelling work formed an action entitled *Prostitution* (1973– 1976), which was given its first controversial public airing at the ICA (see Figure 3.1). The success of Tutti's action hinged on the gamble that censorship of pornography, whether conservative or feminist, would be seen by the liberal artworld establishment simply as a product of the desire to guard high culture and to regulate non-culture for fear that the distinction between the two might be too close to call. Faced with the stifling populist anti-avant-garde atmosphere of 1976, the ICA took the bait and presented Cosey's pornography as art. For the ICA, this did not constitute the attack on populism that the press held it to be; on the contrary, the ICA was eliminating 'elitist' boundaries between high and low, good and bad taste. On the left, the ICA exhibition was celebrated as a political attack, problematizing the middle class's life-world by merging it with its opposite. Such was the official 'institutionalized' avant-garde interpretation, as outlined by ACGB Arts Panelists Conrad Atkinson and his wife Margaret Harrison:

> Cosey introduced to the ICA, a space which was reserved for the showing of 'art', the reality of her won struggle for economic survival, her own sexuality as object, her necessity to pose for pornographic pictures [to supplement her performances].[18]

> By bringing these photographs into the artworld, they exposed the double standards existing in the media and society in general. An activity which debases women as sexual objects is fine when bound up in marketing and making money, but shocking in the artworld, a reflection of the attitude that art should be above and separate from the preoccupations of society. The very papers which feigned puritanical shock showed near-naked women posing on the bonnets of motor cars at the opening of the Motor Show.[19]

usual things – court orders, repossession, jail. And in the end, Judith fluttered her eyes at me and asked was there any suggestion I could make to help her out of her temporary difficulties? So I suggested a touch of the other for a week's grace and Judith said, "I knew you'd say that."

Shame on me I suppose but I rather enjoyed ordering her about. I could never be cruel to a woman but I'm a sadist at heart and like them to know who's boss. She decided we'd have it off in the bedroom and I insisted that she led the way.

"So I can look up your mini as we go upstairs," I ex-plained.

When we got to the bedroom, Judith kicked off her shoes and tossed herself onto the bed, knees touching, looking a little mournful. There were a few photographs on the mantlepiece turned away from the room – they turned out to be mainly wedding photographs when I checked and, nasty sod aren't I, I turned them all round to face the bed. Her husband gave me a surprise for on the photos he was depicted as a rather small middle eastern type. I thought that sort were all rolling in oil money and not given to knocking warehouses over in their spare time.

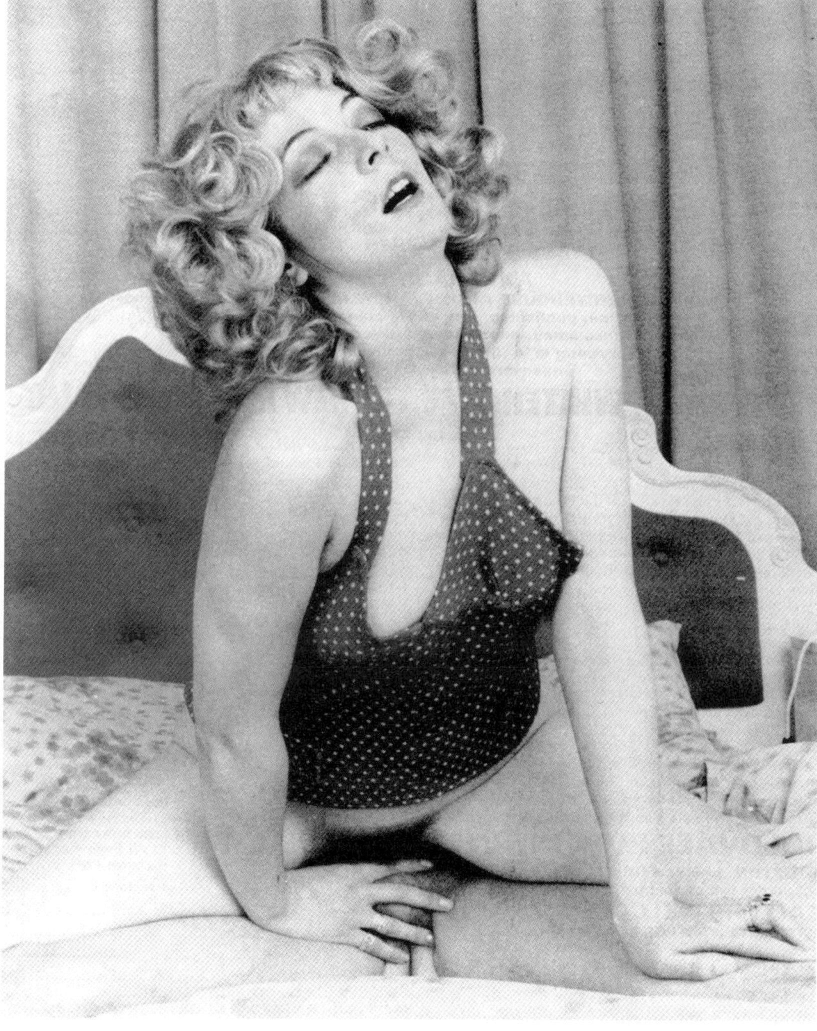

3.1   Cosey Fanni Tutti, *Exhibit No. 32* (1976), image from Mary Millington's *Blue Book*, No. 1, Kelerfern Ltd.,/ Roldvale Ltd., London, 1974, exhibited in 'Prostitution', Institute of Contemporary Art, London, 1976

A major oversight involved in this position was that it failed to recognize the manner in which Tutti's action remained dependent upon the institutions of the artworld in order to achieve its effect. Having entered the ICA, the subversiveness of Tutti's action became questionable, for it is only within such situational modalities that Tutti's agency could be recognized. Tutti's action, nonetheless, produced noteworthy results.

The 'Prostitution' exhibition directly followed the ICA New Gallery's display of Mary Kelly's iconoclastic *Post-Partum Document*, a work which had been constructed over approximately the same period as Tutti's. Kelly's involvement with the women's movement during the 1970s informed her work as an artist, causing her to make a distinctively feminist contribution to aesthetics. *Post-Partum Document* was a collection of objects, images and texts which mapped her own experience of motherhood in relation to her son as he progressed through his early development, from the beginnings of self-consciousness and speech to the age of seven. The work transformed the genre painting of mother and child by exploring the experience from the mother's perspective. While Kelly did not consider that there could be *a* feminist art, only art informed by different feminisms, her text/installation articulated her experience very specifically through the use of psychoanalytic theory based on the work of Freud and contemporary developments in the writings of, among others, Julia Kristeva and Jacques Lacan, building the 'remarkably self-sufficient and smooth-running mechanism' within which it has been discussed.[20]

It is enlightening to consider Tutti's liberal proto-'bad girl' action adjacent to Kelly's particular theoretical reservations concerning the use of the body as a medium:

there's a category of art which foregrounds what you might call feminine 'experience'. Most European performance artists are involved in that. Usually the artist uses herself as signifier, as object, and of course necessarily as a fetish. *The danger is that woman-as-sign is ultimately so recuperable, particularly with theatrical lighting, the mirrors, the video, and what have you.* Right. The artist needs some very powerful means of distancing. This usually takes the form of the text, or of the word as an intervention.[21]

For Kelly, the need to establish critical distance was paramount, hence the use of pseudo-structuralisms such as psychoanalysis. Tutti's action functioned as a more direct threat to such distancing, using institutions to toy with artworld hierarchies. This is implicit in the differences between Kelly's and Tutti's responses to the populist assault on their work. Following the exhibition of Kelly's *Post-Partum Document* at the ICA New Gallery, the press responded automatically: 'After the Tate Gallery's famous bricks, the new art is – dirty nappies.'[22] Kelly's response was equally reflexive, as she sought to defend her work on its own terms (against the field of the artworld and her brand of feminist theory): 'I know that it makes people hostile, but I want this to be taken seriously. I am not doing this as a joke. I am doing it because I have been influenced by the women's movement, because I am an artist and a mother.'[23] Despite the objective resolve of deconstructive feminists such as Kelly, they were no less mythic than the phallocentric aesthetics they displaced. Interpreted as supporting deconstructive feminist arguments, Kelly's *Post-Partum Document* has since become paradigmatic in postmodernist theory. From Kelly's reaction to the press, it is not entirely ironic that the piece should have become an historical artefact of iconic significance. For committed audiences, the objects, images and texts which constitute the *Document* emanate a sacred aura.

Although Tutti used herself as a signifier, her work opened onto the discourses of art, feminisms *and* their populist critique. By encouraging radical members of the artworld to read her actions as art, Tutti allowed them the critical approbation of participating in an attack on both the populist press and the artworld's middle-class hypocritical values. Having adopted this liberal view, however, the institutionalized avant-garde was forced to suppress its reactionary aspect as outlined by feminist iconoclast Andrea Dworkin:

Leftist sensibility promotes and protects pornography because pornography is freedom … Freedom is the mass marketing of woman as whore. Free sexuality for the woman is being denied an individual nature, denied any sexual sensibility other than that which serves the male. Capitalism is not wicked or cruel when the commodity is the whore; profit is not wicked or cruel when the alienated worker is a female piece of meat … The new pornography is a vast graveyard where the Left has gone to die. The Left cannot have its whores and its politics too.[24]

Equally, we cannot have the action as artwork and the action as critique of bourgeois values, for if we take such a 'liberal position' (viewing pornography as an artwork), we risk eradicating Tutti's agency by turning her into commodity, paradoxically denying the action's critical existence as an (anti-)artwork. If, on the other hand, we seek sanctuary by opting for the 'middle-class position' (denying art status to the action), as viewers we effectively become responsible for creating pornography.[25]

For COUM's retrospective at the ICA, Tutti's research in pornographic modelling, striptease and music was also utilized in a COUM collaboration in the form of the 'industrial' pop group Throbbing Gristle (TG). Ostensibly, TG attacked the music-world orthodoxy of the late 1970s with exaggerated Punk amateurism: 'None of us can play, even now we can't even play *Three Blind Mice*.'[26] However, while Punk positioned itself in direct opposition to 'higher education and technical expertise',[27] TG were attempting to operate an elaborate 'crossover', 'to apply the analysis of the artworld to a popular cultural archetype and not frighten off the kids, so without them realising, we were in a way educating them or presenting to them concepts which they would normally just poo-poo and ignore because of the way they are usually packaged'.[28] Rather than see themselves as a pop group, TG described themselves as an art-group, dedicated to non-allied political mischief. TG's 'art' lineage lay in their similarities with Antonin Artaud's Theatre of Cruelty, The Velvet Underground–Andy Warhol's *Exploding Plastic Inevitable*, Captain Beefhart and Art & Language who, in the spring of 1976, had released an anti-Semio-Art LP entitled *Corrected Slogans*. Like many Dada-inspired groups, TG actively assisted in their own mythologization, encouraging conspiracy, speculation and scandal about their activities.

On a formal level, TG had truly crossed the barrier between self-mutilation and actual physical violence, incorporating 'subliminal information, metabolic frequency and different control techniques used by other organisations' into their live public performances.[29] The 'Prostitution' opening night party, according to P-Orridge,

went brilliantly. The stripper came and stripped. I got attacked by a guy from the *Evening News*. He came up behind me and smashed me over the head with a beer glass without saying a word … Then he went mad: he kicked somebody else in the balls, and then attacked three policemen outside with a brick. He got let off with a fine and then wrote this long vehement slag which triggered all the media off.[30]

The scandal of the opening night signalled a possible direction, a way in which performance artists could 'use existing situations to actually affect society from the inside, to subliminally infiltrate popular culture aware of their perception as art but realising their redundancy'.[31] Following in the wake of 1976's major art scandals, COUM's 'Sex Show' deliberately provoked public scandal, the overwhelming press attention giving the whole affair a spectacle status at odds with the Fluxus ideology from which it evolved.[32] Yet 'Prostitution' as a whole emphasized a need for directness, dealing with sex and (sexual) violence since these were the malignant lifeblood of the society of the spectacle. The press, as COUM were well aware, was unable to produce an unglamorized report of their activities. This created a situation which not only highlighted the media's lack of integrity but demonstrated the ways in which power produces meaning and cultural history.[33] As proof of their satirical mastery of the situation, COUM included numerous cuttings of their own 'bad press' as part of the exhibition.

Drawing on Herbert Marcuse's critique of collagist anti-aesthetics, Stuart Morgan identified one of the major problems arising from this approach:

Throbbing Gristle take their opponents' propaganda and turn it against them. It is a dangerous technique. Orridge has been misunderstood, well nigh broken by the British press ... to suggest that the prerogative of art is simply to touch on possibilities without comment surely shows an insufficient grasp of visual rhetoric ... Surely he must see that no amount of manipulation of context can redeem the use of the [Auschwitz] gas-chamber logo [for Throbbing Gristle's Industrial Records Label[34]]; in purely artistic terms, which he cannot escape, there are such things as a sense of diminished responsibility and a law of diminishing returns.[35]

Indeed, as Morgan seemed to suggest, the rhetorical inconsistencies of actions and events such as the 'Prostitution' affair enabled the press to sustain its attacks on the artworld. This remained a major problem in that TG still failed to convincingly eliminate their high art credentials. Tutti remarked that the 'lack of united commitment to protecting an artist's right to exist in what ever area of expression he/she chose by the vast majority of other artists, allowed a regression to empty repetition of old safe movements and techniques, a new conservatism. So now, because the artist of today is often afraid to create and say what he/she feels, we are subjected constantly to work that is dishonest, heartless and therefore completely worthless.'[36] However, there is a sense in which COUM's dreams of 'artistic freedom' were responsible for this lack of solidarity, the space between their work and the ideology of which it formed a critique being too close to call. As sheriffs of the last bastion of aesthetic purity, COUM saw no prospect of productive achievement and thus developed into the very culture they opposed, exemplifying the worst overindulgences of decadent Western capitalism. Yet there lies a more dangerous problematic within the aesthetics of subversion and ineffectiveness. The militant refusal to signify might motivate non-converted consumers of the avant-garde to vent their anger by striking at the economic and ideological systems which sustain 'high art'. More commonly, legitimization crises encourage viewers to seek old reassurances, to attack the liberal institutions which succour the avant-garde. COUM, in effect, helped to justify and popularize the right-wing attack on the Arts Council which took place throughout 1976, and may have been a contributing factor in creating the legitimization crises that ensured a Conservative election victory in 1979.[37]

One strategy designed to prevent legitimization crises and recuperation was to adopt a fully nihilistic stance and refuse to signify entirely. In 1977, Gustav Metzger – painter, performance artist and writer – called for an art strike. For three years he produced no art or criticism:

The use of art for social change is bedevilled by the close integration of art and society. The state supports art, it needs art as a cosmetic cloak to its horrifying reality, and uses art to confuse, divert and entertain large numbers of people … Art in the service of revolution is unsatisfactory and mistrusted because of the numerous links of art with the state and capitalism.[38]

Metzger's cause was doomed to failure as he received no support from fellow radical artists in the Artists' Union, founded in 1972 to support artists and enhance their standing. The most extreme stance against the consensus of '70s cultural and political life had emerged from the fall-out of '60s Situationist-inspired revolt:

Brothers and Sisters, what are your real desires? Sit in the drugstore, look distant, empty, bored, drinking some tasteless coffee? Or perhaps BLOW IT UP OR BURN IT DOWN. The only thing you can do with modern slave-houses – called boutiques – IS WRECK THEM. You just can't reform profit capitalism and inhumanity. Just kick it till it breaks. Revolution.[39]

For many, the Angry Brigade's turn to violence signalled the end of the '60s experiment. With the reactionary popular press whipping up panic, Britons soon countered the tide of political 'extremism' by narrowly electing a Conservative government in 1971. The international oil crisis and resulting inflation, unemployment and energy shortages, and the series of miners' strikes in 1973, just as swiftly led to the defeat of Edward Heath's administration, as Wilson disingenuously promised the most revolutionary Labour government to date as means of appeasing the miners. However, as everyone quickly discovered, the international economic crisis meant that the cultural and political optimism of the affluent '60s baby-boomers had to be severely curtailed. From 1972, mass youth unemployment became a new phenomenon, and no amount of 'culture' could disguise the economic situation. Youths who grew up after the 1976 IMF crisis were the first recent generation in which many were forced to grow up without work, to be defined by the government as a new under-class, a permanent source of 'cheap surplus labour' perpetually excluded from society in order to squeeze down wages and inflation. Leaving much of the younger population with little to do, the economic crisis of the late 1970s spawned a peculiar subcultural mix of '60s arty revolt and early '70s nihilism.

While their methods were controversial, and the results debatable, the legacy of '60s radicalism was an intriguing one. Punk fashioned a cultural posture even more uncompromising than COUM's. In comparison to Throbbing Gristle, whose 'art' credentials remained conspicuous, Punk was decisively anti-art. Goading and occasionally assaulting their audiences, Punk bands created a setting which blurred the line between spectators and performers. As a visual culture, Punk combined the image-consciousness of the 1980s with the radical aspirations of the '60s counter-culture. Although trained as a printmaker at Croydon College, Jamie Reid chose to work outside the artworld, contributing visuals to the *Suburban Press* (1970–1975) 'zine. The *Suburban Press* had been Reid's response to his growing disillusionment 'at how jargonistic and non-committal left-wing policies had become'[40] during the early '70s:

I found Situationist texts to be full of jargon – almost victims of what they were trying to attack – and you had to be really well educated to understand them ... I wasn't so much attracted to the Situationist theory as to how they approached media and politics. The slogans, for instance, were so much better than the texts. They were very immediate, very direct and quite classless. They became part of the language ... there was also a sense of humour there, and of turning the media back on itself.[41]

As with COUM, central to Reid's work was his recognition that power depends upon controlling information. While working for the *Suburban Press*, however, Reid made several significant attempts to break out of the mould of Situationist artiness and the left's agit-prop in-fighting by merging both forms of practice:

We always had a fear that the posters would end up as decor for trendy lefties' bedroom walls. So we did images for specific situations ... We plastered Oxford Street with the *This Store Welcomes Shoplifters* stickers late one Sunday night [during the miners' strike of 1973], and spent the Monday watching the reactions. Friends of ours went and shoplifted quite openly and then, when stopped, pointed out the stickers to the store detectives in the poshest tones possible. They got away with it.[42]

As the Sex Pistols' art director, Reid's graphics, typography and black and white photography consisting of letters and pictures cut out from newspapers continued to ape the appropriational photomontage encouraged by *Camerawork et al.* Unlike the Camerawork group, however, Reid indicated distaste for politically determinate and determining work. Reid took a more politically ambivalent approach, adopting a visual vocabulary and style which was recognizable, knowable and entertaining, yet brimming with acid absurdity. Utilizing the Situationist concept of *détournement*, Reid 'found' other people's graphics and adapted them to the Pistols' context, taking pictures from a 'Belgian Holidays' brochure for the scathing *Holidays in the Sun* record sleeve: 'The result was very successful: bright, unpunky until you looked at it carefully; and complementary to the song's global political hysteria. The Belgian tourist company sued of course, and Jamie had to destroy the original work in front of a solicitor.'[43]

Unlike the Camerawork group, Reid's 'rip-off' graphics and Helen Wellington-Lloyd's 'ransom note' lettering[44] constituted a formidable political menace, directly challenging bourgeois values such as 'property rights' and 'bad taste'. Reid's graphics for the *Never Mind the Bollocks: Here's the Sex Pistols* album sleeve were also subject to a heavily publicized court action. Unlike the obscenity trials of the early '70s (such as the OZ trial) Reid and Virgin Records managed to defeat the obscenity laws in a Nottingham court, the zenith of their defence being when James Kingsley, a Professor of English Studies at Nottingham University, solemnly elucidated the 1000-year history and use of the Anglo-Saxon term 'bollocks'.[45]

Writing in 1980, Peter York noted the significance of such contributions to popular culture: 'The main thing that punk introduced was the idea of cut-ups, montage – a bit of Modern Artiness – to an audience who'd never heard of eclecticism. Punk was about changing the meanings of things.'[46] Peter York's grinning approval confirmed Punk's recuperation into the spectacle; by drawing a critical and historical comparison between Reid's work and anti-fascist montage of the late 1970s such as MINDA's designs for the Campaign Against Racism and Fascism,[47] we are forced to recognize that Reid's 'Modern Artiness' constituted a radical form of political 'art'. Before MINDA began to confront the rise of fascism by drawing parallels between the images of the Conservative Party, the National Front and the Nazis in the late '70s, Reid had carried out a sustained assault on the *iconography* of fascism which made MINDA's strategies appear almost propagandistic. From placing a swastika in place of the Queen's eyes (on the sleeve of the 7-inch single *God Save The Queen*) to forming a swastika from marijuana leaves (on *Never Trust a Hippy*), Reid ridiculed fascism by striking at its very heart, de-centring its power by problematizing the meaning of its imagery. In addition, Reid's paradoxical use of capitalist modes of production (album sleeves, tee-shirts and stickers) to disseminate such imagery pointed the way for the institutionalized avant-garde of the 'New Times' left of the '80s. Throughout his involvement with the Sex Pistols, Reid's political intent remained clear – the ability to change meanings empowers the dispossessed. While artists such as Burgin and journals such as *Camerawork* had advocated this, Reid enacted it, disseminating guerrilla semiotics *en masse*.

Reid's associate Malcolm McLaren, meanwhile, adapted tactics of shock and agitation to revolt against musical expertise and the corporate machinery of pop. This allowed him to capitalize on the radical claim that swiping at the music business – a perfect example of consumer capitalism – would encourage the audience (the society of the spectacle) to force change. Commercially inspired by the Situationist belief that life should be creative and spontaneous, McLaren encouraged the Sex Pistols to display anti-social behaviour. Like COUM Transmissions, McLaren quickly became a (self-proclaimed) master at *creating* spectacles. 'By [1978], a lot of revisionist stuff was going on, it was getting really difficult to grasp what exactly 1976 was all about, whether punk was an Art movement or a political one or, indeed, just a big con, put on by Malcolm McLaren … ', wrote York.[48] While the situations created by the Sex Pistols revealed a critical obsession with systems of control similar to that of COUM Transmissions, both McLaren and Reid subsequently claimed that prompting warnings about renewed teen barbarism simply gave the Sex Pistols a lot of publicity, enabling them to get more gigs and make 'Cash Out of Chaos', McLaren's slogan. Punk certainly was a blessing for British tabloids who could act as moral guardians to great financial profit.[49]

Another avant-garde movement had been commodified and institutionalized, yet what remained disconcerting was that its protagonists had been a party to their own movement's co-option.[50] Had the aesthetics of indifference been played out? Certainly, using capitalist tactics to fight capitalism resulted in a stalemate of sorts.[51] At the end of the 1970s Glitterbest Punk – the name of the management company McLaren bought to run the Sex Pistols – claimed to have produced the ultimate situation, the death of Art. COUM's nihilism had simultaneously been a suppression of nihilism, finding meaning despite the fact that nothing has meaning. Their anger that no morals existed concealed their desire for a new moral code (as in P-Orridge's argot). If COUM were truly nihilistic they would have 'Cease[d] to Exist', as their stickers advocated, rather than extending their activities within TG, 'Psychic TV', 'Temple ov Psychic Youth' and 'Chris and Cosey', various names they used. In this, they failed to recognize that the only alternative form of 'purist' nihilism, as explored by Glitterbest Punk, would be to perform out of crass materialism. Similarly, erstwhile King Mob members, the Wise Brothers, missed the point of Glitterbest's extreme pursuit of nihilism: 'Punk is the admission that music has got nothing left to say, but money can still be made out of total artistic bankruptcy with all its surrogate substitutes for creative self-expression in our daily lives. Punk music, like all art, is the denial of the revolutionary becoming of the proletariat.'[52] Of course, being truly nihilistic, Punk had to be a denial of *all values*, whether 'conservative' or 'revolutionary'.

Those who sought to continue in the same way found that the use of rock to shock quickly became predictable, and hence not very shocking. 'Far deadlier is punk's atavism. Since refinement and style were perceived as props for social control, punk's shoddy musical luddism entails a stubbornly static form of rock conservatism', wrote Jim Miller, rather than the carnivalesque prank McLaren had envisaged.[53] The anti-art stance became a set of rules as limited as what had been negated, as Simon Frith pointed out: 'Punk's lasting contribution to rock criticism has been musical moralism. Records are judged for their intentions not their effects; credibility is the necessary virtue, hypocrisy the most damning vice.'[54] Continual arguments arose in the music press about 'punk posers', bands who had adopted a Punk image and sound because it had become marketable, rather than because they believed in the 'punk cause'. The assumptions underlying such critical debates were somewhat misconstrued.

Reformed music critics had praised Punk for its emancipatory impulse while maintaining a populist distaste for 'academic' theories of popular culture. Consequently, Punk was seen to answer to the Frankfurt Hochschule's negative critique of popular music, a critique outlined in Theodor Adorno's famous essay 'On Popular Music' (1941). Adorno here argued that popular music merely served to pacify the masses and ensure their acquiescence in increasingly oppressive social relations. However, being a critique of the form and content of bourgeois culture, Punk appeared to negate social control. Hence, for many critics it was *potentially* a revolutionary movement.[55] While Punk critics were correct to praise Punk as a socio-political concept, in concentrating on its Benjaminian 'shock effect' they were overlooking the importance of its aesthetic dimension. What McLaren and Reid seemed to have recognized from the beginning was that the Punk delinquent subculture, since it was created through the channels of the mass media, could only simulate revolution.[56] Despite their anti-art tendencies, counter-cultures were aesthetic; since their acts of defiance were primarily symbolic they would be repressively tolerated rather than resisted by force.[57]

It now seems absurd to think that Punks might have valued their 'subcultural' status to the extent that they imagined their existence might change the social, economic and political topography of Britain. Moreover, for Punks to regard their culture as a possible solution to the problem of the artist's contribution to the perpetuation of an oppressive system would make them guilty of the egotism and elitism they deplored. Hence, while elevating themselves to the status of tragic heroes, Punks simultaneously had no delusions about their effectiveness. In a recognition of the limitations of subculture, Punk did not arise spontaneously from the 'frustrations of the working class'; it was constructed using an organized, 'hip-capitalist' approach.[58] This is clear from the behaviour of the Sex Pistols, who went beyond traditionally defined delinquency, their violations being not so much illegal as knowing attacks on style and form. The Punk stance is a parody of delinquency, utilizing mock violence, masochism and theatrical breaks with 'straight' culture:[59]

When punk brandished class credentials it studiously avoided the flat cues of the respectable white working class. With its tattered clothing, public swearing and spit, it chose the marginalised vestments of the urban damned: the lumpen proletariat ... Proud of its 'dumbness', punk was yet the most articulate of subcultures: anti-art in intention it adopted a politics of ruptural aesthetics; denying the prevailing sense of 'class' and 'politics', it offered the most explicit social radicalism.[60]

This would seem to confirm that Punk 'anarchy', in contrast to other forms of anti-social behaviour, contained a strong aesthetic component. Thus, in line with McLaren's 'pop-Situationist'[61] intent, Punk anarchy was more about aesthetic than political insurgency. As Caroline Coon demonstrated, Johnny Rotten did not write 'protest songs, as such. He is protest. In *Anarchy in the U.K.* he is not advocating anarchism. He is anarchism. It's a subtle shift of emphasis.'[62] Hence, despite its proud display of primitivism, Punk retained a peculiarly nebulous 'artiness'. Since artistry *per se* was suspect, the conventions of Punk didn't invite departures; McLaren had sought to guarantee that art had no future.

Writing in *The Book With No Name* (1981), the first book of the 'New Romantics', Ian Birch identified the Punk legacy:

Come 1977 the punk explosion was everywhere and, at first, the soul set were excited. True to form, it wasn't McLaren's socio-political shenanigans that attracted them but the Sex Pistols' youth and uniforms. Johnny Rotten wasn't an ideological iconoclast as much as a clotheshorse for his interpretation of McLaren and Vivienne Westwood's togs ... to claim that they [the Sex Pistols] had any political significance is stupid. If they did anything, they made a lot of people content with being nothing. They certainly didn't inspire the working classes.[63]

Clearly cut off from its pseudo-political referents, Punk culture was seen as fabrication. By 1978 it seemed that, from its inception, Punk typified what George Melly adroitly characterized as the drift from 'revolt into style'.[64] As Punk nihilism vanished, style made a hedonistically triumphant return, with dramatic consequences:

There was more Art around – Art business, Art Therapy, Art fashion, Art planning – in the seventies than ever in the history of the world. This was a development that was out of line with what Marx had said or common sense had ever observed, which was simply this: that culture became pluralist (or shot to bits) even if the 'cultural hegemony' or, broadly, the notion that the dominant style at a given time is that of the ruling class, had always been such a self-evident one that hopeful left wingers had always taken the converse to be true.[65]

As Peter York hoped, visual culture after Punk had to cope with a major dilemma, namely the lack of a unitary culture to counter. To a number of post-Punk artists it seemed that McLaren's aesthetic tricks had dealt a death blow to both 'affirmative' and 'counter' culture, closing the gap between them. The political and critical hierarchies which had sustained the project of the avant-garde, it seemed, could no longer operate as an index of value for 'advanced art'.

Perhaps, then, it is reasonable to claim that Punk's anti-design stance had always made the whole enterprise peculiarly *arty*? According to popular myth, Punk designers were untrained, anonymous figures, their designs raw and uncouth, using anything that came to hand – biros, Xeroxes, aerosols and scissors. It is true to say that many designers remain anonymous, were self-taught. Yet many celebrated Punk designers *were* trained at art school, and for them plagiarism was more of a carnivalesque prank than political art terrorism.[66] Malcolm Garrett began designing sleeves for the Buzzcocks while still a graphics student at Manchester Polytechnic, where he had developed a taste for International Style typography by reading Herbert Spencer's newly republished *The Pioneers of Modern Typography*: 'I began merging a number of things I liked, the pioneering type of graphic experiments like Futurism and Bauhaus from earlier in the century with stuff from pop art and Andy Warhol.'[67] In the summer of 1977, Garrett's fellow student (and future Assorted iMaGes co-designer) Linder Sterling was finishing her dissertation on the sanitation of Punk. Her photomontage for the sleeve of the Buzzcocks' *Orgasm Addict* (1977), while having obvious precedents in Dada and Surrealism, most closely mirrored the kinds of anti-consumerist montage then produced by feminist community photographers, satirizing imagery from magazines such as *Woman's Own* (see Figure 3.2). Certainly such Punk designs were formally chaotic, irregular and harsh, while as

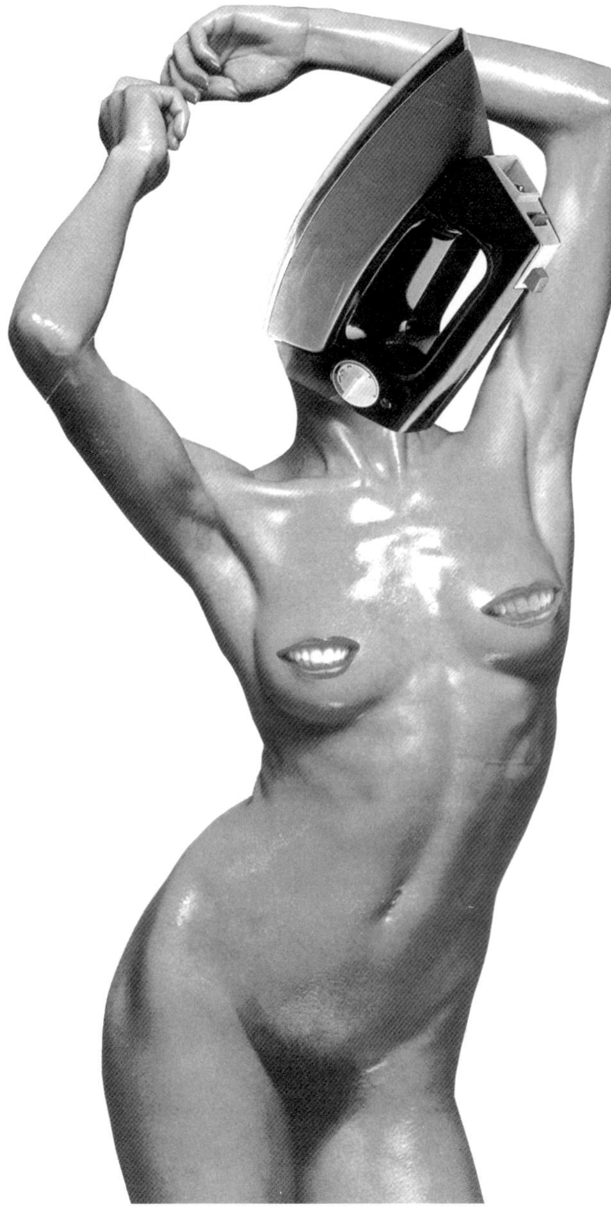

3.2   Linder Sterling, *Orgasm Addict* record sleeve (1977), photomontage, 17.8 × 17.8 cm

'cultural productions' they appeared subversive in intent: all laudable credentials for any aspiring subculture. Far from being anarcho-syndicalists, Assorted iMaGes were a duet of graphic designers who, as students, had been inspired by Punk to cast aside their airbrushes and set squares in revolutionary ferment, along the lines of 'This is *The Evening Standard*. This is *Fiesta*. This is a pair of scissors. Now form an advertising Consultancy.' Hence, Assorted iMaGes 'will use any style; avoids fashion, ignores trends; dismisses fads; deplores dogma; remains oblivious to politics; adores

American cars; eats at McDonalds; and sleeps irregularly'.[68] If anything, the cult of the individual designer was reinforced by Punk's 'version of the credo *quia absurdum est*: you don't like it but you do it anyway; you get used to it and you even like it in the end'.[69] Copyright, an issue previously of little interest to graphic designers, became *the* hot topic (and battles continue to take place over the attribution of many Pistols graphics). Who was the best designer outlaw; who was the least individual? Generating such contradictions, of course, was the whole point.[70]

On the other hand, not everyone revelled in the ambiguity. From 1978, it was clear that a greater number of record-sleeve designs were becoming more absolute, while others looked like baroque creations fit to challenge the collection of souvenirs of art history that inspired them. In most cases, however, the carnivalesque and agitational side of Punk seemed to convert to an emphasis upon record-design-as-historicist-commodity.[71] Given that many sleeve designers had quickly abandoned the anti-aesthetic, the emphasis on commodity fetishism was an ingenious means of ensuring that records did not lose their newly acquired art status. The ironic 'Industrial' style, which had been initiated by TG in the lead-up to 1978's Winter of Discontent, was reformulated and taken literally by designers such as Ben Kelly[72] and Neville Brody who were largely behind the 'Motorway Aesthetic'.[73]

Ultra-elegant 'Industrial' sleeves inspired a plethora of designers to lovingly refine the utopian aspirations of ubiquitous modernist schools of design.[74] Drawing on Garrett's successful appropriation of the International Style, his former school-mate and Manchester Polytechnic graduate Peter Saville turned his back on felt-tip and photomontage, and injected a melodramatic sentiment of Romantic disintegration into the late 1970s by hijacking modernist design for a new generation of 'pale boys' raised on Kraftwerk and Berlin Bowie. Following his first poster for Manchester's Russel Club in 1978, *FAC 1*, Saville was committed to fashioning a new poetry of intelligent commodities. Designing everything that bore the 'Factory' hallmark, he promoted a self-referential index for products ranging from audio and visual releases to clubs and Christmas cards. This vision was unequivocally pitched with *FACT 75*, his elegant design for New Order's second LP, *Power, Corruption and Lies* (May 1983; Figure 3.3). Inspired by Dutch designer Gert Dumbar's posters for the Rijksmuseum, the reverse contained a wheel that deciphered the meaning of the coloured squares on the *Blue Monday*, *Confusion* and *Power, Corruption and Lies* sleeves. Literal references to computational sequences are juxtaposed with sumptuous Romanticism; the colour code that frames Henri Fantin-Latour's *A Basket of Roses* (1890) translating mutely as '*FACT 75*', an apposite graphic response to the opulent electro-existentialism that established New Order's identity.

The implications of this for 'high art' were clarified as early as 1977 with the publication of Charles Jencks' *The Language of Post-Modern Architecture*. Although Jencks' book dealt primarily with architecture, his theoretical commitments were to become increasingly important for a number of artists attempting to

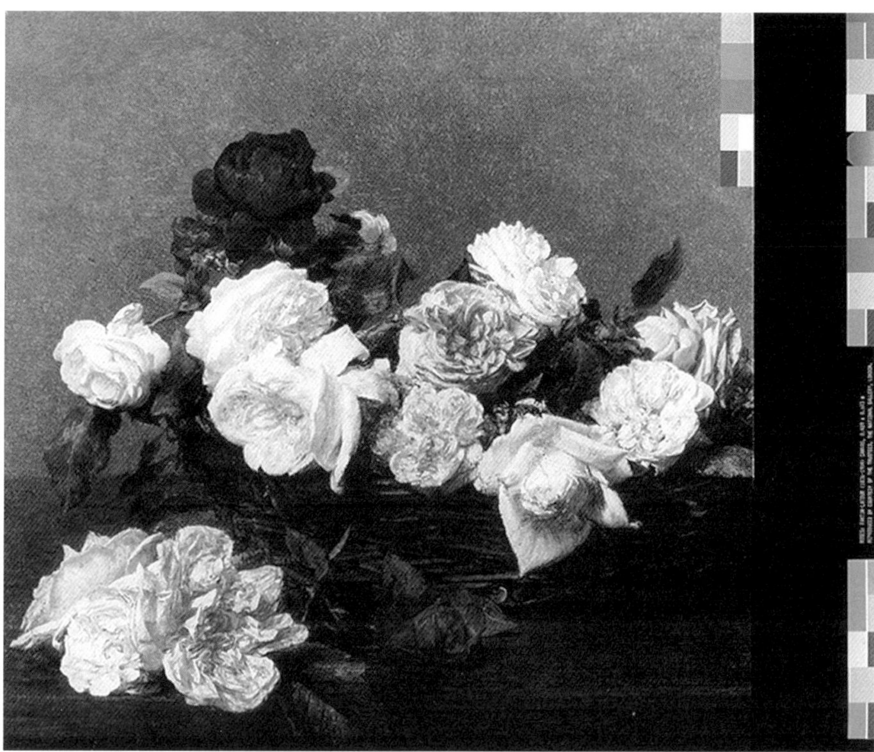

3.3   Peter Saville Associates, album cover of *Power, Corruption and Lies* (1983), typography and photography, 30.5 × 30.5 cm, Factory Records (painting by Henri Fantin-Latour)

force a way through the Punk cul-de-sac. According to Jencks, postmodernism was beginning to beckon architects and artists towards a rich cultural heritage rejected by modernism, placing art back within logocentric traditions which would assist, rather than discourage, iconographic and allegorical readings. Adopting an attitude of amused, agnostic pragmatism, Jencks celebrated what he regarded as the waning of the rhetoric of opposition and critique in postmodernism. Postmodern architecture often functioned as an ironic critique of the heroics of past achievements, altering quotations from established landmarks and classical structures in a totally detached and self-conscious manner. That such elements were often used as building blocks, without accepting their accompanying explanatory systems, suggests that post-modernists had adopted demythologizing tactics.

Punk's stylistic cannibalism of the very recent past added a different mentality to this equation: 'Laurie Ray Chamberlain denounces Hockney in very much the style of Johnny Rotten reviling Mick Jagger or The Who. Some affinities are too close for comfort.'[75] On graduating from the Royal College of Art, Chamberlain had been a contestant in Andrew Logan's 1975 Alternative Miss World Competition. Following his encounter with such London society figures he became a Xerox artist, gaining recognition for his colour photocopies of '70s icons such as David Bowie, before becoming a gossip columnist and fashion editor of the *International Times* in 1977.[76] By the late 1970s, Chamberlain found that aspects of his Xerox work had been adopted by sectors of the post-

Punk pop scene, most notably by Adam and the Ants, whose 'slogan "Ant Music for Sex People"' summarized their 'highly entertaining evolutionary dead end for the Punk Rock sub-genre'.[77] Adam and the Ants' second single *Zerox*,[78] the sleeve of which was designed by Adam Ant himself, paid homage to Chamberlain. Subsequently, Chamberlain was enlisted to select stills from Clive Richardson and Stephanie Gluck's *Zerox Machine* video for the sleeve of the Ants' third single *Cartrouble*.[79]

The integration of the art, music and fashion scenes had also emerged in the neo-kitsch of Duggie Fields (Figure 3.4). As a student at Chelsea School of Art during the mid-1960s, Fields had experimented with Minimalism, Conceptualism, Constructivism, before developing 'a more hard-edge post-Pop figuration'.[80] By 1975 Fields began to merge '60s style with what he saw to be the '70s Style', the Body-Art preoccupation with fetishism and self-abuse, severing the heads and limbs of his figures.[81] Fields' first use of this device came in 1977 with *Against the Inertia of the Seemingly Static Whole Each New Harmonic Incorporation of Life Seemingly Impinges as a Dynamic Perversity*, a painting titled after a quote from the architect Buckminster Fuller:

> The central figure comes from an advertisement in a fashion magazine of the late 1950s ... Then, with the memory of the missing limbs of the Victory of Samothrace, ... he painted this figure with a flying skirt. Behind her (missing) head was originally a plain black square, perhaps a nod in the direction of Ad Reinhardt. Whilst the picture was still a sketch Fields saw in New York an exhibition of Lucio Fontanta which he found powerful and unexpectedly moving, and as a result he decided to slash the black square.[82]

Dynamic Perversity mocked the allegedly radical cutting actions not only of Punk and 1970s performance art, but of the avant-garde as a whole. Unsettled patterned relationships between pictorial elements were deliberately over-stated, and sources absurdly eclectic, making the pointed suggestion that style and content were both subservient to the vagaries of fashion. Fields signals the figure's loss of identity, substituting darkness for light, as she becomes a stylistic icon, disappearing into the undistinguished surface of self-image. The painting suggests that to be reduced to nothing is an end, that it represents a kind of stability, whilst establishing an ironic clash with the latent violence in the treatment of the figure.

In 1978, James Faure Walker obliquely suggested that Fields was dealing with the 'question of how to correlate style and function when both are in an indeterminate context, of how to make art without being preoccupied with the appearance of making art'.[83] Fields had planned to conquer the fashion industry, producing hand-painted shoes and cut-up, breastless dresses, challenging the artworld's hostility to style. 'Johnny Rotten would wear a velvet collared drape jacket (ted) festooned with safety pins (Jackie Curtis through the New York scene punk), massive pin-stripe pegs (modernist), a pin-collar Wemblex (mod) customised into an Anarchy shirt (punk) and brothel creepers (ted).'[84] Fields adopted similar tactics of erosion, estranging historical art forms in order to subvert and deny the value systems that accompanied them. Although flavoured with stylistic clichés and motifs

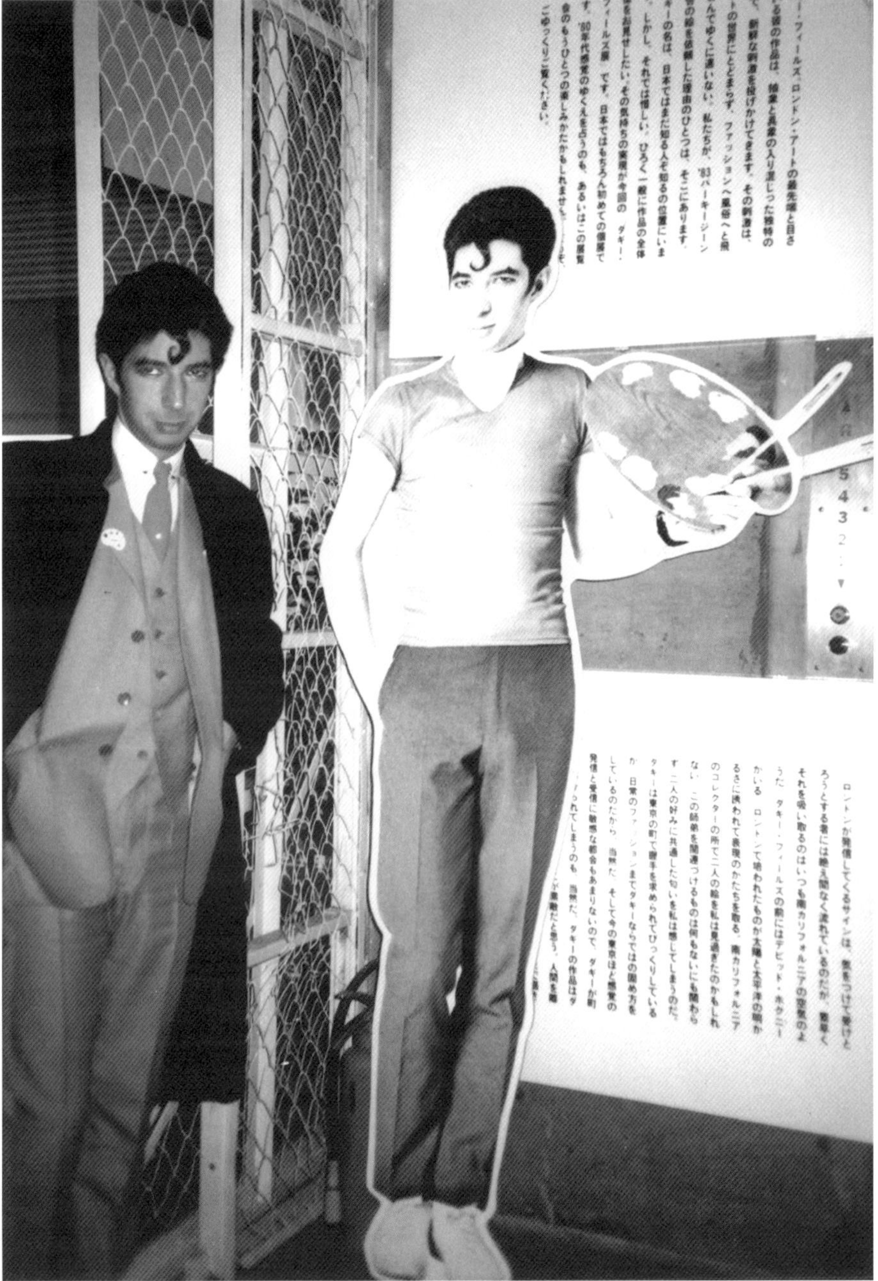

3.4   Duggie Fields at Shiseido Exhibition, Tokyo (1983)

from artists he admired – Miro, Mondrian, Dali, Bacon, Pollock, among others – Fields' reverence for them seldom influenced the style of his work. At his home in Earls Court Square, London, he spent twenty years recontextualizing all recognized markers of art in the same instantly recognizable, brash Pop style; using flat areas of vivid colour on which forms were outlined in matt black produced an aggressive, hard-edged quality.

Fields lovingly refined the abstract aspirations of the ubiquitous Mod-Bauhaus home and institutional design of the 1950s and '60s, with their penchant for petroleum-based plastics, vinyl leatherette and acrylic fibres. Windows were covered with red and black plastic strips; some walls were painted to simulate wood, others with small versions of his landscape paintings and relieved with found objects such as the torso of a mannequin, a wickerwork plantholder in the shape of a pair of plaster legs, and plaster hands. The coffee table, firescreen, telephone and power sockets were painted in *tachisme*, while black paint was splattered on the floor, Jackson-Pollock-style. Given that the exuberant, period colours and fantastic designs of such works emphasized design over structural efficiency, everything that Fields touched was reduced to the common aesthetic denominator of surface, giving the impression that style was infinitely more important than taste: 'impartiality and exploitation of the artificiality of painting goes along with Field's [*sic*] stated interest in style as an autonomous force, quite capable of surviving in the twentieth century media-landscape whilst severed from its original roots'.[85] Fields' vocabulary ceased to be attached to any message, this semantic disengagement underscored by manneristic historical citation. In this Fields had much in common with his Pop predecessors, especially Andy Warhol, yet there remain factors which link him directly to his time.

Like McLaren, Fields used the Situationist concept of *détournement* to pick away at the threads of cultural history in order to produce a slickly co-ordinated consumer package, celebrating cultural stereotypes, rather than disrupting and exposing them as a product of alienation: 'It is hardly surprising, given the strength of the Situationist International's narcissism, that this current could be developed in the 1970s and 1980s into an apolitical aesthetic of extremism.'[86] In the New Romantic pop world, this concept was having a similar effect as New Romantics maligned the nihilism and amateurism of Punk, while placing increasingly greater emphasis on image and 'product'. From this emerged a superficiality that would often border on neurosis.

Steve Strange, ex-frontman of Punk outfit the Moors Murderers,[87] formed the 'collective studio project' Visage in 1979 with Blitz nightclub DJ Rusty Egan, Midge Ure and Billy Currie of Ultravox and John McGeoch, Dave Formula and Barry Adamson from Magazine. Announcing that it was 'leisure time for the pleasure boys', they quickly found themselves invited to all the right cosmopolitan parties with rich high-profile social termites so despised by Punk, and henceforth became the music press's whipping boy. Robotic beats, banks of varied synthesizers, flattened vocals and the message of terminally repeated choruses concealed the void between dead-end daily jobs and night-time fantasies of the 'New Darlings of Decadence' who, deriding the conventionality of fashionable outrage, heralded the new order of posing. The 1982 retrospective album *The Anvil* (on the Polydor label), named after New York's infamous leather 'n' bondage dive, was launched at Strange's very own Paris fashion show. The album cover saw Strange in a Luchino Visconti movie still, photographed by the master of soft porn and presentation incarnate, Helmut Newton. Inevitably, Saville was responsible for the ceremonial graphics.

Yet Fields' desire to substantiate and enrich his own image by depicting his own body as the source of his style had preceded this quintessentially New Romantic trait. When Fields' highly stylized image was not cropping up in his pictures, the belligerent lines of his Punkish clothes and hairstyle were being mirrored in the equally contrived signature of his draughting manner. Fields 'pushed the boat out for the new sensibility, self-conscious, equivocal, eclectic, Post-Modern'.[88] While seeming to jettison the well-worn Pop Art preoccupation with the mass media's account of glamour and stardom, Fields was in fact presenting himself as the luminary, as his own product endorsement. In 1980 his acrylic painting *Acquired Mannerisms* (1973) achieved for Fields some degree of fame when it became available as a poster published by Motif editions and was reproduced on the sleeve of *Careful*, by Californian New Wave band the Motels. Meanwhile, his kiss-curl androgyny, bondage fetishism and souvenir-collecting mentality were being echoed by Soft Cell's Marc Almond.[89] The media having acquired his tastes, Fields was celebrated in the early '80s as an exemplar of the laissez-faire, postmodern artist. Although his work was featured in a number of art magazines, it was more common to find him in *Vogue, Interview, Harpers & Queen, High Fashion, Elle, The Face, Marie Claire, Cosmopolitan* and *Playboy*. In 1983 the Shiseido Perfume Corporation of Tokyo was so impressed by his profile that it created a gallery especially for him. Forty pictures were shown between 19 and 30 January, at Suzue Gumi, Dai San 3 Soko, Takeshiba, Toyko. The artist and his work were simultaneously featured in a television, magazine, billboard and subway advertising campaign for Shiseido throughout Japan.

Considering Fields' move in the wake of Conceptualist and poststructuralist critiques of the author, the colourful costume which formed Fields' disguise was grudgingly denounced by a number of artists and critics as a corrupt device for exploitative artists to initiate an ingeniously covert 'justification' for the artist's re-participation in the heavily authorial game of modern Western art. Fields was accused of infusing the market place by transforming painting into a vacillating performance of vacuous motifs, indulging in aimless history-hopping rather than exercising a serious and long-established critique of representation. The nihilistic vision portrayed in Po-Mo was a dying myth from its inception: 'the irony and inauthenticity of much recent painting is a carnival celebration of the artist as trickster. Whether done in the name of "popular culture" as in the work of Duggie Fields et al., or in the name of "high culture" in the historical eclecticism of recent German and Italian painting, the effect is the same: the re-presentation of history as farce.'[90] York regarded Fields as an important guide 'to the new [Thatcherite] Leisure Class that came up after'[91] him, a new moneyed class which rejected the academic values of the middle classes, replacing the 'pedantic rationality of "good taste" [with] a pluralism of pleasure'.[92] Although this appears to undermine York's claim that Fields' particular brand of postmodernism denied 'cultural hegemony', it does so in a highly oblique fashion. Eclectic Po-Mo became the dominant style at the turn of the 1980s, before it became the style of the new ruling class, the YUPPIES. However, Thatcher's emphasis on self-fulfilment, authenticity and freedom of choice had an obvious appeal to participants in the '60s cultural revolution, many of whom were impresarios such as Fields. Hence, in Po-Mo liberalism, the consumer is king, driven by the desire to maximize pleasure. Fields was a part of the raw, uncouth and socially, psychologically and sexually insecure new elite who were unwilling to attain the 'academic values' associated with citizenship.

Such changes easily swept through all aspects of visual culture at the end of the 1970s. The felt-tip graffito and typewritten amateurism of Xeroxed Punk fanzines such as *Sniffin' Glue*,[93] *South London Stinks*, *Ripped and Torn*, *London's Outrage*, *Vomit* and *Rotten to the Core* could be detected in the early issues of Terry Jones' *iD* (an acronym for 'Instant Design'). However, this magazine was quickly transformed into a market leader, as the editorial emphasis switched entirely to fashion, its Punky credentials distancing it from advocates of the 'graphix' style found in anti-*Vogue* fashion journals of the late 1970s such as VIZ: *Visual Arts, Fashion, Photography*. With Garrett occasionally helping out with design, *iD* succeeded in switching the British fashion press's emphasis away from prosaic interviews with 'Them' designers such as Zandra Rhodes and the Logan Brothers, and their artist friends Fields and Dick Jewell.[94] Instead there was lucid reportage of the outrageous fashions being worn by unknown revellers on 'the streets' and at venues such as Blitz in London's Covent Garden, where night-clubbers had been turning up as living works of art, dancing and trying to be seen.[95] Here was a sharp, timely contrast to the grubbiness of Punk. Theatrical get-ups, swashbuckling pirate clothing, Kabuki masks, make-up and transvestites were all welcomed. Fields, Jewell and Andrew Logan were all regulars alongside sad Pierrot clowns, majorettes, toy soldiers, puritans and Carmen Mirandas hailing from the suburbs. Following two entire editions of *The Face* devoted to them, a host of Romo clubs such as St. Moritz, Hell, Le Kilt and Le Beetroot were spawned. 'The Now Crowd' suddenly became an international movement, 'The Cult with No Name', with an article in *Time*, and lavish spreads in magazines from *Stem* to *Vogue*.

Such Po-Mo plays with the odd, the surprisingly kitsch and the historically redundant openly invited the erasure of historical claims to knowledge made by the academic estate. Punk's corrupt zone of mediation and cross-pollution was further diluted to scepticism, irony and the replaying of pre-established formulas. The wholesale denial of 'authenticity' might be seen to have provided a powerful practical guide for the aesthetic masking of the effects of Thatcherite economics by a plethora of ostentatious Po-Mo embellishments. With hindsight, however, it might appear that such criticisms would have been unfairly waged at New Romantics such as Fields: 'I think most of us are very brutalized by the environment we happen to live in. It's nobody's fault particularly, but, certainly what you label glamour, can be a counteracting force. So it can be used and needs to be used as such.'[96] Po-Mo was more than a mere formula for renewed economic and cultural success in Britain through reinvigoration of the supply side of the economy; to read it as such would be to coarsely parallel form and ideological content. It would also require neglecting the ways in which Fields' brand of Po-Mo differed from the neo-Victorian conservatism of some defences of 'British' painting and sculpture in the early '80s. As I shall show in the following chapter, the increasingly fragmented opposition to the imposition of the Anglo-American model of populist capitalism saw Thatcher's (contradictory) fierce devotion to predatory capitalism and parochial nationalism as linked. This reading vastly overestimated the allegedly unifying cultural and political consequences of Thatcherism while underestimating the ultimate volatility of its contradictory 'modernizing' and antediluvian tendencies. Nonetheless, many radical critics saw Thatcherite ideology as 'reflected' in very different artistic practices, thereby fuelling and legitimizing deep antipathy towards the idea of a 'return' to traditionally sanctioned art practices and the carousing of British parochialisms.

4

The shock of the old

At last, artists are coming out from under the modernist dogma of purist-reductionism which has, in its final stages, so impoverished the great tradition of creative imagery in Western art. Neo-Platonist mysticism, flowering in a period of cultural decline and disillusion, lent a systematic ideology to justify the retreat from depiction … Now, perhaps, we are ready for a neo-Aristotelianism.[1]

The young artist today is 40, because he has not been looked at for two decades.[2]

In the mid-1970s the case for a return to narrative figuration began to emerge with the formation of the Brotherhood of Ruralists by Peter Blake on 21 March 1975, a group of painters who would spend a working holiday together every year at Coombe in Cornwall. Blake had become increasingly absorbed by the mythical aspects of the countryside in the early '70s, showing a great deal of interest in fairytales, folklore, legends and nineteenth-century British art. A number of fairy paintings followed, mixing William Blake with Victorian and Pre-Raphaelite fantasies. Despite his change from flat acrylic paint to oil, Blake's distinctively sensual Pop style remained evident, albeit in a more early-Netherlandish manner. *Titania* (1976), for example, was painted as a sexually aware adult, complete with pubic hair and a distinctly mid-'70s coloured perm. The result was an uncomfortable contradiction between fantasy and verity, similar to that found in magical realist literature. The Brotherhood of Ruralists had no manifesto and no promotional strategy, and held no bureaucratic positions, and therefore made little impact on the institutionalized British artworld. Moreover, given that they described themselves as a 'Brotherhood', it was assumed that they had no true populist agenda, hence they received no attention from the 'crisis critics', Peter Fuller, Andrew Brighton and Richard Cork. Their first exhibition, at the 1976 Royal Academy Summer Show, seemed only to reinforce the critics' somewhat misconstrued notion that they were a reactionary organization.

The same year Ron Kitaj voiced a somewhat similar position to the Brotherhood of Ruralists *vis-à-vis* the status of International Modernist art. Kitaj's opinions were more audible and controversial since the Arts Council of Great Britain had asked him to curate 'The Human Clay', an exhibition of works by various British artists who had been actively celebrating the primacy of the human form in visual art. Clearly antagonistic to the conceptual, minimal and political art espoused by institutions such as the Tate Gallery, Kitaj's assertions seemed to prefigure the *populist* polemics of the crisis critics, albeit from a different intellectual pedigree. At Oxford, Kitaj came under the influence of the Renaissance expert Edgar Wind, in addition to the writings of Erwin Panofsky, Fritz Saxl and Aby Warburg – art historians who 'worked by examining motifs within a work, rather than giving primary concern to its overall stylistic character', analysing 'the way in which visual motifs were connected with social life outside art' by drawing 'analogies between visual and literary examples of the same subject'.[3] Like such iconological scholarship, Kitaj's early practice revealed his preoccupation with providing a context as a means both of modifying the viewer's response and connecting his artworks back to the world. Following the iconological method, Kitaj worked with a plethora of disparate texts both visual and verbal – Kafka, the thirteenth-century mystic Ramon Lull, Erasmus, Nietzsche, '60s popular culture – in an attempt to create a profound intellectual record of his dialogue with culture as a whole.[4]

It is important to note that the iconological method that influenced Kitaj was largely a humanist phenomenon, as Panofsky argued in *The History of Art as a Humanistic Discipline* (1955). Of central importance to neo-Kantian humanists such as Panofsky was the belief that the artist necessarily orders reality.[5] According to humanists, even artists who wish to express disorder must organize their modes of expression in a manner that will suit their particular world-view. In practice, this led Kitaj to juxtapose visual and verbal fragments from historical and contemporary cultures in a meaningful manner, even if the meanings often remained obscure to his audience. While, on a superficially formal level, Kitaj conformed with the Neo-Dada contention that 'there was neither a socially and morally charged imagery which he could take for granted and deploy, nor a range of factual reference which he could assume his spectator could take for granted and draw upon',[6] the epistemological conclusions of prioritizing Dadaesque indeterminacy over artistic agency were discarded. Kitaj wished to 'sail through less nihilist waters than those navigated' by his contemporaries 'towards an (ungraspable?) redemptive art'.[7]

While developing the impression of his working-self as intellectually *engaged*, Kitaj became increasingly concerned with provoking a similar effect on his audiences. Allusive titles were supported with source documentation in his exhibition catalogues, encouraging viewers to investigate meanings which transcend the empirical evidence of the work. By the mid-'70s, however, Kitaj was beginning to tire of some of the more radical aspects of his working process.[8] His change in attitude appears in transitional works such as *If Not, Not* (1975–1976; Figure 4.1). On first inspection of such works it seems as though he was moving towards a High Modernist position. For example, Kitaj was clearly continuing to declare his modernity in his ready borrowings from modernist literature, albeit in less recondite fashion. Kitaj based the work on both the mood and the collaged division of images found in T. S. Eliot's *The Wasteland*. Like Eliot's poem, *If Not, Not* stresses its own internal

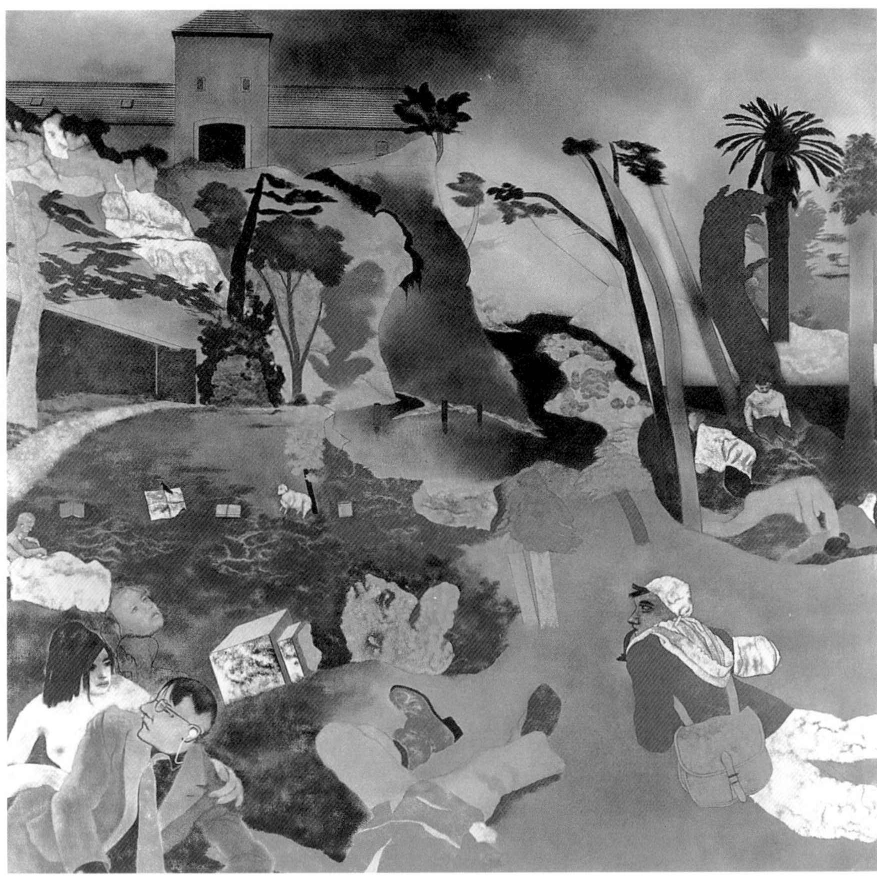

4.1   R. B. Kitaj, *If Not, Not* (1975–1976), oil on canvas, 152.4 × 152.4 cm

factors, the patterned relationships between figures imparting a sense of metonymy rather than metaphor. Moreover, Kitaj was becoming increasingly modernist in the ways he applied paint – in some images thinning it to little more than a wash, in others daubing it over a ground with expressionistic fervour, revealing an overwhelming preoccupation with process. Although he maintained an interest in literary sources and titles, Kitaj began to experience less of a compulsion to buttress his work with exceedingly complex materials of that character. On a formal level, Kitaj extended the links between the present and past through an astonishing array of allusions to the paintings of Motherwell, Van Gogh, Giorgione, Michelangelo, Cézanne, Goya and Bacon, among others, and the drawings of Degas.

Kitaj, then, was seeking ways in which to make the realization of the subject of equal importance to the form of the work: 'Ultimate skill and imagination would seem to assume a plenitude in painting when the "earthed" human image is compounded in the great compositions, enigmas, confessions, prophecies, sacraments, fragments, questions which have been and will be peculiar to the art of painting.'[9] Hence the piecemeal quality of Kitaj's early collage works was soon superseded by balanced compositions, illusionistic space and 'draughtsmanly dexterity' as he endeavoured to refract his times. Kitaj's turn to what might be considered a more academic method was not wholly for the sake of an empty traditionalism; rather it allowed him to create works which would underscore the tragic twisting of humanist goals which occurred during the twentieth century. For example, the 'gatehouse at Auschwitz actually figures in *If Not, Not,* as one of a number of sinister intrusions in an otherwise idyllic landscape inspired by Giorgione's *La Tempesta*'.[10] In this, Kitaj obliquely refers to the 'First Great German Art Exhibition' at Munich in 1937, a show which was dominated by pastoral landscapes, depictions of a pre-industrial, 'healthy' world (unblemished by Nazi autobahns and munitions factories). Drawing on the hypocrisy evident in the Nazis' glorification of the idyllic 'simple life', *If Not, Not* presents a superficially utopian landscape populated with the innocent victims of an all-powerful dystopian populism. Thus the efficacy of *If Not, Not* might be seen to lie in its allusion to the dangers of the intellectual naivety it depicts, its formal and practical conservatism being compatible with Kitaj's long-standing belief that artworks should *actively* make viewers aware of the historical reality of their situation. It was in providing points of access using images which could be more readily understood that Kitaj aimed to make his work more accessible to the 'masses' it was intended to 'cure'.[11]

While Benjamin and the Frankfurt Hochschule's sociology of culture played a significant role in shaping Kitaj's ideas about painting – their model of popular high art leading him to question the disrespect for figurative art – we should regard Kitaj's increasing emphatic insistence as resulting from his growing awareness of a 'fundamental condition' of the artist's venture: 'To put it a simple way: many of us like to make pictures of people because people and their lives interest us more than anything else.'[12] Kitaj's commonsensical theorizing (misleadingly) suggests that he had little time for the philosophical intricacies of the Frankfurt Hochschule: 'My Kulcher ain't as cultivated as most of the streetsmart theorists, from Greenberg and Judd to the post-Lacanian *pishers,* even though I've done some theoretical *pishing* myself.'[13]

Nonetheless, we should note that while Kitaj was advocating a less reflective approach to theoretical matters, his shift to a more 'comprehensible' mode of communication in fact was no more than a move from obscure literary references to more readily available and easily consumable art historical sources, again a move much against the grain of the times.[14] Although this seemed superficially plausible, when it came to the matter of interpretation, as Fuller pointed out, both sets of references required a great deal of prior knowledge and developed critical ability on behalf of the viewer: 'when all this has been said and done about how art should break out, acquire a new subject matter, and all the rest, what does he [Kitaj] paint? Portraits of John Golding, painter and art historian and *The Orientalist,* a fantastic imaginary figure, superimposed with literary and art references. He makes the same mistake as he opposes himself to.'[15]

In order to circumvent this problem, Kitaj increasingly made use of his own leitmotifs, recycling images, including figurative characters, from one work to another: 'I like the idea that it might be possible to invent a figure, a character in a picture the way novelists have been able to do – a memorable character like the people you remember out of Dickens, Dostoyevsky, Tolstoy.'[16] The figure with the hearing-aid depicted in *The Jew Etc*, who had also made an appearance in *If Not, Not*, was again to appear in *Bad Faith* (1980), *The Jewish School* (1980), *The Listener* (1980) and *Cecil Court, London WC2 (The Refugees)* (1983–1984). While he has identified the character as 'Joe Singer', a friend of his mother's whom he remembered from childhood, Kitaj has sought to make him into 'an archetype representing a condition of man, and more specifically of the Jew, in the twentieth century'.[17] Singer became a leitmotif that Kitaj could control and manipulate, changing context to change meaning. Although audiences now had to be familiar with Kitaj's personal iconography in order to make sense of his new works, they were simultaneously new realms of meaningful possibilities: 'Pound's great advice was enough: that demarcation he spoke of between a symbol which in effect exhausts its references and a sign or mark of something which constantly renews its reference.'[18]

While Kitaj's critics believed that such unorthodox tendencies made his work increasingly inconsistent, Kitaj scholars held this quality to be the most alluring and compelling aspect of his work. A consummate example of the most substantial and long-running critique concerning the value of Kitaj's work is the argument initiated by Peter Plagens: 'Kitaj is "interesting" because he's tricky, ambiguous and complex … Kitaj doesn't do more than embellish narrative enigmas with graphic deftness; his work – unlike [Francis] Bacon's – doesn't move you or scare you *as painting*.'[19] Plagens seems to point to Kitaj's inherent weakness, namely, his inability to develop an *affective* mode of communication. Kitaj scholars such as Michael Podro have, nevertheless, sought to counter this view, arguing that 'the effect of having stained the canvas with paint evokes the exposure of a light-sensitive photographic plate, to which is added the drawn marks of the graphic journalist. This is part of his documentary immediacy. He does not invite attention to the cuisine of painting but to the nerve of subject matter.'[20] This, however, seems to imply a contradiction, not least in relation to Kitaj's professed allegiance to the 'Great Tradition' of 'Giotto, Piero, Michelangelo or hundreds of years later Ingres, Delacroix, Goya, Degas, Cézanne, or in our own time Matisse and Picasso'.[21] How could Kitaj produce artworks with a 'documentary immediacy' which were also thick in their textual references? For many of his critics, he clearly could not, his affected technique ultimately forming a deterrent to the 'interesting' aspects of his work. Yet, as Andrew Brighton pointed out, Kitaj's critical failure may in fact result from the failure of critics, for it was Kitaj who 'stuck with imaginative culture when so many of us were afflicted with theoreticist hubris – whether by way of Greenberg or Marx'.[22]

'Now a lot of the newest wave is quite literary (ugh) but I guess that will pass too and I'll be left behind again like a schmuck. Don't you feel sorry for me?'[23] Towards the end of the '70s, Kitaj found sympathy from David

Hockney. Like Kitaj, Hockney's backward glance was partly inspired by the confusion endemic in the late-'70s British artworld.[24] When asked by Fuller to defend his work against the critical ruminations of the period, Hockney responded in line with Kitaj: 'You can interest people who don't know much about painting; the figure is the most important thing in people's lives.'[25] Such populist polemic was given its most controversial tone earlier in 1977 when Hockney and Kitaj appeared naked on the cover of *New Review*.[26]

Like Kitaj, Hockney was chastised for his efforts. Most vehement were the comments in the normally conservative *Arts Review* where it was argued that it was too late to revert to the primacy of the figure because the 'boundaries of content, or making pictures of people' had been irrevocably 'extended beyond recognition'.[27] It is unsurprising to find that Kitaj's and Hockney's stance should have aroused the suspicions of modernists and postmodernists alike; especially if we consider that a central tenet of twentieth-century anti-aesthetics has been the notion that art may only continue to carry conviction by distancing itself from the Ptolemaic certainties of the pre-modern era. Consequently, those who objected to Kitaj's and Hockney's concerns were making a well-versed philosophical protest against their apparently conservative agenda of reimposing a stultifying centre in a post-Copernican era: '[To] conduct a dispute around phrases like "depiction of people and things in the visible world" implies a great narrowing-down and misrepresentation of what has actually happened in twentieth-century art. It was exactly the conception of the homogeneous "visible world" handed down from the Renaissance that was broken by modern art, and not only by art but also by science, by physical and social science, and by modern experience generally.'[28]

Hockney's approach was in fact quite complex in its relationship with the dominant art paradigms of the late '70s. In speaking broadly of making 'the diversity of modernism into a synthesis',[29] he was seeking a practical escape from the claustrophobic critical debates of the period. This much is depicted in his portrait of the formalist art historian and curator Henry Geldzahler, *Looking at Pictures on a Screen* (1977; Figure 4.2). When asked to describe this work Hockney repeatedly sought to underscore his Kitaj-like contention that 'it is always figures that look at pictures. It's nothing else ... You don't get *Red and Blue Number Three* looking at *Blue and Brown Number Four*.'[30] However, Hockney largely avoided the interpretative liability of art historical appropriation or of personal iconography found in Kitaj's work.

The most important branch of British art to develop from Kitaj's and Hockney's pronouncements came in the shape of 'Narrative Painting', selected by Timothy Hyman for the Arnolfini Gallery in Bristol where it was shown from September to October 1979, before travelling to the ICA in London, Stoke-on-Trent and Edinburgh. This alerted artists to the continuing importance of figurative Pop Art while drawing attention to artists such as Peter de Francia, Jeffrey Camp and Ken Kiff. It was rather prophetically suggested that exposure of such work might induce 'naive', less obtusely theoretical forms of art than the kinds of social art produced for Cork's exhibitions. Like Brighton, Hyman

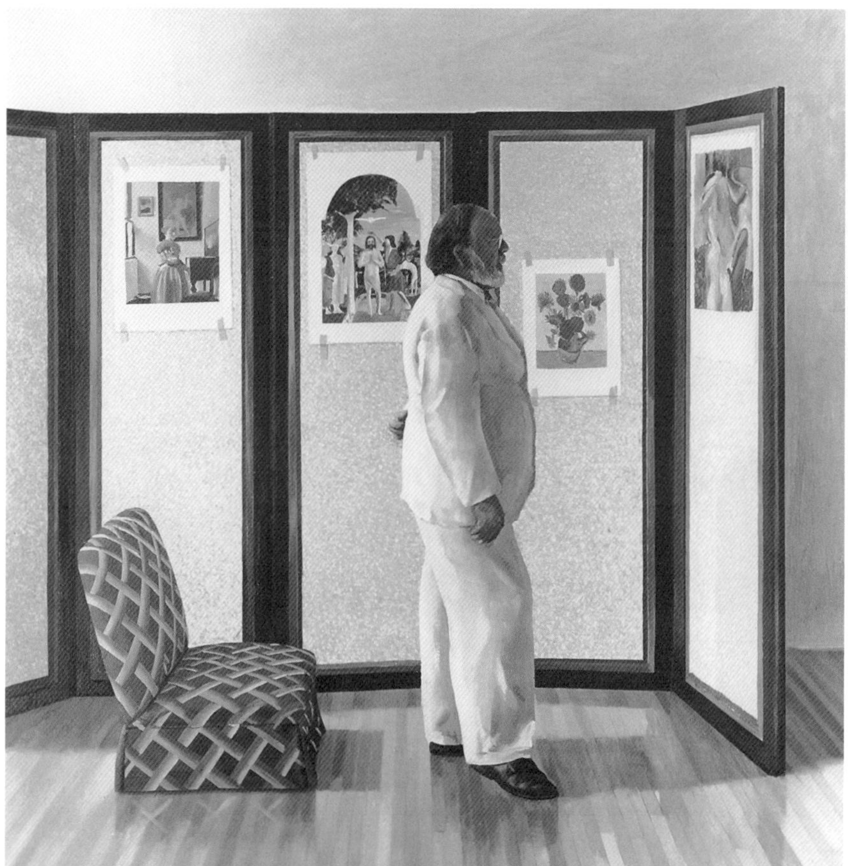

4.2   David Hockney, *Looking at Pictures on a Screen* (1977), oil on canvas, 188 × 188 cm

also hoped to encourage artists to explore alternative, non-modernist, art histories. Unsurprisingly this merely amounted to an alternative white, male, Eurocentric vision of modern art, placing strong emphasis on the lessons of Léger, Beckmann and Balthus since *they* made 'a nonsense out of all those schema by which the art of our time has been viewed as a progress to, or "beyond", abstraction'.[31]

On the one hand, this created some interest in a new generation that included Anthony Green, one of the few contemporary artists who represented middle-class urbanites without attempting to criticize them. On the other hand, the exhibition gave exposure to the Scottish Marxian narrative painter Alexander Moffat who had a profound effect on Scottish painting in the 1980s. Hyman's pluralism was pre-empted by Andrew Brighton and Lynda Morris's relativist exhibition 'Towards Another Picture' (Nottingham Castle, 10 December 1977–26 January 1978). Brighton had got the idea for the exhibition from his varied experience of the different facets of the artworld: as a student at the conservative Royal Academy Schools, as a sales assistant in a popular-print shop and as a research student at the Royal College of Art (where he investigated the divisions between high and low 'fine art'). As a

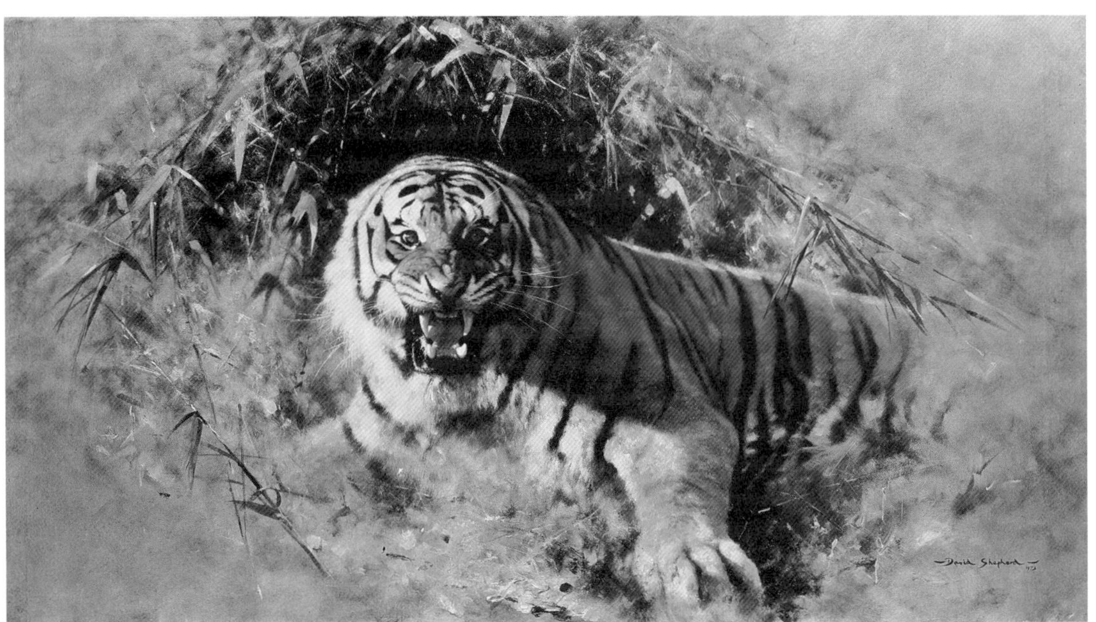

4.3   David Shepherd, *Tiger Fire* (1973), oil on canvas, 99.1 × 55.9 cm

means of blurring these distinctions, the exhibition was hung thematically with sections devoted to war, landscape and various human activities (pastoral, sporting and industrial), and several groupings of abstract paintings hung according to subject matter. Notable inclusions in the exhibition were the works of academic and populist painters such as Terence Cuneo, who depicted Lord Mayors and steam trains, and David Shepherd, who specialized in steam trains and African wildlife – especially elephants. (See Figure 4.3.) To ignore such popular prints, Brighton and Morris proposed, was to distort the history of Western art by excluding works which the vast majority of Britons held to be precious examples of fine art. In this, Brighton and Morris were far from reactionary.

While the 'social functionalism' promoted by Cork was particularly amenable to the control and committee procedures favoured by the Arts Council, Brighton's and Morris's selection was vigorously resisted by the artworld's managerial sectors who saw it as a threat to the premises upon which they had staked their reputations. 'Towards Another Picture' successfully demonstrated that culture is the product of contradictory and contesting ideologies, leaving the problems as unresolved as they are in practice. The exhibition was also important in that it opened up unwritten histories of art. For example, were there not important distinctions and hierarchies to be observed *within* the popular-print world?

Cuneo had trained as an illustrator, and in the 1950s was famous for his illustrations of trains in boys' comics. During this period he also painted official royal portraits and numerous commemorative propaganda-on-canvas illustrations of public or state events. By the 1970s, however, his original works were mainly collected by toy-train enthusiasts, although they remained popular in poster format, printed and sold through independent companies. In contrast, ex-Stowe public schoolboy Shepherd did not come to popular painting by way of illustration but by producing framed paintings for sale at small London galleries and the Open Air Show at the Victoria Embankment Gardens in the early 1950s. Following rejection by the Slade, he trained under ex-Slade student Robin Goodwin, 'learning the hard way, which is always the best'.[32] Prints of his elephant painting *Lords of the Jungle* were published *en masse* in 1963, followed by *Wise Old Elephant*, *Winter* and *Plough Elephants at Amboseli*, all achieving vast sales through Boots the Chemist, guaranteeing a fame he clearly disdained: 'If I stayed at Boots the Chemists, I might make a quick and considerable financial killing, but after a few years, my work would probably be worthless. This was not my idea of being a professional artist – art meant a great deal more than money.'[33]

It is enlightening to consider Brighton's and Morris's claims alongside *The Burlington Magazine*'s attack on the Tate's purchasing policy *qua* Andre's 'Bricks':

if they really intended to show what is being created in the 1970's, in all its variety, the Tate should be looking just as hard at painters working in a more academic tradition, like Seago or Cuneo, whose work is very popular, as at the latest *avant garde* productions. But then the Tate never had the slightest intention of doing full justice, in an almost sociological way, to the variety and range of 'art' in our time.[34]

By stressing the show's 'grass-roots appeal' with precisely such inclusions, the organizers of 'Towards Another Picture' were plainly attempting to claim a non-artworld audience and thereby create a radical alternative to the Tate Gallery and Arts Council perspective on British art: 'art history, properly practised, is part of cultural history. The task of those constructing a history of our own times is to examine and understand the uses of art in our culture, not to reinforce the evaluation of one section of the art market by giving them doubtful historical lineage.'[35] In some ways the anthology which accompanied the exhibition achieved this aim, promoting recognition that there is a distinction to be observed between art's histories and an art historical text.[36] In 1978, the overall reception of the exhibition, however, was not favourable. Reviewing the show for *Artscribe*, Adrian Searle asked what 'kind of critic nods silent approval at it *all*, as though there were good in everything, and he would not change it?'.[37]

Spending much of the late 1970s working at Goldsmiths College on the Gulbenkian Foundation's 'Enquiry into the Economic Situation of the Visual Artist', Brighton never managed to retain the high profile of his friend Fuller. 'Towards Another Picture' and the 'The State of British Art' conference of 1978[38] nonetheless encouraged the British Arts Council to commission another relativist exhibition. In 1979 they asked Derek Boshier to curate 'Lives: An Exhibition of Artists Whose Work is Based on Other People's Lives'. In his introduction to the catalogue, Boshier (a leading Pop artist in the early 1960s) followed Kitaj's and Hockney's lead, explaining that he had intended to mount a populist exhibition 'concerning or open to all or any people'.[39] Since everyone can relate to images of other people without the need for specialist art historical knowledge, he argued, an exhibition with figurative-humanist content was bound to be popular.

If Brighton and Morris courted controversy with the shrewd juxtaposition of Cuneo and Shepherd, Boshier deliberately enraged the cognoscenti with his inclusion of Norman Hepple's work. Hepple, educated at Goldsmiths and the Royal Academy Schools, was a former war artist to the fire service and painter of many royal portraits. His paintings parallel the spectacular fascist art of the Third Reich; as he put it, 'the illiterate can be moved by the poetry and magic of pictures'.[40] Surely such art was more in need of critique than promotion? Was Boshier being satirical with the penultimate line in Hepple's potted biography: 'Spends winter in Spain painting landscape and the peasants'? Perhaps not.[41] The real criticism was not intended to come from Boshier himself, but from the other exhibits. Included alongside Hepple's reactionary drudgery was Margaret Harrison's *Rape* (1978). Harrison's Bergerian appropriational painting stood in ideological opposition to Hepple's jingoistic canvases, despite the fact that both artists were trained at the conservative Royal Academy Schools. In this, Harrison opened up painting as a possibility for feminist artists who had previously been preoccupied with the scripto-visual mode. Its inclusion in 'Lives', however, returned visitors to the question of form raised by 'Towards Another Picture': how, precisely, could the viewer distinguish the value of Harrison's illusionism from Hepple's? How was it possible for Harrison's use of the 'European painting tradition' to carry any critical weight?

Other inclusions helped to complicate matters. Sue Wells contributed photographs of a *Welsh Farming Community* (1979), taken in the 'slice-of-life' convention much discredited by Photoconceptualists. Formally indistinguish-able from these, Desmond O'Neill's society photographs for *Tatler*, *Vogue* and *Harpers & Queen* were windows into a wealthy urban ruling class. Given that Wells and O'Neill were both advocates of obsolete 'verist' photographic practices, and photographers of (different) societies, what were viewers to make of their relative merits? To the average gallery-goer, the world represented in O'Neill's photographs was no more or less 'real' than that seen in Wells', both being, in effect, the 'Other'. The inclusion of Dick Jewell's found photograph projects helped to magnify such contradictions. Jewell initially received some critical attention in 1977 for his artists' book *Found Photos*, which was produced as an ironic response to people's fascination with photographs of the famous. (See Figure 4.4.) Jewell's book was comprised solely of reproductions of anonymous, discarded instamatic portraits that he had been collecting from photo-booths since the late 1960s. Significantly, these reproductions were *not* accompanied by texts; the abandoned pictures were simply presented for viewers to flick through perceptively or myopically, however they wished. A similar approach had been used in the silkscreen print *Cosmo Babies* (1976) in which Jewell juxtaposed the front covers of women's lifestyle magazine *Cosmopolitan* with equally glamorous images of newborn baby girls. Despite the obvious Althusserian overtones, there was never any explicit suggestion that this work could be critical of the media,

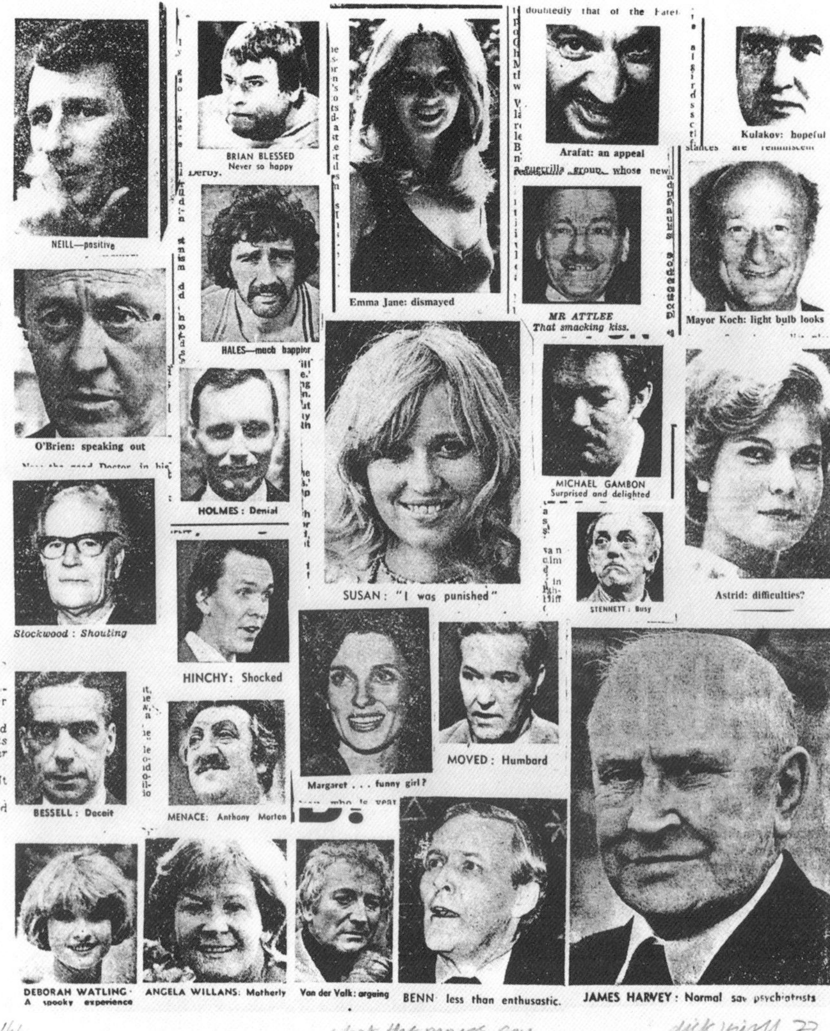

4.4   Dick Jewell, *What the Papers Say* (1977), silkscreen print, dimensions unavailable, Arts Council Collection, Hayward Gallery, London

Jewell being mainly interested in the flat aesthetics of the pun. Within the context of 'Lives', the *Jewell Family* (1977) participative project formed a pun in relation to O'Neill's society pictures (Jewell Family = Family Jewels). Jewell simply wrote to everybody in the London telephone directory who shared his surname, asking their permission to display any photographs which they chose to return to him. 'It's nice seeing from you', he innocuously concluded in the accompanying text piece.

In 'Lives', Jewell's depoliticized works were forced to contend with Peter Marlow's 'agitational' reportage photojournalism: 'Distributing pictures via agencies leaves the photographer's work open to all kinds of misuses. The control the photographer has over the end result is small. Magazines can, and frequently do, disregard or change the emphasis of the accompanying text and the captions', as Boshier wrote in the catalogue. The mere ability to recognize this fact, of course, had long been elevated into an art form by Photoconceptualists. Boshier's 'Lives' forced the artworld cognoscenti to question why they should ever have been so readily impressed by what commercial image-makers took for granted. This point was finally driven home by Boshier who included the Duffy Agency's advertisements for Smirnoff, Clark Shoes, *Elle* and Benson & Hedges, all of which were influenced by Semio-Art's use of text–image juxtaposition. Such contradiction emerged everywhere. Gerald Scarfe's satirical caricatures of the puissant and Posy Symonds' cartoon comedies of manners of middle-class life were exhibited alongside numerous anonymously designed Punk fanzines whose titles celebrated cultural and economic impotence: *Bored Stiff*, *Scrapheap* and *Ripped & Torn*. While major class divisions were pinpointed here, self-criticism and biting burlesque appeared common to both camps.

In the event, 'Lives' did prove popular with the public. For the critical sectors of the artworld, however, this popularity was achieved at the expense of 'cleansing' the exhibits of their political impetus. 'Lives' celebrated contradiction at the expense of totalitarian complacency and smooth political transaction. Unfortunately, the exhibition took place at a time in which the forces of reaction had significantly grown in strength within the British artworld. The refusal of critical factions of the artworld to deal with the difficult questions raised by Boshier can be judged only when considered against the predominant cases put for the return of the figurative at the end of the 1970s. The combative anti-avant-garde assertions made by Ron Kitaj, David Hockney, Peter Fuller and Timothy Hyman served as the main catalyst for the reactionary elements in British art in the early 1980s, a corollary of which was the suffocation of allegedly 'critical postmodernist' discourses on British practices. Feminist, Marxist and performance-led critics who had dominated the 1970s found themselves forced to compete against a 'new' reactionary voice, much to the discredit of criticism:

Cynics would be forgiven for concluding that the whole [Arts Panel] operation is a kind of ritual dance in which partners occasionally change positions but no one ever leaves the floor. The 1978/9 major [Arts Council of Great Britain] awards and bursaries present a useful example: two of the three £6000 bursaries and nine of the sixteen £2000 awards went to conceptualists or performance artists. The remaining winners were all of the most narrow minimalist species of abstraction. Not a single figurative artist received an award. Out of the total of nineteen winners, no fewer than eight were associated with one of the three London avant-garde galleries, the Lisson, the Robert Self and the Acme (which is one of the Council's own galleries).[42]

While it is true that figurative painters continued to be shunned by *some* members of the ACGB between 1975 and 1980, examination of the ACGB's annual reports and accounts over the period reveals that traditional art forms generally received by far the bulk of funding in terms of both exhibitions and artists' bursaries. Curated by William Packer, art critic for the *Financial Times*, the first 'British Art Show' opened at the Mappin Art Gallery, Sheffield in December 1979, implying to non-metropolitan audiences that British art had been behaving itself all along. Similar 'views' of British art were quickly put on show in France and the USA, exhibitions depicting 'the English as a group of eccentric romantics dropping wood and slate and walking through "timeless" landscapes, such as "Un Certain Art Anglais"' at the Musée d'Art Moderne de la Ville de Paris in 1979.[43] The 1980 Hayward Annual finally sounded the death knell for the Arts Council's '70s experimentation, establishing instead something remarkably similar to Fuller's elitist brand of mysticriticism: 'Painting is not easy to write about and I cannot describe or explain these works … real art cannot be grasped, learned or understood quickly. Real art evades easy description, discourages amusing anecdotes, confronts glamour and camp with a stony unblinking eye, and is not welcome in colour supplement land.'[44]

The organizers of the 1980 Hayward positioned their ideological response to British art in a way which would accord with the audience's ideological assumptions, thereby securing their consent to their own subjection and to the hegemony of 'serious culture'. The most successful and influential curatorial press-gang of the early Thatcher era came the following year, 'A New Spirit in Painting' at the Royal Academy of Art in London. By grouping Freud, Frank Auerbach, Leon Kossoff, Howard Hodgkin and Michael Andrews alongside Kitaj and Bacon, *within an international context*, the 'New Spirit' organizers suggested that these painters formed a group by merit of their shared isolation from the international avant-garde. Although there is some truth in this claim, it is apparent, even from a brief examination of their work, that these artists were far from being consciously nationalistic. The organizers' promotion of the *Zeitgeist* as an escape from the 'art crisis', however, suggested that the isolated position of this 'School of London' allowed them to harbour specifically 'British' qualities.[45] Critical niches were easily carved for any opportunistic critic willing to refute International Modernism in favour of an 'authentic British Art'.[46] Much of this school of criticism directly misappropriated the radical academic challenge to the canon:

The revision that is desirable does not involve demotion of the currently accepted giants but significant expansion of the pantheon, and recognition of the 'mainstream' does not follow the pattern of a railway line but rather the wide-flowing river fed by many tributaries and composed of interweaving currents.[47]

The implication here is not that the assumptions underlying 'the canon' needed to be destabilized or abandoned, but that a new canon had to be created, a canon based on 'British National Identity'.[48] This was not a new development. Earlier in the 1970s, Patrick Heron had voiced his dissatisfaction that New York was dominating the artworld. As Terry Atkinson remarked, 'What was really rich about Heron was that it wasn't the phenomenon of hegemony that worried him, but that it was NY-based and not British. Forward the Light Brigade! He set out an intra-modernist almanac of who really ought to be famous – and it certainly isn't those nasty New York modernists.'[49] A similar 'alternative' set of assumptions about the virtues according to which British art was to be understood were more explicitly outlined by Fuller throughout the 1980s. According to art critic Alan Gouk:

The 'British Tradition' apparently consists of Constable, Bomberg, Kossoff, Hoyland and Hockney … the 'peculiarly British empirical tradition which can be traced back to Constable, Hume, Locke, Bacon and beyond' (one painter and four philosophers). What happened to it between 1837 and the 1950s? How did it leap from an early nineteenth century Suffolk farmer's son [Constable] to the arms of an 'immigrant Polish Jewish leatherworker's son'?[50]

Nonetheless, for many, the humanist perspective from which the Royal Academy had examined the history of recent painting was vindicated as precisely the re-evaluative context that this work required. Typical of many of the School of London's detractors when faced with Richard Morphet's 'Hard-Won Image'[51] exhibition at the Tate Gallery in 1984, John Roberts created a conceptual weld between the humanist *interpretation* and support of the group with the *work* of the group:

drawing, the integrity of the human figure, and the 'intense' relationship between subject and object are intended to act as closure against the critical and projective assumptions of self-modernising art. The argument therefore is never about representation as a self-conscious, public and political act, but about the resilience of certain kinds of genre painting in the face of more novel forms of representation. Discussion of the body, the landscape, the community is stuck within the frozen terms of humanist subject matter.[52]

Thus, the School of London were criticized for attempting to provide a putative escape from modernity. While it is wise to insist that they be judged within history, the problem remained in that Roberts judged them against the group definitions given by their conservative supporters, thereby failing to check his experience of their work against such accounts. Such was the nature of Brighton's critique of such uncompromisingly materialist stances: 'some contemporary art stems from and invites a professional discourse that does not value the embodied or the expressive and what cannot be said. Rather it claims to be cleansed by theory of the mouldy rhetoric of the heroic artist and to produce "pieces" with clean handed precision.'[53] As Brighton suggested, critics such as Roberts failed to respond to Auerbach's work because it celebrates 'the idea of inarticulate experience, of things beyond textual discourse'.[54] Accepting the notion that Auerbach paints something beyond textual discourse does not entail a denial of history; it does not so much deny the disparate claims of postmodern theory as resist them.

Central to critical postmodernist theory of the late '70s and early '80s was the belief that individual subjects are denied the possibility of knowing the world since they are constructed by various texts and discourses, through which subject positions are created for them. Hence, material reality was regarded not only as unknowable but as unchangeable by conscious intervention. To varying degrees, Freud, Auerbach and Kossoff sought to resist such aspects of critical postmodernist theory: 'Powerfully present though the subject already is to the artist as he begins work, he nevertheless has in a sense to discover it in the independent terms of his material, which has a reality of its own. In order that a work should be truly new, it must be thoroughly *wrought*.'[55] Such a view would appear to correspond to the modernist doctrine decreeing that a work of art transcends the 'chaos' of modern life and the contradictions by being an autonomous object.

Following the example of his mentor, David Bomberg, Auerbach sought not merely to capture 'reality' in paint but to recreate 'quotidian facts' on the canvas. It is nonetheless clear that Auerbach, like Bomberg, was aware that painting does not passively 'reflect reality' but actually contributes to the definition and production of our sense of the real. This is implicit in Auerbach's famous description of intent: 'What I'm not hoping to do is to paint another picture because there are enough pictures in the world. I'm hoping to make a new thing for the world that remains in the mind like a new species of living thing.'[56] To produce 'a new species of living thing' is not only to actively shape the conditions of others' perceptual devices but to acknowledge that our cultural productions are *the world*. Were the kinds of deep significance read into Auerbach's paintings literally superficial components of the paintings' material surface? Although the twisted, smeared and flayed flesh of Auerbach's paintings appears to suggest that he approaches his work with the daubed fervour of the Expressionists, he in fact carefully *builds* his paintings. Auerbach's friend and critical apologist Michael Podro suggests that this signifies a search for formal-conceptual closure, 'a final comprehensive formulation', rather than an unpredictable outcome.[57] (See Figure 4.5.) The evidence for this is drawn from Podro's personal formal observations of Auerbach's works and statements: 'The problem of painting is to see a unity within a multiplicity of pieces of evidence … When the conclusion occurs and I feel I've been lucky enough to find some sort of whole for this overwhelming and unmanageable heap of sensations and impressions, I think the previous attempts have contributed.'[58] While accepting this, however, Podro has attempted to deny that Auerbach's technique proclaims the fact that our modes of representation and cognition are continually shifting. The reason for this lies in Podro's methodological assumptions. Although he is 'committed to enlarging on the phenomenological character of painting in a way which may help to chart its diversities in this century [he wishes to do this] in a way which will preserve the sense of continuity of earlier and later procedures'.[59] In this, Podro reveals himself to be a 'perceptualist'. Predicating his thoughts on logical positivism, he suggests that representations and the represented are logically separable, that painting is a visual adjunct to the primary event. This belief enables Podro to claim that since the basic 'reality' does not change, some representational systems can be 'truer' than others. The truth-value of these representations can be measured against the basic reality and the art of the past that had a similar goal. This explains why Podro and many supporters of the School of London insist not only that formal unity is eventually achieved in Auerbach's pictures but that this unity is an index of their success as works of art.

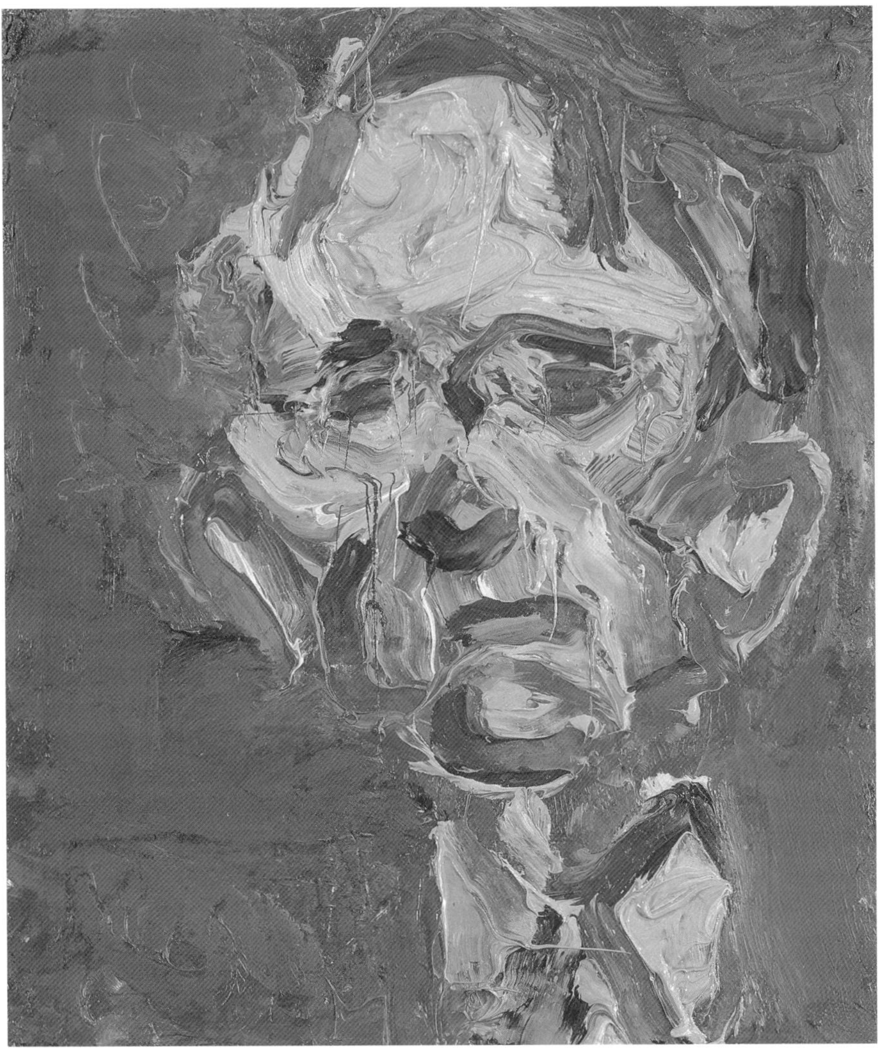

Although in some of his statements Auerbach speaks of his efforts to subsume flux into the harmonious structure of his pictures, he, in fact, believes this to be an impossible task:

When I see the great pictures of the world paraded in my mind's eye they are great images which don't leak into other images, they are new things … One hopes somehow to make something that has a similar degree of individuality, independence, fullness and perpetual motion to these pictures. But actually one hopes, although of course one won't achieve it, one actually hopes in vain.[60]

This is not merely a practical issue. It is not that Auerbach lacks the technical skill to produce great 'individual' pictures, but that such pictures are themselves only *seemingly* great; in their perfect state they exist only as products of consciousness 'paraded in [his] mind's eye'. The implication is that great pictures are great because we need them to be. Thus, in arguing the case for continuity of approach between pictures from the past and the present, Podro in fact constructs the analytical criteria with which to evaluate the achievements of the past and the present, overestimating Auerbach's faith in his own cultural agency. Far from being 'formal resolutions', Auerbach's drawings and paintings establish a conflict between the implied pursuit of a centre and the latent violence in the treatment of his chosen motif, remaining bound by the postmodernist distrust of the 'speculative imagination'.[61] This leaves Auerbach open to a major criticism. If he questions the existence of the centre, why does he continue to search for it? Since his entire life's work amounts to nothing more than a futile pursuit, is his modesty ('of course one won't achieve it') entirely false? Perhaps for Auerbach to voluntarily stop making pictures would represent the kind of closure that cannot come. This, if anything, would be false modesty.

In comparison to Auerbach's work, it is apparent that Leon Kossoff's pictures represent less of a departure from the example of Bomberg. Kossoff's unreconstructed positivism resides in the complex surface of his painterly webs. For Kossoff, the painted surface can reveal truths, not only about an allegedly 'alien reality' but about the people and places it connotes. His practice reveals his Expressionist intent: 'the surface is usually laid down quickly: often in a matter of hours. Kossoff lays the board on the floor, and the disposition of the painting across the surface owes much to rapidly performed body movements'.[62] Kossoff clearly intends his mark-making to be *evocative*. In allusion to Constable's English pastoralism, he paints recognizable places and events (*Inside Kilburn Underground: Summer 1983, Children's Swimming Pool: Autumn Afternoon*), appending the season in which they were painted to his literalist titles. As such, he seeks to wed Impressionist notions of 'truth to site' with Expressionist notions of subjective and atmospheric construction.

Lucien Freud's practice involved a more complex approach to the question of 'the real': 'I would wish my paintings to be *of* the people, not *like* them. Not having a look of the sitter, *being* them … As far as I am concerned the paint *is* the person. I want it to work for me just as flesh does.'[63]

Certainly, Freud seeks a 'direct' route, transforming his painting from an intensification of reality to the Aristotelian ideal of '*being*' reality. (See Figure 4.6.) At the same time, however, Freud clearly maintains some interest in the 'independence' of painting, strictly underlining the autonomous nature of his paintings with his contention that 'the paint *is* the person'. In claiming that 'reality' *can* be both found and captured, Freud begins to invite the more serious accusation of conceits. What he desires is a kind of representational Minimalism, an 'art of the real'. His paintings are intended to be both iconographically and emphatically disengaged. Freud's human figures do not look at the viewer: many look away passively; others close their eyes as though sleeping or dead. His non-hierarchical representation, paying equal care and attention to every*thing* depicted on the surface of his canvases, reinforces this inertness while discouraging interpretation. Formally, Freud's paintings evoke Minimalist values of honesty and clarity by way of an illusory

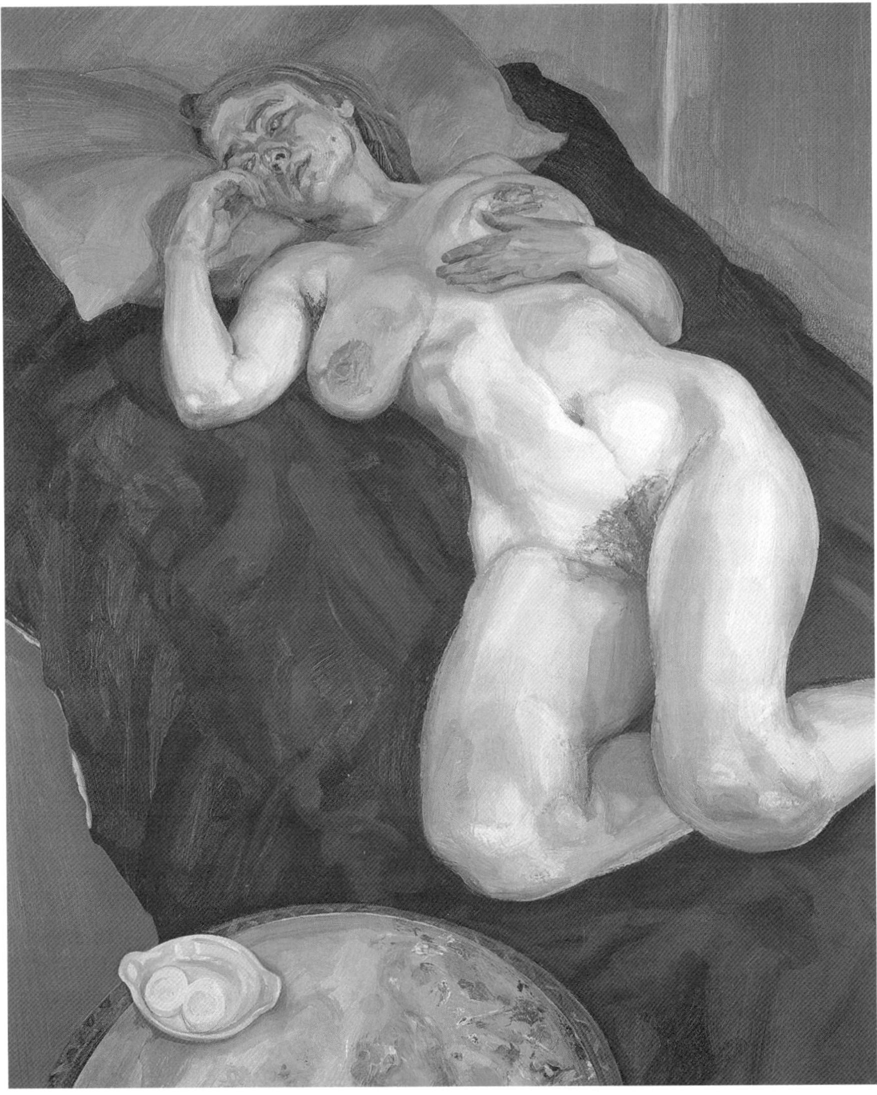

4.6   Lucien Freud, *Naked Girl with Egg* (1980/81), oil on canvas, 75 × 60.5 cm

simplicity and coolness of tone. The result is paintings in which humans, animals, plants and inanimate objects are rendered one; as Freud put it, 'the head must be just another limb'.[64] Despite the claims of painting connoisseurs, Freud's frigid painting process does not invite approbation; rather it suggests that to be reduced to nothing is an end, that it represents a kind of formal stability. Do Freud's paintings therefore represent a radical break with the Realist tradition of humanist empathy associated with the School of London? Freud has often been guilty of leading the viewer to allocate 'themes' of alienation and sexuality to his paintings using such symbolically charged elements as fried eggs, dogs and rats. Hence, despite his attempts to eradicate humanist concepts, Freud, in fact, is ultimately reliant on conventional, captivating humanist iconography to produce his mulish images. As such, the radical aspects of his work are somewhat compromised, the 'transparency' of his method being such as to allow us to easily mistake it for the passé Realism that he intends to denigrate.

Ever grander and more ludicrous claims were made for such work throughout the 1980s than in the late '70s. Fuller suggested that Kossoff and Auerbach created a kind of 'redemption through form', an aesthetic reparation. Read weakly, Fuller's theory appears to be remarkably close to what Auerbach and Kossoff were attempting to achieve. For Fuller, however, Auerbach's and Kossoff's paintings were 'formally redemptive' since they produced the kind of optical quality of frisson which Roger Fry described as being like an 'internal ejaculation'. The manner in which this thesis was argued was remarkably similar to certain Formalist claims that abstraction entailed a critique of culture by creating an alternative universe: '[Kossoff's pictures] are permeated by an undeniable sense of sadness, and awareness of the anguish, frailty and impermanence of life. And yet the energy, intensity, and sensuousness of the way they are painted provides a celebratory transcendence of their subject matter.'[65] For Fuller, aesthetic autonomy could be won by returning to the 'shared symbolic order' of 'Nature', yet only if this was discovered within the *tradition* of British painting stretching back in an unbroken line to the 'great days' of Ruskin.

The question of tradition suggests a fundamental contradiction in Fuller's brand of Ruskinian moralism. To fully return to the 'shared symbolic order' of 'Nature' is clearly impossible unless the artist believes that tradition can be ignored. The School of London, however, manifested an even greater involvement with the conventions of past art that were found in historicist New Image painting (see Chapter 5). Although it can easily be demonstrated that these artists subscribed to the postmodern intertextual sensibility, the main difference is the complete absence of the irony, or 'double coding', found in most postmodernist culture in the work of the School of London. The greatest difficulties arise from the fact that, on the one hand, this practice was regarded by intertexual postmodernists as signalling the School's lack of postmodern inauthenticity while, on the other, it was lauded by conservatives as proving their authenticity and sincerity as 'serious' painters. It was perhaps not so much that the School of London were somehow *too* influenced for postmodernist tastes, but that they were influenced by the wrong artists, 'The Great Tradition of Rembrandt's humanist painting'[66] rather than the tradition of the new initiated by Duchamp.

Freud, for example, often cites the work of Watteau. Rather than reading Watteau's paintings as a celebration of the centred subject, Freud has concentrated on their anti-humanist aspects, the sense that his paintings may be ultimately meaningless. In the paintings of Chardin, for example, characterized by the use of the contemplative mode, Michael Fried claimed that the figures were directly immersed in their own world and activities, so that they in no way form a state of consciousness with the composition or the necessary presence of the spectator: they are physically impenetrable.

The opposite was said by Fried to be true of Watteau's theatrical mode: figures appear to play in their world rather than inhabit it, and the presence of the spectator is no longer denied.[67] In *Large Interior W11 (After Watteau)* (1981–1983) Freud reads Watteau's Commedia dell'Arte painting *Pierrot Content* as establishing a space for contemplation; he seeks to ensure that the spectator cannot penetrate without a feeling of intrusion: 'In Freud's picture his son has become Pierrot, Pierrot the comedian, the public performing persona, but Freud paints his son as if caved in upon himself, introspective, avoiding the stare of the artist and viewer.'[68] While Freud's response to Watteau may be questionable *as art history*, in relation to Freud's practice we must consider Watteau's pictures as being of no more importance than Freud's sitters and settings. This demonstrates that the hierarchies of art historians and artists are not identical.

Women's issues were taken up briefly last year and then dropped in favour of this year's topic, working-class art. Shouldn't both be vital and continuing areas of concern? Ironically the women's movement is still considered politically marginal at a time when most male practitioners of 'social purpose art' are political voyeurs, but most women artists have shared a grass-roots involvement in the Women's Movement, have felt their political commitments deeply and have fought for them daily in their personal lives.[69]

For many, the 'return to painting' – with its attendant rhetoric of 'tradition', 'value' and 'authenticity' – in the late 1970s was an exclusively male affair, the denunciations of painting as a commodity and negatively gendered media having helped to foster the dematerialization projects – use of alternative media, non-media and Conceptual practices – of the earlier 1970s. However, the end of the 1970s also saw a number of women within conventional artworld circles becoming increasingly dissatisfied with radical academicism. Spence for one had suggested a critique of Kelly's iconoclasm. Critical photographers' confronting of pictorial rhetoric and Spence's Barthesian interest in myth provided a ground for women's intervention in painting and more traditional forms of sculpture.

The 1978 Hayward Annual consolidated these views. Following a suggestion by Lucy Lippard, an entirely female jury chose the second Hayward Annual, held in 1978. Unlike in the 1977 exhibition, the catalogue provided extensive information about the artists and their work, written by Sarah Kent. Included were canonical works such as Mary Kelly's *Post-Partum Document* (1973–1979), Alexis Hunter's *Approaches to Fear* (1976–1978) and Susan Hiller's *Fragments* (1976–1978). Hiller, who trained as an anthropologist, used found cultural artefacts as the raw materials for her artworks. Focusing her attention on broken pieces of pottery made by Pueblo Indian women, she sought to question cultural context, comparing her role as an artist with theirs. Such work had been underrated by anthropologists by being relegated to the status of 'craft'. Hiller pointed out that Pueblo women derived their ideas from an interaction between tradition and innovation, just as a contemporary Western fine artist might: 'Curiously, the practices of artists within our own culture are rarely investigated by anthropologists, whose opinions may perpetuate certain assumptions derived from art-historical descriptions of the art of previous eras, which are then projected on to the situations of other societies.'[70]

For some, the dilemma with such work was that it recreated many of the problems associated with the 'universal intellectual', implying that any examination of the givens of culture must arise from a sense of being outside it, studying 'society as though it were some remote hill tribe'.[71] However, Hiller's works differed substantially from the paternalistic rationalism of social functionalism in the late '70s, in employing subjective processes such as dreaming, automatism and improvisation. The 1978 Hayward Annual was a valuable opportunity to frame her work within the context of a distinctly feminist discourse supportive of such critical practices. Contentiously, the politically feminist work of Kelly, Hiller and Alexis Hunter was shown alongside work which was not feminist in intent, but simply *by* women, as the organizers sought to testify to the diversity of women's art. Each artist was separated off into their own exhibition space, reinforcing notions of artistic autonomy, separating women's artistic activity from men's. The popular press responded in its usual flippant manner, 'revelling in their coy belittlement and safe humorous superiority – The Female Twist, Wayward Gallery, Girl's Own Annual, No Deadlier than the Male, Ladies First, Ladies Night at the Hayward, Distaff Side'.[72] Accusations of bandwagon-jumping and tokenism were rife in both gutter press and feminist circles.

The political climate was changing rapidly for feminist artists. Coming to power in 1979, Margaret Thatcher proved that 'women', as ideological imperatives, could be as materialistic and matriarchal as any paternalists or patriarchs, and could certainly be more cruel, damaging and blinkered. In a stand against the reactionary climate of 1980, the ICA staged 'About Time', an exhibition of women's video performances and installations, and 'Issue: Social Strategies by Women Artists', an international show chosen by Lucy Lippard. Both shows were largely continuous with the politicized forms of art politics explored in exhibitions organized in 1978 by Richard Cork. Like Cork, Lippard emerged as a critic by supporting the latest developments in Conceptual art, before converting to endorse more 'socially purposeful' feminist and community art practices. While Cork, at the time, had largely ignored the contribution to political art made by women, it gave second wind to Lippard's critical career. The ICA at last was redressing the balance with a series of issue-based shows organized by women and containing work by women. It was, however, too late, unwittingly taking up where the crisis critics had failed:

The 'Issue' artists, armed with articulate jargon and backed, sometimes unwittingly, by strong Left theoretical positions, presented their socio-political *outreach* work as the new feminist dawn. Operating within a hierarchical scale of progress and correctness in women's art and a degree of cultural chauvinism (both tacitly endorsed by the ICA), they attempted to marginalize most other positions. Figurative painting and sculpture, female imagery, the female imagination and sensibility, subjectivity and expressiveness ... were now regarded as inappropriate to the ideological cause and ten years out of date.[73]

Despite its merit, the curatorial stance taken in 'Issue' had already received a bashing in the British art press. Being based in the USA, Lippard lacked a clear grasp of how her pet critical issues might have related *specifically* to the controversies that had arisen around the British Arts Council over the previous four years. Much of the rhetoric, therefore, seemed as idealist and outdated as the biological feminism that its producers attacked. The incorporation of theoretical discourse, and the playing between verbal and visual discourses, were taken to exemplify not only *the* agenda to be followed by feminist artists, but also the *form*, suggesting that practice is simply scripted by theory, that work serves only to exemplify the master text. The critique of domination productively made by politically feminist artists increasingly looked like examples of the misappropriation of theory, where its all-encompassing ambition actually mystifies the operations of specific oppression and detracts from the more focused arguments.

British critics Sarah Kent and Jacqueline Morreau, being more in tune with the prevalent spirit of reaction in Britain, were far more adept at responding to the critical opportunity offered to them by the ICA when they organized 'Women's Images of Men'. 'Our ... point was that a substantial group of women artists were using figuration and narrative to explore their ideas in highly personal ways; they were neither represented by the feminist avant-garde which like the male mainstream rejected figuration or by the more directly feminist artists.'[74] 'New Image feminists' continued to produce within the vigorous political and theoretical debates created by the women's movement during the early 1970s, actively incorporating theory and reflection into their working processes. However, Post-painterly Media – Text-as-Commentary, Text-as-Object and Photo-as-Text – were no longer intrinsic to the construction of 'feminist', as they had been succeeding Kelly's work. Although she did not actually exhibit in 'Women's Images of Men', the results of this paradigm shift were clearly visible in the practice of Alexis Hunter, a Photoconceptualist who emerged from the SPACE organization in East London and the Women's Workshop of the Artists' Union.[75]

While working at the Women's Arts Alliance in 1976, Hunter appropriated advertising techniques, experimenting with fetishistic reportage and staged sequential photo-narratives in her deconstructive *Approaches to Fear* series. Rejecting the cerebralism of Kelly and Hiller, Hunter sought to lure viewers with references to trashy B-movie iconography and the S&M aura of Punk divas such as Siouxsie Sioux, exploiting the rhetoric of popular culture to advocate feminist ideas beyond the converted cognoscenti. Hunter exhibited *The Marxist's Wife (Still does the Housework)* and *A Young Polynesian Considers Cultural Imperialism (Before she Goes to the Disco)* in 'Issue', sardonic works which 'directly challenged the po-faced political orthodoxy at the time' from a feminist standpoint.[76] By 1981 her growing interest in psychology and psychoanalysis led her to commence the *Male Myths* series, exposing the

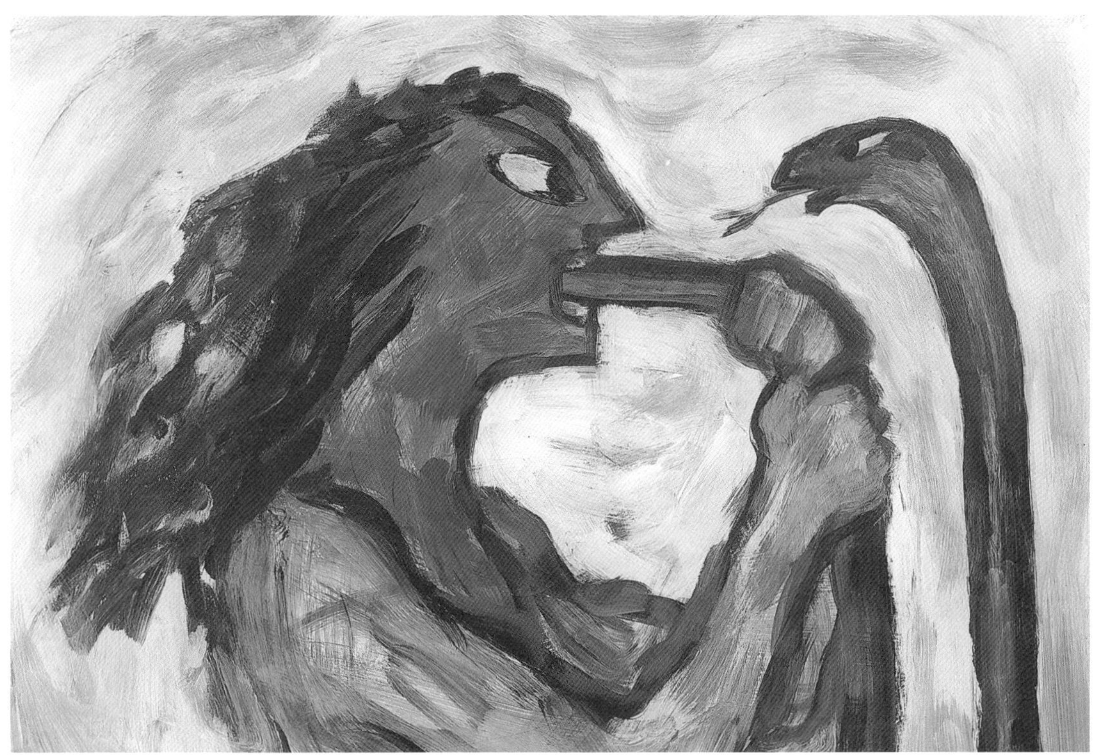

patriarchal basis of Greek mythology with a wry twist of humour. These tactile works were painted swiftly with acrylics on canvas. Some works were executed in a schizophrenic, quasi-automatic naive style, others were painted left-handed. Hunter meditated to achieve desired moods, and like Hiller she drew on disparate cultural, mythological sources and advocated abject subjectivities. This was a significant departure from dry, systematic Photoconceptualism:

4.7   Alexis Hunter, *Passionate Instincts VI* (1983), oil on canvas, 115 × 26 cm

[Hunter has] returned to painting, using it as a vehicle for virulent attacks on patriarchal values. *Considering Theory* (1982) shows a woman in mortal conflict with the phallic serpent that has been the instrument of her own downfall and the excuse for restricting her potential. The painting's title also encourages one to read it as an attack on the academicism that stifled individual expression throughout the 1970s and discouraged painting and sculpture.[77]

Certainly, Hunter, whose populism had been criticized in the late '70s by some feminists, had no interest in merely illustrating academic theory. This encourages us to ascertain whether Hunter's paintings were a critique or a product of the ideology of expressive individualism long discredited by feminists. On the one hand, her inclusion in 'Women's Images of Men' was designed less to ensure a comprehensive account of women's representational art than it was to provide a polemic calling for its recognition as a *subversive* art practice. Hunter's figurative representations were celebrated as an art of desire and the unconscious which nonetheless interrogated the 'real', as a means to ask fundamental questions about the relationship of reality to unreality, self to not-self or Other and conscious to consciousness.

Concerted efforts were made to assert this claim by suggesting that the New Image work by women displaced the male New Image. Male New Image artists were accused of cynically infusing the market place by transforming painting into a vacillating performance of vacuous motifs. Far from announcing a Neo-Expressionist loss of faith, Hunter's paintings were a search for conviction: 'This destruction of social clues by mixing them up was Post-modernist. I wanted to capture that strange, defiant animal beauty that came out of such despair despite the dissolution of a culture based on hope.'[78] In 1983, Hunter started using mythical animals to represent the dichotomies of human emotions, struggles between ambition and desire, reason and passion, logic and instinct. In her *Passionate Instincts* series, creatures copulate violently, yet they remain unable to reproduce, signifying the sterility and pomp of the New Image. (See Figure 4.7.) For Morreau, such paintings formed part of a radical, innovative painterly critique of representation:

The exhibitions made a huge impact on the British art scene. It can be claimed that *Women's Images of Men* accelerated the adoption of the New Image as the new avant-garde ... New Image took from women's art a characteristic for which it has been condemned – eclecticism, previously known as plagiarism. But where women re-work old styles and traditional craft skills to project their ideas within a feminist framework, New Image indulges in aimless history-hopping or plunders popular culture for no particular purpose ... The failure of the New Image artists to say anything new confirms that women artists working with figuration and narrative are the true innovators of the 1980s.[79]

By establishing a critique of the character and politics of their representations with regard to feminist politics, narratives and myths, women were seen to have produced an effective set of feminist possibilities in art. Unlike the male New Image, it was claimed, Hunter did not create an alternative world, nor did she assert the purity of the medium. Instead she aimed to articulate the void we experience when forced to confront the impossible, representing the unrealizable task of reversing her own cultural formation. As such, the women's New Image succeeded in dissolving an order experienced as oppressive and insufficient.

The claim that feminism's greatest contribution to early '80s art was its lack of contribution to the New Image was somewhat tenuous. Feminists greatly aided in the creation of '70s pluralism, but the very possibility of feminism existing as a political force necessitated that it resist the absolute relativism this intimates. On the other hand, the idea that women were able to (or wanted to) escape the marketable fashions of the male artworld is something of a myth. Hunter's work clearly had something in common with readings of the New Image which stressed its optimism and clearly benefited from the international interest in trans-avant-garde work.[80] The subversive, and by implication the revolutionary, aspect of women's New Image work was simply identified as that which transgresses and contradicts the dominant ideological order, an idea that has its ancestry in Romanticism.

Moreover, it was effectively equated with misrule, chaos and unconscious irrationality. The irruption of the repressed is itself seen as a radical event leading to real social transformation. However, as Punk had already proven, the notion that resistance to the social order can be generated simply through the development of the 'negative' is one which presented no challenge to patriarchy in the double-think age of hip monetarism. Indeed, like the 1978 Hayward Annual, 'Women's Images of Men' was not repressively tolerated, but repressively celebrated. Once more, the 'coy belittlement'[81] of the press signalled that it had not even been 'subversive' enough to encourage the conservative backlash which met the Tate 'Bricks', or the moral panic that followed in the wake of 'Prostitution'. 'Subversively' speaking, 'Women's Images of Men' was not so much an insurrection against the artworld as a cautious attempt to modernize it.

There was a more substantial danger for women in equating them with the unconscious and irrational. 'Women's Images of Men' suggested that practice and debates concerning representation were so abstruse as to be irrelevant to most people's lives. The alternative case was put for value in the feminine, in women's already overdetermined position as 'Other' as a means to radicalize marks of feminine difference for consciousness-raising. As such painting for women 'tended to be reclaimed in *opposition* to claims for art's cognitive significance. The result, in a number of instances, is women artists identifying their painting with a repressed, intuitive, feminine Other.'[82] In this context, the publicity that arose from the New Image feminism was illuminating: 'although much of the work was politically naive, the exhibition could, ironically, be said to have greater political impact than all the theoretically sophisticated, "alternative" manifestations put together'.[83] In the context of these responses, the exhibition could be celebrated as providing a barometer of patriarchy, highlighting the media's ability to assimilate or negate any critique of its patriarchal values. The work was not seen as a threat to the status of 'art', but rather as a threat to male values of aesthetic beauty and feminine decorum. As such, it could not be seen as a wholly subversive strategy, the press effortlessly recuperating the event as spectacle, the reception of the exhibition indicating 'why some feminists consider that introducing novel content is in itself insufficient'.[84]

At what cost was the ICA show's success purchased?[85] Was it acceptable for female artists to become more prominent after compromising the feminist project? Kent's quest for critical acclaim for female artists was often indistinguishable from the quest for commercial success. Two years earlier, she had staged an exhibition of Allen Jones's fetishistic paintings at the ICA. Anger at the content of Jones's work led to a tit-for-tat proposal that women should be given an opportunity to present *their* images of men. Thus protest, in part generated by Kent towards her own exhibition, provided the impetus for her to organize another show.[86] There is little doubt that much of the outraged response to Jones's sado-masochistic work (then a hot favourite among the more liberal art-house milieu of Punk) was genuine. Kent's response, however, reeked of the worst excesses of artworld careerism. The desire for women to reach the highest level of achievement clearly exploited the long-discredited notion of 'generic woman'. For Kent to claim that women suffer artistically *as* women more acutely than they suffer under other denominators that mark them as socially 'less than' or threatening – or that the artist's primary allegiance should be as a woman in solidarity with other women – was inherently conservative, appertaining to the Romantic fantasy of total self-expression, and the signification of the gesture as a mark of the painter's presence. Kent's pro-active feminism was bound to be acceptable to the British art establishment since its basis was compatible with Thatcherite Social Darwinism. Yet 'Women's Images of Men' remains a justifiable cultural intervention in so far as it extended the debate by taking it into the (male capitalist) market place:

Lisa Milroy's rapid rise to attention would have been unthinkable five years ago, especially given her subject matter – items of household use or of dress that would no doubt have been denounced as 'feminine' or 'domestic'. Amanda Faulkner's confrontative women would doubtlessly have provoked anger rather than delight. Therese Outlon's ambitious and elegiac landscapes would probably have passed unnoticed or even gone unmade.[87]

As I will discuss in the following chapter, despite such challenges to male hegemony in the British art market, the overwhelming focus of British art in the 1980s, both at home and abroad, fell on a group of predominately male painters and sculptors associated with the New Image style to which many feminist painters had been opposed. This grouping was far from coherent, especially when compared with the hard-won battles over oil painting found within conservative and feminist circles. New Image painting and object sculpture in Britain owed a great deal to the rising power of a new breed of publicly funded curators in the early '80s, who rejected the parochialism of the British tradition promoted by Fuller and others in favour of this international style of the early '80s. They also cast aside the reservations of radical artists in their willingness to collaborate with and legitimize the portfolios of private galleries and prominent wealthy right-wing collectors.

Who am I? Where am I going? How much will it cost? Will I need any luggage?

Approaches have become more eclectic, there are moments of a certain anarchic humour, and many of the statements are personal and direct. The artists have little reason to see their work as consciously avant-garde any more, and the self-confidence that this affords has allowed them to make work which can connect in a variety of more interesting ways with other parts of the world. The thunderclouds of an over-self-conscious avant-garde in sculpture have rolled away to reveal a clearer sky.[1]

If the contemptible pretence that figurative imagery is new and that an all embracing 'new spirit' can be derived from the seeming apotheosis of Picasso remains unchallenged then those allied to this irresponsible lyricism in which the figuration of mental chimeras and irrelevant abstract concepts deceitfully promising ecstasy, will forever be destined to serve under the auspices of multi-national big business – to be in the employment of fashion and advertising entrepreneurs.[2]

Hit by the 'winter of discontent', many private galleries that had shown the new art of the 1970s, such as Robert Self, began to close towards the end of the decade. Nicholas Logsdail had gained respect from the public sector of the artworld by exhibiting and selling new art such as Minimalism and Conceptualism at the Lisson Gallery in London. When the New Image came onto the market, Logsdail refused to cash in. He looked around for an alternative set of practices, a movement which did not appear to imply such a wholesale rejection of late modernism. Given that the emphasis had been on the politics of representation and art for social purpose, there had been little or no place for 'sculpture' (as object) during the late 1970s. There might be a case for establishing a heritage for the 'St Martin's School' of 'sculptors': Barry Flanagan, Gilbert & George, Richard Long and Bruce McLean. Locating this gap in the market, Logsdail lent his support to a group of mainly figurative sculptors who had began to produce work in the mid-'70s: Richard Deacon, Antony Gormley, Anish Kapoor, Bill Woodrow and Tony Cragg (included in group Lisson shows in 1977 and solo Lisson shows in 1979, 16 July–9 August 1980).[3] Like the St Martin's School, the Lisson Group also rejected the welding techniques of Anthony Caro, as well as the carving and modelling tradition of Henry Moore. However, unlike the St Martin's School – whose work did not consist of sculpture as such, but of performances, temporary installations or photography – the new sculptors had no reservations about producing *objects*.

In the early 1980s important sectors of the public artworld appeared to embrace and manage the International New Image, while others scrambled around in an attempt to find an alternative 'British' tradition, looking at painters such as the School of London. At the same time, a rather different generation of curators was emerging in Britain. Rather than look backwards, Lewis Biggs, Mark Francis and Sandy Nairne worked with their peers – Cragg, Woodrow and Deacon. Again, while most promotional areas of the artworld were beginning to celebrate a return to painting, this group looked for a sculptural equivalent of the New Image. They did not have to look much further than Logsdail's gallery. 'Objects & Sculpture'[4] – at the ICA in London and the Arnolfini Gallery in Bristol between 24 April and 1 May 1981 – was based around the Lisson Gallery stable of Edward Allington, Deacon, Gormley, Kapoor, Margaret Organ, Peter Randall-Page, Jean-Luc Vilmouth and Woodrow, but did not include any examples of Cragg's work. Despite the fact that the group had already been broken out into the artworld by the Lisson Gallery, this exhibition marked the beginning of a boom in British sculpture based on the following principles:

The work appears to be decidedly 'impure' in utilising either base or rejected materials and with the frequent incorporation of actual real objects or images of real objects. It has strongly human connotations either in its scale, in its tactile qualities, in its images or through the evident ways in which it was made. The work expresses a rejection of space and form as areas of pure exploration, and is not directly connected with the environment in which it is seen. It does not involve a concern with the planar expression of mass and volume, and indicates little interest in a simply aesthetic rendering of line, colour or material. The work is neither figurative nor abstract, nor could it simply be termed as abstracted. It *is* associative, and in some cases is also symbolic or metaphorical. Although every work has different meanings, and different ways of signifying those meanings, together they seem to refer both to *objects* in the world, and to *sculpture* given some status as a category of special objects separated from the world.[5]

This was not a straightforward rejection of the avant-garde. In fact, much of the new sculpture emerged from concerns of the late 1970s.[6] Such principles are clearly discernible in Cragg's sculptural experiments of the 1970s when he studied at the RCA. Here he produced a series of ephemeral works under the influence of the St Martin's School, taking a strong interest in nature and the landscape, drawing on the examples of Richard Long, Hamish Fulton and Roger Ackling (Ackling taught at the RCA), in addition to the work of Gilbert & George and Bruce McLean, and Susan Hiller's anthropological research-based activity.

For Cragg, the semiology of vernacular objects of 'culture' (as opposed to 'nature') that had preoccupied numerous British photographers since the translation of Barthes' *Mythologies* in 1973 became his *sculptural* preoccupation towards the end of the decade as he sought to relocate the fine arts within culture as a whole. 'Popular culture, the mass media, new technology have marginalized art's mediation of culture as a whole. If Late Modernism was complicit with this – wanted, as Carl Andre said of his work, to create objects that had no equivalent in the world – post-modernism has thrown itself back into sorting out signs and icons and rituals.'[7] For example, the pseudo-scientific nomenclature of Cragg's *Four Plates* (RCA, 1976) seemingly refers the viewer unproblematically to the medium and subject matter until we are confronted with the sculpture in question: 'Using four identical plates, Cragg broke three, spreading farther apart the fragments of each successive plate. While challenging the identity of these arranged fragments as plates, they are still perceived as plates because the model (the unbroken plate) is supplied and because in each group of fragments the circular outline is retained despite the expanding diameter.'[8] Cragg thereby draws our attention both to the instability of our semiotic categorizations and to the impossibility of non-categorization. A note of irony is added when we consider that the artist is responsible for 'mis-shaping' the plate. True to the deconstructive bent of the later 1970s, Cragg envisaged his role as an artist in terms of shattering given forms and conventions. Yet Cragg differed in his intimation that the logos can never be eradicated, but in fact sustained the project of the late avant-garde. Although Cragg's work may have retained the self-referentiality of the modernist art which preceded it, it added a subversive twist of self-deprecating ambivalence, striking a difficult balance between an awareness of modernism's serious purpose and the element of 'play' common to much '80s art.

In addition to creating a developmental break with modernist sculpture, Cragg's experiments also established a subtle dialogue with the Jencksian brand of postmodernism[9] found amongst exponents of the New Wave:

What is at stake in this new sculpture, and what takes it far in advance of the 'neutrality' of their generation's concerns, is the possibility of making some kind of sculpture which not only retrieves some sense of what it is like to be surrounded by objects and their signs but puts their effects to work. It is the putting-of-effects to work which distinguishes what I would call a 'critical' postmodernism. This centres on a familiar distinction between making and taking. The job of the postmodernist artist is not simply to *make* things, to capture a likeness or identify with a particular emotional state, but literally to *take* things, to displace their identifications.[10]

By following John Roberts' concept of 'putting effects to work', we can formulate a distinction between Cragg's *bricolage* and Jencksian post-modernism. Duggie Fields sought to stress the triviality of art in the postmodern era, adopting a semiological approach as a basis for a deconstructive theory of the image. By imposing on the viewer a significance that was merely an appropriational insistence on the presence of what he could not produce, Fields expressly thematized art's inadequacy in relation to articulating the complexity of postmodern existence. In some senses Cragg's work radicalized Jencksian Po-Mo, the collapse of any available symbolic code leading to his use of the atavistic found object. However, the manner in which Cragg puts his fragments to work suggests that he aimed to transcend Jencksian agnosticism by constructing a speculative sculpture from modernism's ruins.

At the very end of the 1970s, Cragg favoured of reconstruction, his procedure becoming predominately one of finding, sorting and organizing fragments of the modern world into an objective and structured form. 'The epistemological construct of reference object and fragments arranged within a related shape, begun in *Four Plates,* continued to operate in Cragg's work for the next two years. It appeared most significantly in 1978 with *New Stones – Newton's Tones,* which for Cragg was a breakthrough, furthering this use of the object ... Here Cragg used broken bits of everyday utilitarian items, predominately those made of plastic. With this work Cragg found a means to endow banal objects with expressive power.'[11] *New Stones – Newton's Tones* (1978) consists of small pieces of coloured plastic arranged in a rectangle following the sequence of Issac Newton's spectrum: dark red, red, orange, yellow, green, blue, dark blue and violet. The suggestion here was that art experience was no different from the experience of colour in everyday life, everyday life being signified by the discarded fragments used by Cragg to create the sculpture. There was also a shift from the Romantic and rustic of Richard Long and Hamish Fulton in place of the urban and domestic environment. As far as materials are concerned, there was now little difference between Cragg's work and Andre's Minimalism, which also *symbolically* evoked a non-art discourse. However, while *Black and White Stack* (1980) clearly mimicked Minimalism formally (being a floor-based geometrical structure), as a structure it was contaminated, constructed from the mangled detritus of modern society, revealing the disorder masked by the slick surfaces of modernist aesthetics.

If *New Stones – Newton's Tones* undeniably referred critically to Andre's floor works, it marked a decisive break with Minimalism's iconophobic disdain for aesthetic decision-making and pictorial representation. This much was confirmed by *Red Skin* (1979) which saw Cragg position a number of red plastic objects on the floor in a more painterly fashion, constructing the image of a Native North American. The iconography of the work seemed to have very clear links with New Image paintings of the same period, particularly Malcolm Morley's paintings based on clichéd Western perceptions of Native Americans. In following works such as *The Streets are Made of Cowboys and Indians* (1980), *Red Indian* (1983) and *African Culture Myth* (1984) Cragg made these links all the more explicit, by placing the fragments on the wall. In this, Cragg's sculpture began to bear an increasingly close resemblance to Julian Schnabel's archaeological plate paintings. Cragg seemed cynical of the Neo-Expressionist trend nonetheless, as his satirical *New Figuration* (1985) wall assemblage insinuated. A simultaneous shift away from such vacuous emblematic cultural icons came with an exhibition of works held at the Whitechapel Art Gallery from 27 February to 22 March 1981 which engaged directly with current social issues: *Postcard Union Jack, Policeman, Riot* and *Britain Seen from the North.*

Cragg's signature procedure reached its apex in the *Five Bottles* installation, exhibited at the Lisson Gallery in 1982 ('Tony Cragg: Sculpture', 2–22 December) and in Tokyo ('Aspects of British Art Today', Metropolitan Art

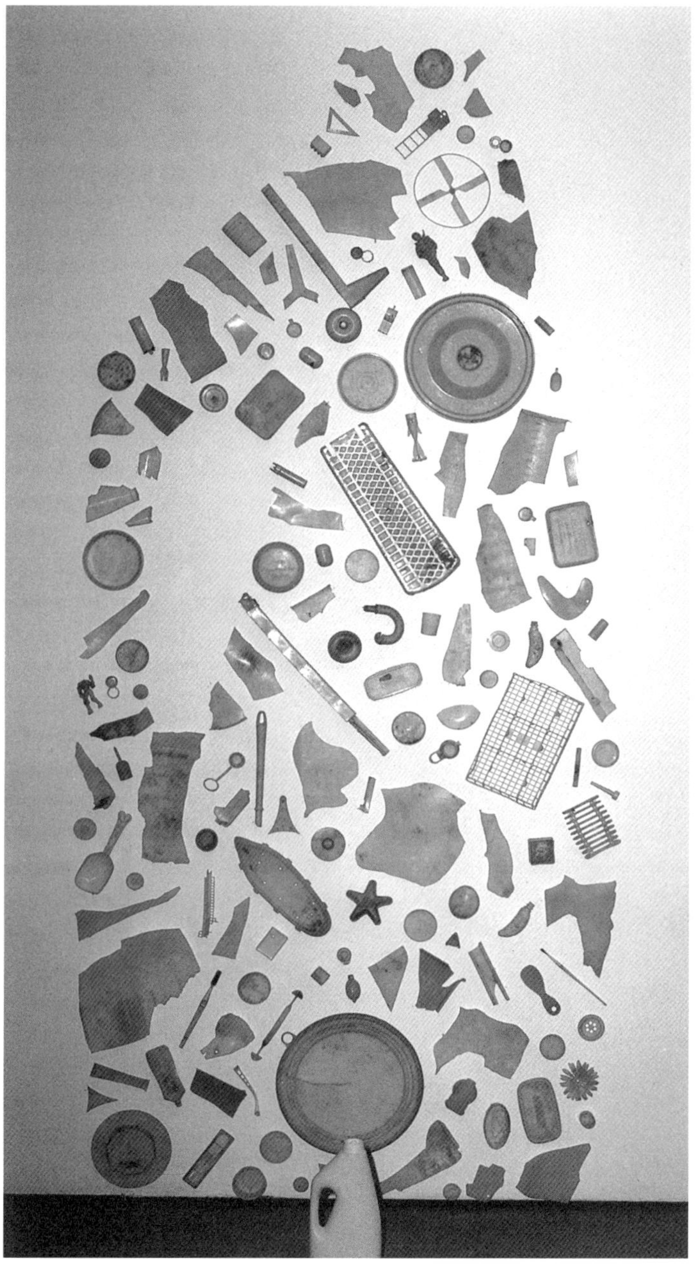

5.1   Tony Cragg, *Five Bottles (Yellow, Green, Orange and Blue)* (1982), installation at the Metropolitan Art Museum, Tokyo, coloured plastic fragments, dimensions variable, Collection Galerie Buchmann, Saint-Gall, 1982

Museum, 27 February–11 April). (See Figure 5.1.) Here, a number of discrete elements, each a fragment of a brightly coloured mass-produced object, were formed into simple, decoratively appealing and easily recognizable shapes. Each silhouetted motif on the wall took its outline from the found plastic bottle on the floor in front of it, so that the image presented was a hugely magnified shadow cast by a three-dimensional artefact. In *Blue Bottle* (1982), a found blue plastic washing liquid bottle served as Cragg's prototype object.

Significantly, the prototype could be seen to comply with the rigorous construction standards of modernist design; it was manufactured according to the Taylorist system of production and clearly displayed its functionality. By setting this object apart, Cragg imbued it with an aura often associated with works by the pioneers of the International Style. While this demonstrated the efficiency and beauty of modernist construction techniques, Cragg simultaneously suggested that the modernist ideal was flawed from its inception by constructing a large reproduction of the prototype object from the debris of similar artefacts. The broken detritus of modernism here provided a 'real metaphor' for the spiritual and physical wasteland created by the structural rationale of mass-production society. Cragg's sculpture thus displayed a love–hate relationship with modernism. While it retained modernist notions both in its Minimalist form and in its refusal to conceal the structure of its realization, it simultaneously undermined this 'liberating' aesthetic by locating it as merely the seedbed of the modern disease of consumer fetishism: 'The distinction between a healthy, natural and a diseased industrial/cultural world lies in the mystification of both. In their insignificance, categories such as these intensify man's powerlessness against a fallacious progress which is solely geared towards either autonomous materiality or scientific specialisation.'[12]

In this there appeared to be some similarities with Cragg's American contemporary Jeff Koons, whose 1981 exhibition 'The New' directly addressed the parallel between the fetishization of new goods in consumer culture and the fetishization of novelty and progress in modernism. Here Koons placed a set of 'found' *New Hoover Convertibles* in Plexiglas cases reminiscent of both display cabinets and the Minimalist sculpture of Donald Judd and Dan Flavin. In this Koons was asking whether the pleasures we receive from new art objects was markedly different from that which we receive from new products.[13] Cragg's silhouette wall sculpture *Hoover* (Museum of Art and Industry, Saint-Étienne, 23 January–8 March 1981) presented a similar set of meanings when read in relation to Conceptualism and Minimalist sculpture. Conceptualist similarities were perhaps most clear in that he also often appropriated 'found objects' in the Duchampian/*assemblage* tradition. Yet for Koons and Cragg there were slightly different iconological concerns. For Koons, the vacuum cleaner was androgynous (it sucks and blows). Its function is to clean, implying Minimalism's sterility. Cragg wallowed in similarly flat irony, the image of a vacuum cleaner being constructed from debris.[14]

Cragg soon added a further twist to what is often called 'parody minimalism', applying the Minimalist concept of systemic procedure to the practice of reproduction. In *Five Bottles*, he created massive reproductions of his prototype objects from other found objects of the same material. He was, therefore, able to reproduce his found source while maintaining a post-modernist stranglehold on his agency as an artist. Nonetheless, in this Cragg reminded us of the modernist notion of a self-contained realm of ideas. Both the prototype object and its representation were constructed from the same material and took on the same form, thereby becoming literal examples of the modernist design concept of 'truth to materials'. At the same time, this concept appeared to be mocked, since the objects forming the representations on the wall, although made from the same material as the source object, clearly took on a series of different shapes and forms. Hence, Cragg appeared to resign the viewer to the poststructuralist notion that we have no hierarchy in which to fix our ideas, that the distinction between ideal form and arbitrary surface is untenable.

Additionally, however, *Five Bottles* also placed Minimalism and Conceptualism under scrutiny. Having negated the concept of artistic agency or expression, *à la* Minimalism, the viewer is left to judge Cragg's work ultimately by the purely external criterion. Having arrived at the notion that his sculptures might demonstrate a critique of modernist design ideology, we remain struck by the idea that the representational objects on the wall appear to *want* to take on the 'true' Platonic form in front of them.[15] Having no recourse to the artist's involvement with the production of the work in order to explain this, we are led to read the work anthropomorphically.[16] It is precisely at this point that the cerebralism of Minimalist and Conceptualist art breaks down. The rule of systems over the realm of ideas is fundamentally shaken. The self-referential ideology underwriting Conceptualism appears neither self-evident (since it involves principles that are pragmatic rather than pure) nor self-contained (since it is incomplete). The Conceptualist economics of contraction are not celebrated, but mocked by imaginative allusion, by way of an emphatic insistence on metaphor and metamorphosis. Although using the systemic procedures of the detached art of the real, Cragg's sculptures created an opposite effect, asking us to 'read metaphorically'. In re-introducing the possibility of iconographic meaning by way of a postmodern dissatisfaction with this concept, Cragg seemed to achieve the impossible, forging a new set of deep structures from an endgame, postmodernist world of surfaces: '[My] initial interest in making images and objects was, and still remains, the creation of objects that don't exist in the natural or the physical world, which can reflect and transmit information and feelings about the world and … [our] own existence.'[17]

The use of mass imagery taking the form of consumer durables and packaging common to the Lisson School in the late 1970s soon became something of an orthodoxy in its own right. Reversing Cragg's procedure, Bill Woodrow took the skin of one styled product and turned it into a hand-crafted image from another, for example a washing machine and a cowboy film: *Car Door, Ironing Board, Twin Tub with North American Headdress* and *Twin-Tub with Guitar* (1981; Figure 5.2). The wit of the transformation was often startling and the underlying sardonic social comment clear. However, it was a form of imagery equally active in the professional advertising world of the early '80s. When 'The Sculpture Show' – co-sponsored by United Technologies and the Greater London Council – opened in August 1983, John Roberts was roused to claim that the 'Lisson boom is dead. Over the past two years since its "launch" at the ICA and Arnolfini its contradictions have become more and more apparent. The conservative nature of the works'

5.2   Bill
Woodrow, *Twin-
Tub with Guitar*
(1981), twin-tub
washing-
machine, 101.6
cm high

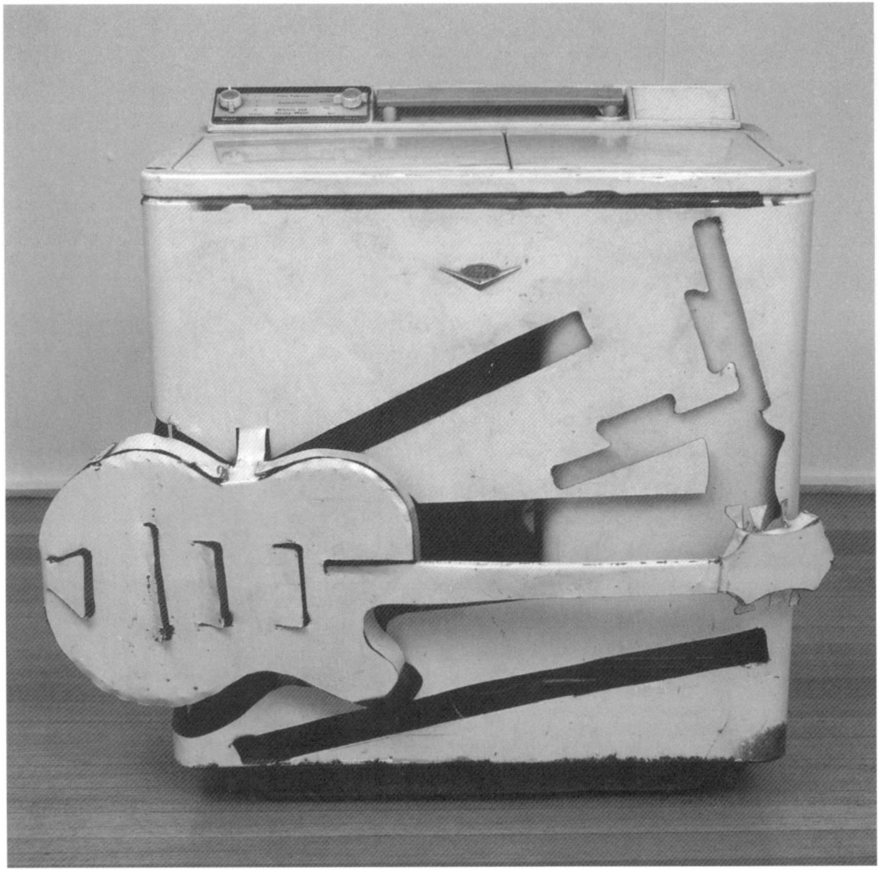

5.2   Bill Woodrow, *Twin-Tub with Guitar* (1981), twin-tub washing-machine, 101.6 cm high

so-called pluralism (or rather arriviste historicism) is revealed in all its blatancy as little more than a British equivalent of American Dekor.'[18] The show – selected by sculptors Paul de Monchaux and Kate Blacker and the critic Fenella Crichton and held at the Hayward Gallery and the Serpentine Gallery – was one of the biggest art shows ever staged in London, being all the more remarkable for being devoted entirely to the new sculpture of Cragg, Woodrow, Vilmouth and Allington and of young then-little-known artists such as David Mach and Julian Opie. This second generation of Lisson sculptors prefigured not only the 'instant' success of artists such as Steven Campbell in the mid-'80s but the entrepreneurial spirit of the warehouse exhibitions pioneered by Damien Hirst at the end of the '80s.

Making It (1983; Figure 5.3) became more important than ever. As Opie put it, 'The new language is more personal than a pile of bricks. Where the Seventies were devoted to making sculpture that couldn't be bought, work now is more accessible and artists are unashamed to make money. Because it is less reverential, it's also more exciting.'[19] However, the show can also be seen as a product of the 1976 art crisis in that it was intended to be yet another PR exercise for public art quangos. With young Scottish sculptor David Mach as the public marker, 'The Sculpture Show' was designed to

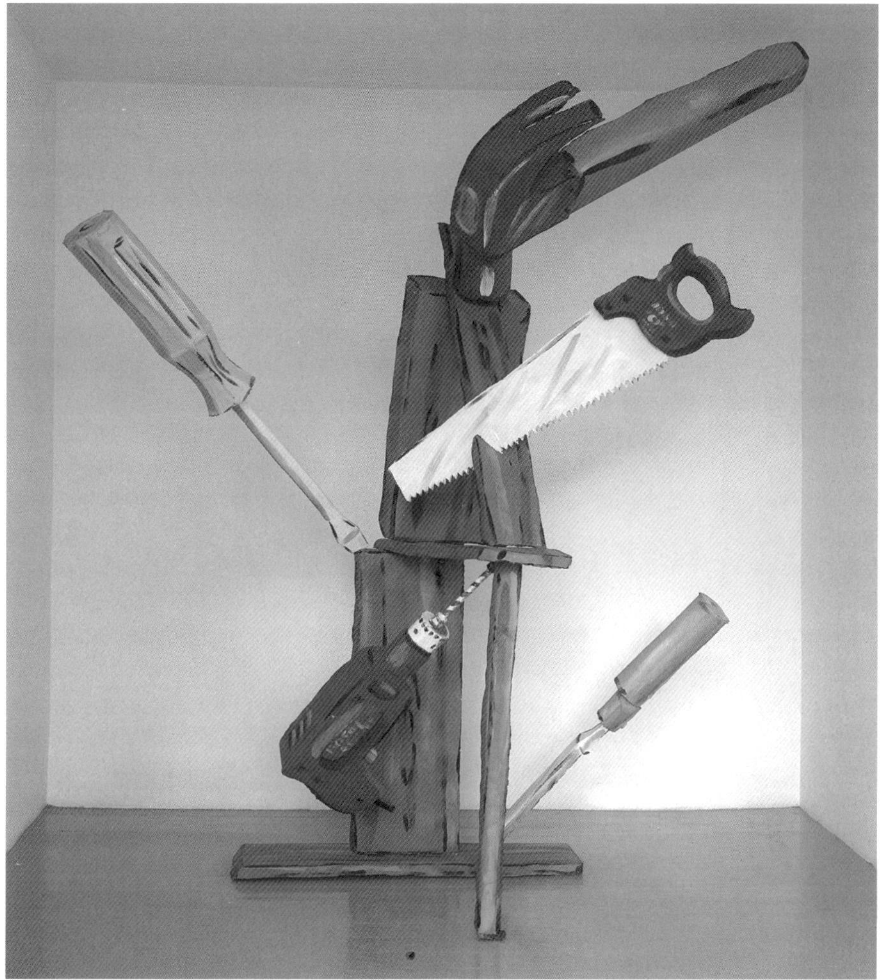

5.3   Julian Opie, *Making It* (1983), oil on steel, 305 × 52.5 cm

promote the notion 'that British sculpture had entered a populist, democratic and accessible phase'.[20] Notwithstanding, precisely by being so high-profile, the show brought out the tabloid scandal-mongers in new force: 'It is almost as if part of the show has been designed to deliberately play into the hands of the person who automatically assumes that what is called sculpture today consists largely of random assemblages of garbage or, at best, of pieces of industrial metal-work. In room after room the pervasive impression is of litter: litter scattered on the floor; litter piled high, litter painted and lovingly displayed or litter left to fend for itself.'[21] Claiming that the latest generation of sculptors had got 'Rubbish Down to a Fine Art', the *Star* and the *Mail* ignored the differences between Minimalism and its newer parody version in order to focus on the 'fact' that Mach had been paid £50,000 for *Polaris*, a 170 × 20 ft sculpture in the shape of a submarine constructed from 6,000 car tyres. This, in actuality, was the cost of the complete exhibition (minus the tyres, which had been donated). On Sunday 21 August 1983, *Polaris* was

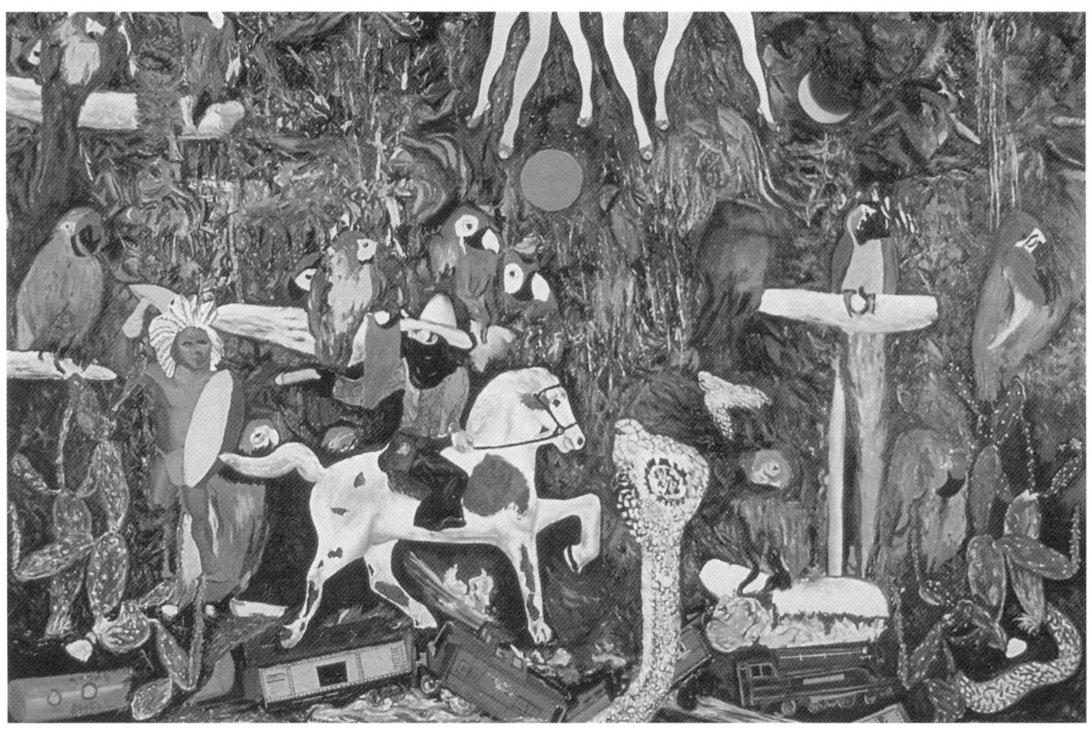

5.4   Malcolm Morley, *Christmas Tree (The Lonely Ranger Lost in the Jungle of Erotic Desires)* (1979), oil on canvas, 182.9 × 274.3 cm, private collection

seriously damaged after being set alight by a 'frustrated [furniture] designer with classical tastes'.[22] 'The most constructive piece of art criticism we have seen this year', was the verdict of George Gale writing for the *Daily Express* the following day. The attacker, James Gore-Graham from West Kensington, suffered 90% burns from the explosion, and died three days later. It was decided not to repair *Polaris*.

Due to the polemicizing of Kitaj and Fuller and the public nature of its art institutions, British art was slower to respond to the International New Image. The 'New Spirit' exhibition in 1981 recruited expatriate Englishman Malcolm Morley to the camp of British painting. For American neo-conservative art critic Hilton Kramer, the polarities of Morley's work arose from an aspiration 'to create an art that addresses the spectator at two levels simultaneously, the mythic/symbolic and the naturalistic'.[23] This, Kramer believed, was the same kind of aspiration that had inspired modernists such as Max Beckmann and T. S. Eliot, offering what Eliot described as 'a way of controlling, of ordering, of giving shape and a significance to the immense panorama of futility and anarchy which is contemporary history'.[24] Certainly, Morley's imaginary scenes of impossible accidents were constructed by his desire to retrieve the magic of childhood icons. (See Figure 5.4.) In this sense, Morley was approaching myth from a psychoanalytic perspective: 'to make painting resonant with wonderment, to make painterly seeing oracular, these were and remain Morley's aims'.[25] Yet, as Michael Compton noted, Morley's paintings lacked the formal unity found in even the most fragmented examples of modernism: 'Representing the literal case directly through [a failure of illusion], Morley dramatises the role of the artist in representing the world … The picture shifts and tends to disintegrate so that the flux and contradiction of the painting can be read as an allegory of the state of the world in which the painter lives.'[26] Indeed, it is surprising to find *any* neo-conservative defence of Morley's work given the willed ruptures in his practice since the mid-1960s.

It has been argued that Morley adapted Semio-Art tactics in relation to his painting practice, adopting a postmodern reading of the world as a system of codes. If his artworks were referential they referred only 'to problematise the activity of reference'.[27] Morley thus seemed theoretically closer to the poststructuralism of the *October* group of critics than to the cultural conservatism associated with the 'New Spirit'. Indeed, in Morley's case it would seem that the melodramatic criticism of Hilton Kramer and Christos Joachimides was more a way of putting pressure on the new painting to measure up to their own standards. Morley was clearly interested in addressing the philosophical issues which conservatives abhorred: meaninglessness, and loss of authenticity. Hence, where Kramer saw mythology and renewed faith in art's symbolic purpose, Robert Hughes comprehended a vast throng of artists fostering a 'Career of Repetition and Glut',[28] recycling old picturesque genres into new saleable genres. Fuller similarly mourned the lack of an 'echo of authentic experience, let alone achieved technical skill, or working through of expressively original forms',[29] perceiving yet another ironic play of codes passing for radicality, a further tiresome example of the flippant reams of cynicism which had been recycled *ad nauseam* by the avant-garde since the 1950s.

There are, however, a number of factors which may have encouraged Kramer's admiration despite the fact that Morley was the poet of a hollow world, intent on making a virtue out of escaping the process of 'making sense'. Although many of his paintings were filled with mythological and archetypal symbols, any attempt to analyse them failed, since the signs were disconnected from any source and therefore only represented themselves. As such they extended the Formalist mode by creating another morphological style, as Morley maintained: 'The anchor in all of it is its realization on a two-dimensional surface. By that I don't mean just the idea of painting as something flat, but rather the mental image in your mind, is two-dimensional or it has no dimension. Imagine the projection of the imagination being almost flat, having no dimension at all.'[30] This suggests that while following the tenets of poststructuralist thought, Morley was simultaneously seeking to subvert them with their opposing force, namely, the apolitical structuralism favoured by Kramer. It would seem that Morley – in making internally self-questioning ambivalence the content of his paintings – was attempting to liberate his art from the dominant critical criteria of the 1980s. Morley's strength over the majority of New Image painting, in this respect, lay in his recognition that the deconstructive method could only subvert the meaning of an artwork after some meaning had been construed. Morley's ingenious method ensured that his paintings were initially read determinately so that, when critically disseminated into post-Expressionist Formalism, they would never appear completely free of iconographic and expressive determinations.

Given that Morley had adopted some of the demythologizing techniques of Semio-Art, it is surprising to find that he also failed to receive the approval of critical postmodernists, many of whom regarded his work as nothing other than a cynical creation of the market.[31] A substantial critique was launched by Craig Owens, who saw that in its use of modernist strategies as a means of attacking modernism's radical impulse itself, the New Image signalled a 're-newed authoritarianism masquerading as anti-authoritarian'.[32] Sandro Chia's paintings, for example, often functioned as ironic comments on the heroics of past art. As Owens observed, Chia's use of altered quotations from established 'masterpieces' and from classical myths functioned 'not as respectful homage, but as an act of mutilation'.[33] Morley's painting did not amount to such a wholly negative revelation of the impossibility of painting meaningfully, but rather to a representation of the constraints upon meaning.[34]

Morley's interest in sensual watercolour encouraged him to make his first trip to England for twenty years in order to make something of the bourgeois civilities connected with the conspicuously sensual medium. He travelled extensively, painting the English landscape *en plein air*: 'It's a way of getting lost – of getting rid of self-consciousness. The problem of this two-dimensional business is that it's constantly creating a type of self-consciousness which, unfortunately, looks very ugly in terms of an individual's idea of something. The idea is to have no idea. Get Lost. Get Lost in the Landscape.'[35] Despite his claim to be 'lost in the landscape', the paintings which Morley produced in this year (*Landscape with Horses Till the Cows Come Home*, *Cows* and *Landscape with Horse*, all 1980) continued to testify to his fascination with the souvenir, an interest which allied his work with *déjà-lu* experience. A curious enchantment with travel and transport had consistently manifested itself in his early paintings of pleasure cruisers, souvenirs and postcards. The search for pastoral bliss was increasingly associated with the innocence of childhood as located in his constant magical-realist references to the toys of his infancy (model aeroplanes and boats, toy soldiers, Indians, medieval knights and so on). This was amplified in his cultivated Expressionism, as he depicted increasingly overt exotic provinces from well-thumbed holiday brochures. In addition to the parrot paintings in Florida, he painted scenes in Costa Rica, Arizona and Central America, and explored the tropical jungles of Africa and the Egyptian deserts. Morley's commitment to the notions of metalanguage is synonymous with his 'tourist' or 'outsider' status, as signified by his paintings of Native American reserves. His distance was made even more literal by his choice of islands as subject matter: the Greek and Caribbean islands, and the Portuguese and Spanish islands of the Atlantic. Given that islands are literally detached from the rest of the world (though not necessarily from civilization) they represent escape, allowing an expansion of the category of the real so as to encompass myth, magic and other extraordinary phenomena in nature which Western rationalism has tended to exclude. Morley's visit to the British Isles, then, should have been a highly significant event. 'Constable Country' was the very source of naturalistic, picturesque and sublime landscape painting. It was also his childhood home, suggesting that the high degree of biographical content found in his work would be emphasized.

In Morley's English paintings, established notions of national identity appear only to be invoked inauthentically. Far from being born of a nostalgic longing for 'naturalistic' descriptions of the countryside, Morley's clichéd visions of English farm landscapes seem to have been born of the contention that places are characterized by their surface characteristics, that we are all tourists who may only see what we are told to see. In effect, these sketches appeared to reverse the emphasis and processes of his earlier photo-realist paintings which were in part designed to 'correct the habit of the eye and mind of perceiving the world in terms of what they know rather than what they see'.[36] However, while the watercolours appeared to be the outcome of a free and subjective impulse, Morley declared that they were simultaneously the result of putting into play the programmatic intellectual processes that were so crucial for the development of his Super-Realist paintings. Having created a series of 'spontaneous' watercolour sketches of the English countryside, Morley proceeded as ever to deny their authenticity by adopting his systemic 'gridding' procedure, treating his loosely sketched sources as 'objective' evidence. However, it is also apparent that by breaking down his 'spontaneous' responses, as symbolized by the watercolours, into a series of squares, Morley was able to focus all of his attention on the colour, gesture and rhythm contained within a small area. In each instance what was insisted on was the surface and materiality of oil paint. The skin of the painting was vibrant and physical. There was no repainting, no scraping away, no building up of layers. Everything was the result of the first layer of colour laid down. A series of such 'improvised gestures' were 'systematically repeated' square by square until the oil paintings were finished. Morley dramatized the relationship between the preliminary and secondary stages of making, tackling painting as 'act': 'In a sense, I'm doing the painting in order to find out what the painting is: it's truly a means of self-discovery … The painting technique of the re-enactment idea is truly method acting … exhausting. I feel very close to Stanislavsky's method, I'm a method painter.'[37] More than an example of 'awkward authenticity', Morley's painting was polyvalent, riddled with unofficial voices contesting, subverting and parodying each of the dominant art discourses of its era.

The success of the Lisson object sculpture and Morley's New Image painting was quickly replicated by a group of painters who emerged from Glasgow School of Art in the 1980s, including Steven Campbell, Adrian Wiszniewski and Ken Currie. All had a hearty distaste for the traditions of Scottish art and a desire to seek an international reputation for their work.[38] 'They were also united in a predilection for figurative imagery as a reaction against the semi-abstract painting that flourished in Glasgow School of Art for years. They differed in the nature of figurative imagery and its aims, ranging from the poetic to the political. They had *no* common programme, rarely exchanged ideas, at times were diametrically opposed in terms of subject matter and content and were fuelled by a passionate, often violent, rivalry.'[39]

In his first few years at Glasgow School of Art, Campbell studied in Roger Hoare's Department of Murals and Stained Glass, a department generally designed for students whose work did not fit into traditional categories (although it was commonly used as a dumping ground for 'trouble-makers' such as Campbell). Campbell fully complied with the remit of the department, producing furniture and sculpture and writing, placing works in various arrangements and finally planning *Gesamptkunstwerk* performances which included all of these elements. 'During and after the performances came a series of figurative paintings featuring a single person ... I called him Hunt. I was painting him at the same time I had all these 1940s murder magazines – I looked down and saw the headline: "Is it Hunt or is it ... ?" He is athletic, wears a raincoat, walks around a lot and falls from great heights.'[40] Campbell's use of the character Hunt has many parallels with Kitaj's use of 'Joe Singer', despite the fact that Campbell's narrative approach was in direct contrast to Kitaj's (obscure literary references rather than readily available art historical sources). If Joe Singer was 'an archetype representing a condition of man, and more specifically of the Jew, in the twentieth century',[41] then Hunt was his postmodern shadow, an incompetent voyager-detective trapped in a painted world. Like Kitaj, Campbell continued to make use of his own leitmotifs, recycling images from one work to another.

Such 'visual art' influences became increasingly important following Campbell's forced transferral to the Department of Painting and Drawing succeeding the closure of Murals and Stained Glass. Campbell's tutor became Alexander Moffat who, in line with Timothy Hyman's narrative-painting thesis, earnestly stressed to students the importance of Léger, Beckmann and Balthus.[42] Analogous art historical references quickly multiplied in Campbell's work, promoting one commentator to describe his paintings as 'Sendak and Glen Baxter and early Balthus on a *Boy's Life* junket to Fuseli-land?'[43] Certain similarities between Campbell and Beckmann were also evident, as Campbell's commentary on contemporary events became increasingly oblique 'tangles of myth, allegory, and dream'.[44] It is, however, absurd to argue that Campbell simply abandoned his performance work in order to absorb Hyman and Moffat's thesis. In direct contrast, Campbell demonstrated that the application of pictorial 'languages' *necessitated* their extension; since all languages are 'impure', the procedures of 'narrative painting' must constantly mutate. By being restricted to paint as a medium, Campbell was ensured that his work would evoke a sense of his struggle to come to terms with an unfamiliar 'language'.

On graduating from Glasgow School of Art in 1982, he promptly gained recognition throughout Britain when four of his large paintings were included in 'Expressive Images', a show of seven young Scottish painters at the New 57 Gallery in Edinburgh. The selector, Moffat, created the impression that such work was both a continuation of the Scottish Expressionist tradition and representative of the International Style of 'New Image' painting, mirroring the disingenuousness of the 'New Spirit' exhibition. Although Campbell was encouraged by the International New Image style, as a student he had mainly been involved in performance work influenced by Gilbert & George and Bruce McLean's Nice Style Pose Band.[45] Rather than a form of Expressionism, Campbell's art was a decidedly *staged* wrestling match with the archaic conventions of narrative painting, as Moffat later pointed out: 'His monumental pictures – vivid in imagery, complex in detail and rich in formal invention – retain the device of the dramatically struck pose from his earlier performance works. Unlike the vast majority of New Painters, Campbell's work remains free of stylistic eclecticism or quotation and has never concerned itself with expressionist angst.'[46]

Campbell's art school performances invoked a conceptual approach to figuration, leading him to treat the image as a sign rather than as an expressive device.[47] Far from being Kitajesque exercises in draughtsmanship, his early paintings were designed to be read as frozen performances wherein the human figure – gesticulating, posing, sometimes over-acting – was arranged in Mannerist, balletic positions. 'There is a tinge of Samuel Beckett in these absurdities, only Campbell isn't gloomy.'[48] Indeed, by representing static 'situations' in the Hegelian sense of the word, Campbell encouraged viewers to recognize that the absurd cannot be represented or performed without resorting to cliché:

First I did the drawings for the *Hiker's Ballet* and I thought it was a marvellous idea of a guy chasing a fern across a stage [trying to flatten it with his knapsack]. Every art 'performance' I've ever seen has always been boring … So that's why I put a yawning child in it, to represent the way most people feel who go along to these things.[49]

Within two days of appearing in 'Expressive Images' Campbell left for New York to study at the Pratt Institute, courtesy of a Fulbright scholarship, where he was able to utilize his skills as an impresario more fruitfully, quickly establishing his reputation with two solo exhibitions, at Barbara Toll Fine Arts and the John Weber Gallery in 1983. Between 1983 and 1984 Campbell's work appeared in thirteen group exhibitions and two solo shows in the USA and one solo exhibition in Munich, before being given a solo exhibition at London's Riverside Gallery. His renown in the USA was such that he did not return to Glasgow until 1986, by which point he had taken on Morley's mantle as Britain's most successful, and most productive, ex-pat painter.

Commuting daily from Manhattan to his studio in Brooklyn in subway cars covered by subway artist Keith Harings, Campbell became enraptured by the tales of P. G. Wodehouse and Bram Stoker. His paintings were soon dominated by pretty vacant young Englishmen in tweeds and plus fours who often appeared to be undertaking experiments or exploring absurd landscapes: all the 'eccentricities' of American expectations of Europe at one false remove. Hollywood clichés of Scottish identity were also favoured, especially the shortbread-tin landscapes of Edwin Landseer: 'I usually paint things that are typically Scottish because apart from Landseer no-one's really done that. And he made such an arse of it – in a wonderful way.'[50] Although American critics keenly described the manner in which the 'fir trees, the ferns, the rugged terrain, the frequent castle ruins in the background distinguish his landscapes as Scottish',[51] they were more than aware that 'the artist, a native of Glasgow … has toured the Scottish Highlands only within the confines of an automobile'.[52] Like Morley, Campbell's travellers and explorers did not seek authentic experiences of the landscape; their journeys were dictated by aesthetic predicates. *The Man Who Climbs Maps* (1984) revealed a world which has collapsed into its own representation, a world that is completely at the mercy of man. The attempt to paint the world is futile; we are reminded of the old chestnut, 'The perfect map would cover the entire kingdom.' Campbell, then, reveals a typically postmodern fascination with clichéd views of nature and culture, the *déjà-lu*. While there is a strong element of Morleian catastrophe, confusion and artifice, 'there's also some order in it and the order tends to be the composition'.[53] Unlike Morley, Campbell was not content to allow man to ascend nature. In a number of drawings and paintings we find nature taking 'revenge' on its human analysts, as in *Fern's Revenge – Pool* (1984).

On an iconographic level, Campbell's emphasis on the performative and temporal character of producing and looking at paintings was explicit in his recurring choice of hikers and pitched tents as symbols which remind us 'that we are but temporary dwellers on this earth'.[54] At the level of practical genesis, by painting at such a furious pace, Campbell's working method increasingly paralleled Wodehouse's.[55] Basically hackneyed plot outlines were adorned with increasingly zany kinds of inventiveness, turning stock situations on their head. Improbable events occurred in seemingly 'realistic' frameworks. Physical traits were singled out for enlargement so that the effect was of a two-dimensional caricature, as in *Two Men Gesturing in a Landscape, Each with the Chin of Joan Sutherland* (1984) and *Nasal and Facial Hair Reactions to Various Disasters* (1985). (See Figure 5.5.) Due to Campbell's rate of production, explorers, architects, footballers, huntsmen, hikers, David Hume (the Scottish empiricist philosopher) and Van Helsing (from Bram Stoker's *Dracula*) soon became recognizable 'stock' characters in the sense that they existed primarily to fill certain narrative functions in the 'plot' of his paintings. Once viewers became familiar with Campbell's characters, each of their actions began to remind them of many other actions, since they constantly recurred and referred. Thus the very individualism and self-centredness of characterization was an obsessively repeated ritual.

Far from being 'Scotland's answer to Sandro Chia',[56] Campbell pastiched New Image trends. His parodies were forms of intellectual in-jokes, as often was his use of quotation and cliché. This again parallels Wodehouse who, in his use of quotations, deliberately underlined their nature as clichés, relying heavily on *Roget's Thesaurus* and the *Dictionary of English Synonyms*. Delighting in the juxtaposition of styles, Wodehouse often juxtaposed different sources into one sentence to invite a type of guessing game, a technique which Campbell turned against the master. Like Wodehouse, Campbell revelled in

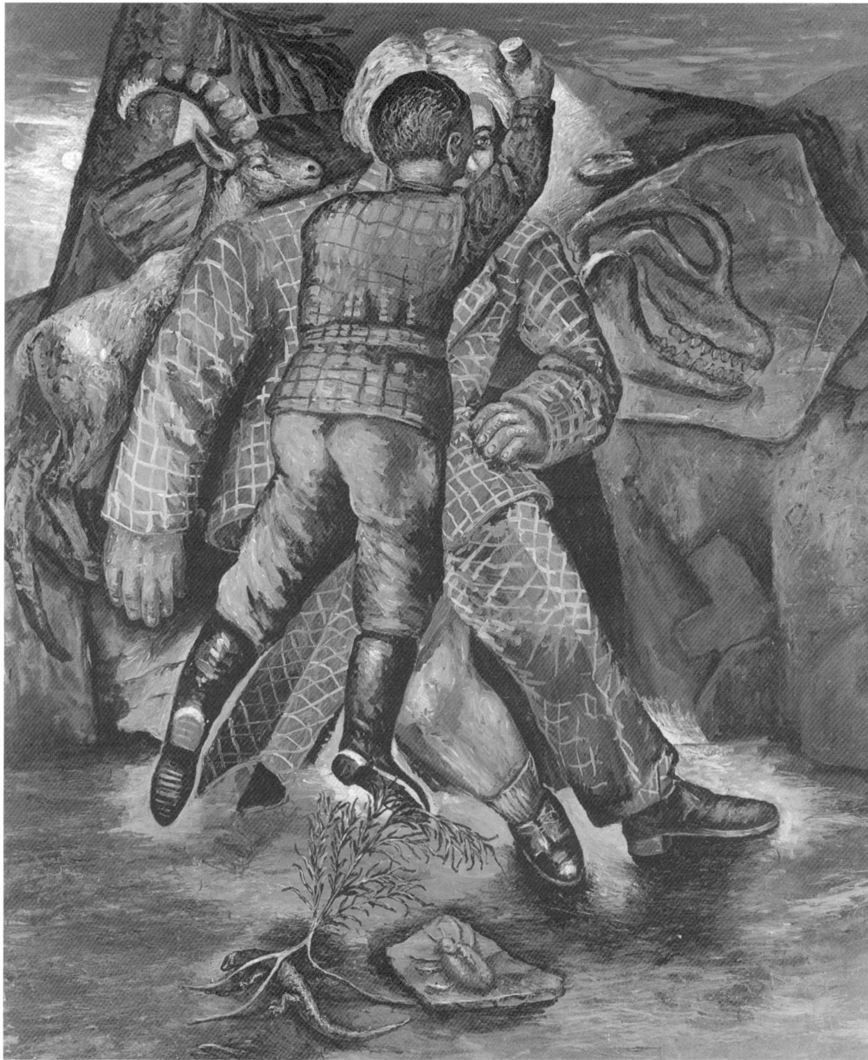

dire puns, describing incidents that don't necessarily mean anything in order to allow his images to masquerade towards something else. 'The awfulness of his puns and the clumsiness of his painting technique frequently totter on the verge of failing yet always pull themselves back from the abyss … ', wrote one critic.[57] Our search for a key to his post-Conceptual painting is really a search for a way to enjoy the pleasure of living in a world that we have made by full understanding, just as the figures the paintings contain are 'people hunting for the meaning of things'.[58]

While the milieu in which performance might define itself was delineated in his paintings, Campbell's characters appeared incapable of initiating measures that impact upon and change their situations in any significant way. Where changes in situation did occur, landscape or buildings, rather than characters, were represented as the chief agents of change. In Campbell's paintings nothing ever turned out as we might expect; if his characters did not always fail or were not frustrated, most of their actions were futile – they were unable to achieve productiveness, break out of the vicious circle of their fate. In short, they failed to become agents of history for themselves. Their only actions were things that related to the structure of the painting, which was therefore the very fabric of their perceived history.

Campbell's construction of his own critical context was summarized most eloquently by Stuart Morgan in his catalogue essay for Campbell's 1984 Riverside Studios exhibition: 'Paradoxically the severance from pictorial conventions which characterises post-painting "painting", running parallel to an increased awareness of textuality in post-structuralist thought, causes a greater awareness of those conventions, which are both cast aside and submitted to scrutiny.'[59] While Morgan was favourable towards this practice, he clearly regarded it as an enigma which might be resolved by modifying critical methods: 'Post-conceptual painting badly needs a critical terminology; art-historical language makes assumptions which do not apply because of its attempt to break with them.'[60] Indeed, Campbell clearly recognized that reverence towards painting could not be restored if the ossified clichés that dominated anti-Conceptual painting were merely ridiculed.

Adrian Wiszniewski graduated from Glasgow School of Art in 1983, one year after Campbell. Like Campbell, Wiszniewski struggled to invent a pictorial language capable of sustaining witty observations, while studying in the Department of Murals and Stained Glass. Wiszniewski's paintings were more graphic than painterly, using exaggerated devices as shortcuts to convey ideas. Although he shared Campbell's desire to compose a rich web of verbal associations, his work was generally more lyrical and less grotesque than Campbell's. Comparisons were made with New Image painters such as Chia and Francesco Clemente, although his work was closely related to illustrations from children's books. This was combined with an interest in clichés and puns, making the title and the work the same thing. In this, Wiszniewski was indebted to McLean, Gilbert & George and Jasper Johns. Pictures of youthful melancholic poets dreaming in emblematic landscapes and idealized interiors are typical of the Romantic tenor of his work, recalling the wartime works of English Neo-Romantics such as John Minton, John Craxton, William Blake, Samuel Piper, the Pre-Raphaelites and Cecil Collins. 'But Wiszniewski's work is not mere indolent escapism: it is an attempt to unite the past with the present and our present lives with all that has been lost. This intention is most apparent in his paintings about an imaginary Jewish brother, a representative of what he has lost through his parents' exile from Poland.'[61] Undeniably, many of Wiszniewski's works were directed against the reactionary voices of the mid-'80s. *Attack of a Right Wing Nature* (1985), for example, examined the Social Darwinism of Thatcherite Britain.

Many critics were less than favourable, as for example Sarah Kent: 'New Image offers a world free from the constraints of the social, political and moral dimensions that circumscribe our actual lives. And this boundless freedom is the source of its insistent and persuasive charm. It portrays a world of hedonistic irresponsibility and indifference, where events are inexplicable, symbols indecipherable and actions free from constraint – a world that exists nowhere – a dreamtime, the realm of the child or the primitive.'[62] Kent suggested that an attenuation of 'reality' underlay the New Image, since it was enmeshed in the chaos of subjectivism. By directing attention away from social 'reality' through 'the denial of history of development, and thus, of perspective', the New Image was seen to establish an assumption that the world is inherently inexplicable and thereby beyond improvement or change:

under the dominance of either conservative or post-structuralist 'post-critical' readings of postmodernism, the eclecticism of reference in much of the new painting has openly contested the possibility of any discursive historical function for painting. As Michael Phillipson, British painter and critic, has said in *Painting, Language and Modernity*, which in many ways represents the most sophisticated defence of this position, the new painting's emphasis on parody and pastiche is essentially a question of mourning and loss.[63]

Perhaps the last nugget of historical consciousness was not entirely being absorbed into a magical sphere. Campbell's attitude was the very opposite of resignation, in that it kept alive the business of historical failure in a rancorous disaffection from the established order of things; critical resistance was not replaced by a mere willingness to escape from history into some magical sphere where problems can be dissolved, but by a permanent psychological insurrection. For critics such as Sarah Kent and John Roberts, to believe, even temporarily, in illusions was to settle for a world that is undecipherable, unknowable and unchangeable. While remaining alert to the ways in which history may be devoured by myth, it must be understood that demystification has its history. If all this entails that the new British painting *was* a denial of history, it still remains to see this as a denial which was itself historically conditioned. The nature of this denial has much to reveal about the nature of what is denied by both artists *and* viewers, about the pressures of history within the contemporary imagination. In varying degrees, Morley, Campbell and Wiszniewski challenged viewers to construct their own worlds, not by entering into a 'creative' collaboration with the artist but by refusing the very possibility of construing meanings and developing significances in relation to their works. This refusal of signification should have been critically enabling, turning the viewer back out on the world.

Art critics, however, were convinced that if the work did not *mean* something then it must be a confidence trick. Brandon Taylor, for example, desperately implicated the art market in order to 'explain' the new painting:

As numerous recent TV appearances attest, these artists enjoy seeming lost in an unreal world of mysterious events which for some reason has followed them into the present from the past. Echoes of their earlier lives in Scotland, Poland or elsewhere dominate the work of these so-called New Image artists – a fact which appears to encourage their being purchased by the Chase Manhattan Bank in New York for its wealthy and anonymous buyers. Frequently attired in 'new conservative' clothing and hairstyles, the *dramatis personae* of these paintings have been incapacitated from making emotional or intellectual contact with the live issues of their day.[64]

In order to substantiate this attack, Taylor binds together two unrelated claims, creating what has become *the* main case against all New Image painting. Firstly, it is suggested the success of the second generation of new painting was *purely* commercial. The artists appear on television and have their work purchased by wealthy patrons, therefore they are simply entrepreneurs promoting a new line in commodities. The practices of painting undoubtedly merge with the politics of exhibition, criticism and the work of dealers, markets, curators and collectors, yet to state this does not dematerialize painting as being outside the possibilities for any form of cultural intervention any more than critiques of cultural paternalism destabilized the integrity of the institutionalized avant-garde at the end of the 1970s.[65] Taylor's critical definition of *all* new painting practices as neo-conservative reinforcements of the machinations of the art market, the acceptance of the pseudo-avant-garde being useful only as another marketing strategy, is simply a reflex reaction to the perceived collapse of cultural paternalism. Taylor's Marxism led him to search for a similar analogy between content and political conviction in the new painting, creating the absurd suggestion that the clothing worn by characters in Campbell's and Wiszniewski's paintings might reveal the painters' unconscious right-wing tendencies. Hence, while claims that its success was based on commercialism might explain the prominence of and critical acclaim for the new painting, they entirely failed to respond critically to the art in question.

Unlike his rivals, Ken Currie, who graduated from Glasgow School of Art in 1985, sought to deal with social and political issues in his work, 'facing up to the realities of modern Glasgow'.[66] To some degree, Currie's work was made in reaction to that of the first generation of New Image painters from Glasgow, re-enacting, under the tutelage of Moffat, the Socialist Realism associated with Muralism in the '70s, producing a contemporary equivalent of the socialist art of Diego Rivera and Fernand Léger as well as the work of Stanley Spencer, Otto Dix and Max Beckmann (while resuscitating the mural movement's attendant contradictions). Exhibitions such as 'Art History: Artists Look at Contemporary Britain', curated by Catherine Lampert at the Hayward Gallery (29 October 1987–10 January 1988), helped to promote the idea of a 'coherent' radical Social Realism at the end of the '80s, displaying Currie's work alongside that of Helen Chadwick, Kitaj, Paul Graham, Michael Sandle, Terry Setch, Peter de Francia, Keith Piper and Alain Miller. Taylor's 'Critical Realism', held at Nottingham Castle Museum in August 1987, had already toured around Scotland and England, profiling the work of 28 artists in seven issue-based sections dealing with matters such as the 'Irish Question' (as seen in Graham's photographs of watchtowers in Northern Ireland), and 'Satire of the Middle Classes' (represented by newspaper cartoonists such as Gerald Scarfe and Steve Bell). On the one hand there was a tendency in such shows to replicate German Expressionism in terms of both form and content,

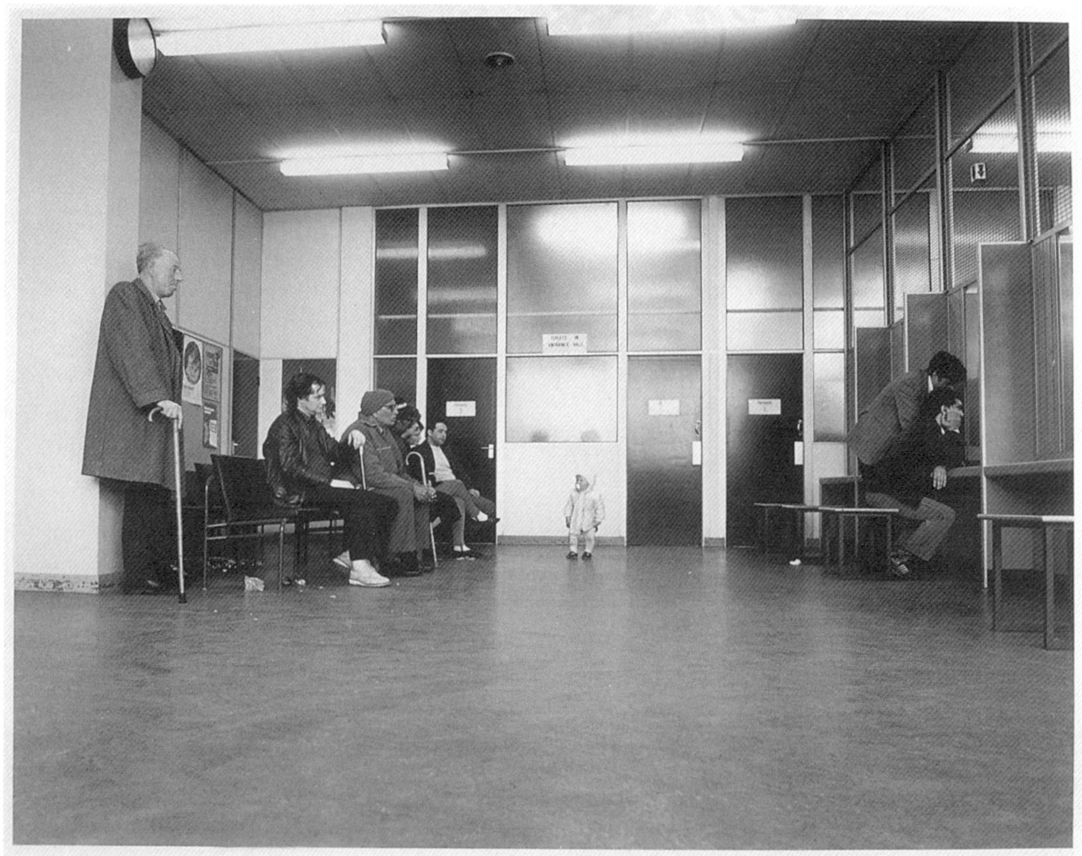

5.6   Paul Graham, *DHSS Office, Birmingham* (*Beyond Caring*, no. 5; 1985), colour coupler print, 88.5 × 106 cm

while other artists continued the largely discredited Photoconceptualist project of exposing 'media myths'. The devices used by participants drew heavily on the pictorial languages of early twentieth-century modernism, and there was little acknowledgement of the impact of the politics of representation. Late '80s Social Realism amounted to little more than a representation of politics: a fatalistic view of a world of DHSS offices, squalor and neglect. (See Figure 5.6.) 'The last thing that is needed in artistic and cultural debate, at a moment of rupture and difficulty in established convention – with all the possibilities that opens up – is for a regressive and prescriptive pseudo-realism to take hold,'[67] wrote Paul Wood.

Currie was also significant in his commitment to establish the Transmission Committee for the Visual Arts in Glasgow in 1983, an artist-run space with the distinct aim of exhibiting politicized art, and encouraging others to do likewise, giving local artists a non-commercial alternative to the London art market. The private-dealer network in Glasgow at this point would not deal in such agit-prop work. Within a short space of time, however, Currie found a dealer in London's Cork Street (RAAB), who could find a market for any New Glasgow Boy, politics and all. While McLean, Campbell and Wiszniewski had, to different degrees, attempted to communicate a pattern of poetic images, Currie aimed to communicate moral and social lessons by painting 'epic' narrative works. Differences between the New Glasgow Boys were put aside for Moffat's influential touring retrospective 'New Image Glasgow', which opened at Glasgow's Third Eye Centre in August 1985.[68] Moffat eagerly outlined the 'group''s relationship to the new wave of international figurative art:

Artists such as Stephen Barclay, Steven Campbell, Ken Currie, Peter Howson, Mario Rossi and Adrian Wiszniewski have all reacted in different ways to the new situation painting finds itself in. Some have seized upon the means of expression initiated by the New Painting to unleash their private obsessions and vivid narratives, exploiting home-made content in ways which were thought barely possible only a few years ago; others have taken a more critical view, pointing out that the New Painting has become all too subservient to capitalist society, but, at the same time, developing a style of painting which benefits from the attention now focused on painting in general.[69]

These trends were also clearly mapped out in the second 'British Art' show held in 1984 – 'The British Art Show: Old Allegiances and New Directions 1979–1984', selected by Marjorie Allthorpe-Guyton, Moffat and Jon Thompson – a far more ambitious project than William Packer's had been in 1979. Moffat and Thompson were selected as representatives of Scottish painting and London-based mixed media work respectively. The subtitle 'Old Allegiances and New Directions' was an indication of diverse approaches emerging in the wake of modernism. The show was pluralistic, divided into seven loosely thematic sections designed to account for the omnidirectional nature of British art in the early 1980s. More than 80 artists and groups were included; however, the range of media was broader than in 1979, including performance, film and video, photography, mixed media and sculpture. The show included stalwarts Auerbach, Kossoff, Caro, Kitaj, John Hoyland and Gillian Ayres in addition to many of the established names of the newer generation such as Wiszniewski, Tony Bevan and Avis Newman. The Lisson Gallery dominated the 'Origins' section, while there was a distinct absence of work by Freud, Ken Kiff, Christopher LeBrun, Opie and Willats.

The anti-Americanism of Jon Thompson's opening essay in the catalogue, 'Reversing the Transatlantic Drift', stressed the literary and poetic aspects of the British tradition as surviving the cultural imperialism of the Americans, and their propaganda for the autonomous art object. For Thompson, European modernism has its roots in Symbolism rather than in the 'reductive' materialism of Manet which dominated American art theory in the post-war era.[70] Thompson's position clearly followed the pluralistic mood of the late '70s, taking it one stage further: 'I try to explode what I think is a dangerous historicist tendency in modernism – to see relationships between different periods of work as causal in some way. The other is to tackle the notion that there is some simple ideological basis for certain kinds of art which makes them antipathetic to other kinds of art … If we can talk about the ideology of art, then we've tried to show that the ideology of art is extremely muddy water.'[71]

The mud produced by the art boom at the turn of the 1980s could most obviously be witnessed in the new mixture of public and private funding, a mixture which was often of mutual benefit. Curators, critics and arts administrators were re-invigorated with the birth of the new movement (Photoconceptualists had written their own critical theory), and dealers had objects to exchange at inflated prices. For the first time in many years, artists were free to profit from their work without being accused of hypocrisy as the Lisson Photoconceptualists and object sculptors had been in the late '70s. This re-invigorated artworld wanted to promote itself as a success, thereby attracting further investment leading to further growth. Following Punk, the 'deregulated' artworld finally learned that it needed scandal less for critical kudos than to attract free publicity, and new money:

As the eighties progress and it becomes increasingly difficult to tell a radical from a conservative the strategy of presenting an 'apolitical' stance has to be considered. This stance, like that of Punk in 1976, however, is a consciously political strategy intended as provocation. As Jean Baudrillard has said, 'Banality, inertia, apoliticism used to be fascist; they are in the process of becoming revolutionary' (*In the Shadow of Silent Majorities*). The notion of an equalisation of all signs calls for a strategy of 'radical eclecticism' designed to raise the issue of the relative rather than absolute nature of human values. To attempt to use the real-life nature of images against the aestheticising formalism of art and at the same time use the authority of art to undermine the reality of real life has become a familiar strategy.[72]

One corollary of this was the establishment of the Turner Prize in 1984 by the Patrons of the New Art, a group of rich contemporary art enthusiasts pledged to promote the visual arts in Britain to a wider (paying) public, awarding £10,000 to the artist who had the finest exhibition in the previous year. Patrons included Nicholas Logsdail and Charles Saatchi. Nominees in the 1980s included Morley, Richard Deacon, Gilbert & George and Howard Hodgkin (all of whom then had works in the Saatchi Collection, Deacon selling through the Lisson). Deacon's work was not so readily commodifiable, nor did it relate directly to the international market for a new spirit in painting. Gilbert & George had been around for some time, and were more closely associated with performance art. Hodgkin, who had also been around for some time, was tainted by his appearance in 'The Hard Won Image'.[73] Hodgkin was too conventional to lend initial credibility to the prize, or British art, as being on the cutting edge of contemporary visual art internationally. In 1984, there were no *established* New Image painters in Britain.[74] As all things to all men, Morley must have seemed the ideal choice for recipient of the first Turner Prize. The jury, of course, was immediately accused of tampering with the laws of geography, given that Morley had lived in New York for twenty years. The choice was seen by neo-conservatives and progressives alike as rewarding Morley's part in the promotion of the 'New Spirit in Painting' show, out of which many dealers, critics and curators were rehabilitating their careers. Unlike awards such as the Prix de Rome which maintained educational and didactic ambitions, the Turner Prize was a quick reward for services rendered to the new establishment. Morley was disgusted at the way the judges told him of his success – by phone at 1:30am – and branded the notion of pitting artists against each other a 'blood sport'. Morley's scepticism towards the prize was confirmed in the following years, in which the initial nominees were all awarded it. Hodgkin won in 1985 – by this time a necessary gesture, given how vociferous the neo-conservative agenda had been in 1984 – Gilbert & George in 1986 and Richard Deacon in 1987. No Lisson or Saatchi artist was left out. Tony Cragg won in 1988 followed by Richard Long in 1989. Anish Kapoor was finally given his honours in 1991 when Channel 4 stepped in as sponsor to save the prize, offering a bounty increased to £20,000.

In the 1980s British art publishing continued to expand, much in line with the influx of private capital in other sectors of the artworld. Following Faure Walker's departure from *Artscribe* in 1983, the magazine edged towards a lifestyle glossiness, moving from essay-based critique to affirmative interviews with rich, successful artist-celebrities. The critical battles of the '70s and early '80s disappeared as democratic artist-led institutions such as the AIR Gallery were superseded by private galleries and Portobello Road art boutiques.[75] With financial support from American tycoons the Butlers, *Artscribe* evolved into an international art glossy under the editorship of Matthew Collings, a painter – trained at London's Byam Shaw Art School in the early '70s – who had worked on the magazine since 1979. Collings was largely supportive of the New Image trends of the '80s, yet had clear affiliations with the critical practice of Art & Language. He gave *Artscribe* an Anglo-American bias, turning it from British-provincialism to international-provincialism, remaining with it until 1988 when, according to Collings, he was forced to resign after 'an office fracas' with the magazine's distribution manager.[76] Collings headed to New York to drum up support for a new London-based magazine, before returning to present art reports for the BBC Late Show. Stuart Morgan became temporary editor of *Artscribe*.

The magazine moved into its final international phase, focusing on the Young British Artists emerging under Saatchi's patronage. Its demise in 1992 fuelled the distribution of two art magazines launched in 1988, both of which were commercially successful. *Modern Painters* – the brainchild of Peter Fuller, who claimed that he needed a new forum for his views, having been systematically excluded from *Art Monthly* and *Artscribe* – became the most popular art journal in the UK. Taking the opposite approach to Richard Cork, Fuller set out to banish discussion of anything *other* than painting and sculpture, much as had *Artscribe* twelve years previously. *Modern Painters'* reactionary voice was something of an embittered last stand in the final battle against cultural modernization, and was saved only by Collings' studied ironic populism. Its irrelevance was marked by the emergence of *Frieze* in the same year. With a market-friendly mix of *Artscribe's* cross-cultural lifestyle features, reviews and glossy adverts formula and *The Face's* fascination with design, *Frieze* would establish the practical and critical terms of British art at the turn of the next decade, focusing predominantly on the work of graduates who had benefited from the most recent radical experiments in fine art education. (See Figure 5.7.) *Frieze's* strength and success lay in its valiant decision to

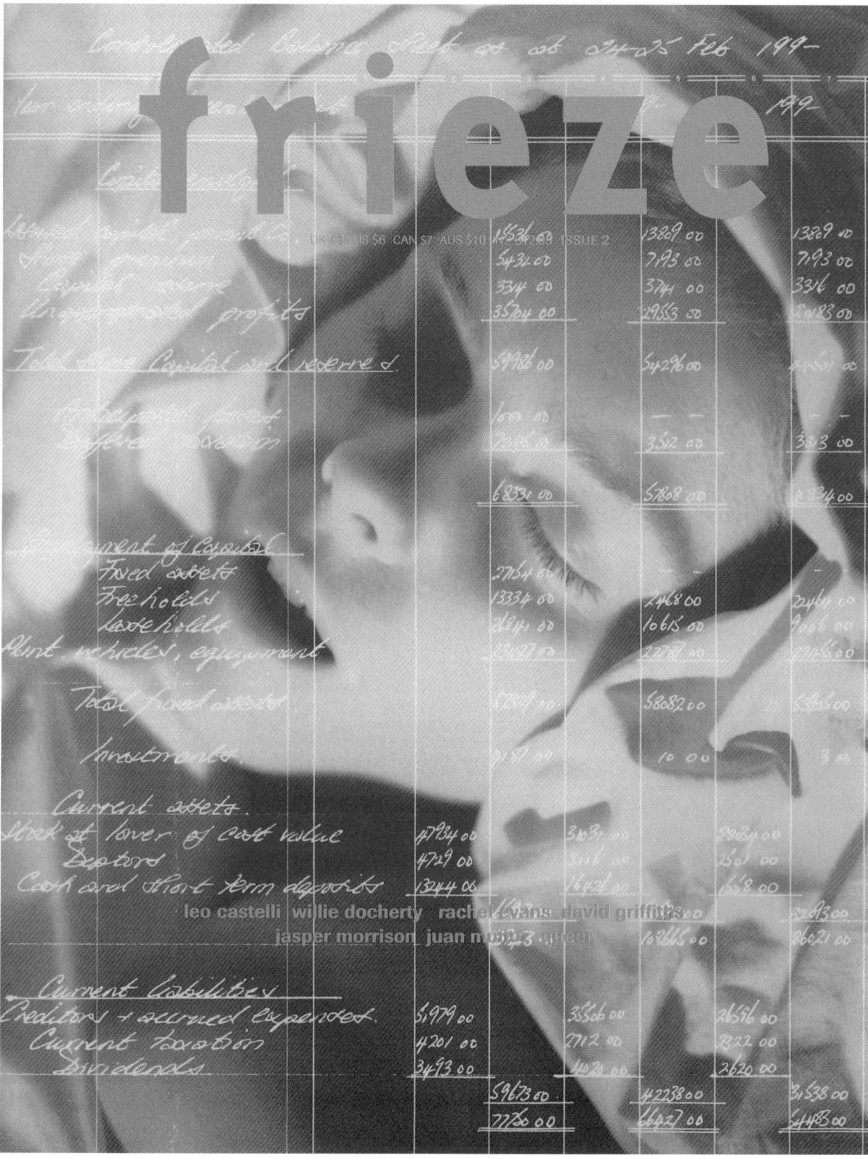

5.7   Issue 2 of *Frieze*, 1988, cover image *I Heard Meaning*, by Rachael Evans

nurture connections with artists who were emerging from art schools in the late '80s to find little coverage or support from the established British art press. As had the launch of *Artscribe* and *Art Monthly* in 1976, *Frieze* signalled and encouraged a seismic shift of focus, as a new generation of artists, dealers, curators, critics and collectors sought to re-align the existing structures of the British art world on their own terms.

Art after Britain?

Now look harder. You're probably saying, 'Hey! That's just a full stop. I've seen one of those before!' But that just goes to show how stupid you are … That black, black circle says a lot about death, it says a lot about modern anxiety, it says a lot about our whole concept of what kind of concept a concept really is, it says a lot about everything and a lot about nothing. And it says a helluva lot about the here and now. Hey! Let's take another look at it: It could be an eye. It could be an arsehole.[1]

In the mid-1980s, radical changes in fine art education were initiated by Keith Joseph, founder of the right-wing think tank the Centre for Policy Studies and Secretary of State for Education in the Thatcher administration. Joseph encouraged higher education to focus on more 'relevant', industry-friendly research and vocational education, by enforcing savage cuts and national academic uniformity. In this harsh climate, fine art struggled to secure funding and to legitimate itself as a sector of higher education which might secure economic growth. Many departments of painting, sculpture, printmaking and photography thus found themselves merged under the auspices of mixed and multi-media Fine Art degrees. Ironically, the Conservative offensive against intellectual dissent and the esoteric specializations of traditional humanist higher education benefited critical postmodernists for whom the sanction against specialisms acted as a means of justifying their disposition towards practices such as intermedia, new media, installation, photography, video and site-specific art. These changes wrought by Thatcherite economic determinism tended to affect peripheral educational establishments, where the need to justify policy and spending in the face of the Conservative reforms was more pressing, than at centralized institutions such as Central St Martin's or the ICA (the Royal College of Art, notably, retains its specialist departments).

As such a peripheral institution, there was a hybrid approach at Goldsmiths College in New Cross, South London. Its school of fine art was not divided into separate departments such as painting and sculpture, and the different year groups were often mixed in the 1980s. Its educational paradigm was a commitment not to an education through the self-expression of innate creativity that many art schools pursued, but to an education in visual culture as a whole. Tutors such as Jon Thompson and Michael Craig-Martin contrasted with each other in terms of taste but they both stressed the value of responding to the history and theory of culture.[2] The traditional master–pupil relationship, representing the transmission or rejection of ideas, was not at the core of Goldsmiths. Rather than elevating the autonomous self, through acts of self-expression and self-discovery, students were encouraged to critically legitimate their work in the currency of cultural theory. The intellectualization of art education in this sense was another anomaly of Thatcherite anti-intellectual educational policy, encouraging artists to accurately measure and justify the existence of their work in terms that might be understood, evaluated and managed by the numerous educational bureaucrats created by Joseph's draconian policies. In the '80s this meant responding to philosophers such as Jean Baudrillard and Fredric Jameson and considering the import of psychoanalytical theory. This, of course, was a paradigm shift which owed a great deal to critical theory and attendant anti-authorialism. In practice it often led to art becoming the illustration of theory in schools as students attempted to jump through educational hoops. Ciphers of self-expression were replaced by ciphers of critical practice. Students were also encouraged to become mercantilists and 'help themselves' as had artists such as Michael Craig-Martin in the 1970s. There was a sense that the Conceptual project might be revisited, opening up artist-run spaces again rather than simply pandering to the saturated '80s art market.

In 1988, a year before he completed his course at Goldsmiths College, Damien Hirst organised 'Freeze', an exhibition of his own and fellow students' work in a Docklands warehouse. 'Freeze' has since been heralded by many of its apologists as constituting a new dialogue with the public while for its detractors it was 'simply a recurrence of the founding myth of modern art: the *Salon des Refusés* of 1863'.[3] Many of the artists associated with 'Freeze' have been subject to a re-enactment of many of the problems and debates associated with the late '70s avant-garde as their work was met with media ridicule. History repeated itself when tank-piece *Away from the Flock* (Figure 6.1) was attacked by an artist in 1994 when on display at the Serpentine Gallery. Like Andre's sculpture, the work itself was attacked with blue ink. In this case, however, the attacker professed that he was attempting to 'improve' the work. The effect this time was not one of universal revulsion on the part of the artworld. Hirst's book *I Want to Spend the Rest of My Life Everywhere, with Everyone, One to One, Always, Forever, Now* contained a pop-out version of the work in question, inviting the viewer to pull a tab which turns the illustration of the work blue.[4] The sensationalism surrounding this work and others entered Hirst, like the 'Bricks' before him, into popular culture. Rather than seeing this as an obstacle, Hirst accepted the publicity. For Hirst, advertising and sculpture were part of the same visual language; people should attend an art gallery as they would a cinema.[5] While Hirst often professed to have abandoned the notion that art might stand in a critical position in relation to the productions of capitalist media, it is clear that his practical work did not engage *directly* with such debates. His art might even be regarded as conservative in that he chose to produce paintings and sculptures,[6] rather than image–text works or performances. By continuing

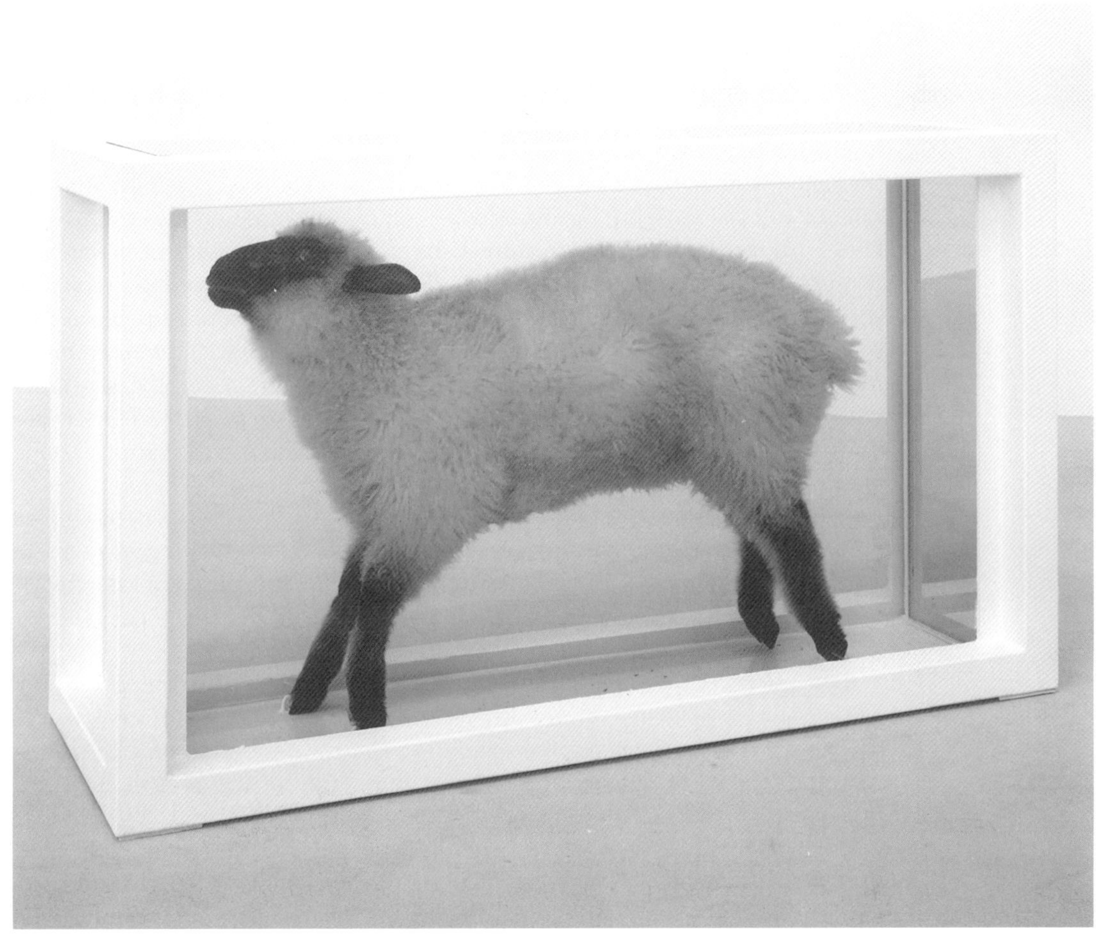

6.1   Damien Hirst, *Away from the Flock* (1994), lamb, steel, glass and formaldehyde, 96 × 149 × 51 cm

with this line of enquiry, however, it is obvious that Hirst's work constituted a complex, yet light-hearted, engagement with '70s issues' of production and commodification. Hirst's installations actively engaged with their own historification in a manner similar to much of the museological art of the late '80s. The Cabinet of Curiosities[7] and the theme of *vanitas* were perhaps most famously reworked in his *The Physical Impossibility of Death in the Mind of Someone Living* (1991). Here, Hirst suspended a 14-foot tiger shark in a formaldehyde solution, the paraphernalia employed in this anatomical diorama harmonizing with a concern with arbitrary schemes of biological categorization and museological spectacle. At the same time he produced a huge trophy of Young British Art, commissioned specifically for Saatchi's court. The pun works nattily: 'What a beauty!', Saatchi might cry at his catch. Simon Ford was entirely correct to claim that the work functioned as a powerful spectacle in nurturing what he called the myth of the Young British Artists (yBas).[8] For Julian Stallabrass, Hirst formulated shallow, 'lite' art: spectacular, clear products and crude puns tailor-made to attract the attention of Saatchi, 'most clearly seen in the prevalence of the one-liner work of art [which] makes its points swiftly with conventional signs'.[9] Was this particular work any more than an expensive ad man's toy?[10]

The tiger shark was one of many attempts made by Hirst to make art that was more 'real', leaving things in a state as close as possible to how they might be found in nature. Early installations for the exhibition 'Modern Medicine' (1990), based on pharmacy cabinets, were predicated on the way science and the museum produced ways of understanding the world.[11] Hirst here both inherited and undermined the modernist centrality of vision and its positivist tenets. As with scientific discoveries, the museum is frequently seen to provide a utopian vision. In Hirst's work the museum's paternalistic role is questioned, the benefit and scope of its taxonometric functions being reduced to 'subjective' themes and preoccupations more generally associated with the history of art: love, death and beauty. Viewers of his work were invited to absorb information in ways which to some extent contradict one another. Hirst's drug cabinets, for example, were 'portraits' of unidentifiable humans, applicable as schemata for a human body. Their reductionism was both serious and amusing, primordial and timely, encouraging viewers to ponder the implications of the museum's role in the acquisition of knowledge in whichever manner they wished: perceptive or myopic, involved or detached, aesthetically fluent or semi-literate.

Ever more complex possibilities of the Cabinet of Curiosities came to lie behind the deceptively limpid appearance of later dissected animal works such as *The Lovers: Spontaneous, Committed, Detached, Compromising …* (1991), two glass cabinets displaying jars containing the organs of a male and a female cow. Prompting the viewer to adopt a number of mutually adverse ways of seeing, Hirst's work deflated and magnified both its meanings and the values by which these meanings are judged, inviting belief by under-cutting it. On the one hand, appealing to the 'animal within humanity', the work invited us to treat the organs non-judgementally. As motifs, the jars and display cabinets also refer to this 'non-judgemental' stripping of nature into a series of discrete objects intended for scientific or aesthetic analysis.[12] Given that the impetus behind Hirst's medicine cabinets and natural history displays was his desire to make people believe in art in the way that they believed in the power of drugs,[13] he therefore encourages us to be lured by the fascination exercised upon us by the title of the work. We readily acknowledge the organs as bovine lovers, and the cabinets and their contents as an artwork, despite the fact that we have no way of knowing whether cows fall in love or whether the cabinets were constructed as a work of art. In so doing we demonstrate our incessant willingness to take up 'reactive' attitudes towards things in the world: praise, blame, love, hate and so on. Equally, for Hirst, science is as reactive as it is non-judgemental, a practice subtly saturated with desire and seduction, the automata of the body. By making internal organs analysable, he dissociates the contents of the body from its form. These bovine lovers live beyond nature and culture; they are literally disembodied; their only territory is the terrain of transgression, affect, death, sex. Although dislocated from their automatic 'natural' bodies, they still appear to have the freedom to recombine and choose their selves, the work now suggesting the *presence* of creative forces.

By allowing visitors to subordinate such traditionally museological forms of knowledge to the elaboration of devices which dislocate perception, Hirst therefore posed the question of whether the primary significance of the information legitimated by science, representation and institutions such as the museum lies in its truth value or whether it is purely relative. Unwittingly, such pragmatic accounts of science and art encourage the wider nihilism which now affects all spheres of knowledge, the belief that the boundaries between consciousness, its products and 'reality' have been totally erased; that there is no more nature, no more reality as such. Hirst draws our attention to the moral issues raised by such inert models of spectatorship, forcing us to recognize the ways in which our consciousness must have moral consequences. Our mythical desires are fictional, manipulable, contingent, but given that there is nothing else, art and fiction, like science, must remain something that we can believe in.

The propensity towards mythologization which Simon Ford identifies as the only unifying characteristic of yBa work is one which is attributed to the institutions of the artworld rather than the work itself. Several critiques of the yBas have focused on their mythological tendencies. Liz Ellis's critique of the 'Britpack phenomenon' condemns its promotion of the 'idea of the dangerous avant-garde while actually remaining unchallenging of the establishment'[14] as mooted in Neville Wakefield's essay for the 'Brilliant!' catalogue,[15] which, like Matthew Collings' writing, aped the style of tabloid newspapers. Wakefield claimed that the mid-'90s artists had grown weary of critical postmodernism. Rather than investigate Wakefield's claim, Ellis's rejoinder emphasizes her repulsion at their alleged rejection of theory:

Sarah Lucas makes it clear that she is not making work of social or political or critical meaning, she says: 'Just look at the picture and think what you like. I knew that everybody would have a response to these pictures, whether they thought I was being gratuitous or whether they thought I was making a feminist point or whether they thought I was actually just carrying on the exploitation' … We are therefore … returned to the old, tired familiar notion of artist as moral relativist, removed from the rest of the world, at liberty to make and say and do without the necessity for explanation or intellectual framework. This role does have social-political implications, and however weary these graduates of Goldsmiths may be, many others are passionately involved in these post structuralist debates. To choose not to join the messy debates over the language of experience, the themes of difference and otherness is to adopt a political and intellectual position. The narcissistic self-referential, free-enterprise nature of the work to the exclusion of any other outside factors ultimately locates the work as politically right wing.[16]

Certainly there is truth in such a critique. Indeed it is a tired truism to say that apolitical stances are political. The problem with this is that it does not tell us in which specific way such models of 'apolitical practice' were political, notwithstanding the fact that Ellis neglect to examine if indeed they are *entirely* intended to be apolitical. The fact that Lucas appears to take no responsibility for the viewer's reactions may mean that she is taking some of the key tenets of critical postmodernism to task, issuing a challenge to anti-authorial theory (can you abdicate *all* responsibility as an artist?). As a project, this has reactionary rudiments. Lucas's early works include *Sod you Gits* (1990), shown at City Racing in Oval, London, which rallied against the bigoted *Sunday Sport* tabloid newspaper by enlarging its report on midget stripper Sharon Lewis. Was Lucas 'exposing' false forms of exploitation or merely creating an avenue for her 'humour' as a model of resistance? Lucas's subsequent shift into using 'everyday' objects such as cigarettes, kebabs and tights marked an iconoclastic negotiation with materials and practices familiar in feminist art practices emergent in the 1970s. In this sense, Lucas's work is unremarkable and perhaps more acceptable to the responsible guardians of critical postmodernity. In retrospect, Lucas's enterprise on the female body was neither serious enough to be critical nor smutty enough to be amusing.[17] Now that they have entered the canon, the subversiveness of sculptures such as *Two Fried Eggs and a Kebab* (1992; Figure 6.2) – a fast-food tableau arranged to resemble a reclining nude – becomes questionable. Such work only functions critically or humorously when viewed as an artwork *by* the bourgeois artworld.

In some ways, such an attack on the yBas repeats the attacks made against the School of London and the New Image in the early '80s by critics such as Sarah Kent and John Roberts.[18] The work must be right-wing because its defenders are lazy critics and/or capitalists. Ford avoided this critical trap by deconstructing the false yBa lineage that linked it with avant-garde groups such as the Situationists and popular movements such as Punk. Much criticism of the yBa phenomenon '"markets" it as avant-garde, even though the yBa clearly have no oppositional intentions'.[19] Ford's critique actively engages with and demythologizes the way in which the yBa movement was created by collectors, critics and dealers from 1988 onwards. There is, nonetheless, a certain irony in the fact that Ford was critical of the success of this process of mythification. While Ford was correct to deny that the yBas were *radical* in the sense that the Situationist mythology might suggest they were, he was unable to entirely deny the Punk legacy. To many, Punk was never politically radical, but a form of stylistic revolt. The yBas were aware that their work would be read from a similar post-Punk position and they organized production accordingly.[20] Much could be said of Gavin Turk's *Pop* (1993; Figure 6.3), a museum cabinet containing a waxwork of the artist dressed as Sid Vicious while adopting the stance of Warhol's gun-slinging *Elvis* – a concise 'report' on the commodification of the avant-garde by the straight artworld. In Ford's schema, Turk's achievement, not exactly an unequalled one, is to have appropriated the aura of radicality to increase the desirability of his exorbitant products. Although Ford is well aware that the failings of the Situationist International are not solely due to the failings of its historians, he remains unduly protective when their name is cited as an influence. It may be misleading to mention Situationism alongside British Punk, but it cannot be denied that some form of *interpretation* of the SI's activities

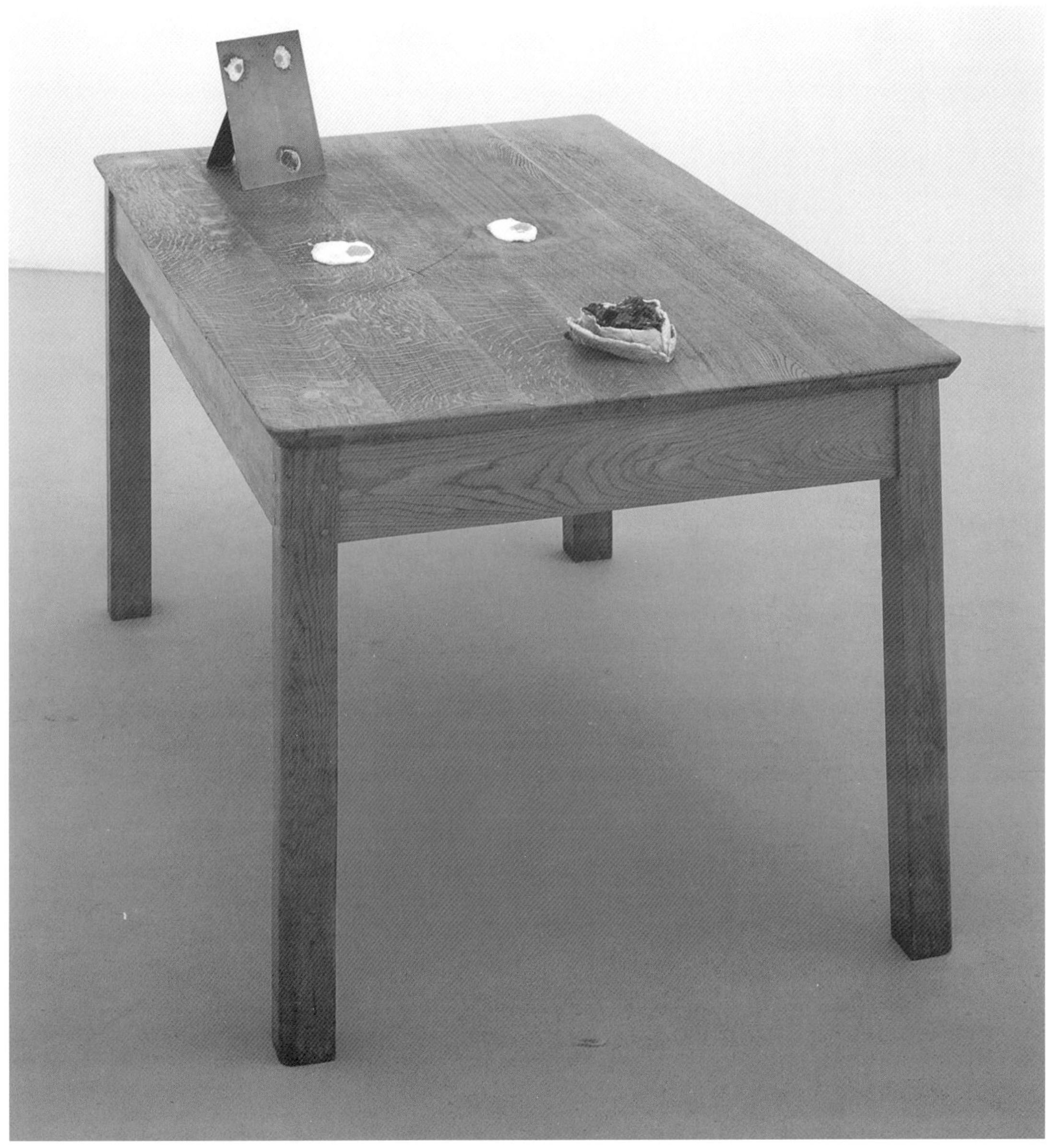

6.2 Sarah Lucas, *Two Fried Eggs and a Kebab* (1992), fried eggs, kebab, table, photo, 76.2 × 152.4 × 89 cm

played a role in its development as a musical genre. There is also a sense in which the yBas' self-conscious mythification coincides, uncomfortably, with the self-promotional tactics of Stewart Home, Jimmy Cauty and Bill Drummond who also seek to capitalize on such a genealogy. Of course, Home's tactics are more obviously transparent than those of the yBas, and as such might constitute a totalizing example of political avant-gardism (see Figure 6.4).[21] But it is equally apparent that Home's tactics are more crude (albeit deliberately) than those of the yBas and their apologists. The yBas' acceptance of commodification was mind-numbing, notwithstand-

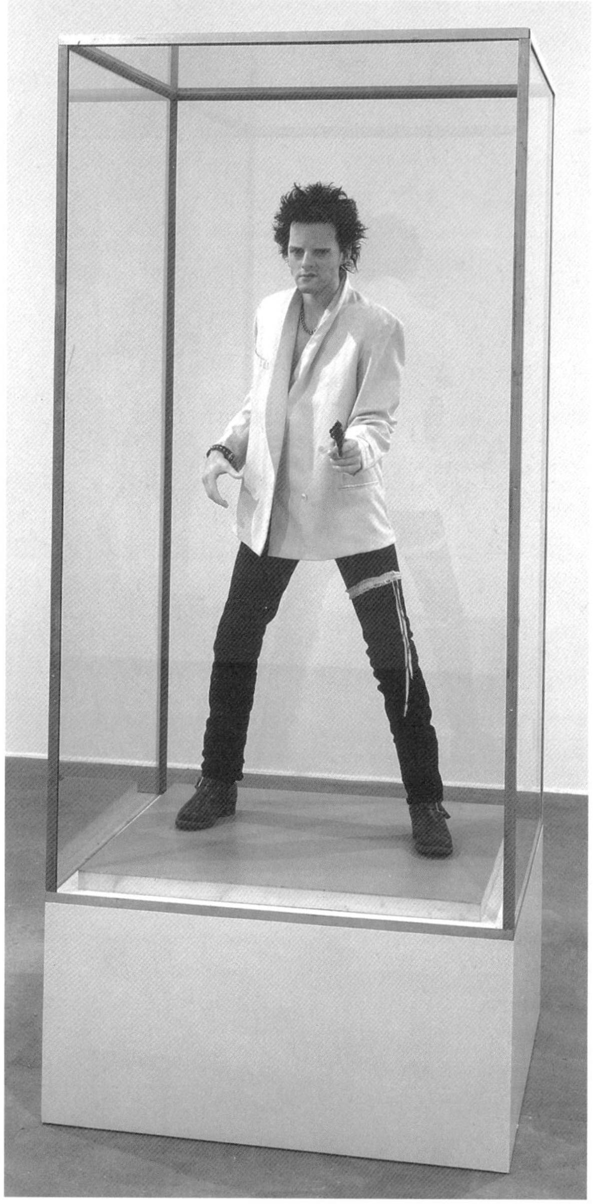

ing the fact that it was always achieved symbolically,[22] and in a less direct manner than Home's critique of art practice.

Another disconcerting aspect of the yBa myth was the mix of private and public sponsorship involved, coupled with celebrity endorsement from figures such as David Stewart and David Bowie. As a re-enactment of '60s Swinging London, the mix of art and celebrity was nothing new. The private–public mix had also been readily exploited by Lisson Gallery sculptors throughout the '80s. Like numerous critics of this period, Ford decried the professionalization

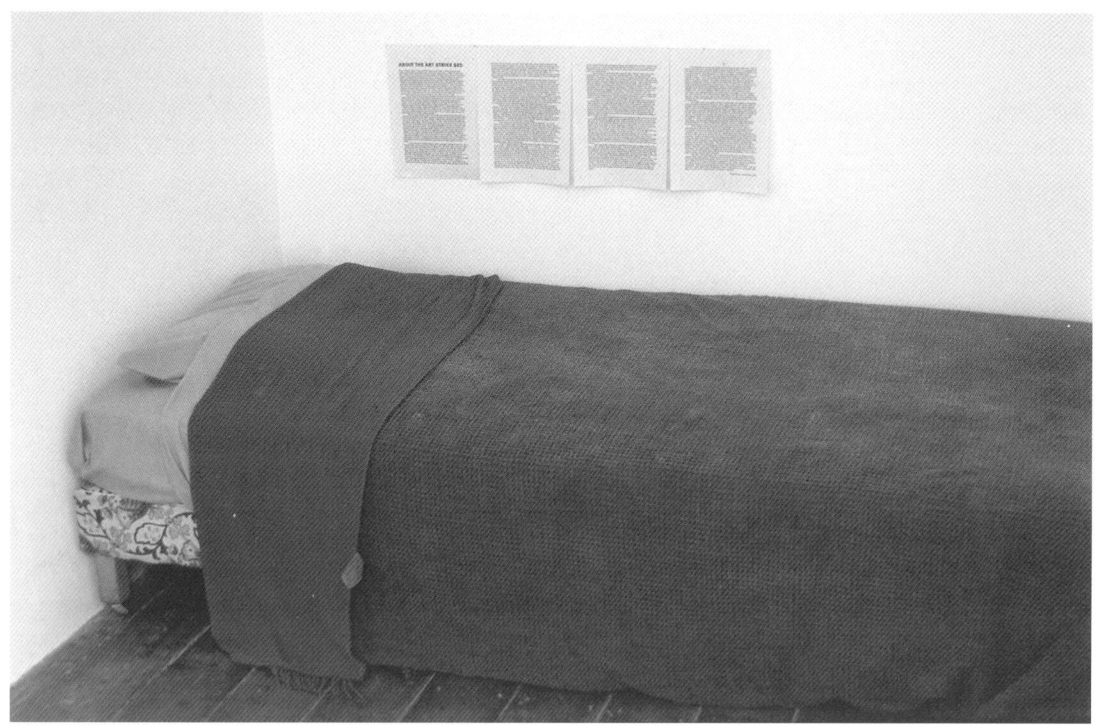

6.4   Stewart Home, *Art Strike Bed* (1993–), any bed endorsed by the artist

and commercialization of all aspects of the cultural climate.[23] Certainly, in London's mercenary climate, the modest, community-based practices popular in the late '70s did not attract corporate sponsorship. Business benefits from spectacular exhibitions of blue-chip art and 'emerging' art with which to associate corporate identities (a combination of opulence and innovation). At the same time, in order to ensure value for money, organizations such as the Association for Business Sponsorship of the Arts had a vested interest in art *appearing* to become popular. This meant pretending to pander to 'the people's taste' by supporting work which contains signifiers drawn from 'popular culture', while retaining the class divisions which generate concepts such as 'high art'.[24] Significant predicaments prevail with Ford's criticism, nonetheless. Flourishing ties between art and capital, between culture and government national branding schemes, are nothing to get excited about. Moreover, as Kevin Davey has pointed out, 'there is the possibility that the contraflow [between American and British culture] is actually a normal and phased feature of the Anglo-American marketplace for music and the arts. Has everybody forgotten the American "Anglomania" that featured early in the Thatcher years?'[25] The '90s saw a new generation of privileged gallerists open their doors in Mayfair, London, most notably Jay Jopling's White Cube space. Dealers seek to exploit holes in the market, whether the artists come from public, private or independent sectors of the artworld. Critiques of the mixed artistic economy in the '90s failed to distinguish between promotional strategies and the nature of the work being produced by such artists, which was of vastly

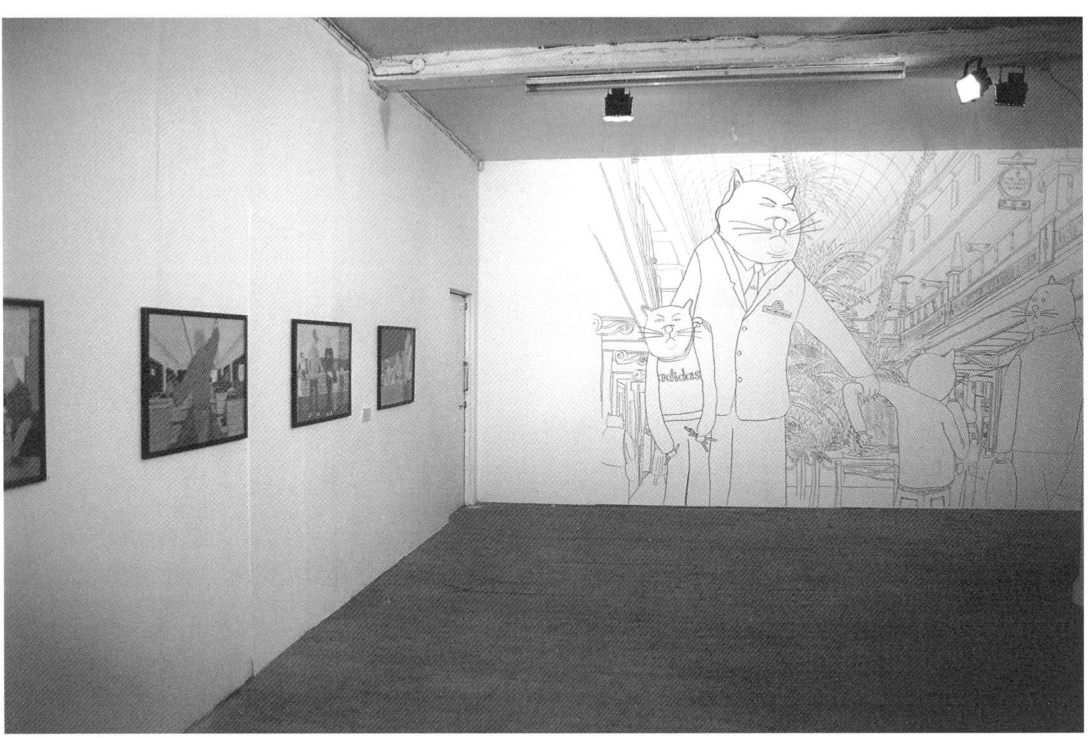

6.5   Jim Medway, installation at The Annual Programme, Manchester (1999)

differing quality.[26] They also failed to give any credit for the work involved in establishing independent spaces in London.

It has been suggested that independent spaces such as Beaconsfield, The Approach, City Racing,[27] Gasworks, 30 Underwood Street, Cubitt, Lost in Space and Factual Nonsense may not have been necessary without the early '90s economic recession which hit private London galleries heavily. With the exception of Beaconsfield, Stallabrass was grudgingly sceptical about the significance of many artist-run spaces.[28] However, to ignore or belittle the importance of such spaces is to suppress the 'unwieldy expansiveness and sheer bloody-mindedness of several Londons off the academically beaten track'.[29] Moreover, the presence of such spaces in cities such as Glasgow (Transmission)[30] and Manchester (The Annual Programme; see Figure 6.5),[31] where the market for contemporary art was a less significant influence on artistic production, denotes the further weakness of such critiques.[32] Essentially, the critique of the 'entrepreneurial' self-help ethos was mean-spirited.[33] The work associated with the yBa tag was made for and supported by capitalists, therefore it must be regrettable.[34] The major problem, it would seem, is that such criticism simply reproduced the kind of factionalism prevalent at the end of the 1970s; indeed its alleged insubordination cannot function outside its given context.[35] The consequences of such criticism for the British artworld of the 1980s should be heeded:

Ironically the conservative trend in the visual arts ran riot. This was due, above all, to the confusion and paranoia left in the wake of an onslaught against modernism launched by pseudo-Marxist-writers, some of whom never understood the basic problems (confusing art with the market). They left destruction in their wake with no practicable alternative. The few theories that did emerge were difficult to apply to the traditional media to which they were by and large addressed, and misinterpretation brought the old reactionaries out in strength.[36]

Assuming that the historically ambivalent attitude of the avant-garde towards consumerism *was* acted out *ad nauseam* by the yBa myth fails to consider the fact that the belief that art can have an unproblematic relationship with the 'political' and the 'ethical' has been thoroughly reworked since the art crisis of 1976. Who in the devolved and privatized artworld was now in a position to decide what was political and ethical? Who should be allowed to manage such aspects of culture? Why are the 'ethical' and 'political' seen to dominate over other aspects of cultural praxis? The yBa did not amount to a marginalization of critical practice, more to a renegotiation.[37] Critical postmodernism was sheep-dip for these artists.[38] Their anti-intellectualism came from knowledge of the history of negation in twentieth-century art. As such, yBa negation can be read simply as a rebellion without a cause, a re-enactment of the passive nihilism popularized in the early '80s following in the wake of socio-political Punk posturing or what Roberts has termed 'the thinking stupidity of the philistine who sees the rejection of the dominant discourses of art as a matter of ethical positioning'.[39]

Roberts' 1996 essays 'Mad for It' and 'Notes on 90's Art',[40] which professed to be theoretically reflexive and critical, attempted to posit this position as an *oppositional* culture: 'The truth is, playing dumb, shouting "ARSE" and taking your knickers down has become an attractive move in the face of the professional institutionalisation of critical theory in art in the 1980s … A younger generation has had to find a way through these congealing radicalisms.'[41] While Roberts certainly remains an opponent of populism (Home has dubbed him a Frankfurt School groupie), he has, nonetheless, attempted to present a theorized defence of the overtly populist yBas, positing their value on his theorization of the 'philistine', a position from which the new generation were seen to have 'fought to renew the conditions of art's passage into the everyday and away from art's academicisation, radical or otherwise'.[42] Clearly the yBas represented an attack on the '80s *critical* establishment, but this signified only the intent to resist a status quo.[43] The stress on supposedly stereotyped 'working-class' culture in yBa was mannered and theatrical as it had to be, given that it took place in an artworld context.[44] In this sense, yBa 'negations' were generally normative. In response, Julian Stallabrass was vocal in attempting to raise the stakes of British art criticism, encouraging a debate on the philistine in the pages of the *New Left Review* while he was assistant editor.[45] While opposed to what he saw as Roberts' hypocrisy and the intellectual vacuity of mainstream British art criticism, Stallabrass did not appear to present an alternative, an effect of denying any autonomy to the art he 'de-mythologized'. However, while Roberts has at least *considered* whether the mainstream blue-chip art of the '90s deserves to be saved from vulgar institutional critique,[46] he has failed to provide a convincing theoretical framework in which this might occur.[47] It is hardly surprising that Roberts and Dave Beech's construction of the 'philistine' as a defence of the yBas was widely taken to task for its patronizing attempt to validate the '"pure pleasures of the body … against the corrupt machinations of the intellect" as though this bourgeois cliché was the "voice of the excluded", a "proletarian" challenge to the hegemony of institutionalized theory in the 80s'.[48] Artist collective BANK's negations were perhaps more complex in that they sought to ridicule the yBa myth while capitalizing on it, a parasitical relationship which made them contenders for Art & Language's position as the police force of the British art world. BANK's success certainly lies in the irresponsibility of their practice, the tabloid tactics used against the mainstream London art scene. Unlike A&L, BANK's antics had little impact on the intellectual framework of critical postmodernism since they had no interest in academia (hence the production of *The Bank* as a tabloid instead of a philosophical journal). Moreover, for BANK, professional curating was the model of totalitarianism, an aristocratic phenomenon which annexes culture and standardizes all opinion. They were, nonetheless, adept at provoking gallerists and art bureaucrats (much easier and more powerful targets than critical postmodernists), most notably with their final project the 'BANK Fax Back Service' show (34 Underwood Street, London, 8–10 January 1999) which involved the group correcting and commenting on press releases and returning them to the senders.[49] While patently open to interpretation, such tactics left little room in which the means of conversation might be examined independently from BANK's provocation. Similarly, while seeking to celebrate the influx of the everyday and the debased into the realm of art, Roberts failed to confront the question of what constitutes an oppositional practice, assuming that emerging artists in the '90s could continue to seek a 'critical function' as they had in the previous decades. It is hardly surprising that BANK were also supported by critics of yBa such as Stallabrass, who sought to promote 'opposition' as an index of value.[50]

Given the changes that took place in the British artworld in the late 1970s relating to the assisted co-option of the 'avant-garde' by the managerial impetus of Semio-Art, such claims make little sense. For example, it can easily be demonstrated that kinds of 'oppositional interventions' such as John Tagg's, which might well have been favoured by mainstream opponents of the yBas, were highly significant in relation to changes which have more recently occurred in curatorial sectors of the British artworld, changes which in turn were of vast benefit to the rise of yBa.[51] It has long since become a truism that much contemporary art practice blurs, or even eradicates, the boundaries between curator and artist. The most frequently celebrated examples of this in Britain are artist-selected exhibitions such as Hirst's 'Freeze' (1988) and 'Some Went Mad, Some Ran Away' (1994). By the end of the '90s it was, however, more commonplace to find exhibitions which were curator-led, as curators sought ever more ludicrous hooks to hang miscellaneous contemporary art by. This spawned the 'cult of the curator', as freelance curators competed for the attention of understaffed galleries thin on ideas for their programmes. Despite their overtly user-friendly façade, the theme-shows of the late 1990s were the offspring of '70s semioticians' anthropological obsessions. Following a decade of Thatcherism, curators learnt how to animate *myths* of iconographic (in)coherence for promotional ends: to construct a theatrical image of the fragmented artworld. In their aim to popularize culture, curators pushed 'executive skills' to the forefront of cultural existence. The dramatized fantasy of 'Schools of Art' imposed by primordial iconologicians became highly lucrative for artists and administrators who successfully and continually re-marketed 'Great Traditions' by dressing deviant art productions in thematic cloaks.[52] Now that critics such as Tagg were much maligned for adopting an overtly sophisticated style of cultural analysis, many curators were at even greater liberty to cultivate the old ploy of presenting 'lack of sophistication' as desirable to sophisticated audiences.

More than any commentator, this view was embodied by Matthew Collings. Like Cork and Fuller before him, Collings was an ambitious critic who went to great lengths to metamorphose with the undercurrents of the new wave. At the turn of the '90s he enrolled for an MA at Goldsmiths College as a means of ensuring that he was in touch with the emergent London scene on its own level, while honing a monotonal, ironic vocal range to wield against the seasoned polemicists of the '70s and '80s. Using a mix of descriptive, anecdotal and diaristic styles, Collings jettisoned the theory-laden prose of '70s and '80s art writing in favour of an agnostic pragmatism, cultivating a self-deprecating irony.[53] Collings' laconic stream-of-consciousness functions as a reflection of the double-think narcissism common to art at the end of the '80s, something that would grow in the 1990s. Collings became, in effect, the Cork of the 1990s, the most prominent defender of the new orthodoxy of Young British Art. Stallabrass argues that this came to be seen as the only available position for criticism in the '90s, a position exemplified by the ironic double-coding of Collings' writing: 'One of the virtues of Matthew Collings' book, *Blimey!*, is that it offers a consistent pastiche of conventional art world talk. His meandering prose, inability to sustain an argument and thinking in soundbites is an exemplification of that talk, and its careless but consistent mislaying of all that is important.'[54] Can Collings' version of events be challenged effectively? Are the parodies of Collings found in magazines such as *Private Eye* are virtually indistinguishable from the real Collings, whose writing is already a 'pastiche of the tyranny of received opinion that governs the art world'?[55] Collings at least did not feign authenticity and cannot consequently be reprimanded for lacking critical distance and intellectual responsibility. If anything Collings was successful in opening up contemporary art criticism to a wide audience without patronizing them with polemics for social functionalism. Was this form of cognition totalizing, or were there alternatives? According to Stallabrass, 'theory's standard configuration of intellectual disciplines may not be the most effective tools to use, since the art has thoroughly inoculated itself against most of them in advance'.[56] Either this picture was correct or we are immoderately close to the culture Stallabrass rebukes.

Stallabrass's doubts were perhaps related more to the limitations of the dominant discourses and institutions of the London artworld in the mid-'90s than to the inherent weakness of '90s British art in general. In Scotland a different model had emerged from the introduction of public art courses at Glasgow School of Art and at Duncan of Jordanston College of Art in Dundee. Public art courses were nothing new in the UK. In Scotland, however, the presence of Malcolm Miles and of national art magazines such as *Alba* raised the profile of public practice in context: 'If there is one lesson to be gained, it is that the consumer, or spectator, is as important as the artist, and may adopt an active rather than a passive role.'[57]

Douglas Gordon began studying at Glasgow School of Art (GSA) in 1984, a period in which the New Glasgow Boys were receiving international critical acclaim. Following his foundation year, Gordon was one of the students admitted to the first year of the newly founded Department of Environmental Art (which had replaced the Murals and Stained Glass Department). When David Harding and Sam Ainsley introduced the new course in 1985, a course document was produced which based the teaching on John Latham's dictum that 'The context is half the work.' The idea, then, was that the new department would generally ascribe to the tactics of the Artists' Placement Group. There would be an emphasis on the kinds of community art and public practices that were popular in the 1970s. As such, the new department would be a tight, socially responsible ship, standing in direct contrast to what were then seen as the trivial antics of the Painting Department. This did not go entirely according to plan. Given that there was no head of department, students rejected the course document, and wrote their own. More than under the Goldsmiths system, these students taught each other. A group posthumously dubbed 'The Irascibles' by Ross Sinclair, including Gordon, Sinclair, Roderick Buchanan, Jacqueline Donachie, Christine Borland and Martin Boyce, formed a tight self-support system (see Figure 6.6).[58]

This group of artists sought to avoid the idea of art as negation of the past:

People also ask us if we were reacting to artists like Steven Campbell and Adrian Wiszniewski, who were prominent when we were at school. But really, nobody could be bothered. They were so far away from what we were trying to do, we just didn't use them as a reference point at all. They were just a tiny, unimportant part of the international art world … Things are happening so quickly now. By the time those artists had left Scotland and begun showing abroad, we were already bored with them. There was no point in setting ourselves against them.[59]

Despite Gordon's professed lack of interest in the New Glasgow Boys, the rise of the 'Scotia Nostra' has many parallels with their success. Of course, many of the New Glasgow Boys had, in fact, flourished in the ill-fated Department of Murals before being forced to tackle painting. The 'Scotia Nostra', therefore, were the direct ancestors of supporters of intermedia at the GSA. Moreover, like the New Glasgow Boys, they have gone on to become important players in the international art world via the support of artist initiatives such as Edinburgh's New 57 Gallery and Glasgow's Transmission Committee for the

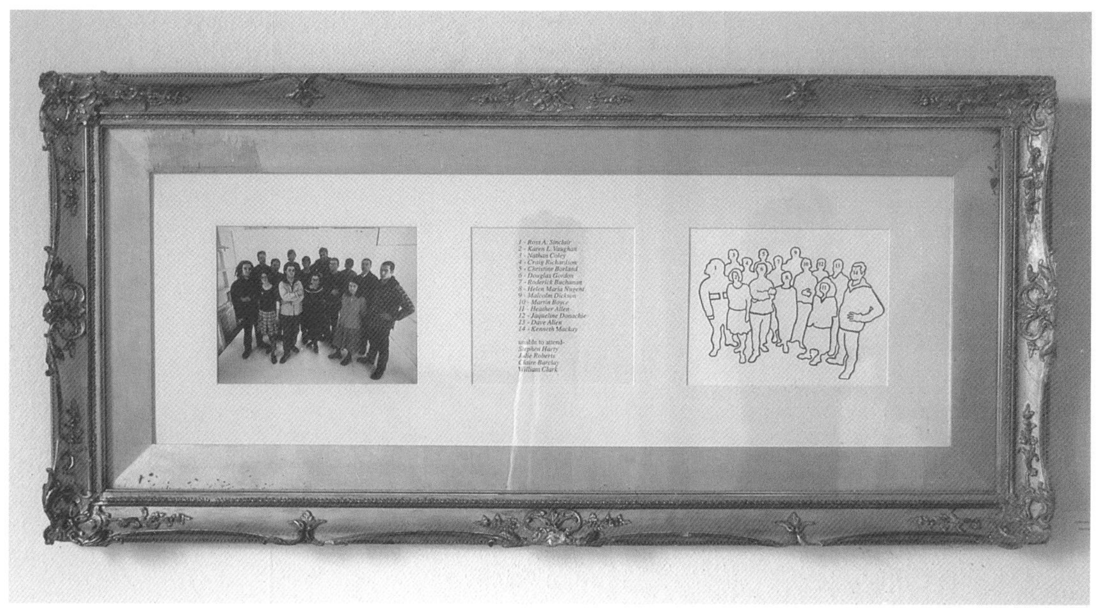

6.6 Ross Sinclair, *The Irascibles* (1991), photograph

Visual Arts.[60] The major difference, however, is that the Environmental Art group did not initially see such institutions as stepping-stones to success in the private artworld: 'Why wait for your work to be approved/validated/ confirmed by some ex public schoolboy in a sharp suit/jeans n' sneakers? (but maybe you knew him already from prep school?) You get out there, do some fucking hot show and invite them over on your own terms.'[61] While many London-based artists in the late 1980s set up warehouse exhibitions with the hope of attracting private buyers and dealers, Glasgow-based artists had less interest in the private artworld. Exhibitions such as 'Windfall', held at the derelict Seaman's Mission in Glasgow in August 1991, were largely the product of Glasgow's public spiritedness and a rancorous disdain for anything vaguely associated with Thatcherite entrepreneurship: 'New Image painting was basically expressionism that had come second-hand from Germany in the late 70s. It embraced the myth of the artist toiling away in his studio, sending his paintings down to the gallery in the big city. Rather than that awful monologue, we wanted dialogue, diversity, context, accessibility, and above all, ideas.'[62]

This was not a novel development. Artist initiatives in Scotland such as Transmission, New 57 Gallery and the Collective Gallery had, rightly or wrongly, long been characterized as democratic and philanthropic, asserting a model of the artist as organized, politicized and active.[63] Edinburgh's Collective Gallery, while 'never achieving the same international profile as Transmission … has always prided itself on being more accountable to its membership as its committee is elected'.[64] In 1984, Malcolm Dickson and fellow students from GSA's Painting Department founded *Variant*, a low-budget magazine – dedicated to Hugh MacDairmid's notion of cross-culturalism – which simultaneously rejected centralism and parochialism. Dickson sought to promote the idea of the 'cultural worker', a figure who crosses media, producing, disseminating and critically consuming culture. This radical model of accountability was aided by Transmission, which from 1985 was run by artists such as Dickson, Carol Rhodes, Gordon Muir, Graham Johnstone and Billy Clark, who modelled the space on the Free University. Video, installation, performance and a commitment to radical politics were favoured – including work by established artists such as Peter Dunn, Lorraine Leeson, Tony Rickaby, Art in Ruins (Glyn Banks and Hannah Vowles), Ralf Rumney and Stuart Brisley – and extra-gallery political activism was encouraged. This trend reached its peak in August 1989 when Transmission hosted the Neo-Situationist 'Fifth Annual Festival of Plagiarism'. Emerging into this milieu, Environmental artists such as Sinclair were equally politicized, marking an attack on the local spectacle of Glasgow's 'European Capital of Culture' celebrations in 1990 with a series of ambient subvertisements.[65] Sinclair's poster marked his global reach by pop cultural allusion. His ornate ongoing mythology of *Real Life* sharply politicized the in/authentic dialectics of (sub)cultural identity. Sinclair's work meditated on the issue of mythologization in relation to his persona as an artist, to the establishment of pop stars and to the myths of national identity, particularly to the creation of a Romanticized 'Sir Walter Scottishness' in the Victorian era. His engagement with self-mythologization parallels the strategies of London yBas concerned with artistic and 'British' national identities such as Turk and Mark Wallinger.

While continuing to support Scottish-based artists, Scottish artist initiatives in the early '90s tended to look further afield than the UK, enhancing the international reputation of Scottish art.[66] 'Windfall' included 25 artists from eight European states. In his catalogue essay, Sinclair stressed the need to bypass the centre: 'Although London will always have a strong pull there exists a valuable and potentially more reciprocal relationship with the European context.'[67] Yet links with the 'centre' were present. 'Windfall' received a great deal of interest from *Frieze*, the new art magazine launched to promote the work of emerging British artists in an international context. 'Windfall' and *Frieze* shared the same designer, arefin&arefin, and Transmission exchanged with City Racing and exhibited work by Simon Patterson. In addition to having been trained in negotiating skills as part of their degrees in public art, early '90s Scottish artists had a clear grasp of the London art scene. On graduating from Glasgow School of Art in 1988, Gordon studied for a postgraduate degree at the Slade School of Art, University College London.[68] It was here that he came under the influence of scopophobic, psychoanalytic Hollywood film theory and its attendant Photoconceptualism – evident in works such as *Twenty Four Hour Psycho* at Glasgow's Tramway (1993) – in particular the writings of Laura Mulvey and the work of John Hilliard, who both lectured at the Slade. Having completed this course, Gordon decided to return to Glasgow. By then, the official art infrastructure was ready to accept and promote the work of this emerging group. In 1990, during Glasgow's year as City of Culture, Christine Borland, Craig Richardson, Kevin Henderson, Roderick Buchanan and Gordon were given a group exhibition at the Third Eye Centre. For numerous critics, this was the answer to the 'New Image

Glasgow' exhibition which had taken place five years earlier. The exhibition, 'Self-Conscious State', also sported a catalogue designed by arefin&arefin. The networking strategies, professional savvy and delegation skills of the new generation were laid bare in Gordon's enormous *List of Names* (1990–present) of everyone he had ever met.

Although spanning a wide range of media such as tattoos, video, installation and mail art, such work was ideas-based and primarily concerned with the art as a conduit for discussion. Gordon's works trigger associative trails in the imagination of the viewer, leaving the narrative open-ended. This places his work firmly in the critical camp of yBa art, which equally learned to abdicate responsibility in the name of poststructuralist unbounded semiosis. In many cases this led him to produce insightful works such as *Three Inches (Black)* (1997), instructions for three inches of an index finger (the distance to make a fatal wound in the human body) to be tattooed black. Gordon successfully revived the rules-based approach popular in Conceptual Art circles in the late '60s, seeing it as an ideal system to produce work in an ever-shrinking information-based world (installation instructions for his works were often faxed to international institutions from his Glasgow tenement).[69] Given its reliance on instructions and the slight re-articulation of found materials, the lack of praxis in much early '90s Scottish Neo-Conceptualism could equally produce work which routinely hit the correct buttons of postmodernist discourses on modernity, spectacle, voyeurism, identity and the body.[70] Gordon's *Twenty Four Hour Psycho* (Figure 6.7) achieved great acclaim for following simple techniques known to under-graduate film students versed in the structural analysis of texts and the basic tools of narratology, slowing down a movie to draw attention to discrepancies between 'real time' and 'narrative time'. Alfred Hitchcock, of course, was the ideal choice of subject matter in that his work provided many points of access for international curators and critics who still admitted an interest in *Screen* theory, Hitchcock's reputation rubbing off on Gordon, the focalizer, by osmosis. As the New Image artists had already suggested, there was no reason why the rejection of closure should have been best served by minimal means; indeed it is simply a truism to say that art can present complex and irreducible readings, aspects of life's wider randomness and confusing copiousness.[71] Neo-Conceptualism in its Scottish variation accepted that multiplicity of meaning emerges from the evaluation of the material, without criticism or further investigation of the social and political consequences of such relativism.[72] Nor did it seek to question its complicity with the unchecked escalation of unaccountable international institutional culture managers and quangos.

To an extent, then, the absence of private support led to the production of institutionally friendly work. This made the new Scottish art different from art bought by Saatchi, which was largely determined by his personal taste. Art in Scotland was increasingly made for a public situation.[73] Indeed, Scottish Neo-Conceptualists produced the kinds of engineered work most eminently compatible with the audience-orientated programming commitments needed

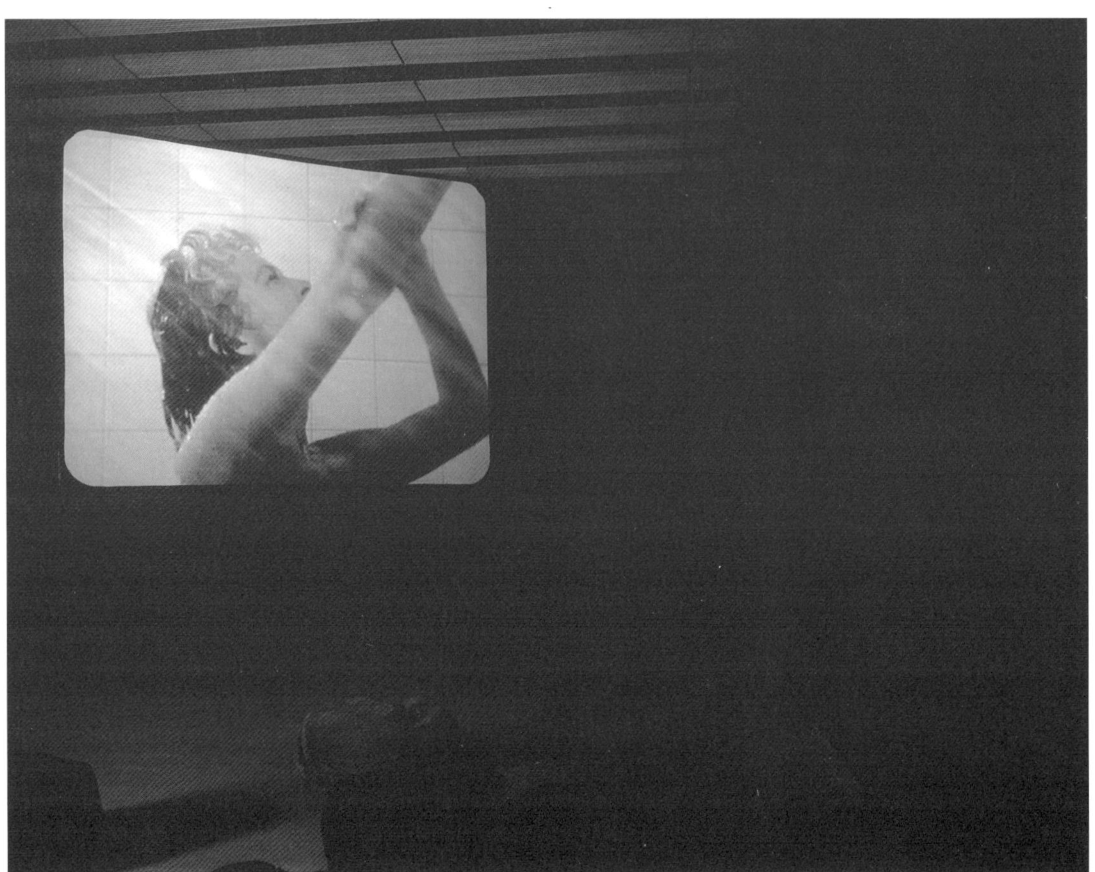

6.7 Douglas Gordon, *Twenty Four Hour Psycho* (1993), Hayward, first shown in 1993 as video installation at Tramway, Glasgow

to keep public institutions afloat. In order to emerge from its parochial house to sip avocado *frappés* at the café-bar, Scottish art had to be readable, clear and relatively popular.[74] The push towards a networked identity for Scottish art in the early 1990s turned many artists' heads to received international concerns. This was delineated in many works via a commitment to the *détournement* of material culture, a project which was most prominent in the museological experiments of Christine Borland. This also often encompassed a concurrent preoccupation with functionalist architecture and design found in the work of Nathan Coley, Martin Boyce and Simon Starling. Semiotic references to internationalism were, nonetheless, often interpreted on a local level, most notably in Buchanan's work, which often centred around the cultural and sporting associations of people living in Dennistoun in the East End of Glasgow.[75] Another internationalist trait in '90s Scottish art was the use of text as a Conceptualist trope, distancing device and index of critical value. This was perfected by Gordon, Buchanan and Jacqueline Donachie, whose promotion of the work of established international figures such as Lawrence Weiner in 1991 at the Transmission helped to secure a belated linguistic turn in much Scottish art. Issue-based practices and signature themes allowed international curators to pick, mix and match. The much-heralded public success of such work quickly spawned a series of private shows such as 'Wonderful Life' at the Lisson Gallery in 1993, for artists such as Gordon.[76]

Other Scottish artists in the early '90s had continued to work in territories which were less confined by globalizing corporatist institutions. While a student at Glasgow School of Art, David Shrigley produced a series of subtle ambient works in the city of Glasgow, *détourn*-ing the local environment with a road sign inscribed with the place name *Hell* (1991), producing a neon sign bearing the legend *Slum* (1994) which was placed in the windows of tenements in Glasgow's bed-and-breakfast-saturated West-end and turning a disused public toilet block into a traditional Scottish pub with the addition of a simple sign reading *The Ship* (1991).[77] Cheaper, more marginal works followed such as *Lost* (1996),[78] a piece of paper stuck to a tree in a park asking for information on a missing 'pidgeon' (*sic*). Simple and unpretentious, such interventions bore a close yet unpatronizing relationship with the history and people of his immediate environment while avoiding the dangers of parachuted public art. Shrigley's work risked not being noticed and in many cases is only available to us through photographic documentation. Unwilling to secure large public commissions, Shrigley began to publish a series of small artist's books, displaying a black sense of dysfunctional humour. Although they appeared in limited editions, the intention of such works was to reach directly into the comic book market, as can be seen in books such as *Merry Eczema* (1992) which feature a mature graphic style.[79] *Ladder Used for Viewing Atrocity* from his book *ERR* (1996; Figure 6.8)[80] is a particularly good example of the erudite wit and *faux-naïf* style he came to be celebrated for, nodding tiredly at postmodernist critiques of the representation of violence by marking a small, absurdist riposte to grandiose anti-war art such as Picasso's *Guernica* (1937). Shrigley reached wide non-art audiences with books such as *Why We Got the Sack from the Museum* (1998) and *The Beast is Near* (1999)[81] and forays into newspaper funnies. A continuing preoccupation with sculpture, painting and photography also allowed Shrigley to exhibit in public and private galleries worldwide.[82]

The situation following the mainstream success of London-based yBa and Scottish Neo-Conceptualism at the end of the 1990s was highly complex. On the one hand there had been a massive growth in artist-led initiatives, which were now to be found in cities such as Newcastle (Waygood Gallery) and Dundee (Generator). This marked an increasing decentralization in terms of activity and funding which contrasted starkly with the situation in British art in the mid-1970s. It is also clear that such spaces took their lead from other international artists' initiatives, seeking horizontal relationships and exchanges of ideas. This coincided with substantial constitutional changes in the UK, the cultural and political implications of which were outlined in Tom Nairne's book *After Britain* (2000); just as the 1976 IMF crisis heralded the end of 'Great Britain', cultural and political devolution created a fresh identity crisis.[83] A crisis was now perceived to lie at the centre. Scottish culture had a

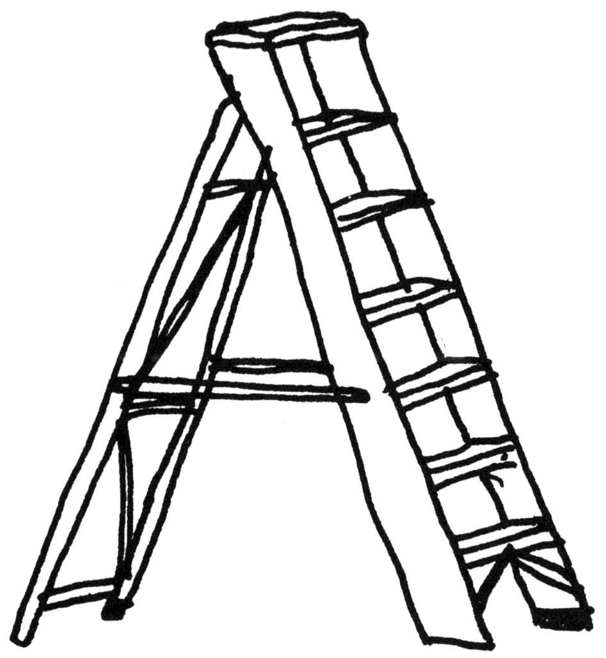

6.8   David Shrigley, *Ladder Used for Viewing Atrocity* (1996), drawing

new-found internationalism and quasi-autonomy which could also be found in large English cities such as Manchester and Liverpool. London artists in the '90s such as Wallinger meditated critically on the 'English imaginary', a culture no longer able to rely on 'Britishness' for its sense of identity. At the end of the '90s, such work was no longer imaginable. The upshot of this for many cultural commentators has been a vain attempt to hold onto a centre, seeing 'Blair's devolved Union and modernising populism' as a 'desperate attempt to relegitimate the British state and the very practice of national politics'.[84] This is bulwarked by the continuing presence of the Turner Prize and the appearance of new commercial prizes such as the Beck's Futures award for young artists, which was first won by Buchanan in 2000.[85] Hence, simultaneously there had been a move to centralize art activity through the construction of large, lottery-funded arts centres such as the New Art Gallery in Walsall,[86] Dundee Contemporary Arts, BALTIC[87] in Gateshead (see Figure 6.9), Tate Modern in Southwark and Tate Britain in Millbank, London. Unfortunately, the presence of such institutions in London, coupled with the flood of private galleries from Mayfair to the East End, forced many artists out of affordable studio accommodation.

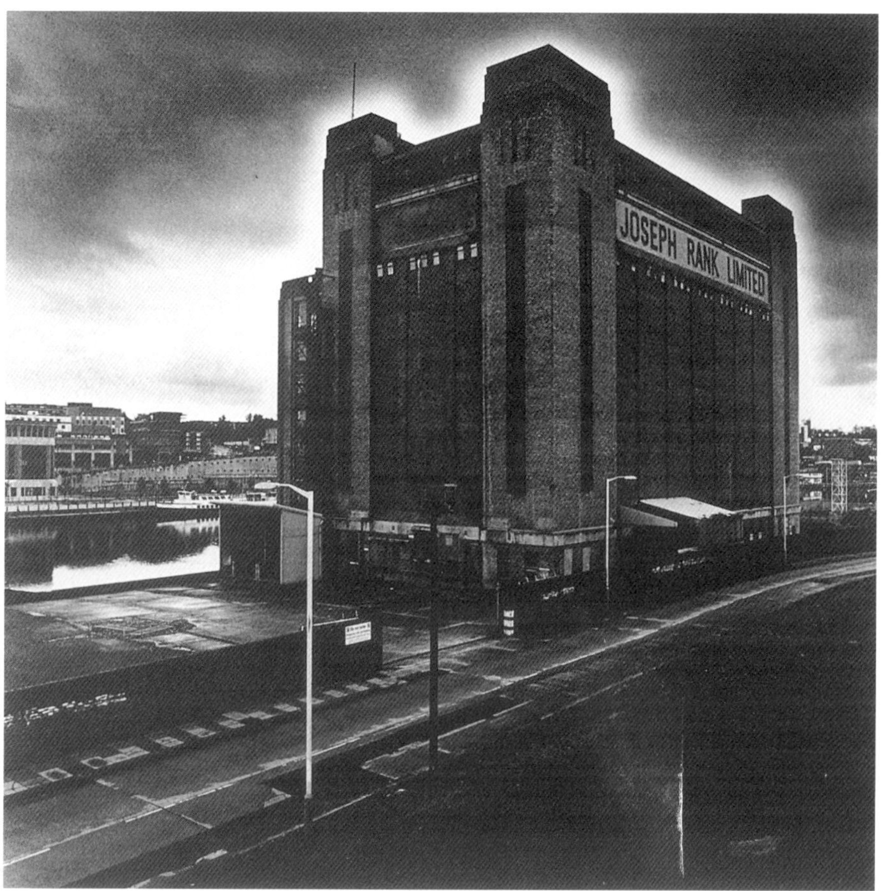

The response to this situation, with its shifting boundaries and the absence of a myth around which to structure a synchronous analysis, was multivalent. On the one hand, established institutions such as the Saatchi Gallery audaciously asserted their hold on the art of the 1990s, arrogantly proclaiming it 'The Saatchi Decade'[88] while presenting more of the same to an eager public with exhibitions such as 'Ant Noises' (August 2000), a reprise of 'Sensation' of 1997.[89] 'Ant Noises'' misplaced bombast, signified by Hirst's 80-foot, £1m sculpture *Hymn* (2000), unmistakably marked the failure of the centre to hold. 'The New Neurotic Realism'[90] was an abortive mythology which claimed that art had entered a post-ironic condition: 'The works put forward a direct and immediate relationship with artistic expression and the imagination. I see a strong expressive quality in the work without that falling into the pitfalls of re-working a crazed expressionism.'[91] Meanwhile prominent artist-curators such as Matthew Higgs[92] searched for alternatives to the yBas' paradigmatic self-indulgence and individualism, experimenting with a return to collaborative, extra-mural (outdoors) political art, which reached beyond the gallery to engage with issues such as globalization, negation, democracy, poverty and consumerism. This tendency was promoted by a number of dialogue-centred exhibitions held in London at the very end of the twentieth century: Stefan Kalmár's 'Urban Islands' at Cubitt (20 November–31 December 1999), 'CRASH! Corporatism and Complicity' at the ICA (24 November–19 December 1999), 'Democracy!' at the Royal College of Art (14 April–12 May 2000) and Higgs' 'Protest and Survive' at the Whitechapel Art Gallery (15 September–12 November 2000), and by the publication of *Art For All?* (2000).[93] Such exhibitions were concerned with what social functionalism might mean in the context of the late '90s, showcasing artistic projects exploring emergent global networks of knowledge, corporatism and resistance. Globalization debates impacted on artists' cross-disciplinary and interactive research into the complex skeins of postmodern geographies and economies. This certainly indicated a decisive break with explorations of parochial 'British' identities that had preoccupied artists in the UK during the '80s and early '90s. In line with New Labour's vision of a 'modernized' Britain, British art was being globalized to enable it to compete in a world culture, the alleged globalist erosion of parochial identity and power being taken as a given rather than as a debate. The infrastructure and language of global knowledge disseminated by such exhibitions instantly posed as the cultural oligarchy of the late 1990s, a fatalistic culture resigned to the clichéd management-speak of the neo-colonial sectors of globalized capitalism. 'The superficial or not-so-superficial similarity of sponsors, curators and artists in relying on modes of pastiche and varieties of subversion just emphasised how ambiguous the return to a critical art might be in the current climate, whatever the convictions of those involved',[94] wrote Benedict Seymour. Certainly, the tendency of such shows was to stress a collapse between 'subversive appropriation' in art and its emergent mirror in global anti-capitalist movements. This project of critical complicity had a pedigree in '80s Simulacral art, but in the late '90s it was closer to the high-tech strategies of culture jammers such as Negativland, Rtmark, Adbusters and Britain's mass-media maestro Chris Morris. In other ways this was business as usual, the exhibitions serving to raise the national profiles of a number of British artists and groups including Jeremy Deller, Inventory, Beagles and Ramsay and Carey Young,[95] while sparking a fresh series of spats concerning art and social purpose in the British art press.[96] 'Protest and Survive' (see Figure 6.10) created a nostalgic lineage with the social functionalism and radical academicism of the late 1970s by exhibiting the work of artists such as Deller, Chad McCail and BANK alongside earlier art by Jo Spence, Cosey Fanni Tutti, the Hackney Flashers, Peter Kennard and Stephen Willats, artists who would not have served well as precedents for the yBas. Yet this was seen as offensive packaged historicism by a number of commentators.[97] Indeed, while the emphasis on unemployment, discrimination, social deprivation and political angst remained relevant, the show tended to iron out the past for curatorial advantage.

The demotion of the visceral in '90s Neo-Conceptualism meant that it was rarely discordant enough. Certainly, the danger with the managerial situation in British curating in the late '90s was that artists might become content with

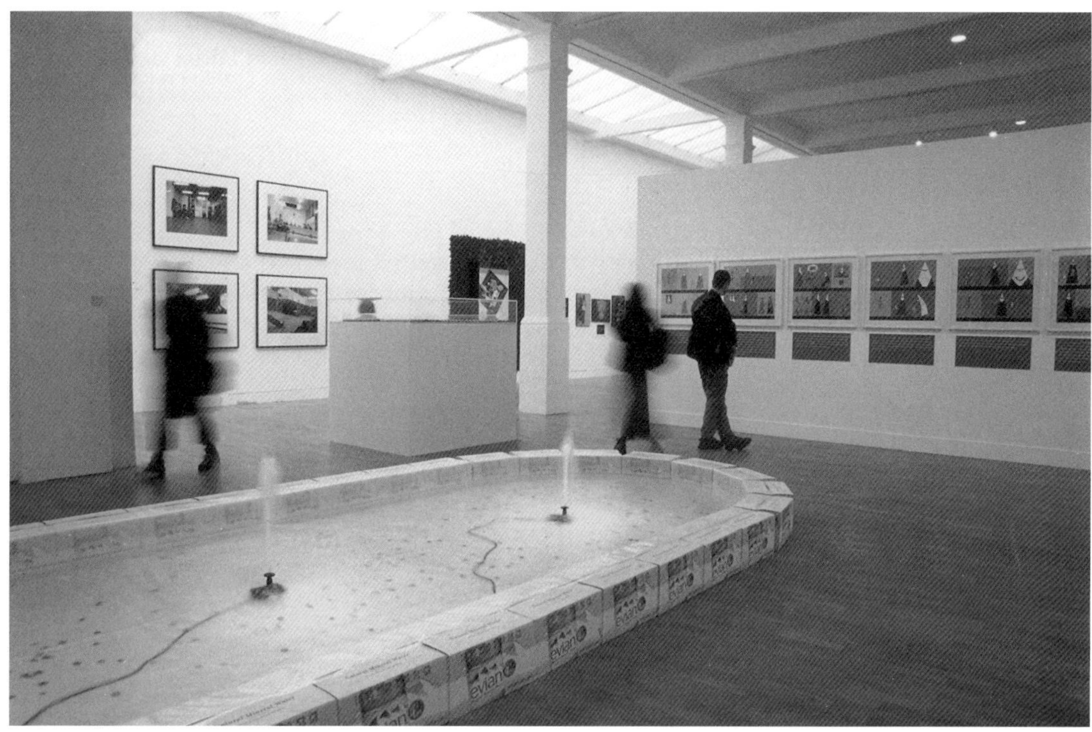

6.10   Installation view of 'Protest and Survive', Whitechapel Art Gallery, London, 2000

their lot rather than continue to explore alternatives. It was therefore crucial that new work should not be slurped back into the administrative establishment and absorbed by it. In some quarters of the UK there was a will to reassert the opacity of art, and to recover anomaly against the virtue of art as 'concept'. 'Heart & Soul', a group exhibition at artists' studios in 60 Long Lane, Southwark, London (30 July–15 August 1999), was a good example of this desire (see Figure 6.11). Featuring work from 36 artists, the exhibition included a wide variety of media, and mixing well-known artists such as Maloney with emerging ones such as Jim Lambie, Enrico David, Dean Hughes, Mark Titchner, David Musgrave and Polly Staple it studiously avoided a curatorial theme or an over-riding aesthetic other than a renewed interest in intuitive practices.[98] While the exhibition was vaguely heralded as the new 'Freeze', its contemporaneity lay in its distance from epoch-building and rebel-rousing. This anti-thematic decentred approach to curating had strong parallels with exhibitions held in Scotland, particularly Joanne Tatham & Tom O'Sullivan's 'Blow Your Mind' at the Collective (January 1998; Figure 6.12) and 'It May be a Year of Thirteen Moons but it's Still the Year of Culture' by Charisma (Lucy McKenzie and Keith Farquhar) at Transmission (11 July–6 August 2000; Figure 6.13). Members of Elizabeth Go (Victoria Morton, Haley Tompkins, Sue Tompkins, Sarah Tripp and Cathy Wilkes) and artists such as Michael Fullerton flutter between media, producing slight and uncompromisingly innate works that would have been largely unthinkable in the early Neo-Conceptualist '90s.[99] The proceduralist mannerisms

Kirsten Berkeley
JJ Charlesworth
Gillian Carnegie
Henry Coleman
Stuart Cumberland
Dexter Dalwood
Enrico David
Steven Dowson
Keith Farquhar
Ewan Gibbs
Brian Griffiths
Steven Gontarski
Luke Gotteller
Jun Hasegawa
Thomas Helbig
Roger Hiorns
Dean Hughes
Max Hymes
Dean Kenning
Elizabeth Kent
Ben Judd
Jim Lambie
Martin Maloney
Lucy McKenzie
Ian McLean
Paul Morrison
David Musgrave
Rupert Norfolk
Michael Raedecker
Polly Staple
DJ Simpson
Tommy Stockel
David Thorpe
Mark Titchner
Gary Webb
Martin Westwood

Heart & Soul
OPENING Friday July 30 1999/7pm to 11pm
60 Long Lane
London SE1/Telephone 0181 788 6089
July 30 to August 15 1999 Wed/Sun/12-6pm
UNDERGROUND Borough

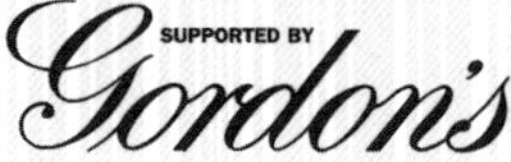

6.11 Invitation card for 'Heart & Soul', London, 1999

of much '90s art appeared to have been contaminated with a wilful negligence intended to incapacitate those with a penchant for the ascetic. The production of such a negotiable art had much more to do with making things than making things up.

If anything, the sheer diversity and international horizontality of art produced and exhibited in Britain at the close of the twentieth century suggests that the battles against modernist homogeneity which marked the situation that this book set out to map are entities of a largely forgotten, irrecoverable past. Selective amnesia willing, current practices can be bracketed as open verdicts. In political terms, the dominant sectors of the British artworld can be seen to have discovered etiquette to the mutual advantage of the emaciated state and the market. British art is a well-behaved model of Blair's vision of Britain: it is modern, accommodating, international and networked. As such – unlike the Conservative and Labour Parties of the '70s and '80s – New Labour has no need to radically reform the expanding British artworld; rather it seeks to manage it responsibly in nebulous obligation to the British people. Decentralization (rather than democratization) and quangos of public–private partnerships (PPPs) are now ubiquitous in the British artworld. Cultural parochialisms are discreetly regulated as British subsidiaries precisely as a means of avoiding inflaming the English, Irish, Welsh and Scottish nationalisms characteristic of the art and politics of the 1980s. By ensuring escalating political, institutional, economic and cultural self-determination by dynamic, enterprising, energizing and transforming

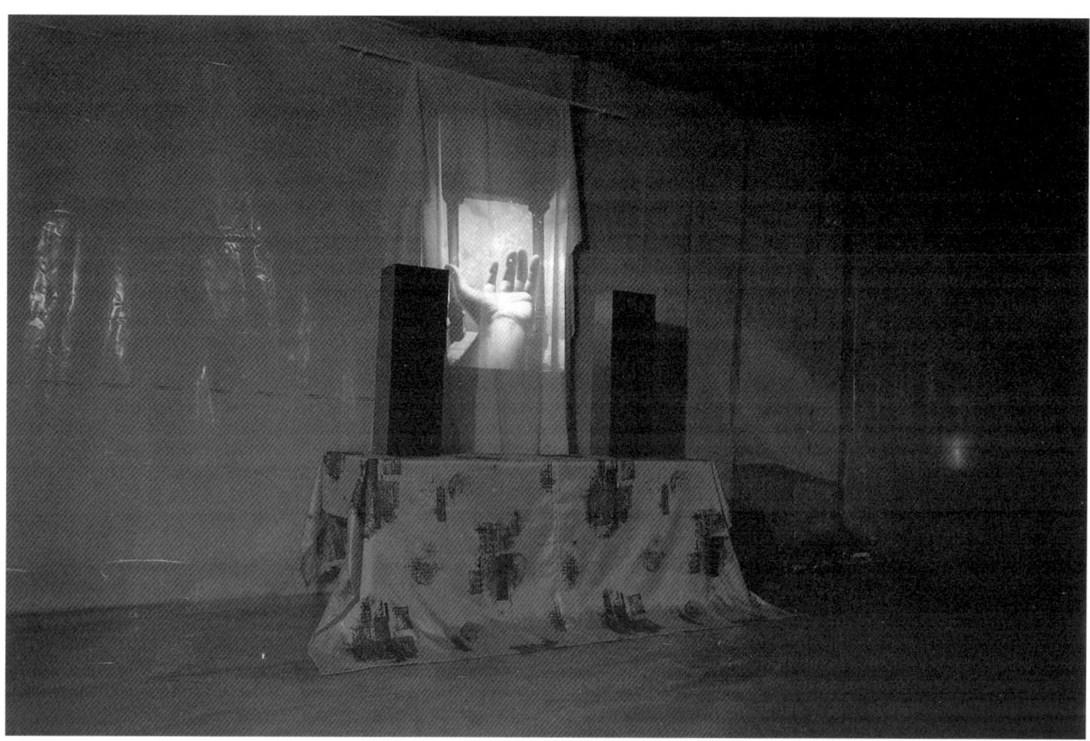

creative forces, contemporary artists living and working in Britain have also ensured that cultural devolution will increasingly be simulated and re-cuperated by sizeable institutions such as BALTIC, ICA and Tate Modern.

6.12   Joanne Tatham & Tom O'Sullivan, *Blow Your Mind* (1998), mixed media installation, Collective Gallery, Edinburgh

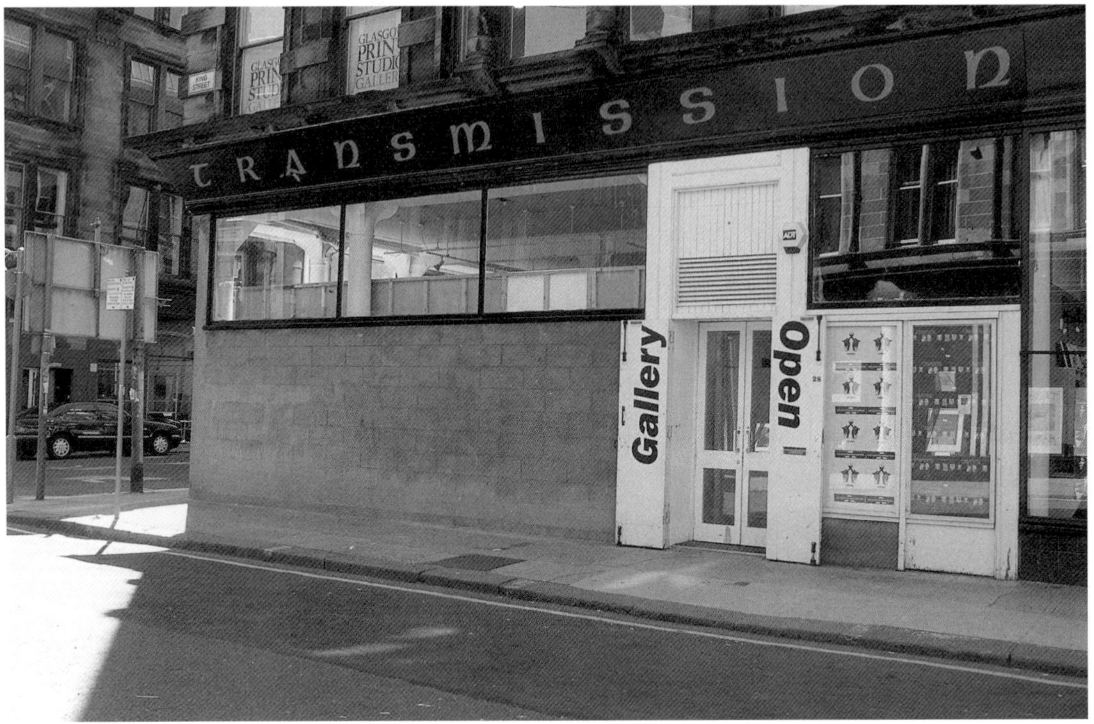

6.13   Installation view of Charisma 'How Long Can We Keep This Up?', altered gallery sign (2000), *It May Be a Year of Thirteen Moons but It's Still the Year of Culture*, Transmission, Glasgow, 2000

Notes

1   The British art crisis

1. Norman Shrapnel, 'Introduction', *The Seventies: Britain's Inward March*, London: Constable, 1980, p. 13.

2. Peter Fuller, 'On Social Functionalism', *Artscribe*, No. 13, August 1978, p. 43.

3. Caroline Tisdall, 'Art Controversies of the Seventies', in Susan Compton, ed., *British Art in the 20th Century*, London: Royal Academy, and Munich: Prestel-Verlag, 1986, p. 84.

4. Colin Simpson, 'Tate Drops a Costly Brick/How the Tate Gallery Spent £1 million in Two Years', *Sunday Times*, 15 February 1976.

5. *Ibid.* Simpson was not the first to write about the purchase – this was achieved by an anonymous employee of the *Basingstoke Gazette* on 13 February 1976.

6. Carl Andre, in Peter Stafford, 'Brick Sculpture Not the Original, Artist Confirms', *The Times*, 18 February 1976, p. 5.

7. Of the numerous articles which appeared in the British press on 16 February 1976, most carried headlines which pointed to this factor: see unsigned articles 'Gallery Stonewalls Bricks Buy', *Evening Standard*; 'Tate Gallery Silent on Price of Artistic Pile of Bricks', *Daily Telegraph*; 'Cost of Tate's Brick Buy Still Secret', *South Wales Argus*; 'The Tate's Brick Wall of Silence', *The News Portsmouth*; 'Tate Stays Silent on Brick Buy', *Jersey Evening Post*; and 'Gallery Stonewalling', *Western Evening News*.

8. Richard Morphet, then Deputy Keeper of the Modern Collection at the Tate, stated this clearly: 'The Tate waited four years before purchasing in 1973 its important Andre sculpture … The other five had already entered the collections of important museums in Europe and America, and the Tate's purchase thus represented its last chance of acquiring any of these six works.' See Richard Morphet, 'Carl Andre's Bricks', *Burlington Magazine*, Vol. 118, No. 884, November 1976, p. 767.

9. 'From the comment this aroused, you would not have dreamed that it was absolutely traditional for a sculpture to occur in several examples, or that Duchamp had run the gauntlet with his ready-mades well over fifty years earlier' (Pat Gilmour, 'Trivialisation of Art by the Press', *Arts Review*, January 1977, p. 50). In Rosalind Krauss's words, Andre's bricks were 'reproductions without originals'. However, it is not clear that Andre would have entirely agreed with Krauss's postmodern reading: 'that pile of bricks is my work, and if you want to get the authentic example or specimen of the work of Carl Andre then you must go to Carl Andre and buy it. I have a monopoly supply' (Andre in Fuller, 'On Social Functionalism', p. 123).

10. Morphet, 'Carl Andre's Bricks', p. 764.

11. See 'Tate Bricks Disfigured', *The Times*, 24 February 1976, p. 1.

12. Andre agreed with the Tate's actions, as is clear in an interview with Peter Fuller: *'You once said, "my works are in a constant state of change. I'm not interested in reaching an ideal state with my work. As people walk on them, as the steel rusts, as the brick crumbles, the materials weather and the work becomes its own record of everything that's happened to it." Do you therefore disapprove the Tate's decision to remove the ink-stain from the bricks?* I *approve* of the removal of it. That statement was not meant to refer to vandalism, but to the fact that I do not polish metal plates … *Isn't vandalism part of history, too?* Vandalism is part of history, but then so is Auschwitz. That does not mean we should approve and continue the practice' (Andre in Fuller, 'On Social Functionalism', p. 117).

13. Andre in Fuller, 'On Social Functionalism', p. 124.

14. ' ... everyone says that bricks cannot stand by themselves, they need an argument, or line of work, to surround them. I absolutely agree; but the *Venus de Milo* would just be a stone woman if nobody knew about sculpture' (*ibid.*, p. 117).

15. Rosetta Brooks, 'Please, No Slogans', *Studio International*, No. 191, March/April 1976.

16. *Ibid.*

17. As Michael Compton, Keeper of the Tate collection, put it, 'I see no reason why we shouldn't be primarily concerned with our own subculture, and just try to spread it a little bit ... The Government is backing my game, my passionate interest, and so long as I can continue to persuade them to do so, I will. I'm on to a good thing, and I would not dream of questioning it' (in Peter Fuller, 'The Tate, the State and the English Tradition', *Studio International*, Vol. 194, No. 988, 1/1978, p. 7).

18. Robert Morris, 'Notes on Sculpture: Part II', *Artforum*, Vol. 5, No. 2, October 1966, pp. 20–23.

19. Carl Andre, 'The Bricks Abstract', *Art Monthly*, No. 1, October 1976, p. 24. This abstract, containing a number of comments on the affair selected by Andre, was presented in table form, strongly resembling Andre's concrete poetry.

20. The Centre for Policy Studies was founded by Keith Joseph on 12 June 1974. See Matthew D'Ancona, *The First Modernisers*, London: Centre for Policy Studies, 1999.

21. See Kathleen Burk and Alec Cairncross, *'Goodbye Great Britain': The 1976 IMF Crisis*, London: Yale University Press, 1992.

22. Roy Shaw, 'Introduction', in his *The Arts and the People*, London: Jonathan Cape, 1987, p. 9.

23. 'The complex history of avant-garde art can be read as the history of a crisis of high imaginative culture. A crisis brought on in reflective culture by the rise of the New Class and by the modern idea of progress, that is, the secular idea of moral and social advance through the growth of instrumental knowledge' (Andrew Brighton, 'Art Currency', in *Current Affairs: British Painting and Sculpture in the 1980s*, Oxford: Museum of Modern Art Oxford and The British Council, 1987, p. 14). See also Alvin W. Gouldner, *The Future of the Intellectuals and the Rise of the New Class*, London: Macmillan, 1979.

24. Shaw, 'What Use are the Arts?', in *The Arts and the People*, p. 20.

25. *Ibid.*, p. 25.

26. Nicholas Fairbairn, quoted by Thomson Prentice, in 'Adults Only Art Show Angers MP', *Daily Mail*, 19 October 1976, p. 1.

27. Ted Little (then Director of the ICA), *ibid*. Roy Shaw, however, condemned the exhibition: 'It is my personal view that this is not the kind of thing which public money should be used for' (in Richard Cork, 'Richard Cork's 1976 Art Review', *Evening Standard*, 30 December 1976).

28. See Jonathan Harris, *New Art History: A Critical Introduction*, London: Routledge, 2001.

29. Briony Fer, 'The Modern in Fragments', in Francis Frascina *et al.*, *Modernity and Modernism: French Painting in the Nineteenth Century*, New Haven: Yale University Press, 1993, p. 43.

30. See Chapter 3, 'Dynamic perversity', below.

31. Throbbing Gristle actually made its debut at the AIR Gallery on Shaftsbury Avenue, London, in July 1976. COUM led the way for the entrepreneurial artists of the 1980s and 1990s. Having given up on state subsidy, COUM simply became a private limited company (Industrial Records).

32. Timothy J. Clark, 'Preliminaries to a Possible Treatment of *Olympia* in 1865', *Screen*, Spring 1980, p. 27.

33. See Keith Joseph, *Monetarism is Not Enough*, London: Centre for Policy Studies, 1976.

34. 'Victorian values' stressed the virtues of authority, hierarchy, discipline and order, all of which were in fact subverted by Thatcher's economic liberalism. Bowing to public pressure, Labour also proposed an end to the Arts Council's (quasi)autonomy. However, considerable ideological differences remained, with Labour, advised by socially engaged artist Conrad Atkinson, proposing a democratic system of 'checks and balances' in order to make the Arts Council publicly accountable, and the Conservatives advocating the end of the Council. See Labour Party, *The Arts and the People: Labour's Policy Towards the Arts*, London: Labour Party, 1977.

35. The Executive Committee of the ABSA included representatives of the Beecham Group, Doulton and Company, IBM (UK), Imperial Tobacco, Legal and General Assurance, Midland Bank, Perkins Engines Group and Phillips Industries.

36. See David Alexander, *A Policy for the Arts: Just Cut Taxes*, London: Selsdon Group, 1978. As Secretary of State for Education and Science in the 1970–1974 Conservative government, Margaret Thatcher had attempted to introduce charges for entry to state museums and

galleries, only to have her policy rejected by Harold Wilson's government on its re-election in 1974.

37.   Colin Tweedy, 'From Maecenas to Manager', in his *A Celebration of 10 Years' Business Sponsorship of the Arts*, London: Association for Business Sponsorship of the Arts, 1986, p. 9.

38.   Prince Charles, in Tweedy, *A Celebration of 10 Years' Business Sponsorship of the Arts*, p. 5.

39.   See Eric Hobsbawm, 'The Forward March of Labour Halted?', in M. Jacques and F. Mulhern, eds, *The Forward March of Labour Halted?*, London: Verso, 1978 (first publ. in *Marxism Today* in September 1978).

40.   See Conservative Political Centre, *The Arts – The Way Forward*, London: CPS, 1978.

41.   Shaw, *The Arts and the People*, p. 20.

42.   'The twelve Regional Arts Associations founded between 1958 and 1973 brought a measure of devolution (together with the Arts Councils of Scotland and Wales) but that did not create any democracy at the centre' (Robert Hewison, 'The Arts in Hard Times', in his *Too Much: Art and Society in the Sixties, 1960–75*, London: Methuen, 1986, p. 228).

43.   Andrew Brighton, 'Official Art and the Tate Gallery', *Studio International* (Review Issue), No. 1, 1977, p. 42.

44.   This view was particularly prevalent in Britain during 1978. See Roger Taylor, *Art: an Enemy of the People*, London: Routledge & Kegan Paul, 1978, and Sue Branden, *Artists and People*, London: Routledge & Kegan Paul, 1978.

45.   'There is a marked difference between the art publications of London and New York. Both *Art Monthly* and *Studio International* have been deep in the fray of analysing the social issues of art. *Artscribe* may deplore some of the analysis but it does not ignore it. In the States, after the removal of Max Kozloff from *Artforum*, there is a total blackout (with the exception of feminist publications such as *Heresies*)' (Rudolf Baranik, 'US/UK Dialogue on Social Purpose', *Artscribe*, No. 14, October 1978, p. 54).

46.   According to Cork in Donald Brook, 'Books: A Cautious Bob Each Way: Richard Cork, *The Social Role of Art*', *Art Monthly*, No. 37, 1980, p. 22.

47.   For a critique of Seymour's catalogue text for this exhibition see William Wood, 'Still You Ask for More: Demand, Display and The New Art', in Michael Newman and Jon Bird, *Rewriting Conceptual Art*, London: Reaktion Books, 1999, pp. 66–87.

48.   Cork, 'Introduction' to his *Beyond Painting & Sculpture: Works bought for the Arts Council by Richard Cork*, exhibition catalogue, London, Arts Council of Great Britain, 1974, p. 3. The exhibition opened at Leeds City Art Gallery on 12 January 1974. It then travelled to the Walker Art Gallery, Liverpool (16 February–17 March) and the Arnolfini Gallery, Bristol (4 May–8 June).

49.   Janet Daley, 'The Arts Council vs. The Visual Arts', *The Literary Review*, October 1981, pp. 40–1. Daley, a cultural conservative in the tradition of Fuller, was one of the crisis critics' fiercest critics. As she pointed out, Victor Burgin (among others at this time) was a member of the Art Advisory Panel and Awards to Artists Sub-committee of the ACGB (1971–1976). Much of the work selected by Cork at this point emerged from this tightly knit milieu.

50.   Peter Fuller and John Tagg, 'Richard Cork and the "New Road to Wigan Pier"', *Art Monthly*, No. 30, October 1979, p. 4.

51.   Cork, 'Art and Social Purpose', *Studio International*, March/April 1976.

52.   John Roberts, 'The Dialectics of Postmodernism: Thatcherism and the Visual Arts 1', in his *Postmodernism, Politics and Art*, Manchester: Manchester University Press, 1990, p. 61.

53.   'I certainly remember reading Williams in the 70s; he was somebody I was conscious of when I was at Cambridge in the 60s as one of the few dons who had something to say' (interview with Cork, Queens Park, London, February 1998).

54.   See Raymond Williams, *Marxism and Literature*, Oxford: Oxford University Press, 1977.

55.   Jeffrey Steele, 'Notes Towards Some Theses Against the New Kitsch', *Art Monthly*, No. 18, July/August 1978, p. 19.

56.   ' … the objective cretinization of painters, opens the door for a further connected system of false ideas about the social function of art – most notably the false idea that it is not itself an indispensable part of the system for propagating the ideology of the bourgeois class' (*ibid.*, p. 19).

57.   Ben Jones, 'Editorial', *Artscribe*, No. 1, January–February 1976, p. 4.

58.   'As an historical note, in 1976/77, when Caryn Faure Walker was employed as a Visual Arts Officer for the Greater London Arts Association, GLAA assistance was awarded to the magazine *Artscribe*, edited by none other than James and Caryn Faure Walker' (Michael Daley, 'Arts Council Awards', *Art Monthly*, No. 49, September 1981, p. 32). Like much anti-Arts-Council

rhetoric of the early '80s, this deliberately overstates the case; *Artscribe* was started with a total of only £70 in revenue awarded to Ben Jones.

59. Jones, 'Editorial'.

60. 'What always struck me about Cork, Fuller, and also Andrew Brighton was their condescension towards "practitioners". They seriously thought they could provide artists (the plebs) with a programme, a theory, the tablet from the mountain. *Artscribe* succeeded because so many "practitioners" absolutely loathed that presumption. It had nothing to do with being conservative or radical' (from my correspondence with James Faure Walker, May 2001).

61. James Faure Walker, 'Towards a Definition of the Progressive in Painting', *Artscribe*, No. 3, Summer 1976, p. 13.

62. See Chapter 2, below, and John Roberts, *The Impossible Document*, London: Camerawords, 1997.

63. Brandon Taylor, 'Writing on the Surface: A Recent Tendency at *Artscribe*', *Art Monthly*, No. 33, February 1980, p. 3.

64. *Ibid.*

65. Correspondence with Faure Walker (see n. 60, above).

66. Brandon Taylor, 'Textual Art', *Artscribe*, No. 1, January–February 1976, p. 7.

67. Brandon Taylor, 'The Avant-Garde and St. Martins', *Artscribe*, 'Education Issue', No. 5, September–October 1976, p. 5.

68. Cork also used this illustration in his editorial for 'Art and Social Purpose', *Studio International*, March/April 1976.

69. 'Editorial', *Studio International*, September/October 1976, p. 155.

70. Taylor, 'The Avant-Garde and St. Martins'.

71. *Ibid.* See John A. Walker, *Left Shift: Radical Art in 1970s Britain*, London and New York: I. B. Taurus, 2002.

72. Taylor, 'The Avant-Garde and St. Martins', p. 6.

73. Faure Walker, 'Richard Cork interviewed by James Faure Walker', *Artscribe*, No. 7, May 1977, pp. 41–4.

74. Rory Coonan, 'Style in the 70s', *Art Monthly*, No. 29, September 1979, p. 14.

75. See 'Peter Fuller Responds to "Painting Now"', *Artscribe*, No. 6, April 1977, pp. 31–4, and 'James Faure Walker Replies', *ibid.*, pp. 34–7. Hyman soon became an influential advocate of *ut pictura poesis*.

76. While editor of *Studio*, Cork had commissioned articles by Brighton, Fuller and John Tagg. For Brighton, Fuller and Tagg's version of events see Peter Fuller and John Tagg, 'Richard Cork and the "New Road to Wigan Pier"', *Art Monthly*, No. 30, October 1979.

77. Fuller, 'The Crisis in Professionalism', *Studio International*, Vol. 194, No. 988, 1978, p. 80. Fuller also wrote in a footnote that 'My central historical perspective on British culture and history has been greatly influenced by Tom Nairne and Perry Anderson' (p. 87). See especially, Tom Nairne, 'The British Historical Elite', *New Left Review*, Vol. 1, No. 23, January/February 1964; Perry Anderson, 'Origins of the Present Crisis', *ibid.*, and Perry Anderson, 'Components of the National Culture', *New Left Review*, Vol. 1, No. 50, July/August 1968.

78. Fuller, 'The Tate, the State and the English Tradition', pp. 7–8.

79. Peter Fuller, 'The Crisis in British Art', *Art Monthly*, No. 8, June 1977, p. 8.

80. 'I reject the idea that there is such a thing as a "science of aesthetics", or a legitimate method of "formal" analysis which can lead a critic to the identification of "objective", "permanent", "culture free", "universal" or "fundamental" aesthetic attributes within a given work of art … Things in the world are without meaning, or signification, or visual relations between their component parts, or "formal" or aesthetic value … my consciousness, and the consciousness of all the other viewers of the work are not identical or fixed. Consciousness is determined by history' (Peter Fuller, 'Problems of Art Criticism', in Brandon Taylor, ed., *Art and Criticism*, Winchester: Winchester School of Art Press, 1979, pp. 22–3).

81. Peter Fuller, 'Preface', in his *Art and Psychoanalysis*, London: Writers & Readers Publishing Co-operative Limited, 1980, p. 242.

82. The general emphasis of Fuller's argument had, at this point, much in common with that of Jurgen Habermas in 'Modernity – An Incomplete Project', in Hal Foster, ed., *The Anti-Aesthetic: Essays on Postmodern Culture*, Port Townsend, USA: The Bay Press, 1983, pp. 3–16.

83. See Sebastiano Timpanaro, 'The Freudian Slip', *New Left Review*, No. 91, May–June 1972, pp. 43–56; Charles Rycroft, 'Review: Freud and Timpanaro's *Freudian Slip*', *New Left Review*, No. 118, November–December 1979, pp. 81–8, and Raymond Williams, 'Problems of Materialism', *New Left Review*, No. 109, May–June 1978, pp. 3–18.

84.   Fuller, 'In Defence of Art', in his *Beyond the Crisis in Art*, London: Writers & Readers Publishing Co-operative Ltd, 1980, p. 242.

85.   ' … my emphasis is distinct from that of Richard Cork; the differences between us are as significant as the areas of agreement' (Fuller, 'Problems of Art Criticism', p. 22).

86.   Fuller, 'On Social Functionalism', p. 43.

87.   Fuller and Tagg, 'Richard Cork', p. 7.

88.   Clive Philpot, 'An Insular View of British Art Mags', *Art Monthly*, No. 1, October 1976, pp. 1–2. Philpot went on to comment: 'The recent bi-monthly newspaper *Artscribe* seems to be attempting some of the things that a weekly or fortnightly publication could usefully provide, but it is difficult to see it as a national organ since its view of art is principally from the standpoint of a particular kind of painting and sculpture.'

89.   Andre, 'The Bricks Abstract', p. 25.

90.   Editorial, 'P-Orridge's Gruelling Days', *Art Monthly*, No. 2, November 1976, pp. 1–2.

91.   *Artscribe* initially sold for 20p and *Art Monthly* for 40p. Both 'inkies' contained writing that rivalled that in the £1.75 'glossy' *Studio* (often by the same critics). Artists and students rather than just institutions could afford both magazines.

92.   Richard Cork, 'Editorial', *Studio International*, Vol. 191, No. 980, March/April 1976, p. 100.

93.   The Brotherhood of Ruralists was formed in 1975 by Blake and a group of six Romanticist friends with the purpose of expressing 'through personal vision and experience of our native heritage a celebration of the English countryside' (Frank Cole, 'Foreword', in Nicholas Usherwood, *The Brotherhood of Ruralists*, London: Lund Humphries, 1981, p. 6; see also Chapter 4, 'The Shock of the Old', below).

94.   On 9 June he was replaced by Edward Lucie-Smith as the *Evening Standard*'s art critic; Lucie-Smith lasted until 1980, when Brian Sewell took over.

95.   'Artists will never succeed in becoming truly popular merely by imposing their work unchanged, on audiences whose needs and attitudes have only been perceived on an abstract and paternalist level' (Cork, 'Art For Whom?', in *Art For Whom?*, exhibition catalogue, London: Serpentine Gallery, 1978, p. 9).

96.   Fuller and Tagg, 'Richard Cork', p. 5.

97.   See Stephen Willats, *Stephen Willats*, London: Chester Beatty Research Institute, 1964, and *Visual Automatics and Visual Transmitters*, Oxford: Museum of Modern Art, 1968.

98.   See also Stephen Willats, *The Artist as an Instigator of Changes in Social Cognition and Behaviour*, London: Gallery House Press, 1973.

99.   Stephen Willats, *Art and Social Function*, London: Latimer New Dimensions, 1976.

100.   Several galleries took part in this experiment: City Art Gallery, Southampton (1973); Whitechapel Art Gallery, London (1974); The Lisson Gallery, London (1975); Midland Group Gallery, Nottingham (1976).

101.   See Stephen Willats, 'Questions about Ourselves', in *I Don't Want to Be Like Anyone Else*, exhibition catalogue, London: Lisson Gallery, 1978. This work was based in the Avondale Estate, Hayes, West London.

102.   Richard Cork, 'Assault by the Facts of Life', *Evening Standard*, 25 April 1974, p. 32.

103.   Conrad Atkinson, 'Interview with Richard Cork', *Studio International*, No. 191, March/April 1976, p. 179.

104.   Conrad Atkinson, 'Industry and Industrial Disease', in Caroline Tisdall and Sandy Nairne, *Picturing the System*, exhibition catalogue, ICA, London: Pluto Press, 1981, p. 10.

105.   Atkinson studied art at Carlisle College of Art 1956–1960, then for a teaching degree at Liverpool College of Art in 1960–1961, and did postgraduate studies at the Royal Academy Schools 1961–1965. Atkinson was a contemporary of members of Art & Language who were at the Slade during this period.

106.   Terry and Susan Atkinson (no relations) thought so: ' … such sloganeering memento making, we believe, holds patronising and disrupting assumptions about the nature of its public. We believe it assumes a public which doesn't have to be made but which is already out there fully formed and wants to hear these things. A public to be in its imagined universalism and not one which will learn complex things. It is a public of simple slogans; it is a public of the worlds of the Conservative and Labour Parties, the world of the *Morning Star* art critic. This is a public which will be told things, a public of fixed and petrified worthiness, and, most patronising of all, an inert band of rote-learner receivers. This public learns nothing but rote, a public which is powerless to proselytise and, in the end, reason for itself. This is deeply patronising' ('British Political Art at Coventry', in *Mute I*, exhibition catalogue, Copenhagen: Galleri Prag; Derry: Orchard Gallery; London: Gimpel Fils, 1988, p. 16).

107.   'In my view there is a difference between a genuinely participatory work made by people in a particular situation, and a work which attempts from a different viewpoint to analyse that situation using those people's experience. I think that in the first five years of the 70s many artists confused the difference between participation and taking the responsibility for the particular viewpoint that was expressed. The problem being that you have to be a specialist in order to demystify the media from form' (Conrad Atkinson, 'People's Imagery: Trade Union Banners 1976', in Tisdall and Nairne, *Picturing the System*, p. 21).

108.   'If we should happen to think that the injustices animating him as an artist might be rectified by the application of (let's say) more enlightened self-interest, or the removal of artificial constraints from the free play of market forces, we shall not be certain why he denies it. The buried foundations of his advertised "Marxism" are as obscure at the surface of his speech as those of his art-theoretical or aesthetic position. There is far too much taken for granted, for a thesis on art and politics' (Donald Brook, 'Reflections on "The State of Art: The Art of the State"', *Art Monthly*, No. 72, December/January 1983/84, p. 3).

109.   Atkinson, 'People's Imagery'.

110.   Allan Wallach, 'Conrad Atkinson: The Dilemma of Political Art', *Arts Magazine*, No. 54, December 1979, p. 153.

111.   *Ibid.*

112.   Charles Harrison and Fred Orton, *A Provisional History of Art & Language*, Paris: Editions E. Fabre, 1982, p. 62.

113.   Mel Ramsden, 'Art & Language: Mike Baldwin and Mel Ramsden, Extracts from a Conversation with Sanda Miller', *Artscribe*, No. 47, July/August 1984, p. 15.

114.   See Art & Language, 'Art for Society?', *Art–Language*, Vol. 4, No. 4 (Banbury: Art & Language Press), June 1980.

115.   Cork's title closely parallels 'Art for the People', an exhibition of photographs of mural paintings held by the anti-fascist Artists' International Association (AIA) at the Whitechapel Gallery in 1939. See R. Radford, *Art for a Purpose: The Artists International Association, 1933–1953*, Winchester: Winchester School of Art Press, 1987.

116.   Harrison and Orton, *A Provisional History*, p. 61. Harrison and Orton were referring to Atkinson's *Thalidomide: Anniversary Print for the Queen Mother* (1978), which exposed what amounted to a royal seal of approval for the multinational company United Distilleries who made profits at the expense of thalidomide victims.

117.   Anon., 'An Exhibition Censored', 10 November 1978, reprinted in 'O God! O Ulster!', *Art Monthly*, No. 22, 1978–1979, pp. 21–2.

118.   Ulster Museum, 'Press Release', 9 November 1978, reprinted in 'O God! O Ulster!' (see n. 117).

119.   Derek Boshier, 'Statement', in his *Lives: An Exhibition of Artists Whose Work is Based on Other Peoples' Lives, Selected by Derek Boshier*, exhibition catalogue, London: Arts Council of Great Britain, 1979.

120.   Atkinson, 'Correspondence: "Lives' Lives"', *Art Monthly*, No. 27, June 1979, p. 28.

121.   Jeff Sawtell, 'Comment', *Artery: A Cultural Journal for Left Unity*, No. 13, Spring 1978.

122.   See Glyn Jones, 'Mur al, mural ist, mural ism', letter printed in *Art Monthly*, No. 18, July/August 1978, pp. 32–3.

123.   Richard Cork, 'The Royal Oak Murals', *Art Monthly*, No. 15, April 1978, p. 10.

124.   *Ibid.*

125.   Sarah Kent, 'Why Not Popular', paper given at the conference on 'The State of British Art', London, ICA, 10–12 February 1978, reprinted in *Studio International*, Vol. 194, No. 988, 2/1978, p. 120.

126.   *Ibid.*

127.   Malcolm Miles, 'Community Murals in Britain', in his *Art for Public Places*, Winchester: Winchester School of Art Press, 1989, p. 72.

128.   It is very likely that Rochfort and Binnington believed that they were working in the midst of a similar economic and cultural crisis to that which Rivera had experienced when working on the USA's Federal Art Project in the early 1930s. Furthermore, their political affiliations (as members of the Communist Party of Great Britain) and influences (especially Mexican Muralism) directly parallels the Muralism of the Artists' International Association, founded in Britain in 1933 in response to the rise of fascism. See Desmond Rochfort, *Mexican Muralists: Orozco, Rivera, Siqueiros*, London: Laurence King, 1993; Radford, *Art for a Purpose*; Tate Gallery, *Mural Painting in Great Britain 1919–1939: An Exhibition of Photographs*, London: Tate Gallery, 1939; and Lynda Morris and R. Radford, *AIA: The Story of the Artists International Association*, Oxford: Museum of Modern Art, 1983. Following the completion of the Royal Oak Murals in 1978, the Greenwich Mural Workshop embarked upon a scheme commemorating *The Battle of*

Cable Street (1978–1983) on the flank wall of St George's Town Hall, Cable Street, Tower Hamlets, London. While again pointing directly to a parallel of the 1930s with the late 1970s and early 1980s, this proved to be more relevant and controversial than the Royal Oak scheme, especially given the number of race riots during the period of its genesis (e.g. in Lewisham in 1977 and Brixton in 1981). See C. Kenna, *Murals in London*, and C. Kenna and S. Lobb, *Mural Manual*, both London: Greenwich Mural Workshop, 1985.

129. Fuller, 'Social Functionalism', *Art Monthly*, No. 19, September 1978, p. 27.

130. David Sweet, 'Artists v The Rest: The New Philistines', *Artscribe*, No. 11, April 1978, p. 38.

131. Cork, 'The Royal Oak Murals', pp. 10–11. Cork here echoed Binnington's view of other mural schemes of the mid-1970s: '[The Eyesights Project] conceived by the Greater London Arts Association (GLAA) and sponsored by Thames Television in 1975, was a simplistic attempt to take art from the gallery context and give it to a wider working-class audience. The scheme basically was to select designs from those submitted to GLAA and plaster the East End with these images using commercial advertising hoardings. Much to the surprise of the organisers, the residents of Tower Hamlets received this benevolent act of patronage with considerable hostility. A local campaign against the project succeeded in stopping it, and the protest's organisers went on from this to found one of the most progressive, effective and comparatively well-financed borough Arts councils in Britain … Eyesights failed, and failed magnificently, for it assumed that all that was necessary to give an avant-garde art a genuine social function was to liberate it from the gallery confines and patronisingly give it to a working-class audience. They were reminded quite ungraciously that established working-class communities have a culture, an art and a series of quite legitimate demands for their artists' (David Binnington, 'A Genuine Social Function for Artists: A Dream or a Reality', in his *Art for Whom?*, exhibition catalogue, London: Arts Council of Great Britain, 1978, p. 56).

132. *Art Monthly*, No. 21, November 1978, p. 31.

133. The GLA was founded in 1971 with the aim of manifesting the spirit of 1968. 'These ideas included a re-affirmation of the importance of art and all creative activity; greater public access to art as well as greater involvement in art activities; a belief in self-help and mutual aid to get things done, rather than passive dependence on "experts" and established authority' (Stan Bell, 'The Spirit of "68"', in *Roots into the 80's: Glasgow League of Artists Yearbook*, Glasgow: John Watson, 1979).

134. ' … the admission under questioning, that the Westway muralists really didn't want members of the community working alongside them and preferred post hoc comments to propter hoc consultations that would allow the community to determine what the community had to look at on its wall … ' (Peter Townsend, 'Editor's Elongated Note [Art for Whom? Discussion]', *Art Monthly*, No. 18, July/August 1978, p. 23).

135. Cork found support for this view: 'These murals and the thinking that goes along with them can be found anywhere in Britain. They are merely decorative motifs placed upon sad gable ends, there to gloss over the slum playgrounds of a city, about as meaningful as a billboard and telling as many lies, saying "this is art"; at best it is a pretty picture competently executed. They do not point in any way to the social and political changes happening in this country' (Eileen Lawrence, 'Greenberg's Scotland', *Art Monthly*, No. 15, 1978, p. 30).

136. Cork, 'The Royal Oak Murals', pp. 10–11.

137. The designs were shown to and discussed by democratic organizations within the district before being displayed on the site, where the public were asked to write down their impressions.

138. 'Rochfort: Tell me, what do you think of it – do you like it? Lady: I think it's very good, very clever. Rochfort: Do you know what it's about? Lady: No. Rochfort: When you go past it, what is the thing that you first notice about it? Lady: Well, I couldn't actually tell you, really, because I only just look at the colours really. I couldn't tell you what it was all on there. Man: Well, I don't know much about it, but it looks all right, it looks nice. It cheers the place up a bit. The flyover don't look nice, but with that it looks a bit decent. I don't mind it but don't know much about it. I walk past it every day and I just look at it. But I don't know much about painting, to be honest with you. Elderly man: It's quite beautiful. It's cheerful, and the canvases didn't cost anything did they? Rochfort: Do you know what it's about? Elderly man: No, that's what intrigues me, you see. I'm not quite sure about that. But it looks very, very cheerful and colourful, you know. Rochfort: What do you *think* it's about? Elderly man: (*after a long pause*) Ah, you beat me there' (Richard Cork, 'The Art We Deserve? Transcript of a Film by Richard Cork, directed by Jeremy Marre for the Arts Council of Great Britain, shown at the ICA at 7pm on 8th November 1978', *Artscribe*, No. 20, November 1979, p. 51).

2 Radical academicism

1. Judd's and Morris's influence on Burgin can be determined in his essay 'Situational Aesthetics', *Studio International*, No. 178, October 1969.

2. Victor Burgin, 'The Absence of Presence: Conceptualism and Post-modernisms', in *1965–72: When Attitudes Became Form*, exhibition catalogue, Cambridge: Kettles Yard Gallery, 1984, p. 39.

3. Burgin, 'Introduction', in his *Two Essays on Art Photography and Semiotics*, London: Robert Self, 1976, p. 2.

4. In 1973 T. J. Clark published two influential studies of French nineteenth-century painting, *The Absolute Bourgeois* and *Image of the People*, both of which analysed the relationship between class struggle and art. This coincided with the French publication of Nicos Hadjinicolaou's *Art History and Class Struggle* (English translation 1977). The following year, Clark published 'The Conditions of Artistic Creation', a call to arms in the *Times Literary Supplement* for a restructured art history that would draw on Althusserian Marxism, semiotics and a close attention to material and ideological factors.

5. T. J. Clark, 'The Conditions of Artistic Creation', *Times Literary Supplement*, 24 May 1974.

6. T. J. Clark, 'On the Social History of Art', in his *Image of the People: Gustave Courbet and the 1848 Revolution*, London: Thames & Hudson, 1973, p. 13.

7. Burgin, *Two Essays*, p. 2.

8. *Ibid.*

9. *Ibid.*

10. 'Interpellation' is like someone calling out, 'Hey you there' in the street, and 'by this one-hundred-and-eighty-degree physical conversion, he becomes a subject' (Louis Althusser, 'Ideology and Ideological State Apparatuses: Notes towards an Investigation', in his *Lenin and Philosophy, and Other Essays*, London: New Left Books (Verso), 1971, p. 163).

11. *Studio International*, No. 191, March/April 1976, pp. 146–7.

12. This is from the same passage by Williams quoted in Burgin's 'Why Photography? Edited transcript of a lecture given at Reading University, Fine Art Department, 4th November 1975', in *Arte Inglese Oggi 1970–76*, exhibition catalogue, Milan: Palazzo Reale, 1976, p. 363.

13. John Stezaker, 'Notes: The Pursuit', *Studio International*, No. 191, March/April 1976, pp. 135–45.

14. Victor Burgin, 'Art, Common-Sense and Photography', *Camerawork*, No. 3, 1976, reprinted in Jessica Evans, ed., *The Camerawork Essays: Context and Meaning in Photography*, London: Rivers Oram Press, 1997, p. 77.

15. John Berger, *Ways of Seeing*, London: BBC, 1972.

16. ' … it's not enough simply to oppose one discourse with another, antithetical, discourse. One has to *know* the discourse that is being opposed in order to assimilate it, transform it within the discourse of "higher logical type"' (Burgin, 'Why Photography?', p. 365).

17. Laura Mulvey, 'Visual Pleasure and Narrative Cinema', *Screen*, Vol. 16, No. 3, 1975, pp. 6–18.

18. Unlike Stezaker, Burgin made 'anonymous' subvertisements for exhibition catalogues and art journals. However, Burgin never crossed over into mainstream lifestyle magazines such as *Harpers & Queen* or *Melody Maker*. See 'Going Somewhere? Class Consciousness you're nowhere without it!', in Fruitmarket Gallery, ROBERT BARRY, VICTOR BURGIN, HAMISH FULTON, GILBERT AND GEORGE, HANS HAACKE, JOHN HILLIARD, KOSUTH/CHARLESWORTH, DAVID TREMLETT, LAWRENCE WEINER, exhibition catalogue, Edinburgh: Fruitmarket Gallery, 3–24 April 1976; 'It's Worth Thinking About … Class Consciousness, Think about It', *Studio International*, No. 191, March/April 1976, pp. 146–7; 'What Does Possession Mean to You?', *Camerawork*, No. 3, 1976, back cover; 'Centrefold', ZG, Vol. 1, 1981, and 'Centre Pages', BLOCK, No. 8, 1983, pp. 34–5.

19. See Robert Breen, 'Foreword', Fruitmarket Gallery exhibition catalogue (see n. 19, above).

20. Self had close links with Michael Spens, who had become a millionaire when Pilkington Glass went public, and decided, in traditional aristocratic fashion, to use his newfound wealth to become a patron of the new 'socially responsible' avant-garde of the mid-1970s, by purchasing *Studio International*.

21. Burgin, *Two Essays*, p. 2.

22. Eirlys Tynan, 'Victor Burgin's "Possession"', *Studio International*, No. 193, September/October 1976, pp. 225–6.

23. Burgin, *Two Essays*, p. 3.

24. ' … history is still conceived as at once "over" (completed) and "over there" (distanced): art historical research is still seen as working on the past in much the same way as certain chemicals work on a latent photographic image, an image which simply needs to be adequately

developed in order to emerge in all its immutable detail' (Victor Burgin, 'Introduction: Something About Photography Theory', in A. L. Rees and F. Borzello, eds, *The New Art History*, London: Camden Press, 1986, p. 42).

25. T. J. Clark, 'Preliminaries to a Possible Treatment of Olympia in 1865', *Screen*, Spring 1980, p. 30.

26. See Jessica Evans, 'Victor Burgin's Polysemic Dreamcoat', in her *Art Has No History!: The Making and Unmaking of Modern Art*, London: Verso, 1994.

27. ' ... it seemed at least a reasonable working hypothesis to assume that other forms of human communication might have evolved along basically similar lines' (Burgin, 'Art, Common-Sense and Photography', p. 81).

28. 'Arguments from language studies may provide useful analogies, but these arguments will be no better and no worse than any argument by analogy – the analogies should not be taken as reflecting an essential identity in the processes involved. Visual representation and languages are logically different in their relationships to represented objects, in that words do not necessarily embody any of the properties of the objects in order to perform their function adequately' (Martin Kemp, 'Seeing and Signs: E. H. Gombrich in Retrospect', *Art History*, Vol. 7, No. 2, 1984, p. 241).

29. ' ... a nicely cooked piece of rationalism ... To talk of the different faculties at work in cognition may serve philosophical clarity, but I believe it casts the processes of image-making in a synthetic light which bears no relationship to the intermingled complexity of the actual mechanisms at work. The essential nature of visual image-making is that it exploits these processes in relation to the perceptual structures *specific to vision*' (*ibid.*, p. 237).

30. Art & Language, 'The French Disease', *Art–Language*, Vol. 3, No. 4, October 1976 (*Fox 4*), p. 33. 'One common assumption was that artists and intellectuals are empowered to create and to uncover meaning by virtue of their occupancy of some higher realm – some level of consciousness above that at which meaning is supposedly determined for the unenlightened mass. The image of the mass in need of enlightenment was necessary to the success of Semio-art; necessary, that is to say, to its claims to be demystificatory, and (thus) "emancipatory"' (Harrison, 'Art & Language', p. 23).

31. The group Art & Language started in Coventry in 1967/68 with four people: Terry Atkinson, Michael Baldwin, David Bainbridge and Harold Hurrell. In 1969 Ian Burn, Mel Ramsden and Charles Harrison became associated with the group.

32. Art & Language, 'In Contradiction', *Art–Language*, Vol. 3, No. 4, October 1976 (*Fox 4*), p. 14. This view had been expressed in the 'Art and Social Purpose' edition of *Studio International* earlier in 1976: 'Such work only reinforces the minorities' cultural belief in its own authenticity by representation of mass ideology in the form of primitive rhetoric. It becomes a manifestation of the same kind of cultural imperialism on the level of style of all forms of ideology and consciousness which is perhaps most manifest in the illustration from *Vogue* incorporated in Jonathan Miles and John Stezaker's *Captions (of Cultural Détente)*' (Rosetta Brooks, 'Please, No Slogans', *Studio International*, No. 191, March/April 1976).

33. Kemp, 'Seeing and Signs', p. 237.

34. Art & Language, 'Us, Us and Away', *Art–Language*, Vol. 3, No. 4, October 1976 (*Fox 4*), p. 1.

35. Art & Language, 'In Contradiction', *ibid.*, p. 13.

36. See Ludwig Wittgenstein, *Philosophical Investigations*, 125.

37. Harrison, 'Art & Language'.

38. See Peter Smith, 'Art & Language at Robert Self', *Art Monthly*, No. 13, December/January 1977–1978, pp. 28–9.

39. Charles Harrison and Fred Orton, *A Provisional History of Art & Language*, Paris: Editions E. Fabre, 1982, p. 59.

40. Art & Language, 'Somewhere to Begin', *Art–Language*, Vol. 3, No. 1: 'Draft for an Anti-Textbook', September 1974, p. 2.

41. Harrison and Orton, *A Provisional History*, p. 54.

42. 'The loyal opposition to Art with Social Purpose, typified by Art & Language (+ lines emanating mainly from Marcel Duchamp) propagates the identical contempt for the working class and for the majority of artists, but this time in its contrary, frankly scholastic/occult form' (Jeffrey Steele, 'Notes Towards Some Theses Against the New Kitsch', *Art Monthly*, No. 18, July/August 1978, p. 20).

43. Charles Harrison, '"Seeing" and "Describing": the Artists' Studio', in his *Essays on Art & Language*, Oxford: Basil Blackwell, 1991, p. 157.

44. *Ibid.*

45. Art & Language, 'In Contradiction', *Art–Language*, Vol. 3, No. 4, October 1976 (*Fox 4*), p. 13.

46. Harrison, 'The Conditions of Problems', in his *Essays*, p. 98.

47. Mel Ramsden, 'Art & Language: Mike Baldwin and Mel Ramsden, Extracts from a Conversation with Sandra Miller', *Artscribe*, No. 47, July/August 1984, p. 14.

48. 'It is empirically false, even absurd to suggest that Conceptual Art's value is supposed to lie in its acceptability as a philosophical thesis' (Art & Language, '"Artists" and "Philosophers"', *Art Monthly*, No. 26, May 1979, p. 34).

49. Victor Burgin in John Roberts, ed., 'Interview with Victor Burgin', in Roberts' *The Impossible Document: Photography and Conceptual Art in Britain 1966–1976*, London: Camerawords, 1997, p. 89.

50. Ramsden, 'Art & Language', p. 15.

51. The Open University course A316, 'Modern Art: Practices and Debates', stands as a testament to the possibilities of critical gerrymandering: ' … there was always a preference whenever anything got written by [Charles] Harrison, to emphasise the historical importance of Art & Language' (Victor Burgin in Roberts, ed., 'Interview', p. 87). There is, of course, nothing new in the deliberate historification of art practice. Most avant-garde groups of the early twentieth century vastly overestimated their importance in their manifestos in order to create an instant genealogy.

52. 'Who cares finally about the definition of art? What does it matter? I can't see it, so ultimately it comes down to this: either you get it or you don't and I just never got it, they were disappearing up their own fundaments, as far as I was concerned. And my argument was precisely that, I said the debate wasn't getting anywhere, you've got to get in to some sort of engagement with the social world', (Victor Burgin quoted in Roberts, *The Impossible Document*, pp. 90–1).

53. Jo Spence, 'The Politics of Photography', *Camerawork*, No. 1, London: Half Moon Photography Workshop, February 1976.

54. *Ibid.*

55. See Paul Carter, 'Photography for the Community', *Camerawork*, No. 13, March 1979, pp. 2–3.

56. Liz Heron, 'Hackney Flashers Collective: Who's Still Holding the Camera?', in T. Dennett, D. Evans, S. Gohl and J. Spence, eds, *Photography / Politics: One*, London: Photography Workshop, 1979, p. 125.

57. Spence, 'The Politics of Photography'.

58. Bob Long, 'Camerawork and the Political Photographer', *Camerawork*, No. 16, November 1979, pp. 10–15.

59. See *Camerawork*, No. 8, a special documentary edition on the race riots initiated by the National Front.

60. See *Camerawork*, No. 14, August 1979.

61. By 1977 the Hackney Flashers consisted of Jo Spence, Sally Greenhill, Margaret Murray (photographers), Ann Decker (graphic designer), Christine Roche (illustrator), Sue Trewelk (silk screen printer) and statistician Liz McGovern.

62. The Hackney Flashers Collective, 'The Hackney Flashers Collective', in Paul Hill, Angela Kelly and John Tagg, *Three Perspectives on Photography: Recent British Photography*, exhibition catalogue, London: Arts Council of Great Britain, Hayward Gallery, South Bank Centre, 1 June–8 July 1979, p. 80.

63. Liz Heron, in Dennett *et al.*, eds, *Photography / Politics: One*, p. 125.

64. Phil Goodall, 'Feministo: Portrait of the Artist as a Young Woman', 1977, reprinted in Rozsika Parker and Griselda Pollock, eds, *Framing Feminism: Art and the Women's Movement 1970–1985*, London: Pandora, 1987, p. 206.

65. See Tricia Davis and Phil Goodall, 'Personally and Politically: Feminist Art Practice', *Feminist Review*, No. 1, 1979, pp. 21–35.

66. 'We use the skills we already have – "female", "domestic" skills – crochet, knitting, sewing as well as more traditional "arty" skills' (Goodall, 'Feministo', p. 206).

67. Rozsika Parker, 'Portrait of the Artist as a Housewife', in Parke and Pollock, *Framing Feminism*, p. 208.

68. 'The symbolic significance craftworks had or have for women is normally overlooked despite the fact that feminist art historians continue to draw attention to the content and social role of craft production' (*ibid.*).

69. Rudi H. Fuchs, 'Introduction', *Languages: An Exhibition of Artists Using Word and Image*, exhibition catalogue, Harlow: Arts Council of Great Britain, 1979, p. 3.

70. See Hill *et al.*, *Three Perspectives*.

71. Tagg, *ibid.*, p. 71.

72. John Tagg, 'Practising Theories: An Interview with Joanne Lukitsh', *Afterimage*, Vol. 15, No. 6, January 1988, reprinted in Tagg's *Grounds of Dispute: Art History, Cultural Politics and the Discursive Field*, London: Macmillan, 1992, p. 74.

73. Stuart Hall's practical proposals are also open to this critique: 'The Left has to look around and see the language that consumer capitalism speaks to people in. It's very up to date with a high stress on technology … The Left has to be professional. Just look at the slickness of adverts designed to appeal to the mass consumer' (Stuart Hall, 'Stuart Hall: Left in Sight', *Camerawork*, Vol. 29, Winter 1983/84, p. 18). This line of enquiry had already been pursued by Punk, to little *political* effect. See Chapter 3, below.

74. Tagg, 'Practising Theories', p. 78.

75. Jon Bird, 'On Newness, Art and History: Reviewing BLOCK 1979–1985', in A. L. Rees and F. Borzello, eds, *The New Art History*, London: Camden Press, 1986, p. 33.

76. BLOCK , 'Introduction', *The BLOCK Reader in Visual Culture*, London: Routledge, 1996, p. xi.

77. 'The "new" art history differs from the old precisely in that it seeks to restore to art history the missing dimension of lived social relations; the expression "new art history" therefore is another way of saying "social history of art". The social history of art is of course not new; what is new (or more correctly *was* new, ten or fifteen years ago) is the promise, or threat, that the "social history" approach might become the dominant one in university art departments' (Burgin, 'Introduction: Something About Photography Theory', in Rees and Borzello, eds, *The New Art History*, p. 41).

78. For a critique of this OU course in the history of modern art see Simon Watney, 'Modernist Studies: The Class of '83', *Art History*, Vol. 7, No. 1, March 1984, pp. 102–110.

79. Open University readers on Modern Art invariably reflect upon their own art historical methodology as part of their discussion of modern art. Conveniently, this makes it difficult to separate such forms of analysis from their object, thereby ensuring their legitimacy as critical tools. For an account of the rise of social and feminist art history (at Leeds) which is reasonably independent of secondary historical tasks, see Fred Orton and Griselda Pollock's lengthy introduction to their *Avant-Garde and Partisans Reviewed*, Manchester: Manchester University Press, 1996.

80. Bird, 'On Newness, Art and History', p. 32. See also Brandon Taylor, 'The New Art History?', *Art Monthly*, No. 100, September 1986.

81. BLOCK, 'Introduction', p. xiii.

82. *Ibid.*, p. xii.

83. BLOCK, 'Editorial', BLOCK, No. 1, 1979, p. 1.

84. Terry Atkinson, 'Materialism, By Jove!', BLOCK, No. 1, 1979, pp. 34–8.

85. Tony Rickaby, 'Fascades', BLOCK, No. 1, 1979, pp. 48–9.

86. BLOCK, No. 2, 1980, pp. 40–44.

87. *Screen* had taken up a radical agenda in the early 1970s, promoting the ideas of the Russian Formalists, Brecht and the Frankfurt School and introducing semiotics and Lacanian psychoanalysis. Most notably, *Screen* introduced Althusser's structuralist Marxism to British cultural studies.

88. 'Whatever the displacements the social history of art has effected upon traditional art-historical discourse, for the most part the body of works loosely representing the "canon" has remained in situ' (Bird, 'On Newness, Art and History', p. 33). Tom Gretton also disallowed art history any disciplinary adequacy 'from which to write the history of ideology articulated by visual material'. Instead he imagined that 'other image histories may have different and more radical potentials' (Tom Gretton, 'New Lamps for Old', in Rees and Borzello, eds, *The New Art History*, pp. 63–74).

89. BLOCK, No. 2, 1980, p. 37.

90. See Jo Spence, 'What Did You Do in the War Mummy? Class and Gender in Images of Women', in Dennett *et al.*, eds, *Photography / Politics: One*. Spence here adopted the techniques of the CCCS to study *Picture Post* (the magazine, launched in 1938, which pioneered photojournalism and achieved great circulation figures during the Second World War), a topic that by this stage was becoming canonical, being dealt with by critics such as Hall and Dick Hebdige.

91. Spence quoted in Roberts, 'Interview with Jo Spence', in John Roberts, *Selected Errors: Writings on Art and Politics 1981–90*, London: Pluto Press, 1992, p. 140.

92. Liz Wells, 'The Words Say More than the Pictures: Jo Spence's Work Reviewed', *Camerawork*, No. 32, Summer 1985, p. 26 (italics in original).

93. See Dennett, Evans, Gohl and Spence, eds, *Photography / Politics: One* and *Two*: there were only two numbers of this journal.

94.   See 'A Statement from the Photography Workshop', *ibid.*, p. II. Spence wrote only one essay for *Camerawork*.

95.   Spence, 'What Did You Do … ?', p. 30.

96.   *Ibid.*

97.   Phototherapy, which Spence developed with Rosy Martin, draws upon co-counselling conventions, yet flouted those conventions by making the work public. The best-known example of such work is *The Picture of Health* (1982–1991), Spence's major collaboration with Maggie Murray of Format Photographers and Yana Stajo.

98.   Wells, 'The Words Say More', p. 27.

99.   Spence, 'What Did You Do … ?'.

100.   ' … as it turned out photo-based practice was not historically incongruous enough, by 1974 it was too conceptually respectable. Hence the turn in starting to look for practices which Western avant-gardism would consider to be intellectually despicable and ideological death, such as Soviet Socialist Realism, and hence in late 1974 after *The Bridging Works*, starting to try to figure out the making of the World War I works' (Terry Atkinson, 'Using Photographs circa 1974', in Roberts, *The Impossible Document*, pp. 73–4).

101.   ' … he seems tempted by facile effects so that his indecision leaves us uncertain how or to what we should attend' (John Tagg, 'Terry Atkinson: History – Drawing, Robert Self Gallery, London', *Art Monthly*, No. 4, February 1977, p. 20).

102.   Terry Atkinson, 'Mutes', in *Terry Atkinson: Mute 3 (Works After 1987)*, exhibition catalogue, Manchester: Cornerhouse, 1989, p. 30.

103.   *Ibid.*, p. 29.

104.   See Chapter 4, below.

105.   Sarah Kent, 'Critical Images', *Flash Art International*, March 1985, p. 24.

106.   Achille Bonita Oliva's term for Italian New Image painting produced by artists including Sandro Chia, Francesco Clemente and Enzo Cucchi. See Oliva's *The Italian Transavantgarde*, Milan: Giancarlo Politi, 1980.

107.   'New Image' had its roots in the Whitney Museum of American Art's 1978 'New Image Painting' exhibition, which featured work by American figurative painters such as Neil Jenney and Susan Rothenberg. The term was popularized worldwide in the 1980s by 'The New Spirit in Painting' at London's Royal Academy in 1981 and 'Zeitgeist' held in Berlin in 1982, large group exhibitions of international figurative painting curated by Christos Joachimides. Although New Image was an international style, it adopted a series of pseudo-nationalistic identities such as Neo-Expressionism (USA), Transavantgarde (Italy) and the New Glasgow Boys (Scotland). See Chapters 4 and 5, below, for more on the British contribution to New Image painting.

108.   Ian Heywood, *Social Theories of Art: A Critique*, New York: Macmillan, 1997, p. 21.

109.   Charles Harrison, 'On *A Portrait of V. I. Lenin in the Style of Jackson Pollock*', in his *Essays on Art & Language*, p. 139.

110.   Matthew Cullerne Bown and Brandon Taylor, eds, *Art of the Soviets: Painting, Sculpture and Architecture in a One Party State, 1917–1992*, Manchester: Manchester University Press, 1993, p. 10. Following the postmodernist revision of Western art in the '70s and early '80s, and *glasnost* in the mid-1980s, books such as Igor Goomstock's *Totalitarian Art* (1990) and Christine Lindey's *Art in the Cold War* (1991) ended the critical embargo on serious discussion of the Soviet art of the post-1920s.

3   Dynamic perversity

1.   Art & Language, 'Correspondence', *Style* (Vancouver), March 1982, pp. 11–12.

2.   Ralf Rumney, 'The End of Art is Not the End', *Art Monthly*, No. 17, 1978, p. 4.

3.   SPACE (Space Provision, Artistic, Cultural and Educational) was created by Bridget Riley and Peter Sedgley in 1968 in St Katherine's Dock, London, to provide affordable studios for artists. It moved to Martello Street in 1970, which remains one of its prime sites.

4.   COUM Transmissions, 'What Has COUM to Mean?: Thee Theory Behind COUM', typewritten statement, undated, COUM Transmissions/Throbbing Gristle Archive, National Art Library, Victoria & Albert Museum, London, purchased in 1990. See also Genesis P-Orridge, 'A Letter', *Vile*, Vol. 3, No. 2, Summer 1977, pp. 30–31.

5.   Philip Pilkington and David Rusherson, 'Don Judd's Dictum and its Emptiness', *Analytical Art*, No. 1, July 1971, p. 4.

6.   Cosey Fanni Tutti, 'Artist's Statement', typewritten information sheet, May 1975, COUM Transmissions/Throbbing Gristle Archive, National Art Library, Victoria & Albert Museum, London, purchased in 1990.

7.   P-Orridge, 'Artist's Statement', typewritten information sheet, 27 August 1974, *ibid.* (my emphasis).

8.   COUM Transmissions, 'What Has COUM to Mean?'

9.   Hugh Adams, 'COUM in Southampton: Lay Assumptions', *Studio International*, Vol. 192, No. 982, July/August 1976.

10.   P-Orridge, 'A Letter'.

11.   P-Orridge quoted in Colin Naylor, 'Couming Along', *Art and Artists*, Vol. 10, 1975, p. 23.

12.   Jeff Nuttall, 'Sick', in his *Bomb Culture*, London: Paladin, 1970, p. 154. See also the works of R. D. Laing.

13.   P-Orridge quoted in Naylor, 'Couming Along'. Artists such as Chris Burden, Gina Pane and Vito Acconci achieved international acclaim in the field of self-mutilation.

14.   Dave Wise and Stuart Wise, *Punk, Reggae: A Critique*, pamphlet published in Glasgow, c. 1978, reprinted as 'The End of Music: The Revolution of Everyday Alienation', in Stewart Home, ed., *What is Situationism? A Reader*, Edinburgh: AK Press, 1996, p. 67.

15.   P-Orridge quoted in Naylor, 'Couming Along', p. 24.

16.   P-Orridge/COUM Transmissions, 'Genesis P-Orridge', exhibition catalogue, Hayward Annual, Arts Council of Great Britain, 13 April 1979, p. 27.

17.   Genesis P-Orridge and Peter Christopherson, 'Annihilating Reality', *Studio International*, Vol. 192, No. 982, July/August 1976, pp. 46, 48.

18.   Conrad Atkinson, 'Art for Whom: Notes', in Richard Cork, *Art for Whom?*, exhibition catalogue, London: Serpentine Gallery, 1978, p. 38.

19.   Margaret Harrison, 'Notes on Feminist Art in Britain 1970–77', *Studio International*, March 1977, p. 218.

20.   Catherine Lupton, 'Circuit-breaking Desires: Critiquing the Work of Mary Kelly', in John Roberts, ed., *Art Has No History! The Making and Unmaking of Modern Art*, London: Verso, 1994, p. 230.

21.   Mary Kelly in Terence Maloon, 'Mary Kelly interviewed by Terence Maloon', *Artscribe*, No. 13, August 1978, p. 18.

22.   R. Morris, 'After the Tate Gallery's Famous Bricks, the New Art Is – Dirty Nappies', *Daily Mail*, 15 October 1976.

23.   Kelly, quoted in Roger Bray, 'After the Tate Bricks – On Show at ICA … Dirty Nappies!', *Evening Standard*, London, 14 October 1976.

24.   Andrea Dworkin, *Pornography: Men Possessing Women*, London: The Women's Press, 1981, pp. 208–209.

25.   Either response would have proved difficult since the ICA decided to store the works in containers, allowing only one image to be viewed at a time.

26.   P-Orridge quoted in William Furlong, 'Four Interviews', in 'Genesis P-Orridge', exhibition catalogue, Hayward Annual, Arts Council of Great Britain, 1979, p. 15.

27.   Caroline Coon, 'Rock Revolution', *Melody Maker*, 28 July 1976.

28.   P-Orridge quoted in Furlong, 'Four Interviews', p. 16.

29.   P-Orridge quoted in Stuart Morgan, 'What the Papers Say', *Artscribe*, No. 18, July 1979, p. 17.

30.   P-Orridge quoted in Jon Savage, *England's Dreaming: Sex Pistols and Punk Rock*, London: Faber & Faber, 1991, p. 251.

31.   P-Orridge and Christopherson, 'Annihilating Reality', p. 47.

32.   Fluxus was a Neo-Dada organization of international artists founded in 1962.

33.   'I think that the distribution of information is the key to change … I am very antagonistic to the whole concept of being controlled by a process that nobody wants. Basically the power in this world rests with the people who have access to the most information and control of that information' (P-Orridge/COUM Transmissions, 'Genesis P-Orridge', p. 27). COUM's strategy, which was deeply indebted to William S. Burroughs, has since become a commonplace amongst 'culture jammers', a term coined by '80s San Franciscan audio-collage band Negativland and popularized by *Adbusters* magazine in the 1990s.

34. Among the artists signed to Industrial Records were: Cabaret Voltaire, Clock DVA, Richard H. Kirk, Monte Cazazza, The Leather Nun, Chris Carter, Thomas Leer and Robert Rental, and William S. Burroughs.

35. Morgan, 'What the Papers Say', pp. 18–19. See also Dick Hebdige's discussion of the use of the swastika in Punk in his *Subculture: The Meaning of Style*, London: Methuen, 1979. Morgan's argument is remarkably similar to Marcuse's critique of Berlin Dada in his *Critique of Marxist Aesthetics*, as 'adapted' by both Stuart Hall and Peter Fuller in the early 1980s: '[Rudi Fuchs] does not understand the imaginative work of the artist, or the way in which he creates a transitional reality, neither objective nor subjective, through transforming his physical and conventional materials into a new and convincing whole … "Renunciation of the aesthetic form", wrote Marcuse, "is abdication of responsibility. It deprives art of the very form in which it can create that other reality within the established one – the cosmos of hope"' (Peter Fuller, 'The Arts Council Collection', *Art Monthly*, No. 39, September 1980, p. 16).

36. Cosey Fanni Tutti, 'Artists' Thoughts on the 70s in Words and Pictures', *Studio International*, Vol. 195, No. 911/2, 1981, p. 17.

37. See Jurgen Habermas, *Legitimation Crisis*, trans. Thomas McCarthy, London: Heinemann, 1976.

38. Gustav Metzger, 'Art Strike 1977–1980', communiqué issued in 1974. Metzger was best known for organizing the international 'Destruction in Art' symposium at the ICA in 1966, attended by members of the Viennese Actionists and Fluxus, among others.

39. The Angry Brigade, Communiqué 8, 1 May 1971, reprinted in *The Angry Brigade*, Glasgow: Bratach Dubh Documents No. 1, 1978.

40. Jamie Reid, in Jon Savage and Jamie Reid, *Up They Rise: The Incomplete Works of Jamie Reid*, London: Faber & Faber, 1987, p. 55.

41. *Ibid.*, p. 38.

42. *Ibid.*, p. 43. This mirrors a stunt pulled by the Motherfuckers in New York when they printed invitations to a major ghetto store in the Lower East Side, claiming to be offering free goods. Fifty Motherfucker activists turned up at the said time, demanding goods to be handed over. See *King Mob Echo*, No. 3, 1969, an issue devoted to Black Mask, the Motherfuckers and the International Werewolf Conspiracy; and Ron Hahne, *Black Mask and Up Against the Wall Motherfucker: The Incomplete Works of Ron Hahne, Ben Morea and the Black Mask Group*, London: Sabotage Editions, 1993.

43. Savage and Reid, *Up They Rise*, p. 72.

44. 'I was told it had to be something quick and we had no money for Letraset. I loved finding letters from different newspapers and making copies of little posters' (Helen Wellington-Lloyd quoted in Craig Bromberg, *The Wicked Ways of Malcolm McLaren*, London: Omnibus Press, 1991, p. 103).

45. 'Even the case was embarrassing, as the Sex Pistols had benefited from the very liberal consensus they ostensibly despised' (Savage and Reid, *Up They Rise*, p. 425).

46. Peter York, 'The Clone Zone (Night of the Living Dead)', in his *Style Wars*, London: Sidgewick & Jackson, 1980, p. 47.

47. MINDA were an anonymous man and woman who made anti-racist montages. See MINDA, 'MINDA', in T. Dennett, D. Evans, S. Gohl and J. Spence, eds, *Photography / Politics: One*, London: Photography Workshop, September 1979, pp. 39–144.

48. York, 'Boys Own', in *Style Wars*, p. 36.

49. There are interesting parallels between the crisis in the British art press and the huge transformations which took place in the British music press between 1976 and 1978, as *New Musical Express*, *Sounds* and *Melody Maker* were drawn away from promoting pop and progressive 'art' rock by the 'social integrity' of Punk. Having created a crisis situation in the 'art rock' press through aggressive promotion, McLaren's reading of Punk in turn created a crisis situation in the reformed 'Punk rock' press, questioning the value and intent of their socio-political criticism that had been hastily developed to promote the new music. For an account of these changes see York, 'Boys Own', in *Style Wars*, pp. 19–39.

50. See Reid and McLaren's 'Ten Lessons', *The Great Rock n' Roll Swindle*, Polygram Video, 1980. 'It is fair to say that McLaren's "use" of his situationist "knowledge", apart from the obvious "borrowing" of graphic styles (*détournement*) and sloganeering rhetoric, centred round the theoretical implications of the Spectacle's ability to recuperate oppositional practices. He knew that the more he refused incorporation, the more they would try to recuperate him (here "they" are the entertainment and leisure industries, "he" stands for the Punk project). In his role as the artist-businessman, McLaren used the insights and analysis of the Situationist International to do "good business" (George Robertson, 'The Situationist International: Its Penetration into British Culture', *BLOCK*, Vol. 14, 1988).

51. The Thatcherite right, of course, had long been mimicking the populist rhetoric of the left. Unlike the New Right's populist tactics, however, it would seem that the left's attempt to burn out the ideology of the New Right was knowingly doomed from the beginning, testifying to the

left's growing pessimism during the 1970s. McLaren's and Reid's subsequent careers indicate that the fragmentation which resulted from this encouraged a *growth* in conservative attitudes, McLaren becoming a consumer/entrepreneur *par excellence* and Reid becoming a mystic 'artist' with interests in ancient Celtic culture.

52. Wise, Dave and Stuart, *Punk, Reggae: A Critique*, p. 73. King Mob was founded by former members of Heatwave, the English counter-cultural group expelled from the Situationist International in 1967.

53. Jim Miller, 'Some Future', *New Republic*, No. 180, 24 March 1979, p. 27.

54. Simon Frith, 'Consuming Passion', *Melody Maker*, 10 March 1979, p. 14.

55. A good example of this kind of writing from the period is David Laing's 'Interpreting Punk Rock', *Marxism Today*, Vol. 22, No. 4, April 1978.

56. McLaren's actions were contemporaneous with the launch of *October*, an American journal of art and theory. McLaren provides one link between the historical avant-garde and the Baudrillardian postmodernism popular in the early to mid-'80s. Baudrillard's theoretical collapsing of the distinction between fiction and reality, as everything enters a market place of consumable signs, was, in a sense, initiated practically by McLaren, finalizing the recuperation of the 'avant-garde', a theme re-articulated in much '80s art theory: 'Since much academic discourse is grounded in notions of the authentic (and its loss), individuals engaged in cultural and media studies find the prospect of assimilating the "radicality" attached to "avant-garde" ideas a very attractive proposition. The book *Recodings: Art, Spectacle, Cultural Politics* by Hal Foster, in which a bastardized version of specto-Situationist theory is wielded in defence of blue-chip art, may be taken as typical of this trend' (Stewart Home, 'Aesthetics & Resistance: Totality Reconsidered', *Smile*, No. 11, London, 1989).

57. See Herbert Marcuse, *Counterrevolution and Revolution*, Boston: Beacon, 1972, p. 132.

58. See Mark Kidel, 'The Hip Capitalist Dream – A Profile of Richard Branson', *The New Review*, Vol. 4, No. 45, December 1977.

59. ' … class is actually a fluid category and the rhetorical use made of this notion by various individuals associated with PUNK can most accurately be described as a form of theatre … This harping on "*épater les bourgeoisie*" [*sic*] misses the point because transvestism is as likely to shock blue-collar workers as their white-collar bosses. Being more firmly rooted in generational than in class differences, rock usually sets out to shock parents in general, and not simply individuals who view themselves as belonging to the middle or upper classes …, pp. 10–11. Of course, the idea that PUNK is underground, or at least "oppositional", is problematic in terms of those postmodern theories that view our epoch as a time of proliferating margins. But then that part of the PUNK audience that has any interest in post-modernism is more than capable of resolving this "contradiction" by adopting a pose of "ironic" consumption. Besides, coherence is death, whereas living cultures are generated from the tensions generated around clusters of contradiction' (Stewart Home, *Cranked Up Really High: Genre Theory and Punk Rock*, Hove: Codex, 1996, p. 17).

60. Ian Chambers, 'Urban Soundscapes 1976–: England's Dreaming', in his *Urban Rhythms: Pop Music and Popular Culture*, Basingstoke: Macmillan, 1985, p. 181.

61. See Simon Frith, *Art into Pop*, London: Methuen, 1987.

62. Caroline Coon, 'Interview with Johnny Rotten', *Melody Maker*, 20 July 1977. Coon refers to the following lyrics from Jones, Rotten, Matlock and Cook's *Anarchy in the U.K.* (1976): 'And I wanna be Anarchy.'

63. Ian Birch, 'In The Beginning', in his *The Book With No Name*, London: Omnibus, 1981, p. 11. The New Romantics rejected Punk's realist austerity for glamour and theatricality, dressing excessively and preferring electronic music; it became associated with pop groups such as Spandau Ballet, Culture Club and The Human League.

64. George Melly, *Revolt into Style: The Pop Arts in Britain*, London: Allen Lane, 1970.

65. York, *Style Wars*, p. 13.

66. For a definition of the role of plagiarism (as opposed to mainstream postmodernist appropriation) within the '80s avant-garde see Stewart Home, 'Plagiarism as Negation in Culture', in *Desire in Ruins*, exhibition catalogue, Glasgow: Transmission Gallery, May 1987, reprinted in Stewart Home, *Neoism, Plagiarism & Praxis*, Edinburgh: AK Press, 1995, pp. 49–50.

67. Quoted in 'Graphics', *Creative Review*, February 1998, p. 37.

68. Assorted iMaGes, quoted in Catherine McDermott, 'New-Wave Graphics: A Manual of Style', in her *Street Style: British Design in the 8os*, London: Design Council, 1987, p. 71.

69. 'The passive nihilist compromises with his own lucidity about the collapse of all values. Bandwagon after bandwagon works out its own version of the credo *quia absurdum est*: you don't like it but you do it anyway; you get used to it and you even like it in the end. Passive nihilism is an overture to conformism' (Raoul Vaneigem, 'Desolation Row', *King Mob Echo*, No. 1, April 1968, p. 7).

70. See Bryan Biggs and Chris Kennedy, *Cover Versions*, Liverpool: Bluecoat Gallery, 1981.

71. See Peter York, 'Culture as Commodity: Style Wars, Punk and Pagent', in J. Thackera, ed., *Design After Modernism*, London: Thames & Hudson, 1988.

72. Kelly's most celebrated commission was the *Hacienda* night-club in Manchester, owned by Anthony H. Wilson (of Factory) and the group New Order. See 'The Hacienda: New Steps for the Leisure Industry', *The Face*, November 1982, p. 50.

73. Brody graduated from the London College of Printing in 1980. He was largely responsible for the revolution in British graphic design caused by his typography on *The Face* from 1981 onwards. See John Wozencroft, *The Graphic Language of Neville Brody*, London: Thames & Hudson, 1988.

74. This, in turn, was to influence the academic artworld: 'Producing BLOCK was labour intensive and drew heavily on the expertise of a recent graphic design graduate [of Hornsey Art College/ Middlesex Polytechnic], Kathryn Tattersall, whose choices reflect a contemporary interest in Russian Constructivist graphics' (BLOCK, 'Introduction', *The BLOCK Reader in Visual Culture*, London: Routledge, 1996, p. xi). Despite this, it took some time before BLOCK took pop culture seriously enough to allow it to appear in its pages. See Dick Hebdige, 'In Poor Taste: Notes on Pop', *BLOCK*, No. 8, 1983, pp. 54–68.

75. Terence Maloon, 'Notes on Style in the Seventies: 1. Modes of Perceiving', *Artscribe*, No. 12, June 1978, p. 15. In fact, with the anarchic on-stage guitar-smashing performances of Pete Townsend, The Who were a formative influence on the Sex Pistols, who often included a version of *Substitute* in their sets.

76. See Patrick Firpo, *Copy Art: The First Complete Guide to the Copy Machine*, New York: Richard Marek Publishing, 1978.

77. Home, *Cranked Up*, p. 71.

78. Adam and the Ants, *Zerox/Whip in my Valise*, Do-It Records DUN 8, June 1979.

79. Adam and the Ants, *Cartrouble/Kick!*, Do-It Records DUN 10, February 1980.

80. Mary Rose Beaumont, 'Biographical Note', in her *Duggie Fields: Paintings 1982–87*, exhibition catalogue, London: Albemarle Gallery, 28 October–20 November 1987.

81. 'In fact, he admits candidly, part of the reasons for the truncations is simply that once, when painting a figure, he had difficulty with the face. "The body was fine, but I just couldn't get the head to work, so I cut it off"' (Elizabeth Toppin, 'Home is Where the Art Is', *Residence*, No. 17, October 1988, p. 37).

82. Beaumont, *Duggie Fields*, p. 2.

83. James Faure Walker, 'The Claims of Social Art and Other Perplexities', *Artscribe*, No. 12, June 1978, p. 20.

84. Jon Savage, 'The New Hippies', in Birch, ed., *The Book With No Name*, p. 40.

85. Michael Billam, 'Duggie Fields at the Roundhouse', *Artscribe*, No. 24, August 1980, pp. 60–61.

86. Alistair Bonnet, 'The Situationist Legacy: It's All So Unfair!', *Variant*, No. 9, Glasgow, Autumn 1991. Bonnet goes on to observe that this 'tendency has been supported by a second feature of situationism, its equation of the spectacle with all-encompassing alienation. The trouble with this idea is that it doesn't leave much room for purposeful struggle but only the directionless mutation of present realities, or what Vaneigem called "active nihilism". The logical conclusion of this theory is exactly the kind of tedious celebration of meaninglessness seen in the work of Baudrillard and many post-modern artists.'

87. The Moors Murderers were formed by Strange and Chrissie 'Hindley' Hynde, later of the Pretenders, in January 1978.

88. Peter York, 'Them', in his *Style Wars*, pp. 127–8.

89. Jon Savage, 'Soft Cell: The Whip Hand', in his *Time Travel: From the Sex Pistols to Nirvana, Pop Media and Sexuality, 1977–96*, London: Chatto & Windus, 1996, pp. 131–8. The group Soft Cell started off as performance artists at Leeds Polytechnic.

90. John Roberts, 'Post-Modernism: Arrivals and Departures', *Art Monthly*, No. 55, April 1982, p. 28.

91. York, *Style Wars*, pp. 127–8.

92. Chambers, *Urban Rhythms*, p. 199.

93. One of the first Punk fanzines, twelve issues of which were written, designed and photocopied and stapled together by former bank clerk Mark P between July 1976 and 1978. It has been reprinted as Michael Dempsey, ed., *The Bible*, London: Big O Publishing, 1978.

94. See 'Zandra Rhodes Talks to her Good Friend Duggie Fields', *Viz: Visual Arts, Fashion, Photography*, No. 6, 1979, pp. 20–22.

95. 'Contrary to many people's assumptions, they weren't spoilt brats who actually had enough

money behind them to own the clubs. They simply took the risk of hiring the places regularly one evening a week and taking enough money out of the receipts to keep themselves in porridge and eye-liner' (Steve Taylor, 'STRANGE TALES ... of Steve Strange (ne Harrington, soul boy, punk rocker, exhibitionist, leader of fashion and leader of Visage)', *Smash Hits*, 22 January 1981).

96. Duggie Fields in Ferry Zayadi, 'Interview with Duggie Fields', *Viz: Visual Arts, Fashion, Photography*, No. 4, April 1979, p. 13. 'I started off with little bits of media and then approaches to have exhibitions. Approaches ... quite extraordinary; like you have an exhibition here, this reception there, a TV documentary – that sort of thing. After a year of different offers eventually one of them did happen and the one that worked had me doing TV commercials. I had a lot of press coverage, national television and news coverage ... It was big business. [This was] Refreshing in some ways but not in others, in some ways it was complete exploitation ... not [just] by me. I hadn't got a clue what I was getting involved in. I got offered money that would pay my bills and all of us have that problem of earning money. Living in England as an artist is very difficult for anyone, and with the amount of support I have had from the English establishment, particularly difficult for me' (Fields interviewed by Mike Von Joel, 'Duggie Fields: Dynamic Perversity and Other Such Stories', *Art Line International – Art News*, Vol. 3, No. 10, 1988, p. 11).

4   The shock of the old

1.   Janet Daley, 'New Figuration: Part III', *Art Review*, Vol. 30, No. 11, 9 June 1978, p. 289.

2.   Christos Joachimedes, 'How They Got it Together', *Art Monthly*, No. 43, February 1981, p. 4.

3.   Michael Podro, 'From Springer to Warburg: Warburg and Botticelli's Mythologies', in his *The Critical Historians of Art*, New Haven: Yale University Press, 1982, p. 158.

4.   For further discussion see Marco Livingstone, 'Iconology as a Theme in the Early Work of R. B. Kitaj', *Burlington Magazine*, Vol. 122, No. 918, July 1980, pp. 488–97, and Tony Del Renzio, 'Style, Technique and Iconography', *Art and Artists*, 11 July 1976, pp. 34–9.

5.   'Humanists believe that persons *create* works of art, not that they are themselves constructed out of language but that they are at the crossroads of its recreation. Such humanist beliefs are, of course, themselves the foundation of the cultural concepts of "imagination", "creation" and "originality" which make it still possible to talk about works of art in general. In this way humanist values are necessary to their very existence' (S. J. Wilsmore, 'The New Attack on Humanism in the Arts', *British Journal of Aesthetics*, Vol. 27, Autumn 1987, p. 336).

6.   Michael Podro, 'Some Notes on Ron Kitaj', *Art International*, Vol. 22, No. 10, March 1979, p. 19.

7.   Kitaj quoted in Andrew Brighton, 'Conversations with R. B. Kitaj', *Art in America*, Vol. 74, June 1986, p. 102.

8.   'Surrealist ideas like bringing images together in unlikely and unfamiliar conjunction (in hope of producing magic), and other such ideas, attracted me when I was young. Now I can see that what may have seemed outrageous and valuable in that practice was often only an exaggerated form of what is substantial and even life-giving in *all* art ... I mean to say that so much of what I care about in art has to do with the unfamiliar, prodigious, surprising character of what a truly original artist does in his pictures anyway' (Kitaj quoted in Marco Livingstone, *R. B. Kitaj*, Oxford: Phaidon, 1985, p. 42, note 4).

9.   R. B. Kitaj, 'Pearldiving', in his *The Human Clay*, exhibition catalogue, Hayward Gallery, London: Arts Council of Great Britain, 1976.

10. Livingstone, *R. B. Kitaj*, p. 35.

11. 'Significantly he blends an acute historical awareness with a contradictory technical achievement which parallels Post-Modernist pluralism while at the same time pursuing the emancipatory and utopian ideal inherent in Modernism' (Jim Aulich, 'The Difficulty of Living in an Age of Cultural Decline and Spiritual Corruption: R. B. Kitaj 1965–1970', *The Oxford Art Journal*, Vol. 10, No. 2, 1987, p. 43).

12. Kitaj, 'Mondrian', in his *The Human Clay*.

13. Kitaj quoted in Brighton, 'Conversations'.

14. In general, postmodernist art has moved from 'presentness' towards 'theatre', literally in the opposite direction to Kitaj; see Michael Fried, 'Art and Objecthood', *Artforum*, Summer 1967.

15. Peter Fuller, 'An Interview with David Hockney. Part II', *Art Monthly*, Nos 12 and 13, November–December/January 1977–1978, p. 6. Kitaj scholar and friend Michael Podro, while lacking Fuller's overt critical agenda, also noted this problem: 'there is, I think, a tension between Kitaj's assumed literary aesthetic and his visual aesthetic, between his concern to make an emotionally charged private art for a small group of initiates, and a publicly resonant art' (Podro, 'Some Notes', p. 23). Lynda Morris, on the other hand, correctly analysed its effect: 'One

gets a bit irritated as books bearing the legend of Wollheim, Gramsci and Leger jostle with an alarm clock and pudding basin on the breakfast table' (Lynda Morris, 'Popular Front', *The Listener*, 26 May 1977, p. 693).

16.   'R. B. Kitaj Interviewed by James Faure Walker', *Artscribe*, No. 5, February 1977, p. 5.

17.   Livingstone, *R. B. Kitaj*, p. 34.

18.   Kitaj quoted in *ibid.*, p. 17.

19.   Peter Plagens, 'European Painting in LA: A Grab Bag of Well-worn Issues', *Artforum*, Vol. 15, No. 5, January 1976, p. 41.

20.   Podro, 'Some Notes', p. 21.

21.   Kitaj in R. B. Kitaj and David Hockney, 'R. B. Kitaj and David Hockney Discuss the Case for a Return to the Figurative', *New Review*, Vol. 3, No. 34/35, January/February 1977, p. 75.

22.   Brighton, 'Conversations', p. 102.

23.   Kitaj quoted in *ibid*.

24.   'There definitely is a kind of crisis in the visual arts … I don't think it's a very serious thing; I know it will be overcome' (David Hockney, 'Realism Turning into Naturalism', in *David Hockney by David Hockney*, ed. Nikos Stangos, London: Thames & Hudson, 1977, p. 130).

25.   Fuller, 'An Interview with David Hockney. Part II', p. 5.

26.   Vol. 3, No. 34/35, January/February 1977.

27.   D. and M. Ackerman, 'Dear Kitaj and David: The Quality of the Creation is More Important than the Content', *Arts Review*, Vol. 29, 29 April 1977, p. 287.

28.   Guy Brett, 'What is the Tradition', *Art Monthly*, No. 38, 1980, p. 2.

29.   Hockney, *David Hockney*, p. 130.

30.   Kitaj and Hockney, 'Kitaj and Hockney Discuss', p. 76.

31.   Timothy Hyman, 'Ten Younger Artists', in his *Narrative Paintings: Figurative Art of Two Generations Selected by Timothy Hyman*, exhibition catalogue, Bristol: Arnolfini Gallery, September–October 1979, p. 28.

32.   David Shepherd, 'Art Training and London Adventures', in his *The Man Who Loves Giants*, London: David & Charles, 1975, p. 22.

33.   *Ibid.*, p. 74.

34.   Benedict Nicolson, 'Editorial: T1534, Untitled 1966', *The Burlington Magazine*, Vol. 118, No. 877, April 1976, pp. 187–8.

35.   Andrew Brighton, 'Very British Triviality', *Art Monthly*, No. 16, May 1978, p. 20.

36.   'While diagnostic in intention, this anthology is only portentous with regard to its title. Its editors felt a need to bridge the autistic hiatus that was appearing between the serried artistic ranks and the similarly serried files of orthodoxy … the work should be bracketed as an open verdict and thereby allow full criticism to run as the final, unwritten chapter' (Kevin O'Shea, 'Book Review: Towards Another Picture', *British Journal of Aesthetics*, Vol. 19, 1979, p. 188).

37.   Adrian Searle, 'Towards Another Picture', *Artscribe*, No. 10, January 1978, p. 48.

38.   The conference was organized by Richard Cork, John Tagg, Fuller and Andrew Brighton at the ICA in London, 10–12 February, and its proceedings were published in *Studio International*, Vol. 194, No. 988, 1/1978.

39.   Derek Boshier, ed. and curator, *Lives: An Exhibition of Artists Whose Work is Based on Other People's Lives*, exhibition catalogue, London: Arts Council of Great Britain, 1979.

40.   'Norman Hepple', in Boshier, *Lives*.

41.   'Out of the 27 artists exhibiting, only one, Norman Hepple, felt unable to sign' the protest letter to the Arts Council of Great Britain over the exclusion of Atkinson's and Rickaby's work from 'Lives' (Boshier, 'Lives', *Art Monthly*, No. 25, April 1979, p. 21).

42.   Janet Daley, 'The Arts Council vs. The Visual Arts', *The Literary Review*, October 1981, p. 41.

43.   Conrad Atkinson, 'The Countryside of the Poor', *Art Monthly*, No. 37, 1980, p. 23. See also Duncan MacMillan, 'Exhibitions: "British Art Now" in New York', *Art Monthly*, No. 34, 1980, pp. 13–14.

44.   John Hoyland, 'An Introduction to the Exhibition', *Hayward Annual 1980*, exhibition catalogue, London: Arts Council of Great Britain, 1980, p. 6.

45.   The authentication of British national identity proved to be a powerful political force in this period. In 1982 Argentine forces occupied the Falkland Islands. Thatcher's ailing, unpopular government sent a task force to throw out the Argentines. Bolstered by the success of her

jingoistic Falkland Islands policy, Thatcher led the Conservatives to a sweeping victory in the parliamentary elections of June 1983.

46. By 1986, Frances Spalding was able to 'authoritatively' claim that *British* art had hitherto gone unnoticed because 'a concern with modernism has blinkered critical evaluation of twentieth-century art, encouraging historians, in its emphasis on innovation, to look for a linear evolutionary development, a tendency which has helped to banish into temporary obscurity much that did not uphold the dominant avant-garde ideology' (Frances Spalding, 'Preface', in her *British Art since 1900*, London: Thames & Hudson, 1986, p. 7).

47. Richard Morphet, 'An Under-rated Art', in his *The Hard-Won Image: Traditional Method and Subject in Recent British Art*, exhibition catalogue, London: Tate Gallery, 4 July–9 September 1984, p. 15.

48. Morphet had, of course, been a spokesperson for the Tate during the 'Bricks' scandal, which he defended unashamedly by evoking the purity of the late-modernist canon.

49. Terry Atkinson, 'Notes: Communities, Artists, Modernism', *Studio International*, March/April 1976.

50. Alan Gouk, 'Peter Fuller, Art Critic?', *Artscribe*, No. 30, August 1981, pp. 42–3.

51. A term coined by Timothy Hyman, narrative painter and art critic.

52. John Roberts, 'The Naked and the Dead', *Art Monthly*, No. 79, September 1984, p. 16.

53. Andrew Brighton, 'Frank Auerbach', *Art Monthly*, No. 141, November 1990, p. 13.

54. *Ibid.*

55. *Ibid.*, p. 26.

56. Frank Auerbach, 'A Conversation with Catherine Lampert', in William Wright and Anthony Bond, *The British Show*, Sydney: Beaver Press, Art Gallery of New South Wales, 1984.

57. Michael Podro, 'Depiction and the Golden Calf', in Norman Bryson, Michael Holly and Keith Moxey, *Visual Theory: Painting and Interpretation*, Cambridge: Polity Press, 1991, pp. 176–7.

58. Auerbach, 'Conversation'.

59. Podro, 'Depiction', p. 177.

60. Auerbach, 'Conversation'.

61. *Ibid.*

62. Peter Fuller, 'Leon Kossoff', in Wright and Bond, *The British Show*.

63. Lucien Freud, quoted in Lawrence Gowling, *Lucien Freud*, London: Thames & Hudson, 1982.

64. Lucien Freud, quoted in Robert Hughes, 'On Lucien Freud', in *Lucien Freud*, exhibition catalogue, The British Council, London, Hayward Gallery, 4 February–17 April 1988, p. 20. See also Lucien Freud, 'Some Thoughts on Painting', *Encounter*, Vol. 3, No. 1, July 1954, pp. 23–4.

65. Peter Fuller, 'Leon Kossoff', in Wright and Bond, *The British Show*.

66. Peter Fuller, 'Auerbach Versus Clemente', in his *Images of God: The Consolations of Lost Illusions*, London: Hogarth Press, 1985, p. 61.

67. See Michael Fried, *Absorption and Theatricality: Painting and the Beholder in the Age of Diderot*, Berkeley: University of California Press, 1980.

68. Andrew Brighton, 'Large Interior W11', *Art Monthly*, No. 72, December/January 1983/84, pp. 9–10.

69. Mary Kelly, 'The Crisis in Professionalism', *Studio International*, Vol. 194, No. 989, 2/1978, p. 82.

70. Susan Hiller, 'Art and Anthropology/Anthropology and Art', lecture given 6 May 1977, reprinted in Barbara Einzig, ed., *Thinking About Art: Conversations with Susan Hiller*, Manchester: Manchester University Press, 1996, p. 209.

71. Sarah Kent, 'Feminism and Decadence', *Artscribe*, No. 47, July/August 1984, p. 57.

72. Griselda Pollock, 'Femininity, Feminism and the Hayward Annual', *Feminist Review*, No. 2, 1979, p. 43.

73. Monica Petzal, 'Questions about Women's Art Conference', *Art Monthly*, No. 42, December/January 1980/81, p. 23.

74. Jacqueline Morreau and Catherine Elwes, 'Lighting a Candle', in Sarah Kent and Jacqueline Morreau, eds, *Women's Images of Men*, London: Writers and Readers Publishing Cooperative Society, 1985, p. 13.

75. Hunter was later included in the book brought out by Kent and Morreau in 1985 (see previous note). The 'Male Myths' series of paintings attached an ironic and theoretical underpinning to the women-centred painting of that time, which it needed. 'I was asked to show the much earlier *Object* painting from 1974 but it became impossible to be in both *Issue* and *Women's Images of*

Men, such was the feeling of exclusivity generated by both camps of theory-based and emotion-based work practices. I was made to feel that it was unfair being in both shows and I think ended up being a bit of a fall-guy between the two' (author's correspondence with Hunter, August 2001).

76. *Ibid.*

77. Sarah Kent, 'Scratching and Biting Savagery', in Kent and Morreau, eds, *Women's Images*, pp. 4–6.

78. Hunter in Elizabeth Eastmond, 'Alexis Hunter Talks to Elizabeth Eastmond', *Art New Zealand*, No. 54, 1990, pp. 50–54.

79. Morreau and Elwes, 'Lighting a Candle', in Kent and Morreau, eds, *Women's Images*, p. 24.

80. For example, see the work of Charles Jencks, Achille Bonita Oliva and Donald Kuspit on Neo-Expressionism, e.g. Charles Jencks, *What is Post-modernism?*, Hanover: Academy Editions, 1989; Achille Bonita Oliva, *The Italian Transavantgarde*, Milan: Giancarlo Politi, 1980; and Donald Burton Kuspit, *The New Subjectivism: Art in the 1980s*, London: UMI Research Press, 1988.

81. Pollock, 'Femininity, Feminism and the Hayward Annual', p. 43.

82. John Roberts, 'Painting and Sexual Difference', in his *Postmodernism, Politics and Art*, Manchester: Manchester University Press, 1990, p. 166.

83. Kent, 'Scratching and Biting Savagery', in Kent and Morreau, eds, *Women's Images*, p. 8.

84. Rozsika Parker, 'Feminist Art Practices in Women's Images of Men, About Time and Issue', *Art Monthly*, No. 43, February 1981, p. 17.

85. 'The ICA season not only gave confidence to individual artists, but encouraged dealers and exhibition organisers to promote women's work' (Kent, 'Scratching and Biting Savagery', in Kent and Morreau, eds, *Women's Images*, p. 8).

86. Tam Giles, 'Women's Images of Men', *Art Monthly*, No. 42, December/January 1980/81, p. 19.

87. Kent, 'Scratching and Biting Savagery', in Kent and Morreau, eds, *Women's Images*, p. 10.

5   Who am I? Where am I going? How much will it cost? Will I need any luggage?

1. Lewis Biggs, Iwona Blaszczyk and Sandy Nairne, 'Introduction', *Objects & Sculpture*, exhibition catalogue, London and Bristol: ICA and Arnolfini, 1981, p. 5.

2. William Clark, *War of Images*, exhibition catalogue, Glasgow: Transmission Gallery/Glasgow School of Art, January 1986.

3. See Ben Jones, 'A New Wave in Sculpture, A Survey of Recent Work by Ten Younger Sculptors. New Prospectors: Shelagah Wakely and Tony Cragg, Lisson Gallery', *Artscribe*, No. 8, September 1977, p. 16.

4. See Biggs, Blaszczyk and Nairne, 'Introduction' to *Objects & Sculpture*.

5. *Ibid.*, p. 5. This stands in stark contrast to Andre's view of sculpture: 'Works of art are fundamentally in the class of landmines rather than signs. That's my own deep feeling. The linguistic aspect of art is tremendously overstressed, especially in the conceptual thing. It's part of the vulgarisation of our culture, "What does it mean?" and all that' (Carl Andre, in Peter Fuller, 'An Interview with Carl Andre', *Art Monthly*, Nos 16 and 17, May/June 1978, reprinted in Fuller, *Beyond the Crisis in Art*, London: Writers & Readers Publishing Co-operative Ltd, 1980, p. 128).

6. '[Bill Woodrow] is reported as saying that many of his colleagues saw *Art for Whom?* at the Serpentine in 1978 and that they thought there was a way of doing it better … Interesting isn't it that of all those exhibitions of the 1970s … a leading young sculptor … should relate however negatively to the issues raised by that particular show *Art for Whom?*' (Conrad Atkinson, 'Introduction', *The State of the Art and the Art of the State: Power Lecture Given to the Power Institute, University of Sydney, Australia, October 1983*, London: Working Press, 1991, p. 24).

7. John Roberts, 'Postmodernism: Arrivals and Departures', *Art Monthly*, No. 55, April 1982, p. 27.

8. Mary Jane Jacob, 'Tony Cragg: First Order Experiences', in her *A Quiet Revolution: British Sculpture since 1965*, London: Thames & Hudson, 1987, p. 58.

9. In the late 1970s, Charles Jencks read 'postmodernism' as an opportunity to re-establish an eclectic continuity with the architectural and artistic traditions that modernists had rejected in their pursuit of the new. Jencks, on the whole, tended to sanction playful works of art and architecture, rather than outright reactionary aesthetics or radical deconstruction. Jencks's version of postmodernism was rooted in the growing architectural revolt against modernist

rationalism that occurred since the late 1960s. Roughly translated into an art context, Jencksian postmodernism came to signify a revolt against modernist reductionism and historical liberty. In practice, this manifested itself in paintings and sculptures that adopted an agnostic, 'grab-bag' approach to the art of the past, kitschy equivalents of their architectural sibling, Las Vegas.

10. Roberts, 'Postmodernism', p. 27.

11. Jacob, *A Quiet Revolution*, p. 58.

12. Annelie Pohlen, 'Possibilities and New Ways: Tony Cragg's Sculptures as Experience "Made Real"', in her *Tony Cragg*, exhibition catalogue, Société des Expositions du Palais des Beaux-Arts de Bruxelles, Düsseldorf: Heinrich Winterscheidt, 1985, p. 20.

13. The theories of Jean Baudrillard were frequently cited in relation to such work. Referring to the 30-second attention span of American televisual culture, Baudrillard announced the collapse of the distinction between fiction and reality, between art and commerce. Such distinctions are allegedly lost as everything enters a market place of consumable signs; art simply becomes another commodity. See Jean Baudrillard, *Simulations*, New York: Semiotext(e), 1983.

14. In Britain, there was the memory of a vacuum cleaner being sent to the Tate at the height of the Tate 'Bricks' scandal.

15. See Germano Celant, 'Tony Cragg and Industrial Platonism', *Artforum* (New York), Vol. 20, Part 3, November 1981, pp. 40–47.

16. 'The success and importance of Cragg and Woodrow's work rests on the incorporation of process-based sculptural values (recycling, improvisation, self-sufficiency) into the ambient world of consumerism … What is so persuasive about Cragg and Woodrow's semiotics of the object and what carries it away from Pop and the host of epigones that this show supports, is that process (appropriation) and product (mythological emblem, symbol) are inseparable' (John Roberts, 'The Sculpture Show', *Art Monthly*, No. 70, October 1983, pp. 14–15).

17. Tony Cragg, 'Pre-conditions', in *Tony Cragg*, Hanover: Kestner-Gesellshaft, 1985, p. 39.

18. Roberts, 'The Sculpture Show', p. 14.

19. Julian Opie, in David Johnson, 'Intro', *The Face*, October 1983, p. 9.

20. Roberts, 'The Sculpture Show', p. 14.

21. John Russell Taylor, 'Playing into the Hands of Those Who Pour Scorn: The Sculpture Show, Hayward/Serpentine', *The Times*, 16 August 1983.

22. Peter Fuller, 'A Black Cloud Over the Hayward', *Art Monthly*, No. 70, October 1983, p. 12.

23. Hilton Kramer, 'Malcolm Morley', September 1983, reprinted in Kramer's *Revenge of the Philistines: Art and Culture 1972–1984*, New York: Macmillan, 1985, pp. 379–80.

24. T. S. Eliot, '*Ulysses*, Order and Myth', *Dial*, No. 85, November 1923.

25. Enrique Juncosa, 'The Flight of Icarus (Or a Pilot among the Angels)', in *Malcolm Morley 1965–95*, exhibition catalogue, Madrid: Sala-Deex Posiciones Dela Fundacion 'La Caixa', 20 September–12 November 1995.

26. Michael Compton, *Malcolm Morley*, exhibition catalogue, London: Whitechapel Art Gallery, 1983, p. 14.

27. Craig Owens, 'The Allegorical Impulse: Towards a Theory of Postmodernism (Part 2)', *October*, No. 13, Summer 1980, p. 80.

28. Robert Hughes, 'Career of Repetition and Glut', *Time*, 9 March 1987, p. 70.

29. Peter Fuller, 'Plus Ça Change', in his *Images of God: The Consolations of Lost Illusions*, London: Hogarth Press, 1985, p. 5.

30. Morley in Arnold Glimcher, 'A Conversation: Malcolm Morley and Arnold Glimcher, Belport, Long Island, 3rd October, 1998', in *Malcolm Morley*, exhibition catalogue, New York: The Pace Gallery, 2 December–7 January 1988–1989.

31. Neo-conservatives were also critical of the New Image for this reason: 'At all the art fairs, Kunst hassles and state-backed cultural binges, *The New Spirit* is being peddled for all its worth which, despite world-wide recession, remains quite a bit … It is now common knowledge that Schnabel was "manufactured" in much the same way Jasper Johns was "manufactured" in 1958, as a way out of the vacuum created by ailing Tenth Street Abstract Expressionism. (Even the cast has not changed entirely; the long arm of Leo Castelli was involved in both operations)' (Peter Fuller, 'Plus Ça Change', in *Images of God*, pp. 6–7).

32. Craig Owens, 'Honour, Power and the Love of Women', *Art in America*, January 1983, repr. in Richard Hertz, ed., *Theories of Contemporary Art*, New Jersey: Prentice Hall, 1985, p. 136. Owens's observation best applies to the 'New Spirit' programme – the 'shock of the old'.

33. *Ibid.*

34. As Jean-François Lyotard wrote, postmodernist art is 'not in principle governed by

predetermined rules', and therefore 'cannot be judged according to a determining judgement by applying familiar categories. Those rules and categories are what the work of art itself is looking for' (Jean-François Lyotard, 'A Response to the Question: What is Postmodernism?', *Critique*, No. 419, Paris, April 1982).

35.   Morley in Les Levine, 'Dialogue: Malcolm Morley', *Cover*, Vol. 1, No. 3, Spring/Summer 1985, pp. 28–31.

36.   ' ... in a way this step by step process of painting, using the grid, allows you to invent a new metaphor for seeing ... It's a way of moving from association and conditioning. Because the moment you say "wave," or "ocean," you have this thing from childhood ... the whole perception is involved with inventing a new metaphor for seeing, for original seeing, without having to see through a kind of filter of conditioning. The paintings are a constant attempt to decondition myself from the associations of imagery. Very often we come to a perception with a tremendous amount of *pre*-perception. In fact people don't really look at things very much at all' (Morley, quoted in Matthew Collings, 'The Happy Return', *Artscribe*, No. 50, January/February 1985, p. 18).

37.   Klaus Kertess, 'On the High Sea and Seeing of Painting', in *Malcolm Morley*, exhibition catalogue, Paris: Musée National d'Art Moderne, Centre Georges Pompidou, 1993, pp. 225–6.

38.   'That's why the whole Scottish Expressionist thing happened. They were all at art school with me. I didn't go to art school to be a teacher, I went to art school to be a professional artist. That was my intention, and a lot of these people learned that stance' (Steven Campbell, quoted in James Collins, 'Interview with Steven Campbell', *Flash Art*, February/March 1987, p. 78).

39.   Ken Currie, 'New Glasgow Painting in Context', *Edinburgh Review*, No. 72, February 1986, p. 73.

40.   Stuart Morgan, 'Soup's On: An Audience with Stephen Campbell', *Artscribe*, No. 48, September/October 1984, p. 33.

41.   Marco Livingstone, *R. B. Kitaj*, Oxford: Phaidon, 1985, p. 34.

42.   See Timothy Hyman, 'Narrative Painting: A Second Generation', *Artscribe*, No. 19, September 1979, pp. 32–7.

43.   Barry Yougrau, 'Steven Campbell', *Arts Magazine*, January 1984, p. 10.

44.   This also differentiates Campbell from Hyman's implicit criterion that narrative painting 'should be in some sense direct or "naive" in its approach – that it should present an imaginative vision of life, rather than taking up a strategic position about art' (Timothy Hyman, 'Another Branch of the Family', in his *Narrative Paintings: Figurative Art of Two Generations Selected by Timothy Hyman*, exhibition catalogue, Bristol: Arnolfini, 1979, p. 5).

45.   See Sarah Kent, 'Bruce McLean', *Art Monthly*, No. 37, 1980, pp. 12–13. 'Campbell's background is in performance, and the catalogue points out his awareness of those English stylists and poseurs Gilbert & George and the Scot Bruce McLean who has had such an influence on new Scottish expressionists, including Mario Rossi' (Caroline Collier, 'Steven Campbell: Riverside Studio', *Flash Art*, March 1985, p. 47). 'I never thought I was an Expressionist. Right from art school I was more bound up with the '70s British conceptual stuff ... McLean, Gilbert & George, those people. I guess it's fashion; there are enough people jumping on the new Minimalism thing because that's in the air. But it seems pretty depressing! Before we have the casualty of Expressionism, we're going to have a helluva lot of people jumping on the new bandwagon ... Now it's abstract appropriation! Not setting the world afire ... this whole thing looks like a reaction. It's not a development but a change to get away from something. Looks like a six month change. A phoney one!' (Campbell in Collins, 'Interview with Steven Campbell', p. 78).

46.   Alexander Moffat, 'Telling Stories: A New Figuration in Glasgow 1980–85', in *New Image Glasgow*, exhibition catalogue, Glasgow: Third Eye Centre, 1985, p. 6.

47.   ' ... "imagination" is so subordinated by "fancy" in Campbell that it is only perceptible, in the spirited rendering of the nickname marks, admissions of the contingent nature of signs. The unseating of imagination in the work is linked to the banishment of "expressionism", still the accepted Modernist stance in his native Scotland' (Stuart Morgan, 'Steven Campbell: The Case of the Waggling Leg', *Artforum*, December 1984, p. 60).

48.   Lisa Liebmann, 'Steven Campbell, Barbara Toll, New York, and John Weber Gallery, New York', *Artforum*, April 1984, p. 75.

49.   Campbell quoted in Peter Hill, 'Steven Campbell interviewed by Peter Hill, Watts Bar, Manhattan, December 1983', *Alba*, January 1984, p. 20.

50.   Campbell quoted in Morgan, 'Soup's On', p. 32.

51.   Marge Goldwater, 'Of Hikers and Humeans', in *Viewpoints: Steven Campbell*, exhibition catalogue, Walker Art Center, New York, 22 September–10 November 1985, p. 2.

52.   *Ibid.*, p. 1.

53.   Campbell quoted in Morgan, 'Soup's On', p. 32.

54.   Goldwater, 'Of Hikers and Humeans', p. 2.

55. In this, Campbell seemed set to rival the productivity of P. G. Wodehouse who produced 96 novels in his lifetime.

56. Jeremy Lewison, 'Steven Campbell at Riverside Studios', *Studio International*, Winter 1984, p. 53.

57. Peter Hill, 'Steven Campbell at Barbara Toll, New York, and John Weber Gallery, New York', *Artscribe*, February/April 1984, p. 56.

58. Campbell quoted in Morgan, 'Soup's On', p. 31.

59. Stuart Morgan, 'Between Oxford and Salisbury', in *Steven Campbell: New Paintings*, exhibition catalogue, London: Riverside Studios, 28 November–30 December 1984; Edinburgh: Fruitmarket Gallery, 12 January–23 February 1985, p. 7.

60. *Ibid.*

61. Tony Godfrey, 'British Painting at the Crossroads', in his *The New Image: Painting in the 1980s*, Oxford: Phaidon, 1986, p. 90.

62. Sarah Kent, 'Critical Images', *Flash Art International*, March 1985, p. 24.

63. John Roberts, *Postmodernism, Politics and Art*, Manchester: University of Manchester Press, 1990, pp. 128–9.

64. Brandon Taylor, *Modernism, Post-Modernism, Realism: A Critical Perspective for Art*, Winchester: Winchester School of Art Press, 1987, pp. 145–6.

65. See John Roberts, 'Fetishism, Conceptualism, Painting', *Art Monthly*, December–January 1984–1985.

66. Currie, 'New Glasgow Painting in Context', p. 73.

67. Paul Wood, 'Critical Realism', *Art Monthly*, No. 113, February 1988, p. 13.

68. Also shown at the AIR Gallery, London, 10 October–10 November 1985; Milton Keynes Exhibition Gallery, 16 November–21 December 1985; Malaurin Gallery, Ayr, 3–20 January 1986; and the Midland Group, Nottingham, 15 February–15 March 1986.

69. Moffat, 'Telling Stories', p. 6.

70. 'My position is quite clear about what Postmodernism is. For me Postmodernism refers to that art which recognises the fact that the vanguardist impulse in Modernism has run out' (Jon Thompson, quoted in John Roberts, 'Morality, Postmodernism and the Pursuit of Metaphor: The British Art Show', *Artscribe*, No. 49, November/December 1984, p. 21).

71. *Ibid.*, p. 18.

72. Glyn Banks, 'Any Old Irony', *Art Monthly*, No. 72, December/January 1983/84, p. 32. On Saatchi see Rita Hatton and John A. Walker, *Supercollector: A Critique of Charles Saatchi*, London: Ellipsis, 2000.

73. 'I don't think of myself as part of a tradition at all. It's simply that the nature of moveable painting, paintings to hang on a wall, has hardly changed in the last four or five hundred years, there have been no new developments, there have been hardly any new colours, other than synthetic and therefore more stable versions of the earlier ones. And the functions of tone and colour, and line, have not changed at all' (Howard Hodgkin, quoted in Sandy Nairne, *State of the Art: Ideas & Images in the 1980s*, London: Chatto & Windus/Channel 4, 1987, p. 116).

74. Before his show at Riverside Studios in 1984, Campbell only exhibited once in Britain. He therefore did not meet the Turner Prize criteria in its first year.

75. AIR Gallery, once the only London gallery committed to the artist's video, closed on 31 March 1989.

76. Matthew Collings, 'Doing It by the Book', *Modern Painters*, Vol. 1, No. 1, Spring 1988, p. 59.

6   Art after Britain?

1. Anon., 'Matthew Collings Diary', *Private Eye*, No. 918, 1997.

2. Thompson, a curator of 'Falls the Shadow', the 1986 Hayward Annual, was something of a Romanticist, while Craig-Martin, who produced *An Oak Tree* – actually a glass of water on a shelf – in 1974, was a Conceptualist.

3. Simon Ford, 'Myth Making', *Art Monthly*, No. 194, March 1996, p. 194. Ford goes on to explain that 'these shows were easily assimilated into the prevailing dealer and gallery system which welcomed them as a form of research and development of new products and personalities'. The myth that there was a yBa group has been further substantiated by group exhibitions such as Saatchi's 'Young British Artists' shows (1992–1996); 'Minky Manky', a reunion of *Freeze* artists held at the South London Gallery in 1995; 'Brilliant!' at the Walker Art Center,

Minneapolis in 1996; 'Sensation' at the Royal Academy in 1997; and 'Ant Noises' at the Saatchi Gallery in 2001.

4. Damien Hirst, ed. Violette Robert, *I Want to Spend the Rest of My Life Everywhere, with Everyone, One to One, Always, Forever, Now*, London: Monacelli Press, 1996. This feature was designed by Jonathan Barnbrook. It is now commonplace for Saatchi yBa catalogues to include reproductions of 'bad press'; see Saatchi Gallery, *Ant Noises at the Saatchi Gallery 2*, exhibition catalogue, London: Saatchi Gallery, 2001.

5. 'The plea for art to become more like advertising is simplistic and embarrassing; at the very least, the sheer complexity and ubiquitousness of advertising demands a more nuanced analysis' (Michael Corris, 'The Triumphant Moment: A research plan for the future now that 'young British art' is dead as a theoretical concept or as a means of developing frameworks influencing how we make and think about art', in David Burrows, ed., *Who's Afraid of Red, White and Blue? Attitudes to Popular & Mass Culture, Celebrity, Alternative & Critical Practice & Identity Politics in Recent British Art*, Birmingham: Article Press, 1998, p. 20).

6. His paintings and sculptures, however, are normally combined to produce an installation, a good example being his 1991 exhibition 'In and Out of Love', in which he stuck butterfly pupae onto canvases. Over the course of the exhibition the butterflies hatched, lived out their short lives and died, in the artificial tropical environment created in the gallery.

7. See David Carrier, 'The Origins of Museums: The Cabinet of Curiosities in Sixteenth- and Seventeenth-century Europe', *Leonardo*, Vol. 20, No. 1, 1987, pp. 83–6.

8. Other artists exhibited by Saatchi under this banner were Sarah Lucas, Chris Offili, Marcus Harvey, Jake and Dinos Chapman, Rachel Whiteread, Gary Hume and Sam Taylor-Wood. Works by artists such as Gillian Wearing and Michael Landy, who were excluded from Saatchi's original yBa shows, were later hastily acquired when Saatchi curated the 'Sensation' retrospective at the Royal Academy in 1997.

9. Julian Stallabrass, 'Dumb and Dumber?', in his *High Art Lite*, London: Verso, 1999, p. 99.

10. See Rita Hatton and John A. Walker, *Supercollector: A Critique of Charles Saatchi*, London: Ellipsis, 2000.

11. The group exhibitions 'Modern Medicine' (1990) and 'Gambler' (1990) were curated by Hirst, Billie Sellman and Carl Freedman at 'Building One', a former biscuit factory in Bermondsey.

12. 'Gilbert & George have their pictures of shit, just as Damien Hirst has worked with maggots. These serve to illustrate the gulf between art and life, a gulf which the totalitarian artist wishes to reinforce, whether it be through the idealised depiction of a Hitler or Mao, or by the use of subject matter drawn from everyday life, which ceases to be ordinary after undergoing an "alchemical" transformation through the medium of art. In fact, such discrepancies serve the totalitarian artist very well, since those who support work of this type expect blatant insincerity' (Stewart Home, 'The Art of Chauvinism in Britain and France', *Everything*, Issue 19, 1996, as reprinted in his *Disputations on Art, Anarchy and Assholism*, London: Sabotage Editions, 1997, p. 10).

13. Damien Hirst in Andrew Wilson, 'Out of Control', *Art Monthly*, No. 177, June 1994, p. 8.

14. Liz Ellis, 'A critique in three parts of the Britpack phenomenon and particularly the critical reception of Bank, Sarah Lucas and Sam Taylor-Wood' (1997), @ http://web.ukonline.co.uk/members/n.paradoxa/ellis.htm.

15. Neville Wakefield, *Brilliant!*, exhibition catalogue, 2 October–7 January 1996 at the Walker Art Center, Minneapolis, USA.

16. Ellis, 'A critique'.

17. Rosemary Betterton suggests that if 'Lucas's work is read as a critical commentary on the sexual politics embedded in both fine art and mass culture, it can be seen as operating in a critical relationship to both traditions' (Rosemary Betterton, 'Undutiful Daughters: Avant-gardism and Gendered Consumption in Recent British Art', *Visual Culture in Britain*, Vol. 1, No. 1, 1999, p. 25). It would seem, however, that it would require a well-informed feminist audience to will this criticality into being. Lucas is perhaps more interested in enjoyment than in displays of critical insight. See David Burrows and Paula Smithard, 'Enjoy Your Alienation!', *Make*, No. 77, September–November 1997, pp. 11–13.

18. Kent and Roberts became major apologists for elements of the London-based 'Britpack' (and were much maligned as a result).

19. Ford, 'Myth Making', p. 9.

20. 'The similarities with the resurgence of young British art are clear; massive surge of energy, self-determination, infectious self-confidence, decentralization, horizontally reciprocally supportive infrastructures, assimilation, and ultimately disillusion. No more heroes, possibly' (Ross Sinclair, 'This is the Sound of the Suburbs: The Glasgow Model and the Cyclical Nature of Arts Communities', *Proceedings of the Global Culture & Arts Communities Symposium*, 13–17 October 1999, University of Alberta, Canada).

21. As the K-Foundation, self-styled art terrorists, Cauty and Drummond created a scandal in 1994 when they set up an alternative £40,000 award to the Turner Prize for the worst British artist, which was won by Rachel Whiteread, the recipient of that year's Turner Prize. See Chris Brook, ed., *K Foundation Burn a Million Quid*, London: Ellipsis, 1997; Jimmy Cauty and Bill Drummond, *The Manual*, London: Ellipsis, 1988; and Simon Ford, 'The Art of Legitimation', *Edinburgh Review*, No. 91, May 1994, pp. 87–97, and 'Clockwork Skinhead: The Systematic Extremism of Stewart Home', *Rapid Eye*, No. 3, 1994, pp. 58–71.

22. A good example of such immediately recuperated symbolic dissent is John Frankland's laminated polythene and wood installation *You Can't Touch This* (1993) which 'exposes' as illusion and spin the kind of corporate politics associated with Saatchi.

23. The fact that New Labour's cultural policy has caught the attention of Andrew Brighton suggests a further parallel with the events of 1976. See Andrew Brighton, 'Command Performance', *Guardian*, 12 April 1999, pp. 12–13, where he argues that Labour is aping the cultural policies of Stalin.

24. In much 'young British art', the meanings of popular culture were disengaged from the ways in which it is consumed as a contest of conflicting value systems, ignoring interpretative communities and viewer competencies. Moreover, rather 'than being something recent, the technological expansion of "art" beyond the confines of "painting" and "sculpture" has been a commonplace for several hundred years, from at least the time of the sixteenth and seventeenth-century masque through to futurist and dadaist film and performance' (Stewart Home, 'From Arse to Arsehole: John Roberts and the Spectres of Philistinism', in his *Disputations on Art, Anarchy and Assholism*, London: Sabotage Editions, 1997, p. 20).

25. Kevin Davey, 'England: An Imaginary Country', in his *English Imaginaries: Six Studies in Anglo-British Modernity*, London: Lawrence & Wishart, 1999, p. 11.

26. 'Yes much "yBa" is laddish, puerile, ignorant and numbingly celebratory of "popular culture", but equally within this murky nebula much is of genuine interest. My worry about the domino effect of a backlash is that in the ferment of its reactionary zeal, it loses sight of facets of artists' work which exist outside the hype' (John Beagles, 'Back to the Old School', *Variant*, Vol. 2, No. 6, Autumn 1998, p. 2).

27. See ICA, *City Racing 1988–1998: A Partial Account*, exhibition catalogue, Institute of Contemporary Arts, London, 25 January–11 March 2001; Lee Rodney, 'Nostalgia and Nationalism/Two London Surveys', *C Magazine*, No. 70, Summer 2001, pp. 6–9, and David Musgrave, 'The Last Show: City Racing', *Art Monthly*, No. 222, December 1998/January 1999, pp. 26–7. Much of the work exhibited at such spaces was distinct from the slickness which characterizes early '90s yBa.

28. 'While there is a certain radical charge in the act of negation against the industry of high culture, nothing is recommended in its place except the loosest and hippest of liberalisms, defended but also defanged by irony … The result is a lot of shows which all claim to be unique but which all say much the same thing: that they are "alternative". The most important claim that these exhibitions make is negative: it is to proclaim what they are not' (Stallabrass, 'Alternatives', in his *High Art Lite*, p. 65).

29. Dave Beech, 'When was London?', *Untitled*, No. 24, Spring 2001, p. 17.

30. See Transmission Gallery, *Transmission*, London: Black Dog, 2001. 'Artist initiated projects are born out of a desire to get out there and do something. To create a context for initiating and exhibiting work *on your own terms*. They express belief in themselves. They are positive examples of the implementation of *self co-determination*' (Ross Sinclair, 'Bad Smells but No Sign of the Corpse', *Windfall*, Glasgow, 1991, p. 10). This widespread ethos of the early '90s brought problems for many artists: 'Given the numbers of practising artists, it is correct to read these trends as aspects of a practical self-help movement, but survival of the fittest no longer seems an appropriate philosophy – if it ever was' (Naomi Siderfin, 'Occupational Hazard', in Duncan McCorquodale, Naomi Siderfin and Julian Stallabrass, eds, *Occupational Hazard: Critical Writing on Recent British Art*, London: Black Dog, 1998, p. 41).

31. See Richard J. Williams, 'Anything is Possible: The Annual Programme 1995–2000', *Life is Good in Manchester*, Manchester: Trice Publications, 2001, pp. 7–15.

32. 'Historically, commercial galleries have never existed in the city [of Glasgow] and no market exists for the kind of work being produced' (Rebecca Gordon-Nesbitt, 'Urban Myths: A Tale of Two Cities', *Contemporary Visual Arts*, Issue 17, February 1998, p. 39).

33. Artist-run spaces in London such as Beaconsfield and City Racing attracted the attention of major collectors such as Saatchi and therefore were cynically condemned as nothing more than discounted yBa laboratories. Of course, this co-operation and integration of artist initiatives, public art institutions and the private market was another revisitation of Conceptualism. Moreover, as in the '70s and '80s, the 'industriousness and inventiveness' of artist-run spaces in Britain in the 1990s was undoubtedly 'founded on an overt if informal solidarity, one which currently suffuses it with an exceptional – and exemplary – energy and power of attraction' (Suzanne Pagé, 'Preface', *Live/Life: La scène artistique au Royaume-Uni en 1996, de nouvelles aventures*, Paris: Musée d'Art Moderne de la Ville de Paris, 1997, p. 8).

34. John Roberts points out that such vulgar Marxism is inadequate as a means of explaining the yBas' success: 'But cultural industries cannot create cultural capital on this scale, without the art having a life and quality beyond its spectacular mediation. Thus whatever corruption of the market may ensue from the monopolistic powers of one major collector or dealer, does not thereby mean the new art is only – and fragilely – sustained by the machinations of the market' (John Roberts, in Burrows, ed., *Who's Afraid*, p. 39).

35. It is less meaningful outside urban and national contexts, suffering as it does from falsely presenting parochial situations as though they were the products of international consensus. For example, Simon Ford and Anthony Davies's article 'Art Capital' (*Art Monthly*, No. 213, February 1998, pp. 1–4) is only relevant to those intimately involved with the machinations of the promotional sectors of the London art scene in which there has been a massive boost of capital from the City's private purse.

36. David Hall, 'Artists' Thoughts on the 70s in Words and Pictures', *Studio International*, Vol. 195, No. 991/2, 1981, p. 31.

37. 'Rather, it treats the aesthetically despised categories and pleasures of the popular – the pornographic, sleazy, abject and facile – as things that are first nature and commonplace and mutually defining of subjectivity and therefore needing no intellectual introduction into art' (John Roberts, 'Mad For It!', *Everything*, Issue 18, 1996).

38. Michael Archer made this point: 'It is not a working through of earlier questions. Certain things have become internalised, accepted' (Michael Archer, 'Reconsidering Conceptual Art', *Art Monthly*, No. 193, February 1996, pp. 12–13). To say that yBas simply rejected 'critical' postmodernism would require a selective reading of the art of the '70s and '80s: '[John] Roberts posits what he styles "recent British art" as a reaction to the critique of representation pursued by a preceding generation. Thus Mary Kelly becomes a paradigmatic example of seventies and eighties feminist art, while work by the likes of [Cosey Fanni] Tutti is pointedly ignored because it disrupts Porno Roberts's reductive revisionism, while simultaneously making a mockery of the claims he has set forth about the originality and radicality of recent "British" art as a reflex against earlier feminist "propriety about the body"' (Stewart Home, 'Prostitution II: The Return of the "Male" "Gaze"', *Multiple Choice*, exhibition catalogue, Cubitt Gallery, London, 7 March–6 April 1996).

39. Roberts, 'Mad For It!'. Roberts has repudiated the claim that this is empty posturing: 'the "dumbing-down" of much of the new art should not be mistaken for an avant-garde outmanoeuvring of what is taken to be advanced. Far from having any intellectual stake in the supercession of 80s critical postmodernism, the new art seeks to adjust the terms of engagement between critical theory and the art of the recent past' (John Roberts, 'Home Truths', *Everything*, Issue 20, 1997, as reprinted in Home's *Disputations*, pp. 13–14). The problem is that there is no ready way of telling when we are looking at 'posturing' and when we are looking at 'readjustment'. This cultivation of such forms of ambiguity was perhaps the crux of the yBa enterprise.

40. Roberts, 'Mad for It! Philistinism, the Everyday and the New British Art', *Third Text*, No. 35, Summer 1996, pp. 29–42; Roberts, 'Notes on 90's Art', *Art Monthly*, No. 200, October 1996, pp. 3–4.

41. Roberts, 'Mad For It!'.

42. John Roberts, 'Notes', p. 4.

43. ' … the professional critique of representation pursued by the likes of Victor Burgin, Mary Kelly and Hans Haacke, began to appear to this generation as censorious. Such moral strenuousness and the intellectualisation of pleasure looked bathetic, gruesome even, the work of bodies at war with themselves despite the critique of identity' (*ibid.*).

44. ' … the new avant garde is largely working class, whatever that means, and *therefore* anti-establishment in character' (Patricia Bickers, *The Brit Pack: Contemporary British Art, the View from Abroad*, Manchester: Cornerhouse, 1995, p. 18). The theatricality of this position is obvious, especially if, as Roberts claimed, this is the revenge of 'proletarian cognition' on the 'bourgeois culture' represented by critical postmodernism. Critical postmodernism placed a great deal of value on transgression, albeit transgression against the bourgeois values of the post-war culturalist consensus. The yBas plainly mirrored knowledgeable disaffirmation.

45. Significantly, the *New Left Review* was also the arena of Fuller's spats with Marxist critics such as Terry Eagleton at the turn of the '80s.

46. 'The working-class philistine may be the excluded disaffirmative presence of art's professional self-ratification, but this does not mean that working-class refusal of art's ratification is the excluded truth of art. This sociological formalism is what is wrong with the post-aesthetic followers of Pierre Bourdieu who takes the truth of art to lie solely with its class exclusions. To denounce the categories of art in the name of a philistine common sense judgement is merely to substitute the non-cognitive realities of the exclusion for the cognitive problems that the realities create. The philistine as proletarian may haunt the conditions of art's production and spectatorship, but the philistine is also necessarily an intra and inter art voice of the excluded.

For there are power relations internal to the institutions and categories of art which makes it imperative that art continually judges what passes for dominant critical taste. The philistine, therefore, is also the voice of art's bid for critical autonomy, the voice that recognises the congealing power of dominant academic positions in the name of art's critical renewal' (Roberts, 'Mad For It!').

47. Stallabrass has effectively demonstrated this point. See Stallabrass, 'Dumb and Dumber?', in his *High Art Lite*, pp. 118–23.

48. Stallabrass quoting Roberts, in Stallabrass, *High Art Lite*, p. 119. See also Malcolm Bull, 'The Ecstasy Of Philistinism', *New Left Review*, No. 219, September/October 1996, a response to John Roberts and Dave Beech's 'Spectres Of The Aesthetic' (*New Left Review*, No. 218, July–August 1996).

49. See BANK, *BANK*, London: Black Dog, 2000.

50. Stallabrass, at the same time, condemns the yBas' disdain for criticism. Ellis thinks that BANK are particularly guilty of this: 'The lack of critical discussion and the silencing of opposition, partly through media complicity and partly through the endorsement of the political hegemony of the current art establishment, prevents an adequate testing of the moral vacuity and inertia of much contemporary practice' (Ellis, 'A critique').

51. 'Throughout the 90s, though, we have become familiar with the contra- or anti-exhibition title, the title that mocks the assiduousness of theory-led curatorship' (Roberts, 'Mad For It!'). Mainstream curators quickly adopted this initial anti-curatorial seam. An obvious way of popularizing theory is to present its concerns under narrower populist thematic umbrellas.

52. 'Curators have also exploited the space created by a generation of artists who have largely disavowed their claims to authorship, who create deliberately "dumb" art that refuses to answer back, that can, therefore, be neatly slotted into any "theme" or group exhibition "authored" by a "big name" curator' (Robert Garnet, 'Britpopism and the Populist Gesture', in McCorquodale, Siderfin and Stallabrass, eds, *Occupational Hazard*, p. 20).

53. See Matthew Collings, *Blimey! From Bohemia to Britpop: The London Art World from Francis Bacon to Damien Hirst*, Cambridge: 21 Publishing, 1997.

54. Stallabrass, 'Dumb and Dumber?', in his *High Art Lite*, p. 106.

55. *Ibid.*, p. 122.

56. *Ibid.*, p. 105.

57. Malcolm Miles, 'Fifth National Mural Conference: Edinburgh May 9th–11th 1986', *Alba*, No. 1, Summer 1986, pp. 31–2.

58. 'Titled as the photograph of Greenberg's protégés taken in 1954, *The Irascibles*, Sinclair had photographs taken of a group of artists living and working in Glasgow at the time, which he exhibited alongside a list of their names and a drawing providing the key to which face matched which name. At the time, the people photographed were all recently graduated from or in their final years of art school, the implication being of the unknown attendant future. Much like the later *Museum of Despair* [an empty shop on the Royal Mile, Edinburgh, which housed Sinclair's 1994 retrospective], this was a simple and quite humorous instant historification, an acknowledgement of an increasingly condensed time-scale of assimilation' (Katrina Brown, 'From the Inside Out', in Nicola White, ed., *Ross Sinclair: Real Life*, Glasgow: CCA, 1996, p. 38). Many of these artists – also known as the Scotia Nostra – were reunited for 'Girl's High', an exhibition held to mark the tenth anniversary of the Environmental Art Department at the Old Fruitmarket, Glasgow, 1996. See also David Harding, ed., *Decadent: Public Art, Contentious Term and Contested Practice*, Glasgow: Foulis Press, 1997.

59. Douglas Gordon, quoted in Thomas Lawson, 'Hello, It is Me', *Frieze*, No. 9, London, March/April 1993, p. 38.

60. Then run by a committee of four painters from Glasgow and Edinburgh, it exhibited paintings by Ken Currie, Peter Howson and Adrian Wiszniewski in 'Urban Life', the inaugural Transmission show which opened on 2 December 1983.

61. Sinclair, 'Bad Smells', p. 10.

62. Sinclair, 'This is the Sound'.

63. See Malcolm Dickson, 'Another Year of Alienation: On the Mythology of the Artist-Run Initiative', in McCorquodale, Siderfin and Stallabrass, eds, *Occupational Hazard*, pp. 81–93.

64. Rob Tufnell, 'A Recent History of Artists' Initiatives in Scotland', in *Open Country: Contemporary Scottish Artists*, exhibition catalogue, Lausanne, Musée cantonal des Beaux-Arts de Lausanne, Switzerland, 20 January–1 April 2001, p. 51.

65. See Ross Sinclair, 'Capital of Culture/Culture of Capital: Representing Representation', *Alba*, 1990, pp. 6–9, an essay based on his undergraduate dissertation. The poster diptychs *Capital of Culture/Culture of Capital* were posted around Amsterdam, Glasgow and Dublin, European Capitals of Culture in 1987, 1990 and 1991 respectively.

66.   See John Calcutt, 'There + Then', in *Here + Now: Scottish Art 1990–2001*, exhibition catalogue, Dundee: Dundee Contemporary Arts, 2001, pp. 11–25.

67.   Sinclair, 'Bad Smells', p. 11.

68.   Craig Richardson, Euan Sutherland and Gordon had performed as 'The Puberty Institution' at Transmission in 1987 and 1988 and Gordon remained an interested party while in London.

69.   'The pseudo-scientific rigor first used by artists in the 1970s has been adopted by him to show a puritanical nature' (Martin Maloney, 'Douglas Gordon, Lisson Gallery', *Flash Art*, No. 182, May/June 1995, p. 114).

70.   Douglas Gordon works are 'produced from found materials, which evoke an underground culture. For the artist, the use of found materials is an art of gradual mutation that reflects the process of memory and the structure of the psyche' (Jerome Sans, 'Douglas Gordon, Centre Georges Pompidou', *Artforum*, Vol. 34, April 1996, pp. 109–10).

71.   Poststructuralist-inspired polyvalence and pluralism became serviceable tools 'for saying everything and nothing, for stamping a work with a mark of value, while never being reductive, never subjecting discourse to closure, never trampling on anyone's subjectivity, never completing a thought' (Stallabrass, 'Dumb and Dumber?', in his *High Art Lite*, p. 123).

72.   'I see ambiguity as a positive thing; it's about giving the viewers enough space (literally and metaphorically) to come to an individual and shifting conclusion, if that's not too much of a contradiction. Perhaps "democratic" is a better word than "ambiguity" – perhaps not (Gordon in conversation with Jan Debbaut, in Douglas Gordon, *Kidnapping*, exhibition catalogue, Amsterdam: Stadelijk van Abbemuseum, Eindhoven/Nai Publishers, 1998, p. 23).

73.   David Burrows, 'Correspondences, Olympic Village, Waves in Particles Out, Beagles & Ramsay', *Art Monthly*, No. 213, February 1998, p. 24. With no commercial gallery infrastructure, the power brokers of the country's art scene are the curators of public institutions and the Scottish Arts Council, which perhaps explains in part Scotland's cultivation of an institution-friendly form of Conceptualism.

74.   'The idea that the lack of private contemporary galleries in Scotland is responsible for the present flowering of artistic production, glosses over the competing and conflicting pressures that exclusive public funding generates' (John Beagles, 'Under the Central Belt', *Variant*, Vol. 2, No. 2, Spring 1997, p. 9).

75.   Buchanan's *Coast to Coast, Dennistoun* (1996–2000), featuring photographs of local youths sporting various American baseball caps, has parallels with Gillian Wearing's *Signs that say what you want them to say and not Signs that say what someone else wants you to say* (1992–1993), which focused on the aspirations and cultural affiliations of Londoners living in and around Peckham and Southwark.

76.   Notably the Lisson was one of the galleries which had determined the '80s *Zeitgeist* for public institutions (see the beginning of Chapter 5, above).

77.   This ambient approach was shared by many Scottish artists such as Peter McCaughey, Jonathan Monk, Jacqueline Donachie and James Thornhill. See Judith Findlay, 'There's Not Much Art that's like a Good Story', *Art & Design*, Vol. 11, January/February 1996, pp. 8–15, and 'Cityscape: Glaswegian Goods', *Flash Art*, No. 188, May/June 1996, pp. 63–4. In the late '90s it became a favourite approach for advertising firms such as London's CAKE, who produced numerous whispering campaigns and ambient publicity stunts.

78.   'David Shrigley's notice for a lost pidgeon, as an advertisement in a world of advertising, is a static image that successfully interrogates itself to death and by doing this, performs deconstructive surgery on its greater technological structure' (Stan Bonnar, 'Context and Provocation', in Harding, ed., *Decadent*, p. 53).

79.   David Shrigley, *Merry Eczema*, Glasgow: Black Rose, 1992. Drawing on the adolescent bedroom art of American artists such as Jim Shaw and Mike Kelly, Shrigley shared this interest with a number of British artists, including Adam Dant, publisher of *Donald Parsnips' Daily Journal*, a small photocopied 'newspaper' which he distributed around Whitechapel each day in the mid-1990s. See David Lillington, 'Comic Art', *Art Monthly*, No. 216, May 1998, pp. 1–6. This was also related to a more general revival of drawing in British art of the late '90s, as featured in the work of Julian Opie, Chad McCail, Paul Noble and David Musgrave, who featured alongside Shrigley in Emma Dexter and Katya Garcia-Ant's 'Surfacing: Contemporary Drawing' at the ICA, London, 18 September–1 November 1998. See David Musgrave, *Surfacing*, exhibition catalogue, ICA, London, 1998, and David Barrett, 'Surfacing – Contemporary Drawing, ICA, London', *Art Monthly*, No. 221, November 1998, pp. 27–9.

80.   David Shrigley, *ERR*, London: Bookworks, 1996.

81.   David Shrigley, *Why We Got the Sack from the Museum*, London: Redstone Press, 1998, and *The Beast is Near*, London: Redstone Press, 1999. See Cathy Courtney, 'Torah Torah', *Art Monthly*, No. 221, November 1998, pp. 43–4.

82.   See Mark Wilsher, 'David Shrigley: Stephen Friedman Gallery, London', *Art Monthly*, No. 246,

May 2001, pp. 32–3; Judith Findlay, 'David Shrigley, Transmission, Glasgow', *Flash Art*, No. 186, January/February 1996, p. 106; Dave Beech, 'David Shrigley, The Photographers' Gallery, London', *Art Monthly*, No. 204, March 1997, pp. 29–30; and Brad Killam, 'David Shrigley, Hermetic Gallery, Milwaukee', *New Art Examiner*, Vol. 25, December 1997/January 1998, p. 59.

83. Tom Nairne, *After Britain*, London: Granta Books, 2000. Following the Labour victory in the 1997 General Election, the prospect of partial self-government for Scotland and Wales was put to a referendum in each country. Stopping very short of federalism, neither nation was granted full fiscal autonomy from Westminster. The Scottish Parliament, which has limited taxation and spending powers, first sat in 1999 in Edinburgh. The Welsh National Assembly in Cardiff, which also opened in 1999, has spending powers over a number of Welsh issues. Northern Ireland was granted its own Assembly in 1999 following the 'Good Friday agreement' between nationalists and loyalists. The prospect of English regional devolution also began to be debated at the close of the century.

84. Davey, *English Imaginaries*, p. 10.

85. See Roderick Buchanan, *Players*, exhibition catalogue, Dundee Contemporary Arts, 25 November–4 February 1999/2000, Dundee; Nicky Bird, 'Roderick Buchanan, DCA', *Art Monthly*, No. 243, February 2001, pp. 37–8; and Judith Findlay, 'Roderick Buchanan, Tramway', *Flash Art*, No. 183, Summer 1995, pp. 131–2.

86. See Peter Jenkinson, 'The New Art Gallery, Walsall', in Gavin Wade, ed., *Curating in the 21st Century*, Wolverhampton: The New Art Gallery Walsall/University of Wolverhampton, 2000, pp. 13–18.

87. See BALTIC, *New Sites – New Art*, Gateshead: BALTIC, 2000.

88. Dick Price and Jonathan Barnbrook, *Young British Art: The Saatchi Decade*, London, Booth-Clibborn Editions, 1999.

89. Tom Nairne's comparison of the cultural devolutionary strategies of the Blair government with the last days of the Hapsburg Empire is equally apposite to Saatchi's late '90s exhibitions: 'Clinging to what was left of greatness therefore entailed a cautious and less ostentatious conservation of the Centre, in order to balance the radicalisation on the periphery' (Tom Nairne, 'Blair's Britain: Stand Alone England', in his *After Britain*, p. 39).

90. 'Even with a periodic measure of scandal, "sensationalists" faded into the kind of repetitive bowdlerised creative anonymity that is the fate of affluent celebrity artists. With the aid of painter and critic Martin Maloney, Saatchi had earlier attempted to create a new movement from scratch: *The New Neurotic Realism*. Art started to look like it was having more fun while artists remained serious in how they reflected their concerns. These new artists started putting themselves into the picture through low-key shows at artist-run spaces. Cynicism was finally *passé* and the art star a bore' (Dick Price, 'Don't Stop 'till You Get Enough', in *The New Neurotic Realism*, exhibition catalogue, London: Saatchi Gallery, 1999, p. 7). Such exhibitions celebrated art history, handcraft, figuration, glamour, the subjective fantasy and a gothic sensibility within the context of the everyday found in yBa: 'Achieving that feeling, monumental sentiment, the rush of the numb. This group revives the intimate, confines their seduction, and within the beauty, creates just a touch of emphatic, glamorous tragedy. In the thrust towards tomorrow, they are racing to immortalise the Now' (Patricia Ellis, 'How Soon is Now', in *Die Young Stay Pretty*, exhibition catalogue, London: ICA, 13 November–10 January 1999, p. 9).

92. Martin Maloney, 'In Conversation with Gemma de Cruz', in *Die Young Stay Pretty*, exhibition catalogue, ICA, London, 13 November–10 January 1999, p. 15. See also Linda Hutcheon, *Irony's Edge: The Theory and Politics of Irony*, London and New York: Routledge, 1995.

93. Along with Pippa Coles and Jacqui Poncelet, Higgs was a selector of the Hayward Gallery's touring 'British Art Show 5', in 2000. See Matthew Higgs and Tony Godfrey, *British Art Show 5*, exhibition catalogue, London: Hayward Gallery, 2000.

93. Mark Wallinger and Mary Warnock, eds, *Art For All?: Their Policies and Our Culture*, London: Peer, 2000.

94. Benedict Seymour, 'Everything Must Go', *Mute*, Vol. 16, 2000, p. 45.

95. See Eleanor Heartney, 'The Hot New Cool Art: Simulationism', *Art News*, Vol. 86, January 1987, pp. 130–7, and Brian Hatton, 'Simulacra at the Riverside', *Artscribe*, No. 39, February 1983, pp. 30–4.

96. See Julian Stallabrass, 'Art I Like', *Modern Painters*, Vol. 13, No. 2, Summer 2000, pp. 36–8. This edition, edited by Matthew Collings, contains a number of eleventh-hour articles on post-yBa fallout.

97. For example, see the correspondence following the publication of J. J. Charlesworth, 'Crash!: ICA; Urban Islands: Cubitt; Peter Kennard: Gimpel Fils; All London', *Art Monthly*, No. 233, February 2000, pp. 19–21.

98. See Sophia Phoca, 'Protest and Survive', *Third Text*, No. 53, Winter 2000/2001, pp. 100–103, and Constance Carol, 'Dear Make', *Make: The Magazine of Women's Art*, No. 90, December 2000/February 2001, p. 2.

99.   See Michael Archer, 'Heart and Soul', *Artforum International*, Vol. 38, No. 3, November 1999, p. 153; and Gilda Williams, 'Heart and Soul', *Art Monthly*, No. 229, September 1999, pp. 23–5.

100.   See Joanne Tatham, Tom O'Sullivan and Will Bradley, *The Glamour*, exhibition catalogue, Glasgow: Transmission Gallery, 2001, and Will Bradley, 'Cathy Wilkes: Quiet Radical', *Untitled*, No. 25, Summer 2001.

Bibliography

Chapter 1.   The British art crisis

Alexander, David, *A Policy for the Arts: Just Cut Taxes*, London: Selsdon Group, 1978.
Anderson, Perry, 'Origins of the Present Crisis', *New Left Review*, Vol. 1, No. 23, January/February 1964.
—— 'Components of the National Culture', *New Left Review*, Vol. 1, No. 50, July/August 1968.
Andre, Carl, 'Views from the Studio', *Artnews*, Vol. 175, No. 5, May 1976.
—— 'Letter', *Artforum*, Vol. XIV, No. 9, May 1976.
—— 'Correspondence', *Studio International*, Vol. 191, No. 981, May–June 1976.
—— 'The Bricks Abstract', *Art Monthly*, No. 1, October 1976.
Anon., 'Minister Hears How the Tate Bought a Pile of Bricks', *Financial Times*, 17 February 1976.
—— 'An Exhibition Censored', 10 November 1978, reprinted in 'O God! O Ulster!', *Art Monthly*, No. 22, 1978–1979.
Art & Language, 'Art for Society?', *Art–Language*, Vol. 4, No. 4, Banbury: Art & Language Press, June 1980.
Artist's Space New York, *British Art from the Left*, New York, 1979.
Atkinson, Conrad, *Strike at Brannans*, London: ICA, 1972.
—— *Work, Wages and Prices*, London: ICA, 1974.
—— *A Shade of Green, An Orange Edge*, Arts Council of Northern Ireland, 1975.
—— *Northern Ireland 1968; Mayday 1975*, Art Net/Midland Group, 1976.
—— 'Interview with Richard Cork', *Studio International*, Vol. 191, No. 980, March/April 1976.
—— *Approaching Reality*, Newcastle: Northern Arts Gallery, 1977.
—— *Radical Attitudes Towards the Gallery*, London: Art Net, 1977/78.
—— 'Polemic: Art for Whom?', *Art Monthly*, No. 19, September 1978.
—— 'Artist's Statement', in Derek Boshier, *Lives: An Exhibition of Artists Whose Work is Based on Other Peoples' Lives, Selected by Derek Boshier*, exhibition catalogue, London: Arts Council of Great Britain, 1979.
—— 'Correspondence: "Lives' Lives"', *Art Monthly*, No. 27, June 1979.
—— 'Passive Action/Active Passion', *Artforum*, 19 September 1980.
—— *Picturing the System*, London: Pluto Press/ICA, 1981.
—— 'People's Imagery: Trade Union Banners 1976', in C. Tisdall and S. Nairne, *Picturing the System*, exhibition catalogue, ICA, London: Pluto Press, 1981.
Atkinson, Terry, and Atkinson, Susan, *Mute I*, exhibition catalogue, Copenhagen: Galleri Prag; Derry: Orchard Gallery; London: Gimpel Fils, 1988.
Ball, Ian, 'Brick Hating Philistines Upset New York Aesthete', *Daily Telegraph*, 21 February 1976.

Baranik, Rudolf, 'US/UK Dialogue on Social Purpose', *Artscribe*, No. 14, October 1978.

Barnett, Alan W., *Community Murals: The People's Art*, London: Art Alliance Press, 1984.

Bell, Daniel, *The Coming of Post-Industrial Society*, New York: Basic Books, 1973.

—— *The Cultural Contradictions of Capitalism*, New York: Basic Books, 1976.

Bell, Stan, *Roots into the 80's: Glasgow League of Artists Yearbook*, Glasgow: John Watson, 1979.

Binnington, David, 'A Genuine Social Function for Artists: A Dream or a Reality', *Art for Whom?*, exhibition catalogue, London: Arts Council of Great Britain, 1978.

—— 'Muralism', *Art Monthly*, No. 17, June 1978.

Birnham, Bonnie, *The Art Crisis*, London: Collins, 1977.

Boshier, Derek, *Lives: An Exhibition of Artists Whose Work is Based on Other Peoples' Lives, Selected by Derek Boshier*, exhibition catalogue, London: Arts Council of Great Britain, 1979.

Branden, Sue, 'Alienation and the ICA', *Studio International* (Review Issue), Vol. 191, No. 980, March–April 1976.

—— *Artists and People*, London: Routledge & Kegan Paul, 1978.

Brighton, Andrew, 'Official Art and the Tate Gallery', *Studio International* (Review Issue), No. 1, 1977.

—— 'The State of British Art', *Art Monthly*, No. 15, March 1978.

—— 'Art Currency', in *Current Affairs: British Painting and Sculpture in the 1980s*, Oxford: Museum of Modern Art Oxford and The British Council, 1987.

Brook, Donald, 'Books: A Cautious Bob Each Way: Richard Cork, *The Social Role of Art*', *Art Monthly*, No. 37, 1980.

—— 'Reflections on "The State of Art: The Art of the State"', *Art Monthly*, No. 72, December/January 1983/84.

Brooks, Rosetta, 'Please, No Slogans', *Studio International*, Vol. 191, No. 980, March/April 1976.

Burk, Kathleen, and Cairncross, Alec, *'Goodbye Great Britain': The 1976 IMF Crisis*, London: Yale University Press, 1992.

Calvocoressi, Richard, 'Mur al, mural ist, mural ism', letter printed in *Art Monthly*, No. 18, July/August 1978.

—— 'External Walls', *Art Monthly*, No. 19, September 1978.

Carey, John, *The Intellectuals and the Masses*, London: Penguin, 1990.

Clark, Timothy J., 'Preliminaries to a Possible Treatment of Olympia in 1865', *Screen*, Spring 1980.

Cockcroft, Eva, *Towards a People's Art: The Contemporary Mural Movement*, London: Dutton, 1977.

Conservative Political Centre, *The Arts – The Way Forward*, London: CPS, 1978.

Coonan, Rory, 'Style in the 70s', *Art Monthly*, No. 29, September 1979.

Cork, Richard, *Beyond Painting & Sculpture: Works bought for the Arts Council by Richard Cork*, exhibition catalogue, London: Arts Council of Great Britain, 1974.

—— 'Assault by the Facts of Life', *Evening Standard*, London, 25 April 1974.

—— 'Editorial', *Studio International*, Vol. 191, No. 980, March/April 1976.

—— 'Art and Social Purpose', *Studio International*, Vol. 191, No. 980, March–April 1976.

—— 'Conrad Atkinson Interview', *Studio International*, Vol. 191, No. 980, March–April 1976.

—— 'Ulster: The Bitter Picture', *Evening Standard*, London, 6 May 1976.

—— ed., 'A Survey of Contemporary Art Magazines: Artscribe', *Studio International*, Art Magazines Issue, September/October 1976.

—— 'Richard Cork's 1976 Art Review', *Evening Standard*, 30 December 1976.

—— 'The Message in a Brick', *Evening Standard*, 30 December 1976.

—— 'Painting Goes Public: Street Murals in Britain', *New Society*, 25 August 1977.

—— and Fuller, Peter, Tagg, John, and Brighton, Andrew, *State of British Art*, Conference at ICA, London, 10–12 February 1978.
—— 'The Royal Oak Murals', *Art Monthly*, No. 15, April 1978.
—— 'Muralism', *Art Monthly*, No. 17, June 1978.
—— 'Art For Whom?, in *Art For Whom?*, exhibition catalogue, London: Serpentine Gallery, 1978.
—— ed., *Art For Society: Contemporary British Art with a Social or Political Purpose*, exhibition catalogue, London: Whitechapel Gallery, 10 May–18 June 1978.
—— 'Richard Cork's Reply to Ralf Rumney', *Art Monthly*, No. 18, July/August 1978.
—— 'External Walls', *Art Monthly*, No. 19, September 1978.
—— 'The Art We Deserve?', *Artscribe*, No. 20, November 1979.
—— *The Social Role of Art*, London: Gordon Fraser, 1979.
—— 'Collaboration without Compromise', *Studio International*, Vol. 195, No. 990, 1/1980.
Crayk, Fred, 'Muralism', *Art Monthly*, No. 17, June 1978.
Daley, Janet, 'The Art Critic's Art', *The Literary Review*, No. 9, 9–22 February 1980.
—— 'The Arts Council vs. The Visual Arts', *The Literary Review*, October 1981.
—— 'Response to Joanna Drew of the ACGB', *Art Monthly*, Number 57, June 1982.
Daley, Michael, 'Arts Council Awards', *Art Monthly*, No. 49, September 1981.
Dickson, Malcolm, 'Conrad Atkinson/Art Activist', *Edinburgh Review*, No. 76, 1987.
Dugger, John, 'Corkers', *Art Monthly*, No. 16, May 1978.
D'Ancona, Matthew, *The First Modernisers*, London: Centre for Policy Studies, 1999.
Elsom, John, 'Whose Side Are They On', *Art Monthly*, No. 42, 1980–1981.
Faure Walker, James, 'Towards a Definition of the Progressive in Painting', *Artscribe*, No. 3, Summer 1976.
—— 'James Faure Walker Replies', *Artscribe*, No. 6, April 1977.
—— 'Richard Cork interviewed by James Faure Walker', *Artscribe*, No. 7, May 1977.
—— 'The State of British Art: Session 4: Why Not Popular', *Studio International*, Vol. 194, No. 989, , 1978.
—— 'The Claims of Social Art and Other Perplexities', *Artscribe*, No. 12, June 1978.
—— 'In Defence of *Artscribe*', *Art Monthly*, No. 34, 1980.
Fer, Briony, 'The Modern in Fragments', in Frascina, Francis *et al.* eds, *Modernity and Modernism: French Painting in the Nineteenth Century*, New Haven: Yale University Press, 1993.
Ford, Simon, 'Doing P-Orridge', *Art Monthly*, No. 197, June 1996.
Foster, Hal, ed., *The Anti-Aesthetic: Essays on Postmodern Culture*, Port Townsend, USA: The Bay Press, 1983.
Fuller, Peter, 'Subversion and the Artists' Placement Group', *Art and Artists*, No. 6, December 1971.
—— 'Responds to "Painting Now"', *Artscribe*, No. 6, April 1977.
—— 'The Crisis in British Art', *Art Monthly*, No. 8, June 1977, and *Art Monthly*, No. 9, July/August 1977.
—— 'Crisis in British Art', unpublished paper given at the Arnolfini Gallery, Bristol, 25 November 1977.
—— 'The Tate, the State and the English Tradition', *Studio International*, Vol. 194, No. 988, 1/1978.
—— 'The Crisis in Professionalism', paper given at 'The State of British Art' exhibition, ICA, London, 10–12 February 1978, reprinted in *Studio International*, Vol. 194, No. 988, 1978.
—— 'An Interview with Carl Andre', *Art Monthly*, No. 16, May 1978, and No. 17, June 1978.
—— 'On Social Functionalism', *Artscribe*, No. 13, August 1978.
—— 'Social Functionalism', *Art Monthly*, No. 19, September 1978.
—— 'Problems of Art Criticism', in Brandon Taylor, ed., *Art and Criticism*, Winchester: Winchester School of Art Press, 1979.

—— *Beyond the Crisis in Art*, London: Writers & Readers Publishing Co-operative Ltd, October 1980.

—— *Art and Psychoanalysis*, London: Writers & Readers Publishing Co-operative Limited, 1980.

—— and Tagg, John, 'Richard Cork and the "New Road to Wigan Pier"', *Art Monthly*, No. 30, October 1979.

Gilmour, Pat, 'Trivialisation of Art by the Press', *Arts Review*, January 1977.

Gouldner, Alvin W., *The Future of the Intellectuals and the Rise of the New Class*, London: Macmillan, 1979.

Harris, Jonathan, 'Capitalist Crisis and Artistic Culture during the 1930s: New Deal Democratic Realism', in Wood, Paul, Frascina, Francis, Harris, Jonathan, and Harrison, Charles, *Modernism in Dispute: Art since the Forties*, London and New Haven: Yale University Press, 1993.

—— *New Art History: A Critical Introduction*, London: Routledge, 2001.

Harrison, Charles, and Orton, Fred, *A Provisional History of Art & Language*, Paris: Editions E. Fabre, 1982.

Hess, Hans, 'Art as Social Function', *Marxism Today*, Vol. 20, No. 8, August 1976.

Hewison, Robert, 'The Arts in Hard Times', in his *Too Much: Art and Society in the Sixties, 1960–75*, London: Methuen, 1986.

Hewitt, John, 'UK Reviews: Conrad Atkinson', *Studio International*, Nos. 189–90, July 1975.

Hobsbawm, Eric, 'The Forward March of Labour Halted?', *Marxism Today*, Vol. 22, No. 9, September 1978.

Jacques, M., and Mulhern, F., eds, *The Forward March of Labour Halted?*, London: Verso, 1978.

Jones, Ben, 'Editorial', *Artscribe*, No. 1, January–February 1976.

Jones, Glyn, 'Mur al, mural ist, mural ism', letter printed in *Art Monthly*, No. 18, July/August 1978.

Joseph, Keith, *Monetarism is Not Enough*, London: Centre for Policy Studies, 1976.

Kenna, C., *Murals in London*, London: Greenwich Mural Workshop, 1985.

—— and Lobb, S., *Mural Manual*, London: Greenwich Mural Workshop, 1985.

Kent, Sarah, 'Why Not Popular', paper given at the conference on 'The State of British Art', London: ICA, 10–12 February 1978; reprinted in *Studio International*, Vol. 194, No. 988, 2/1978.

Labour Party, *The Arts and the People: Labour's Policy Towards the Arts*, London: Labour Party, 1977.

Lawrence, Eileen, 'Greenberg's Scotland', *Art Monthly*, No. 15, 1978.

Levitas, R., ed., *The Ideology of the New Right*, Cambridge: Polity, 1986.

Lucie-Smith, Edward, 'Do We Need Toys Like This at the Tate', *Evening Standard*, 17 February 1976.

—— 'The Art of Bricklaying', *Art Review*, April 1996.

Maloon, Terence, 'Notes on Style in the Seventies: 1. Modes of Perceiving', *Artscribe*, No. 12, June 1978.

Miles, Malcolm, 'Community Murals in Britain', in his *Art for Public Places*, Winchester: Winchester School of Art Press, 1989.

Minihan, Janet, *The Nationalisation of Culture – The Development of State Subsidies to the Arts in Great Britain*, London: Hamish Hamilton, 1977.

Moore-Gilbert, Bart, *The Arts in the 1970s: Cultural Closure?*, London: Routledge, 1994.

Morphet, Richard, 'Carl Andre's Bricks', *Burlington Magazine*, Vol. 118, No. 884, November 1976.

Morris, Lynda, and Radford, R., *The Story of the Artists International Association*, Oxford: Museum of Modern Art, 1983.

Morris, Robert, 'Notes on Sculpture: Part II', *Artforum*, Vol. 5. No. 2, October 1966.

Nairne, Sandy, ed., *Conrad Atkinson: Picturing the System*, exhibition catalogue, London: Pluto Press/ICA, 25 November–23 December 1981.

Nairne, Tom, 'The British Historical Elite', *New Left Review*, Vol. 1, No. 23, January/ February 1964.

Overy, Paul, 'This is So, Isn't It?', *The Times*, 24 February 1976.

—— 'The "Specialness" of Art and Artists', *Art Monthly*, No. 23, 1979.

Packer, William, 'Carl Andre's Bricks', *Financial Times*, 3 May 1977.

—— 'Carl Andre's Bricks', *Financial Times*, 17 March 1978.

Perrong, Jeff, 'Carl Andre: Art vs. Talk', *Artforum*, Vol. xiv, No. 9, May 1976.

Philpot, Clive, 'An Insular View of British Art Mags', *Art Monthly*, No. 1, October 1976.

Pick, John, ed., *The State and the Arts*, London: City Arts, 1980.

Pye, Patrick, 'Social Ideologues', *Art Monthly*, No. 31, November 1979.

Radford, R., *Art for a Purpose: The Artists International Association, 1933–1953*, Winchester: Winchester School of Art Press, 1987.

Ramsden, Mel, 'Art & Language: Mike Baldwin and Mel Ramsden, Extracts from a Conversation with Sanda Miller', *Artscribe*, No. 47, July/August 1984.

Roberts, John, *Postmodernism, Politics and Art*, Manchester: Manchester University Press, 1990.

—— *The Impossible Document*, London: Camerawords, 1997.

Rochfort, Desmond, *Mexican Muralists: Orozco, Rivera, Siqueiros*, London: Laurence King, 1993.

Rodway, David, 'Muralism', *Art Monthly*, No. 16, 1978.

—— 'Social Art?', *Art Monthly*, No. 18, July/August 1978.

Rumney, Ralf, 'The End of Art is Not the End', *Art Monthly*, No. 17, 1978.

—— 'Cultural Revolution or Art For Social Democracy?', *Art Monthly*, No. 18, July/ August 1978.

Rycroft, Charles, 'Review: Freud and Timpanaro's *Freudian Slip*', *New Left Review*, No. 118, November–December 1979.

Sawtell, Jeff, 'The Royal Oak Murals, Harrow Road', *Artscribe*, No. 11, April 1978.

—— 'Comment', *Artery: A Cultural Journal for Left Unity*, No. 13, Spring 1978.

Searle, Adrian, 'State of the Art Debate at the ICA', *Artscribe*, No. 11, April 1978.

Shaw, Roy, 'The Arts Council's Deliberation (and Disgust) about the ICA Exhibition', letter to *The Guardian*, Saturday 23 October 1976.

—— *Elitism vs. Populism in the Arts*, London: City University, 1978.

—— *The Arts and the People*, London: Jonathan Cape, 1987.

Shrapnel, Norman, *The Seventies: Britain's Inward March*, London: Constable, 1980.

Simpson, Colin, 'Tate Drops a Costly Brick', *Sunday Times*, 15 February 1976.

Skidelsky, Robert, *The End of the Keynesian Era: Essays on the Disintegration of the Keynesian Political Economy*, London: Macmillan, 1977.

Stafford, Peter, 'Brick Sculpture Not the Original, Artist Confirms', *The Times*, 18 February 1976.

Steele, Jeffrey, 'Notes Towards Some Theses Against the New Kitsch', *Art Monthly*, No. 18, July/August 1978.

Sweet, David, 'Artists v The Rest: The New Philistines', *Artscribe*, No. 11, April 1978.

Tate Gallery, *Mural Painting in Great Britain 1919–1939: An Exhibition of Photographs*, London: Tate Gallery, 1939.

—— *The Tate Gallery Biennial Report and Illustrated Catalogue of Acquisitions 1972–4*, London: Tate Gallery, 1975.

—— *The Tate Gallery Biennial Report and Illustrated Catalogue of Acquisitions 1974–6*, London: Tate Gallery, 1976.

Taylor, Brandon, 'Textual Art', *Artscribe*, No. 1, January–February 1976.

—— 'The Avant-Garde and St. Martins', *Artscribe*, Education Issue, No. 5, September–October 1976.

—— 'Writing on the Surface: A Recent Tendency at *Artscribe*', *Art Monthly*, No. 33, February 1980.

Taylor, Roger, *Art: an Enemy of the People*, London: Routledge & Kegan Paul/ Harvester Press, 1978.

Taylor, Shaun, 'A New Way of Looking at Art', *Art Monthly*, No. 34, 1980.

Timpanaro, Sebastiano, 'The Freudian Slip', *New Left Review*, No. 91, May–June 1972.

Tisdall, Caroline, 'Art Controversies of the Seventies', in Compton, Susan, ed., *British Art in the 20th Century*, London: Royal Academy, and Munich: Prestel-Verlag, 1986.

Townsend, Peter, 'P-Orridge's Gruelling Days', *Art Monthly*, No. 2, November 1976.

—— 'Half Marx is Worse than None', *Art Monthly*, No. 17, June 1978.

—— 'Editor's Elongated Note [Art for Whom? Discussion]', *Art Monthly*, No. 18, July/August 1978.

Tweedy, Colin, 'From Maecenas to Manager', *A Celebration of 10 Years' Business Sponsorship of the* Arts, London: Association for Business Sponsorship of the Arts, 1986.

Walker, John A., *Art in the Age of Mass Media*, London: Pluto Press, 1983.

—— *Left Shift: Radical Art in 1970s Britain*, London and New York: I. B. Taurus, 2002.

Wallach, Allan, 'Conrad Atkinson: The Dilemma of Political Art', *Arts Magazine*, No. 54, December 1979.

Willats, Stephen, *Stephen Willats*, London: Chester Beatty Research Institute, 1964.

—— *Visual Automatics and Visual Transmitters*, Oxford: Museum of Modern Art, 1968.

—— *The Artist as an Instigator of Changes in Social Cognition and Behaviour*, London: Gallery House Press, 1973.

—— *Art and Social Function*, London: Latimer New Dimensions, 1976.

—— 'Questions about Ourselves', in *I Don't Want to Be like Anyone Else*, exhibition catalogue, London: Lisson Gallery, 1978.

Williams, Raymond, *Keywords: A Vocabulary of Culture and Society*, Glasgow: Fontana, 1976.

—— *Marxism and Literature*, Oxford: Oxford University Press, 1977.

—— 'Problems of Materialism', *New Left Review*, No. 109, May–June 1978.

—— *Problems in Materialism and Culture*, London: Verso, 1980.

Wolff, Janet, *Hermeneutic Philosophy and the Sociology of Art*, London: Routledge and Kegan Paul, 1975.

Wood, William, 'Still You Ask for More: Demand, Display and The New Art', in Newman, Michael, and Bird, Jon, *Rewriting Conceptual Art*, London: Reaktion Books, 1999.

Chapter 2.   Radical academicism

Allthorpe-Guyton, Marjorie, 'Terry Atkinson: Art For the Bunker', *Arts Review*, No. 13, September 1985.

Althusser, Louis, *Lenin and Philosophy, and Other Essays*, London: New Left Books (Verso), 1971.

Art & Language, *Art–Language*, Vol. 3, No. 1, September 1974.

—— *Art & Language 1966–1975*, exhibition catalogue, Oxford: Museum of Modern Art Oxford, September 1975.

—— *Art–Language*, Vol. 3, No. 4, October 1976 (*Fox 4*).

—— '"Artists" and "Philosophers"', *Art Monthly*, No. 26, May 1979.

Atkinson, Conrad, 'The State of the Art and the Art of the State', BLOCK, No. 10, 1985.

Atkinson, Terry, 'Looking Back – Going On', *Fox*, Nos 1 and 2, New York, 1975.

—— 'Notes: Communities, Artists and Modernism', *Studio International*, Vol. 191, No. 980, March/April 1976.

—— 'Materialism, By Jove!', *BLOCK*, No. 1, London, 1979.

—— 'Happysnap 3', *Art in America*, Vol. 72, September 1984.

—— 'The Art of the New Jerusalem', *Artscribe*, No. 53, 1985.

—— *Terry Atkinson: Mute 3 (Works After 1987)*, exhibition catalogue, Manchester: Cornerhouse, 1989.

—— 'Notes on Tourism 1 & 2, Re-Writing and Re-Reading "Tourism 1 & 2"', exhibition catalogue, Contemporary Art Gallery, Vancouver, 1990.

—— 'Phantoms of the Studio', *Oxford Art Journal*, Vol. 13, No. 1, 1990.

Barthes, Roland, *Mythologies*, trans. Annette Lavers, London: Paladin, 1973.

—— *S/Z*, trans. Richard Miller, London: Jonathan Cape, 1975.

—— 'Image – Music – Text' , trans. Stephen Heath, London: Fontana, 1977.

Berger, John, *Ways of Seeing*, London: BBC, 1972.

Best, Ron, 'Sketch for a Sociology of Art', *British Journal of Aesthetics*, Vol. 17, No. 1, Winter 1977.

Bird, Jon, 'The Politics of Representation', *BLOCK*, No. 2, 1980.

—— 'Politics and Resources of Expression: An Interview with Terry Atkinson', *Art Monthly*, June 1983.

—— 'On Newness, Art and History: Reviewing *BLOCK* 1979–1985', in A. L. Rees and F. Borzello, eds, *The New Art History*, London: Camden Press, 1986.

BLOCK, 'Editorial', *BLOCK*, No. 1, 1979.

—— *The BLOCK Reader in Visual Culture*, London: Routledge, 1996.

Bown, Matthew Cullerne, and Taylor, Brandon, eds, *Art of the Soviets: Painting, Sculpture and Architecture in a One Party State, 1917–1992*, Manchester: Manchester University Press, 1993.

Brett, Guy, 'Terry Atkinson', *City Limits*, 6–12 May 1983.

Brooks, Rosetta, 'Please, No Slogans', *Studio International*, Vol. 191, No. 980, March/April 1976.

—— 'Victor Burgin: Interview', *ZG*, No. 1, 1981.

Burgin, Victor, 'Situational Aesthetics', *Studio International*, No. 178, October 1969.

—— 'Photographic Practice and Art Theory', *Studio International*, Vol. 190, July/August 1975.

—— *Two Essays on Art Photography and Semiotics*, London: Robert Self, 1976.

—— 'Socialist Formalism', *Studio International*, Vol. 191, No. 980, March/April 1976.

—— *Studio International*, Vol. 191, No. 980, March/April 1976.

—— 'Art, Common-Sense and Photography', *Camerawork*, No. 3, 1976.

—— 'Why Photography? Edited transcript of a lecture given at Reading University, Fine Art Department, 4th November 1975', in *Arte Inglese Oggi 1970–76*, exhibition catalogue, Milan: Palazzo Reale, 1976.

—— *Victor Burgin: Work*, exhibition catalogue, Eindhoven, Netherlands, 1977.

—— 'Images of People', *Studio International*, No. 989, 2/1978.

—— 'Looking at Photographs', *Screen Education*, No. 24, Autumn 1977, reprinted in *Hayward Annual*, London: Hayward Gallery: 1979.

—— 'Photography, Fantasy, Function', *Screen*, Spring 1980.

—— *Thinking Photography: Essays in the Theory of Photographic Representation*, London: Macmillan, 1981.

—— 'Centrefold', *ZG*, Vol. 1, 1981.

—— 'Centre Pages', *BLOCK*, No. 8, 1983.

—— 'The Absence of Presence: Conceptualism and Post-modernisms', in Kettles Yard, *1965–72: When Attitudes Became Form*, exhibition catalogue, Cambridge: Kettles Yard Gallery, 1984.

—— *The End of Art Theory: Criticism and Postmodernity*, Atlantic Highlands, New Jersey: Humanities Press International, Inc., 1986.

Burn, Ian, 'Utopian Prayers and Infantile Marxism', *Artforum*, April 1975.

Cambridge Darkroom, *Jo Spence, Review of Work 1950–85*, Summer 1985.

Carter, Paul, 'Photography for the Community', *Camerawork*, No. 13, March 1979.

Clark, Timothy J., *The Absolute Bourgeois: Artists and Politics in France 1848–1851*,
    London: Thames & Hudson, 1973.
—— *Image of the People: Gustave Courbet and the 1848 Revolution*, London: Thames &
    Hudson, 1973.
—— 'The Conditions of Artistic Creation', *Times Literary Supplement*, 24 May 1974.
—— 'Preliminaries to a Possible Treatment of Olympia in 1865', *Screen*, Spring 1980.
—— *The Painting of Modern Life: Paris in the Art of Manet and his Followers*, New York:
    Alfred Knopf, 1985.
Cork, Richard, 'Anger and Barbed Wire [Terry Atkinson]', *Evening Standard*, 10 May
    1983.
Corris, Michael, 'The Irish Museum of Modern Art, Dublin; Terry Atkinson Exhibit',
    Artforum, Vol. 31, March 1993.
Davis, Tricia, and Goodall, Phil, 'Personally and Politically: Feminist Art Practice',
    Feminist Review, No. 1, 1979.
Debray, Regis, 'Image of the People', *New Left Review*, No. 94, November–December
    1975.
Dennett, T., Evans, D., Gohl, S. and Spence, J., eds, *Photography / Politics: One*,
    London: Photography Workshop, 1979.
Dormer, Peter, 'Using Photographs at the Sharp End', *Art Monthly*, No. 44, March
    1981.
Evans, Jessica, 'Victor Burgin's Polysemic Dreamcoat', in her *Art Has No History!:
    The Making and Unmaking of Modern Art*, London: Verso, 1994.
—— ed., *The Camerawork Essays: Context and Meaning in Photography*, London: Rivers
    Oram Press, 1997.
Feaver, William, 'The Sculptures of McLean, Atkinson's Paintings', *The Observer*, 8
    May 1983.
Foster, K., 'Critical History of Art, Or Transfiguration of Values?', *New Literary
    History*, Vol. 3, No. 3, Spring 1972.
Fruitmarket Gallery, ROBERT BARRY, VICTOR BURGIN, HAMISH FULTON, GILBERT AND GEORGE,
    HANS HAACKE, JOHN HILLIARD, KOSUTH/CHARLESWORTH, DAVID TREMLETT, LAWRENCE WEINER,
    exhibition catalogue, Edinburgh: Fruitmarket Gallery, 3–24 April 1976.
Fuchs, Rudi H., *Languages: An Exhibition of Artists Using Word and Image*, exhibition
    catalogue, Harlow: Arts Council of Great Britain, 1979.
Godfrey, Tony, 'Sex, Text, Politics: Interview with Victor Burgin', BLOCK, No. 7, 1982.
Hadjinicolaou, Nicos, *Art History and Class Struggle*, London: Pluto Press, 1977.
Hall, Stuart, 'The Social Eye of the Picture Post', *Working Papers in Cultural Studies*,
    Centre for Contemporary Cultural Studies, University of Birmingham, No. 2,
    Spring 1972.
—— 'Rethinking the Base-and-Superstructure Metaphor', in Bloomfield, J., ed.,
    Class, Hegemony and Party, London: Lawrence & Wishart, 1977.
—— *Culture, Media, Language Working Papers in Cultural Studies, 1972–79*, London:
    Hutchinson in association with the Centre for Contemporary Cultural Studies,
    University of Birmingham, 1980.
—— 'Stuart Hall: Left in Sight', *Camerawork*, Vol. 29, Winter 1983/84.
—— *The Hard Road to Renewal: Thatcherism and the Crisis of the Left*, London: Verso,
    1988.
—— and Jefferson, Tony, *Resistance through Rituals: Youth Subcultures in Post-war
    Britain*, London: Hutchinson in association with the Centre for Contemporary
    Cultural Studies, University of Birmingham, 1976.
—— and Jaques, Martin, eds, *The Politics of Thatcherism*, London: Lawrence and
    Wishart in association with *Marxism Today*, 1983.
—— and Whannel, Paddy, *The Popular Arts*, London: Hutchinson Educational, 1964.
Harding, Robert, 'Camerawork's Overall Project', *Art Monthly*, No. 45, April 1981.
Harrison, Charles, 'Art & Language: A Commentary on the Work of the Second

Decade, Black Propaganda 1977–78', Art & Language Information File, National Art Library, Victoria & Albert Museum, London, 1990.
—— *Essays on Art & Language*, Oxford: Basil Blackwell, 1991.
——, Baldwin, Michael, and Ramsden, Mel, 'Manet's *Olympia* and Contradiction', *BLOCK*, No. 5, 1981.
—— and Orton, Fred, *A Provisional History of Art & Language*, Paris: Editions E. Fabre, 1982.
Hebrige, Dick, 'In Poor Taste: Notes on Pop', *BLOCK*, No. 8, 1983.
Hertz, Richard, 'Philosophical Foundations of Modern Art', *The British Journal of Aesthetics*, Vol. 18, 1978.
Heywood, Ian, *Social Theories of Art: A Critique*, New York: Macmillan Press, 1997.
Hill, Paul, Kelly, Angela, and Tagg, John, *Three Perspectives on Photography: Recent British Photography*, exhibition catalogue, London: Arts Council of Great Britain, Hayward Gallery, South Bank Centre, 1 June–8 July 1979.
Jeffrey, Ian, 'Three Perspectives on Photography', *Artscribe*, No. 18, 1979.
Kemp, Martin, 'Seeing and Signs: E. H. Gombrich in Retrospect', *Art History*, Vol. 7, No. 2, 1984.
Kent, Sarah, 'Critical Images', *Flash Art International*, March 1985.
Kettles Yard, *1965–72: When Attitudes Became Form*, exhibition catalogue, Cambridge: Kettles Yard Gallery, 1984.
Laing, David, *The Marxist Theory of Art*, Sussex: Harvester Press, 1978.
Lippard, Lucy, *From the Center: Feminist Essays on Women's Art*, New York: Dutton, 1976.
—— 'Hot Potatoes: Art and Politics in 1980', *BLOCK*, No. 4, 1981.
Long, Bob, 'Camerawork and the Political Photographer', *Camerawork*, No. 16, November 1979.
Miller, Sanda, 'Art & Language: Mike Baldwin and Mel Ramsden, Extracts from a Conversation with Sanda Miller', *Artscribe*, No. 47, July / August 1984.
Morreau, Jacqueline, and Kent, Sarah, *Women's Images of Men*, London: Writers and Readers Publishing Cooperative Society, 1985.
Mulvey, Laura, 'Visual Pleasure and Narrative Cinema', *Screen*, Vol. 16, No. 3, 1975.
Nairne, Sandy, *State of the Art: Ideas and Images in the 1980s*, London: Chatto and Windus / Channel 4, 1987.
Nead, Lynda, *Missing Persons/Damaged Lives*, exhibition catalogue, Leeds: Leeds City Art Galleries, Jackson Wilson Limited, 1991.
Oliva, Achille Bonita, *The Italian Transavantgarde*, Milan: Giancarlo Politi, 1980.
Orton, Fred, and Pollock, Griselda, *Avant-Garde and Partisans Reviewed*, Manchester: Manchester University Press, 1996.
Parker, Rozsika, and Pollock, Griselda, eds, *Framing Feminism: Art and the Women's Movement 1970–1985*, London: Pandora, 1987.
Pollock, Griselda, 'Three Perspectives on Photography', *Screen Education*, 'Interventions', No. 31, Summer 1979.
—— 'Feminism, Femininity and Hayward Annual Exhibition 1978', *Feminist Review*, No. 2, 1979.
—— 'Vision, Voice and Power', *BLOCK*, No. 6, 1982.
Ramsden, Mel, 'Art & Language: Mike Baldwin and Mel Ramsden, Extracts from a Conversation with Sanda Miller', *Artscribe*, No. 47, July / August 1984.
Rees, A. L. and Borzello, F., eds, *The New Art History*, London: Camden Press, 1986.
Rickaby, Tony, 'Fascades', *BLOCK*, No. 1, 1979.
Roberts, John, 'Terry Atkinson: Facing Realities in Art', *Studio International*, August 1983.
—— 'Postcard from the Front', *Parachute*, August 1984.
—— 'Imaging History: The History Painting of Terry Atkinson', in his *Postmodernism, Politics and Art*, Manchester: University of Manchester Press, 1990.
—— *Selected Errors: Writings on Art and Politics 1981–90*, London: Pluto Press.

—— *The Impossible Document: Photography and Conceptual Art in Britain 1966–1976*, London: Camera*words*, 1997.

Smith, Peter, 'Victor Burgin', *Studio International*, Vol. 191, No. 980, March/April 1976.

—— 'Art & Language at Robert Self', *Art Monthly*, No. 13, December/January 1977–1978.

Spence, Jo, 'The Politics of Photography', *Camerawork*, No. 1, 1976.

—— 'What Did You Do in the War Mummy? Class and Gender in Images of Women', in Dennett, T., Evans, D., Gohl, S. and Spence, J., *Photography / Politics: One*, London: Photography Workshop, 1979.

—— 'What is a Political Photograph', *Camerawork*, No. 29, Winter 1983/84.

—— *Cultural Sniping: The Art of Transgression*, London: Routledge, 1995.

—— and the Photography Workshop, 'Beyond the Family Album, Private Images, Public Conventions', in *Three Perspectives on British Photography: Recent British Photography*, exhibition catalogue, London: Arts Council of Great Britain, Hayward Gallery, 1 June–8 July, 1979.

Steele, Jeffrey, 'Notes Towards Some Theses Against the New Kitsch', *Art Monthly*, No. 18, July/August 1978.

Stezaker, John, 'Notes: The Pursuit', *Studio International*, Vol. 191, No. 980, March/April 1976.

Tagg, John, 'Terry Atkinson: History – Drawing, Robert Self Gallery, London', *Art Monthly*, No. 4, February 1977.

—— 'Marxism and Art History', *Marxism Today*, June 1977.

—— 'Art History and Class Struggle by Nicos Hadjinicolaou', *Art Monthly*, No. 22, December/January 1978–1979.

—— 'Art History and Difference', *BLOCK*, No. 10, 1985.

—— 'Postmodernism and the Born Again Avant-Garde', *BLOCK*, No. 11, 1985/86.

—— 'Should Art Historians Know Their Place', *New Formations*, No. 1, 1987.

—— *Grounds of Dispute: Art History, Cultural Politics and the Discursive Field*, London: Macmillan, 1992.

Taylor, Brandon, 'Terry Atkinson', *Art Monthly*, No. 95, April 1986.

—— 'The New Art History?', *Art Monthly*, No. 100, September 1986.

Tynan, Eirlys, 'Victor Burgin's "Possession"', *Studio International*, No. 193, September/October 1976.

Waite, Lorna, 'Towards Disrupting the Silence: The Images of Jo Spence', *Variant*, No. 4, Winter/Spring 1988.

Wallace, Brian, ed., *Art After Modernism: Rethinking Representation*, New York: Godine, 1984.

Watney, Simon, 'Modernist Studies: The Class of '83', *Art History*, Vol. 7, No. 1, March 1984.

Wells, Liz, 'The Words Say More than the Pictures: Jo Spence's Work Reviewed', *Camerawork*, No. 32, Summer 1985.

Williams, Raymond, 'Marxism, Structuralism and Literary Analysis', *New Left Review*, No. 129, September/October 1981.

Williamson, Judith, *Decoding Advertisements*, London: Boyars, 1978.

Chapter 3.   Dynamic perversity

Adams, Hugh, 'COUM in Southampton: Lay Assumptions', *Studio International*, Vol. 192, No. 982, July/August 1976.

Allen, Richard, *Punk Rock*, London: New English Library, 1977.

Angry Brigade, The, *The Angry Brigade*, Glasgow: Bratach Dubh Documents No. 1, 1978.

Anon, 'The Man in the Drip-Dry Suit', *The Face*, No. 26, 1982.

Art & Language, 'Correspondence', *Style* (Vancouver), March 1982.

Beaumont, Mary Rose, *Duggie Fields: Paintings 1982–87*, exhibition catalogue, London: Albemarle Gallery, 28 October–20 November 1987.

Berland, J., 'Popular Music and the Post-Pop Avant-Garde', *Art and Text*, No. 6, 1982.

Biggs, Bryan, and Kennedy, Chris, *Cover Versions*, Liverpool: Bluecoat Gallery, 1981.

Billam, Michael, 'Duggie Fields at the Roundhouse', *Artscribe*, No. 24, August 1980.

Birch, Ian, ed., *The Book With No Name*, London: Omnibus, 1981.

BLOCK, *The BLOCK Reader in Visual Culture*, London: Routledge, 1996.

Bonnet, Alistair, 'The Situationist Legacy: It's All So Unfair!', *Variant*, No. 9, Glasgow, Autumn 1991.

Bray, Roger, 'After the Tate Bricks – On Show at ICA … Dirty Nappies!', *Evening Standard*, 14 October 1976.

Bromberg, Craig, *The Wicked Ways of Malcolm McLaren*, London: Omnibus Press, 1991.

Brooks, R., 'Art Machine', *ZG*, No. 3, 1981.

Calkin, Jessamy, 'Image Maker: Malcolm Garrett and Assorted iMaGes', *The Face*, No. 23, March 1982.

Chambers, Ian, *Urban Rhythms: Pop Music and Popular Culture*, Basingstoke: Macmillan, 1985.

Clark, T. J., 'Preliminaries to a Possible Treatment of Olympia in 1865', *Screen*, Spring 1980.

Cook, L., 'Popular Culture and Rock Music', *Screen*, No. 24, May/June 1983.

Coon, Caroline, 'Rock Revolution', *Melody Maker*, 28 July 1976.

—— 'Interview with Johnny Rotten', *Melody Maker*, 20 July 1977.

—— *1988: The New Wave Punk Rock Explosion*, London: Orbach & Chambers, 1977.

Cork, Richard, ed., 'Performance Art Issue', *Studio International*, Vol. 192, No. 982, July/August 1976.

—— 'Mary Kelly', *Evening Standard*, 14 October 1976.

—— ed., 'Women's Art Issue', *Studio International*, Vol. 193, No. 987, 1977.

COUM Transmissions, 'What Has COUM to Mean? Thee Theory Behind COUM', typewritten statement, undated, COUM Transmissions/Throbbing Gristle Archive, National Art Library, Victoria & Albert Museum, London, purchased in 1990.

—— 'Coum 34 Missions', *Flash Art* (Milan), December 1976.

Crawford, A., 'The Pagan Art of Malcolm McLaren', *Tension*, No. 2, September/October 1983.

Davis, D., 'Post-Performancism', *Artforum*, Vol. 20, No. 2, October 1981.

Debord, Guy, *Society of the Spectacle*, Detroit: Black & Red, 1970.

Dempsey, Michael, ed., *The Bible*, London: Big O Publishing, 1978.

Dennett, T., Evans, D., Gohl, S., and Spence, J., eds, *Photography / Politics: One*, London: Photography Workshop, September 1979.

Dworkin, Andrea, *Pornography: Men Possessing Women*, London: The Women's Press, 1981.

Faure Walker, James, 'The Claims of Social Art and Other Perplexities', *Artscribe*, No. 12, June 1978.

Firpo, Patrick, *Copy Art: The First Complete Guide to the Copy Machine*, New York: Richard Marek Publishing, 1978.

Ford, Simon, 'Fluxshoe Shuffle', *Art Monthly*, No. 176, May 1994.

—— 'Doing P-Orridge', *Art Monthly*, No. 197, June 1996.

Frith, Simon, 'Consuming Passion', *Melody Maker*, 10 March 1979.

—— 'Youth in the Eighties: A Dispossessed Generation', *Marxism Today*, November 1981.

—— *Art into Pop*, London: Methuen, 1987.

Fuller, Peter, 'The Arts Council Collection', *Art Monthly*, No. 39, September 1980.

Furlong, William, 'Four Interviews', in 'Genesis P-Orridge', exhibition catalogue, Hayward Annual, Arts Council of Great Britain, 1979.

Garrett, Malcolm, 'Graphics', *Creative Review*, February 1998.

Grey, Christopher, *Leaving the Twentieth Century*, London: Free Fall, 1974.

Habermas, Jurgen, *Legitimation Crisis*, trans. Thomas McCarthy, London: Heinemann, 1976.

Hahne, Ron, *Black Mask and Up Against the Wall Motherfucker: The Incomplete Works of Ron Hahne, Ben Morea and the Black Mask Group*, London: Sabotage Editions, 1993.

Harrison, Margaret, 'Notes on Feminist Art in Britain 1970–77', *Studio International*, March 1977.

Hebdige, Dick, *Subculture: The Meaning of Style*, London: Methuen, 1979.

—— 'In Poor Taste: Notes on Pop', BLOCK, No. 8, 1983.

Home, Stewart, *Plagiarism: Art as Commodity and Strategies for its Negation*, London: Aporia Press, 1988.

—— 'Aesthetics & Resistance: Totality Reconsidered', *Smile*, No. 11, London, 1989.

—— *The Assault on Culture: Utopian Currents from Lettrisme to Class War*, Stirling: AK Press, 1991.

—— *Neoism, Plagiarism & Praxis*, Edinburgh: AK Press, 1995.

—— *Cranked Up Really High: Genre Theory and Punk Rock*, Hove: Codex, 1996.

Homes, T., *Electronic and Experimental Music*, New York: Scribners, 1985.

Hornsey Students and Staff of Hornsey College of Art, *The Hornsey Affair*, Harmondsworth: Penguin Education Special, 1969.

Ikon Gallery, *Paintings and Drawings by Duggie Fields*, exhibition catalogue, Birmingham: IKON Gallery, 1 March–3 April 1980.

Israel, Frank, 'Earl's Court Elegance', *Progressive Architecture*, September 1977.

Jameson, Frederick, 'Postmodernism, or the Cultural Logic of Late Capitalism', *New Left Review*, No. 146, July–August 1984.

—— 'The Politics of Theory: Ideological Positions in the Postmodernist Debate', *New German Critique*, Vol. 11, No. 3, Fall 1984.

Joel, Mike Von, 'Duggie Fields: Dynamic Perversity and Other Such Stories', *Art Line International – Art News*, Vol. 3. No. 10, 1988.

Kendal, Ena, 'A Room of my Own: Duggie Fields', *The Observer Magazine*, 8 April 1984.

Kent, Sarah, 'Mary Kelly', *Time Out*, No. 342, 1976.

—— 'Prostitution Didn't Pay', *Time Out*, No. 353/4, January 1977.

Kidel, Mark, 'The Hip Capitalist Dream – A Profile of Richard Branson', *The New Review*, Vol. 4, No. 45, December 1977.

King Mob, *King Mob Echo*, Nos 1–6, London, 1968–1970.

Kitsis, K., 'Icons of Glamour: Echoes of Death', *ZG*, No. 8, 1983.

Krauss, Rosalind, 'Sculpture in the Expanded Field', *October*, No. 8, Spring 1979.

—— *The Originality of the Avant-Garde and Other Modernist Myths*, Cambridge, Mass.: MIT Press, 1985.

Kuspit, Donald Burton, *The Cult of the Avant-Garde Artist*, Cambridge: Cambridge University Press, 1993.

Laing, Dave, 'Interpreting Punk Rock', *Marxism Today*, Vol. 22, No. 4, April 1978.

—— 'The Music Industry in Crisis', *Marxism Today*, July 1981.

—— *One Chord Wonders: Power and Meaning in Punk Rock*, England: Open University Press, 1985.

Livingstone, Marco, 'Eat Dirt Art History: Neo-Pop in the 1980s', *Pop Art: A Continuing History*, London: Thames & Hudson, 1990.

Lupton, Catherine, 'Circuit-breaking Desires: Critiquing the Work of Mary Kelly', in Roberts, John, ed., *Art Has No History! The Making and Unmaking of Modern Art*, London: Verso, 1994.

Maloon, Terence, 'Notes on Style in the Seventies: 1. Modes of Perceiving', *Artscribe*, No. 12, June 1978.

—— 'Mary Kelly interviewed by Terence Maloon', *Artscribe*, No. 13, August 1978.

Marcuse, Herbert, *An Essay on Liberation*, Boston: Beacon, 1969.

—— *Counterrevolution and Revolution*, Boston: Beacon, 1972.

McDermott, Catherine, *Street Style: British Design in the 80s*, London: Design Council, 1987.

Melly, George, *Revolt into Style: The Pop Arts in Britain*, London: Allen Lane, 1970.

Metzger, Gustav, 'Art Strike 1977–1980', communiqué issued in 1974.

Miller, Jim, 'Some Future', *New Republic*, No. 180, 24 March 1979.

Morgan, Stuart, 'What the Papers Say', *Artscribe*, No. 18, July 1979.

Morris, R., 'After the Tate Gallery's Famous Bricks, the New Art Is – Dirty Nappies', *Daily Mail*, 15 October 1976.

Naylor, Colin, 'Couming Along', *Art and Artists*, Vol. 10, 1975.

Needs, K., 'Throbbing Gristle', *ZigZag*, No. 82, March/April 1978.

Nelson, Elizabeth, *The British Counter Culture 1966–73; A Study of the Underground Press*, London: Macmillan, 1989.

Nuttall, Jeff, *Bomb Culture*, London: Paladin, 1970.

Nyman, Michael, 'Music in Fine Art Departments', *Studio International*, Vol. 191, No. 981, May/June 1976.

O'Brien, G., 'Mozart, Puccini, Bizet and McLaren', *Artforum*, December 1984.

Owens, Craig, 'The Allegorical Impulse: Towards a Theory of Postmodernism', *October*, Nos 12 and 13, Spring–Summer 1980.

Parsons, Tony, 'But Mutilation is so Pass/e', *New Musical Express*, 30 October 1976.

Pilkington, Philip, and Rusherson, David, 'Don Judd's Dictum and its Emptiness', *Analytical Art*, No. 1, July 1971.

P-Orridge, Genesis, *G.P.O. versus. G.P-O: A Chronicle of Mail Art on Trial Coumpiled by Genesis P-Orridge*, Geneva: Ecart, 1976.

—— 'A Letter', *Vile*, Vol. 3, No. 2, Summer 1977.

—— 'Intermedia Exile', interview with Malcolm Dickson, *Variant*, 1993.

—— and Christopherson, Peter, 'Annihilating Reality', *Studio International*, Vol. 192, No. 982, July/August 1976.

—— and Naylor, Colin, *Guide to Contemporary Artists*, London: St. Martin's Press, 1977.

Ramball, Paul, 'How the West was Won', *The Face*, No. 38, June 1983.

Rhodes, Zandra, 'Zandra Rhodes Talks to her Good Friend Duggie Fields', *Viz: Visual Arts, Fashion, Photography*, No. 6, 1979.

Rimmer, David, *Like Punk Never Happened: Culture Club and the New Pop*, London: Faber, 1985.

Roberts, John, 'Performance Art at the Hayward', *Artscribe*, No. 19, September 1979.

—— 'Post-Modernism: Arrivals and Departures', *Art Monthly*, No. 55, April 1982.

Robertson, George, 'The Situationist International: Its Penetration into British Culture', BLOCK, Vol. 14, 1988.

Robertson, Sandy, 'New Musick: TG', *Sounds*, 26 November 1977.

—— 'Art Throbs', *Sounds*, 6 January 1979.

Rumney, Ralf, 'The End of Art is Not the End', *Art Monthly*, No. 17, 1978.

Salewicz, C., 'Malcolm McLaren and Bow-Wow-Wow', *The Face*, No. 13, May 1981.

Savage, Jon, 'T.G.', *Search and Destroy*, No. 6, April 1978.

—— 'Industrial Paranoia ... T.G.', *Sounds*, 3 June 1978.

—— *Throbbing Gristle*, London: Fetish, 1981.

—— 'Guerilla Graphics: The Tactics of Agit Prop Art', *The Face*, October 1983.

—— *England's Dreaming: Sex Pistols and Punk Rock*, London: Faber & Faber, 1991.

—— *Time Travel: From the Sex Pistols to Nirvana, Pop Media and Sexuality, 1977–96*, London: Chatto & Windus, 1996.

—— and Reid, Jamie, *Up They Rise: The Incomplete Works of Jamie Reid*, London: Faber & Faber, 1987.

Scott, G. J., 'Genesis at LAICA', *Vile*, 1977.

Smith, Peter, 'Art into Capital', *Oxford Art Journal*, Vol. 12, No. 1, 1989.
Taylor, Paul, *Impresario: Malcolm McLaren and the British New Wave*, London: MIT Press, 1988.
Taylor, Steve, 'Strange Tales', *Smash Hits*, 22 January 1981.
—— 'Rising Strange', *The Face*, No. 14, June 1981.
Thackera, J., ed., *Design After Modernism*, London: Thames & Hudson, 1988.
Tickell, Paul, 'John Cooper Clarke', *The Face*, No. 23, March 1982.
Tickner, Lisa, 'The Body Politic: Female Sexuality and Women Artists Since 1970', *Art History*, Vol. 1, No. 2, June 1978.
Tisdall, Caroline, 'Mary Kelly', *The Guardian*, 16 October 1976.
—— 'Arts Guardian', *The Guardian*, 22 October 1976.
Toppin, Elizabeth, 'Home is Where the Art Is', *Residence*, No. 17, October 1988.
Truman, James, 'Adam Ant and the Selling of Blitz Culture', *The Face*, No. 15, July 1981.
Tutti, Cosey Fanni, 'Artist's Statement', typewritten information sheet, May 1975, COUM Transmissions/Throbbing Gristle Archive, National Art Library, Victoria & Albert Museum, London, purchased in 1990.
—— 'Artists Thoughts on the 70s in Words and Pictures', *Studio International*, Vol. 195, No. 911/12, 1981.
—— Transcript of lecture and debate, Leeds: Leeds Polytechnic, 1982.
Upshaw, L., 'Old Punk and New Wave', *New Art Examiner*, Vol. 8, No. 3, December 1980.
Vaneigem, Raoul, 'Desolation Row', *King Mob Echo*, No. 1, April 1968.
—— *The Revolution of Everyday Life*, London: Practical Paradise, 1975.
Vermorel, Fred and Judy, eds, *The Sex Pistols*, London: Tandem, 1978.
—— *The Sex Pistols: The Inside Story*, revised edition, London: Allen/Star, 1981.
Walker, John A., *Cross-overs: Art into Pop/Pop into Art*, London: Methuen, 1978.
—— 'Pop Music: The Art School Connection', *Theatrephile*, Vol. 1, No. 2, March 1984.
—— 'McLaren and the Sources of Punk', *Variant*, Summer 1985.
Watson, E., 'Portrait of the Artist as a Saleable Commodity', *Camerawork*, No. 12, January 1979.
Welch, Chuck, *Networking Currents: Contemporary Mail Art Subjects & Issues*, Boston: Sandbar Willow Press, 1985.
Wise, Dave, and Wise, Stuart, *Punk, Reggae: A Critique*, pamphlet published in Glasgow, c. 1978, reprinted as 'The End of Music: The Revolution of Everyday Alienation', in Stewart Home, ed., *What is Situationism? A Reader*, Edinburgh: AK Press, 1996.
Wozencroft, John, *The Graphic Language of Neville Brody*, London: Thames & Hudson, 1988.
York, Peter, *Style Wars*, London: Sidgewick & Jackson, 1980.
—— *Modern Times*, London: Heinemann, 1984.
Zayadi, Ferry, 'Interview with Duggie Fields', *Viz: Visual Arts, Fashion, Photography*, No. 4, April 1979.

Chapter 4.   The shock of the old

Ackerman, D. and M., 'Dear Kitaj and David: The Quality of the Creation is More Important than the Content', *Arts Review*, Vol. 29, 29 April 1977.
Adams, Hugh, 'Anonymous was a Woman: The Work of Margaret Harrison', *Art Monthly*, No. 44, March 1981.
Atkinson, Conrad, 'The Countryside of the Poor', *Art Monthly*, No. 37, 1980.
Atkinson, Terry, 'Notes: Communities, Artists, Modernism', *Studio International*, Vol. 191, No. 980, March/April 1976.

Auerbach, Frank, 'A Conversation with Catherine Lampert', in Wright, William, and
    Bond, Anthony, *The British Show*, Sydney: Beaver Press, Art Gallery of New South
    Wales, 1984.
Aulich, Jim, 'The Difficulty of Living in an Age of Cultural Decline and Spiritual
    Corruption: R. B. Kitaj 1965–1970', *The Oxford Art Journal*, Vol. 10, No. 2, 1987.
Baranik, Rudolf, 'A Socialist Formalist View on Berger and Fuller', *Art Monthly*, No.
    60, October 1982.
Biggs, I., 'Recent Paintings: Use and Abuse of Myth', *Artscribe*, No. 38, December
    1982.
Boshier, Derek, *Lives: An Exhibition of Artists Whose Work is Based on Other Peoples'
    Lives, Selected by Derek Boshier*, exhibition catalogue, London: Arts Council of Great
    Britain, 1979.
Brett, Guy, 'What is the Tradition', *Art Monthly*, No. 38, 1980.
Brighton, Andrew, 'Towards Another Picture', unpublished PhD thesis, Royal
    College of Art, 1976.
—— 'Books: The New Humanism and The Man Who Loves Giants', *Studio
    International*, July/August 1976, Performance Issue.
—— 'Very British Triviality', *Art Monthly*, No. 16, May 1978.
—— 'Nicos Hadjinicolaou's Art History and Class Struggle', *British Journal of
    Aesthetics* (Oxford University Press), Vol. 19, 1979.
—— 'Large Interior W11', *Art Monthly*, No. 72, December/January 1983/84.
—— 'Commercial Galleries, The Art World and Business Sponsorship', in *The
    Economic Situation of the Visual Artist*, London: Gulbenkian Foundation, 1985.
—— 'Conversations with R. B. Kitaj', *Art in America*, Vol. 74, June 1986.
—— 'Frank Auerbach', *Art Monthly*, No. 141, November 1990.
—— and Morris, Lynda, *Towards Another Picture: an Anthology of Artists by Artists
    Working in Britain 1945–1977*, Nottingham: Midland Group, 1977.
—— and Pearson, Nicholas M., 'The Specialness of Art and Artists', *Art Monthly*, No.
    21, November 1978.
Brook, Donald, 'Criticism About What? Art and Criticism: A Symposium Held at
    Winchester School of Art 1976', *Art Monthly*, No. 39, September 1980.
—— 'Art and Socialism (Again)', *Art Monthly*, No. 45, April 1981.
—— 'Peter Fuller's Aesthetics After Modernism: The 1982 Power Lecture in
    Contemporary Art', *Art Monthly*, No. 57, June 1982.
Bryson, Norman, Holly, Michael, and Moxey, Keith, *Visual Theory: Painting and
    Interpretation*, Cambridge: Polity Press, 1991.
Buchloh, Benjamin, 'Figures of Authority, Ciphers of Repressions: Notes on the
    Return of Representation in European Painting', *October*, Spring 1981.
Cieszkowski, Krzysztof Z., 'Hockney's *Artist's Eye*: Government Art Collection', *Art
    Monthly*, No. 49, September 1981.
Clark, William, 'The New Spirit in Art Marketing', *Edinburgh Review*, No. 73, 1986.
Cork, Richard, 'Misplaced Swipe', *Art Monthly*, No. 13, December/January 1977–
    1978.
—— 'Collaboration without Compromise', *Studio International* (Art Galleries and
    Alternative Spaces), Vol. 195, No. 990, 1/1980.
Corrigan, Philip, 'Response to Peter Fuller', *Art Monthly*, No. 40, October 1980.
Cox, Neil, 'Frank Auerbach', *The British Journal of Aesthetics*, Vol. 31, October 1991.
Crowther, Paul, *Critical Aesthetics and Postmodernism*, Oxford: Clarendon Press, 1993.
Daley, Janet, 'R. B. Kitaj', *Arts Review*, Vol. 29, No. 9, 29 April 1977.
—— 'New Figuration: Part III', *Art Review*, Vol. 30, No. 11, 9 June 1978.
—— 'The Arts Council vs. The Visual Arts', *The Literary Review*, October 1981.
Daley, Michael, 'A Post-Modernist Programme', *Art Monthly*, No. 23, 1979.
—— 'Arts Council Awards', *Art Monthly*, No. 49, September 1981.
Davis, Tricia, and Hall, Catherine, 'The Forward Face of Feminism', *Marxism Today*,
    Vol. 124, No. 10, October 1980.

Deepwell, Katy, 'In Defence of the Indefensible: Feminism, Painting and Postmodernism', *Feminist Art News*, No. 2, 1987.

Del Renzio, Tony, 'Style, Technique and Iconography', *Art and Artists*, 11 July 1976.

—— 'Instant Critic: Peter Fuller in 1980', BLOCK, No. 4, 1981.

Dunning, William V., 'Post-modernism and the Construct of the Divisible Self', *The British Journal of Aesthetics*, Vol. 33, April 1993.

Eagleton, Terry, 'Aesthetics and Politics', *New Left Review*, No. 107, 1978.

—— *The Ideology of the Aesthetic*, Oxford: Basil Blackwell, 1990.

Eastmond, Elizabeth, 'Alexis Hunter Talks to Elizabeth Eastmond', *Art New Zealand*, No. 54, 1990.

Einzig, Barbara, ed., *Thinking About Art: Conversations with Susan Hiller*, Manchester: Manchester University Press, 1996.

Faure Walker, James, 'R. B. Kitaj Interviewed by James Faure Walker', *Artscribe*, No. 5, February 1977.

Feaver, William, 'Inside Freud's Minds', *Art News*, Vol. 92, September 1993.

—— 'Frank Auerbach', *Art News*, Vol. 94, December 1995.

Feist, Andrew, and Hutcheston, Robert, eds, 'Central Government', *Cultural Trends in the Eighties*, London: Policy Studies Institute, 1990.

Ford, Michael, 'Susan Hiller', *Arts Review*, Vol. 32, No. 4, February 1980.

Foster, Hal, 'Postmodernism: A Preface', *The Anti-Aesthetic: Essays on Postmodern Culture*, Port Townsend, Washington, USA: The Bay Press, 1983.

—— 'The Expressive Fallacy', *Art in America*, January 1983.

Freud, Lucien, 'Some Thoughts on Painting', *Encounter*, Vol. 3, No. 1, July 1954.

Fried, Michael, 'Art and Objecthood', *Artforum*, Summer 1967.

—— *Absorption and Theatricality: Painting and the Beholder in the Age of Diderot*, Berkeley: University of California Press, 1980.

Fuller, Peter, 'An Interview with David Hockney', *Art Monthly*, Nos 12 and 13, November–December/January 1977/78.

—— 'Leon Kossoff', *Art Monthly*, No. 26, May 1979.

—— 'Problems of Art Criticism', in Taylor, Brandon, ed., *Art and Criticism: A Symposium Held at Winchester School of Art 1976*, Winchester: Winchester School of Art Press, 1979.

—— 'Towards a Theory of Expression', *Art Monthly*, No. 36, May 1980.

—— *Art and Psychoanalysis*, London: Writers & Readers Publishing Cooperative Ltd, June 1980.

—— *Seeing Berger: A Revaluation*, London: Writers & Readers Publishing Cooperative Ltd, 1980.

—— 'David Hockney by Marco Livingstone', *Art Monthly*, No. 49, September 1981.

—— 'Art and Biology', *New Left Review*, No. 132, March–April 1982.

—— *Aesthetics after Modernism*, London: Writers & Readers Publishing Cooperative Ltd, 1983.

—— *The Naked Artists*, London: Writers & Readers Publishing Cooperative Ltd, 1983.

—— *Images of God: The Consolation of Lost Illusions*, London: Hogarth Press, 1985.

—— and Eagleton, Terry, 'The Question of Value: A Discussion', *New Left Review*, No. 142, November–December 1983.

Gablik, Suzi, 'The Human Clay: Reviewed by Suzi Gablik', *Studio International*, Vol. 193, No. 985, January 1977.

—— 'Nude Review', *The Sunday Times*, 20 February 1977.

Geelhaar, Christian, 'Looking at Pictures with David Hockney', *Pantheon*, Vol. 36, July/September 1978.

Giles, Tam, 'Women's Images of Men', *Art Monthly*, No. 42, December/January 1980/81.

Godfrey, Tony, *The New Image: Painting in the 1980s*, Oxford: Phaidon, 1986.

Gouk, Alan, 'Peter Fuller, Art Critic?', *Artscribe*, No. 30, August 1981.

Gowling, Lawrence, *Lucien Freud*, London: Thames & Hudson, 1982.

Hall, Stuart, and Jaques, Martin, eds, *The Politics of Thatcherism*, London: Lawrence and Wishart, 1983.

Harrison, Andrew, 'Aesthetics after Modernism', *The British Journal of Aesthetics*, Vol. 25, Autumn 1985.

Hill, Andrea, 'The Hayward Annual', *Artscribe*, No. 19, September 1979.

Hockney, David,*David Hockney: Travels with Pen, Pencil and Ink*, London: Petersburg Press, 1976.

—— *David Hockney by David Hockney*, ed. Stangos, Nikos, London: Thames & Hudson, 1977.

—— 'The State of British Art: Session 2, Who Needs Training?', *Studio International*, Vol. 194, No. 2, 1978.

Hoyland, John, 'An Introduction to the Exhibition', *Hayward Annual 1980*, exhibition catalogue, London: Arts Council of Great Britain, 1980.

Hughes, Robert, 'The Last History Painter: Expatriate R. B. Kitaj Brings Home the Bacon', *Time*, Vol. 113, No. 17, 23 April 1979.

—— *Lucien Freud*, London: Thames & Hudson, 1988.

—— *Frank Auerbach*, London: Thames & Hudson, 1990.

Hyman, Timothy, 'Narrative Art at Arnolfini', *Art Monthly*, No. 19, September 1978.

—— 'Painting 1979: A Crisis of Function?', *London Magazine*, Vol. 19, April/May 1979.

—— 'Narrative Painting: A Second Generation', *Artscribe*, No. 19, September 1979.

—— *Narrative Paintings: Figurative Art of Two Generations Selected by Timothy Hyman*, exhibition catalogue, Bristol: Arnolfini Gallery, September–October 1979.

—— 'Narrative Painting 1', *Art Monthly*, No. 30, October 1979.

—— 'Kitaj: A Prodigal Returning', *Artscribe*, October 1980.

Jencks, Charles, *What is Post-modernism?*, Hanover: Academy Editions, 1989.

Joachimides, Christos, 'A New Spirit in Painting', in *A New Spirit in Painting*, exhibition catalogue, London: Royal Academy of Arts, 1981.

—— 'How They Got it Together', *Art Monthly*, No. 43, February 1981.

Kelly, Mary, 'The Crisis in Professionalism', *Studio International*, Vol. 194, No. 989, 2/ 1978.

Kent, Sarah, 'Feminism and Decadence', *Artscribe*, No. 47, July/August 1984.

—— and Morreau, Jacqueline, eds, *Women's Images of Men*, London: Writers and Readers Publishing Cooperative Society, 1985.

Kitaj, R. B. 'On Associating Texts with Paintings', *Cambridge Opinion*, January 1964.

—— *The Human Clay*, exhibition catalogue, London: Hayward Gallery, Arts Council, 1976.

—— 'Introduction', *The Artist's Eye: An Exhibition Selected by R. B. Kitaj*, London: National Gallery, 1980.

—— 'Hockney', *Vogue* (UK), Vol. 144, No. 8, August 1988.

—— and Hockney, David, 'R. B. Kitaj and David Hockney Discuss the Case for a Return to the Figurative', *New Review*, Vol. 3, No. 34/35, January/February 1977.

——, Hamilton, Richard, and Hockney, David, 'Censorship of Erotic Art', *The Sunday Times*, 20 February 1977.

Kramer, Hilton, *The Revenge of the Philistines: Art and Culture 1972–1984*, New York: Free Press, 1985.

—— ed., *The New Criterion Reader: The First Five Years*, New York: Free Press, 1988.

—— 'In Defense of Painting', *Modern Painters: A Quarterly Journal of the Fine Arts*, Vol. 6, No. 1, Spring 1993.

—— 'The Importance of Peter Fuller', *Modern Painters: A Quarterly Journal of the Fine Arts*, Vol. 6, No. 2, Summer 1993.

Kuspit, Donald Burton, *The New Subjectivism: Art in the 1980s*, London: UMI Research Press, 1988.

—— 'The Other Freud', *Art & Antiques*, Vol. 16, January 1994.

Lee, Rosa, 'Resisting Amnesia: Feminism, Painting and Postmodernism', *Feminist Review*, No. 26, 1987.

Livingstone, Marco, 'Iconology as a Theme in the Early Work of R. B. Kitaj', *Burlington Magazine*, Vol. 122, No. 918, July 1980.

—— *R. B. Kitaj*, Oxford: Phaidon, 1985.

MacMillan, Duncan, 'Exhibitions "British Art Now" in New York', *Art Monthly*, No. 34, 1980.

Marcuse, Herbert, *The Aesthetic Dimension: Towards a Critique of Marxist Aesthetics*, Boston: Beacon Press, 1978.

Marle, Judy, 'The Hayward Annual', *Artscribe*, No. 14, October 1978.

Marx, Karl, *Grundrisse*, trans. M. Nicolaus, Harmondsworth: Penguin, 1976.

Maurice, Cairne, 'Women's Images of Men', *Arts Review*, 24 October 1980, Vol. 32, No. 21.

McEwen, John, 'Everybody on "Hockney on Hockney"', *Art Monthly*, No. 3, December/January 1976–1977.

—— 'Half-Marx is Worse than None', *Art Monthly*, No. 17, 1978.

—— 'Towards Another Picture', *The Spectator*, December 1978.

—— 'Southbank Summer: The Hayward Annual', *Art Monthly*, No. 29, September 1979.

—— 'How They Got it Together: A New Spirit in Painting', *Art Monthly*, No. 43, February 1981.

Morley, Catherine, 'Against A Theory of Expression', *Art Monthly*, No. 44, March 1981.

Morphet, Richard, *The Hard-Won Image: Traditional Method and Subject in Recent British Art*, exhibition catalogue, London: The Tate Gallery, 4 July–9 September 1984.

Morris, Linda, 'The Human Clay', *The Listener*, 19 August 1976.

—— 'Popular Front', *The Listener*, 26 May 1977.

Nairne, Sandy, *State of the Art: Ideas and Images in the 1980s*, London: Chatto and Windus, 1988.

Newman, Michael, 'Eight Women Artists: 1980 Acme Gallery', *Arts Review*, Vol. 32, No. 22, 7 November 1980.

Nicolson, Benedict, 'Editorial: T1534, Untitled 1966', *The Burlington Magazine*, Vol. 118, No. 877, April 1976.

October, Cambridge, Mass., 'Rendering the Real: An 8 Article Special', No. 58, Fall 1991.

Oliva, Achille Bonita, *The Italian Transavantgarde*, Milan: Giancarlo Politi, 1980.

O'Shea, Kevin, 'Book Review: Towards Another Picture', *British Journal of Aesthetics*, Vol. 19, 1979.

Overy, Paul, 'Paintings of Kitaj', in 'Letters to the Editor', *The Times*, 10 September 1975.

—— 'How Good is Contemporary Art?', *The Times*, 17 August 1976.

—— 'Filibuster for the Figurative', *The Times*, 10 May 1977.

—— 'The Specialness of Art and Artists', *Art Monthly*, No. 23, February 1979.

Owens, Craig, 'Honour, Power and the Love of Women', *Art in America*, No. 71, January 1983.

Parker, Rozsika, 'Feminist Art Practices in Women's Images of Men, About Time and Issue', *Art Monthly*, No. 43, February 1981.

Peppiatt, Michael, 'Could There Be a School of London?', *Art International*, No. 1, Autumn 1987.

—— 'Frank H. Auerbach: Going against the Grain', *Art International*, No. 1, Autumn 1987.

Petzal, Monica, 'Questions about Women's Art Conference', *Art Monthly*, No. 42, December/January 1980/81.

Plagens, Peter, 'European Painting in LA: A Grab Bag of Well-worn Issues', *Artforum*, Vol. 15, No. 5, January 1976.

Podro, Michael, 'Some Notes on Ron Kitaj', *Art International*, Vol. 22, No. 10, March 1979.

—— 'From Springer to Warburg: Warburg and Botticelli's Mythologies', in his *The Critical Historians of Art*, New Haven: Yale University Press, 1982.

Pollock, Griselda, 'What's Wrong with Images of Women?', *Screen Education*, No. 24, Autumn 1977.

—— 'Femininity, Feminism and the Hayward Annual', *Feminist Review*, No. 2, 1979.

Roberts, John, 'The Naked and the Dead', *Art Monthly*, No. 79, September 1984.

—— *Postmodernism, Politics and Art*, Manchester: Manchester University Press, 1990.

Rothon, Tony, 'The Hayward Annual', *Art Monthly*, No. 8, June 1977.

Rycroft, Charles, 'Freud and Timpanaro's Freudian Slip', *New Left Review*, No. 118, November–December 1979.

Schwartz, Barry, *The New Humanism: Art in a Time of Change*, London: David & Charles, 1974.

Scruton, Roger, *The Meaning of Conservatism*, London: Macmillan/Penguin Books, 1980.

—— *The Aesthetic Understanding*, Manchester: Carcanet, 1983.

—— *The Politics of Culture*, Manchester: Carcanet, 1983.

—— *The Philosopher on Dover Beach*, Manchester: Carcanet, 1990.

Searle, Adrian, 'Towards Another Picture', *Artscribe*, No. 10, January 1978.

—— 'The State of the Art Debate at the ICA', *Artscribe*, No. 11, April 1978.

—— 'Thermodynamics: Thoughts on Four Artists at the Hayward', *Artscribe*, No. 13, August 1978.

Shepherd, David, *The Man Who Loves Giants*, London: David & Charles, 1975.

Shone, Richard, 'Leon Kossoff', *The Burlington Magazine*, Vol. 130, November 1988.

Sless, R. D., 'Lives', *Arts Review*, Vol. 32, No. 1, 18 January 1980.

Spalding, Frances, 'Hayward Annual', *Arts Review*, Vol. 32, No. 18, 12 September 1980.

—— *British Art since 1900*, London: Thames & Hudson, 1986.

Spender, Stephen, *R. B. Kitaj: Pastels and Drawings*, exhibition catalogue, London: Marlborough Fine Art Catalogue, 1980.

Steele, Jeffrey, 'Notes Towards Some Theses Against the New Kitsch', *Art Monthly*, No. 18, 1978.

Steyn, Juliet, 'R. B. Kitaj', *Art History*, Vol. 18, March 1995.

—— and Cherry, Deborah, 'Putting the Hayward Annual Together', *Art Monthly*, No. 19, September 1978.

Tickner, Lisa, 'Attitudes to Women Artists', *Art Monthly*, No. 23, February 1979.

Timpanaro, Sebastiano, 'The Freudian Slip', *New Left Review*, No. 91, May–June 1972.

Tuten, F., 'Neither Fool, nor Naive, nor Poseur-saint: Fragments on R. B. Kitaj', *Artforum*, Vol. 20, No. 5, January 1982.

Usherwood, Nicholas, *The Brotherhood of Ruralists*, London: Lund Humphries, 1981.

Waddington, Leslie, 'Towards Another Picture: An Anthology of Artist's Writings, Midland Group, Nottingham, 1977', *Art Monthly*, No. 15, 1978.

Williams, Raymond, 'Problems of Materialism', *New Left Review*, No. 109, May–June 1978.

Wilsmore, S. J., 'The New Attack on Humanism in the Arts', *British Journal of Aesthetics*, Vol. 27, Autumn 1987.

Withers, Jane, 'Therese Outlon: British Art's Hottest New Star', *The Face*, No. 59, March 1985.

Wright, William, and Bond, Anthony, *The British Show*, Sydney: Beaver Press, Art Gallery of New South Wales, 1984.

Chapter 5.   Who am I? Where am I going? How much will it cost? Will I need any luggage?

Althorpe-Guyton, Marjorie, 'Tony Cragg', *Flash Art*, No. 134, May 1987.

Atkinson, Conrad, *The State of the Art and the Art of the State: Power Lecture Given to the Power Institute, University of Sydney, Australia, October 1983*, London: Working Press, 1991.

Banks, Glyn, 'Any Old Irony', *Art Monthly*, No. 72, December/January 1983/84.

Baudrillard, Jean, *Simulations*, New York: Semiotext(e), 1983.

Biggs, Lewis, Blaszczyk, Iwona, and Nairne, Sandy, *Objects & Sculpture*, exhibition catalogue, London and Bristol: ICA and Arnolfini, 1981.

British Council, *Transformations: New Sculpture from Britain, Tony Cragg, Richard Deacon, Antony Gormley, Anish Kapoor, Alison Wilding, Bill Woodrow*, catalogue of exhibition held at the XVII Bienal de Sao Paulo, 5 October–18 December 1983 and in Rio de Janeiro, Mexico and Lisbon, 1984.

Bumpus, Judith, 'Tony Cragg, Hayward Gallery, London', *Arts Review*, Vol. 39, 13 March 1987.

Celant, Germano, 'Tony Cragg and Industrial Platonism', *Artforum* (New York), Vol. 20, Part 3, November 1981.

Clark, William, *War of Images*, exhibition catalogue, Glasgow: Transmission Gallery/ Glasgow School of Art, January 1986.

Collier, Caroline, 'Steven Campbell: Riverside Studio', *Flash Art*, March 1985.

Collings, Matthew, 'The Happy Return', *Artscribe*, No. 50, January/February 1985.

—— 'Doing It by the Book', *Modern Painters*, Vol. 1, No. 1, Spring 1988.

Collins, James, 'Interview with Steven Campbell', *Flash Art*, February/March 1987.

Compton, Michael, *Malcolm Morley*, exhibition catalogue, London: Whitechapel Art Gallery, 1983.

Cook, Lyne, *Tony Cragg*, London: Hayward Gallery, 1987.

Cragg, Tony, 'Pre-conditions', in *Tony Cragg*, Hanover: Kestner-Gesellshaft, 1985.

Currie, Ken, 'New Glasgow Painting in Context', *Edinburgh Review*, No. 72, February 1986.

Eliot, T. S., '*Ulysses*, Order and Myth', *Dial*, Vol. 85, November 1923.

Francis, Mark, 'Objects and Sculpture', *Art Monthly*, No. 48, July/August 1981.

Fuller, Peter, 'An Interview with Carl Andre', *Art Monthly*, Nos 16 & 17, May/June 1978.

—— 'A Black Cloud Over the Hayward', *Art Monthly*, No. 70, October 1983.

—— *Images of God: The Consolations of Lost Illusions*, London: The Hogarth Press, 1985.

Glimcher, Arnold, 'A Conversation: Malcolm Morley and Arnold Glimcher, Belport, Long Island, 3rd October, 1998', in *Malcolm Morley*, exhibition catalogue, New York: The Pace Gallery, 2 December–7 January 1988–1989.

Godfrey, Tony, *The New Image: Painting in the 1980s*, Oxford: Phaidon, 1986.

—— 'Tony Cragg, Hayward Gallery, London', *The Burlington Magazine*, Vol. 129, May 1987.

Goldwater, Marge, 'Of Hikers and Humeans', in *Viewpoints: Steven Campbell*, exhibition catalogue, New York: Walker Art Center, 22 September–10 November 1985.

Graham-Dixon, Andrew, 'Cragg's Way', *Art News*, Vol. 88, March 1989.

—— 'Great Britain Neo, No: Still Faithful to the Old Guard', *Art News*, Vol. 88, September 1989.

Harrison, Charles, 'Art & Language: A Commentary on the Work of the Second Decade, Black Propaganda 1977–78', typewritten document in Art & Language Information File, National Art Library, Victoria & Albert Museum, London, 1990.

Hatton, Rita, and Walker, John A., *Supercollector: A Critique of Charles Saatchi*, London: Ellipsis, 2000.

Hill, Peter, 'Steven Campbell interviewed by Peter Hill, Watts Bar, Manhattan, December 1983', *Alba*, January 1984.

—— 'Steven Campbell at Barbara Toll, New York, and John Weber Gallery, New York', *Artscribe*, February/April 1984.

Hughes, Robert, 'Career of Repetition and Glut', *Time*, 9 March 1987.

Hyman, Timothy, *Narrative Paintings: Figurative Art of Two Generations Selected by Timothy Hyman*, exhibition catalogue, Bristol: Arnolfini, 1979.

—— 'Narrative Painting: A Second Generation', *Artscribe*, No. 19, September 1979.

Jacob, Mary Jane, *A Quiet Revolution: British Sculpture since 1965*, London: Thames & Hudson, 1987.

Jencks, Charles, *The Language of Post Modern Architecture*, London: Academy Editions, 1977.

Johnson, David, 'Intro', *The Face*, October 1983.

Jones, Ben, 'A New Wave in Sculpture, A Survey of Recent Work by Ten Younger Sculptors. New Prospectors: Shelagah Wakely and Tony Cragg, Lisson Gallery', *Artscribe*, No. 8, September 1977.

Juncosa, Enrique, 'The Flight of Icarus (Or a Pilot among the Angels)', in *Malcolm Morley 1965–95*, exhibition catalogue, Madrid: Sala-Deex Posiciones Dela Fundacion 'La Caixa', 20 September–12 November 1995.

Kent, Sarah, 'Bruce McLean', *Art Monthly*, No. 37, 1980.

—— 'Critical Images', *Flash Art International*, March 1985.

Kertess, Klaus, 'On the High Sea and Seeing of Painting', in *Malcolm Morley*, exhibition catalogue, Paris: Musée National d'Art Moderne, Centre Georges Pompidou, 1993.

Kirshner, Judith Russi, 'Tony Cragg, Richard Deacon', *Artforum*, Vol. 23, Summer 1985.

Kramer, Hilton, *Revenge of the Philistines: Art and Culture 1972–1984*, New York: Macmillan, 1985.

Levine, Les, 'Dialogue: Malcolm Morley', *Cover*, Vol. 1, No. 3, Spring/Summer 1985.

Lewison, Jeremy, 'Steven Campbell at Riverside Studios', *Studio International*, Winter 1984.

Liebmann, Lisa, 'Steven Campbell, Barbara Toll, New York, and John Weber Gallery, New York', *Artforum*, April 1984.

Livingstone, Marco, *R. B. Kitaj*, Oxford: Phaidon, 1985.

Lynton, Norbert, 'Tony Cragg Fifth Triennale India, New Delhi, 15 March–7 April', London: Fine Arts Department, The British Council, 1982.

Lyotard, Jean-François, 'A Response to the Question: What is Postmodernism?', *Critique*, No. 419, Paris, April 1982.

McEwen, John, 'Tony Cragg, Hayward Gallery, London', *Art in America*, Vol. 75, July 1987.

Moffat, Alexander, 'Telling Stories: A New Figuration in Glasgow 1980–85', in *New Image Glasgow*, exhibition catalogue, Glasgow: Third Eye Centre, 1985.

Morgan, Stuart, 'Soup's On: An Audience with Stephen Campbell', *Artscribe*, No. 48, September/October 1984.

—— 'Steven Campbell: The Case of the Waggling Leg', *Artforum*, December 1984.

—— 'Between Oxford and Salisbury', in *Steven Campbell: New Paintings*, exhibition catalogue, London: Riverside Studios, 28 November–30 December 1984; Edinburgh: Fruitmarket Gallery, 12 January–23 February 1985.

Musée National d'Art Moderne, *Malcolm Morley*, Paris: Centre Georges Pompidou, 1993.

Nairne, Sandy, *State of the Art: Ideas & Images in the 1980s*, London: Chatto & Windus/Channel 4, 1987.

Newman, Michael, 'Irony and the Amazonians: Post-Modernism in the Media Jungle', *Art Monthly*, No. 61, November 1982.
Owens, Craig, 'The Allegorical Impulse: Towards a Theory of Postmodernism (Part 2)', *October*, No. 13, Summer 1980.
—— 'Honour, Power and the Love of Women', *Art in America*, January 1983, reprinted in Hertz, Richard, ed. *Theories of Contemporary Art*, New Jersey: Prentice Hall, 1985.
Pace Gallery, The, *Malcolm Morley*, New York: The Pace Gallery, 2 December–7 January 1988–1989.
Pohlen, Annelie, *Tony Cragg*, exhibition catalogue, Société des Expositions du Palais des Beaux-Arts de Bruxelles, Düsseldorf: Heinrich Winterscheidt, 1985.
Porges, Maria, 'Tracing a Different Path: a Survey of Recent British Sculpture', *Artweek*, Vol. 18, 11 July 1987.
Roberts, John, 'Postmodernism: Arrivals and Departures', *Art Monthly*, No. 55, April 1982.
—— 'Post? Modern? Ism?', *Art Monthly*, No. 60, October 1982.
—— 'The Sculpture Show', *Art Monthly*, No. 70, October 1983.
—— 'Morality, Postmodernism and the Pursuit of Metaphor: The British Art Show', *Artscribe*, No. 49, November/December 1984.
—— 'Fetishism, Conceptualism, Painting', *Art Monthly*, December–January 1984–1985.
—— *Postmodernism, Politics and Art*, Manchester: University of Manchester Press, 1990.
—— *Selected Errors: Writings on Art and Politics 1981–90*, London: Pluto Press, 1992.
Taylor, Brandon, *Modernism, Post-Modernism, Realism: A Critical Perspective for Art*, Winchester: Winchester School of Art Press, 1987.
Taylor, John Russell, 'Playing into the Hands of Those Who Pour Scorn: The Sculpture Show, Hayward/Serpentine', *The Times*, 16 August 1983.
Third Eye Centre, *New Image Glasgow*, exhibition catalogue, Glasgow: Third Eye Centre, 1985.
Transmission, *War of Images*, exhibition catalogue, Glasgow: Transmission/Glasgow School of Art, January 1986.
Walker Art Center, *Viewpoints: Steven Campbell*, exhibition catalogue, New York: Walker Art Center, 22 September–10 November 1985.
Whitechapel Art Gallery, *Malcolm Morley*, exhibition catalogue, London: Whitechapel Art Gallery, 1983.
Wood, Paul, 'Critical Realism', *Art Monthly*, No. 113, February 1988.
Yougrau, Barry, 'Steven Campbell', *Arts Magazine*, January 1984.

Chapter 6.   Art After Britain?

Anon., 'Matthew Collings Diary', *Private Eye*, No. 918, 1997.
Archer, Michael, 'Reconsidering Conceptual Art', *Art Monthly*, No. 193, February 1996.
—— 'No Politics Please, We're British?', *Art Monthly*, No. 194, March 1996.
—— 'Heart and Soul', *Artforum International*, Vol. 38, No. 3, November 1999.
—— 'Lucy McKenzie', *Artforum International*, Vol. 40, No. 1, September 2001.
BALTIC, *New Sites – New Art*, Gateshead: BALTIC, 2000.
BANK, *BANK*, London: Black Dog, 2000.
Barrett, David, 'Surfacing – Contemporary Drawing, ICA, London', *Art Monthly*, No. 221, November 1998.
Beagles, 'Under the Central Belt', *Variant*, Vol. 2, No. 2, Spring 1997.

—— 'Make Me Wanna Holler, Throw Up Both My Hands', *Variant*, Vol. 2, No. 5, Spring 1998.

—— 'Back to the Old School', *Variant*, Vol. 2, No. 6, Autumn 1998.

—— Vincent, Martin, Brook, Andrew, Nichol, Janie, and Wilkinson, David, 'Your Place or Mine?', Vol. 2, No. 3, Summer 1997.

Beasley, Mark, 'The City Racing Decade (*City Racing 1988–1998: A Partial Account*, ICA, London January 25–March 18 2001)', www.untitledonline.co.uk.

Beech, Dave, 'David Shrigley, The Photographers' Gallery, London', *Art Monthly*, No. 204, March 1997.

—— 'When was London', *Untitled*, No. 24, Spring 2001.

Betterton, Rosemary, 'Undutiful Daughters: Avant-gardism and Gendered Consumption in Recent British Art', *Visual Culture in Britain*, Vol. 1, No. 1, London, 1999.

Bickers, Patricia, *The Brit Pack: Contemporary British Art, the View from Abroad*, Manchester: Cornerhouse, 1995.

Bird, Nicky, 'Roderick Buchanan, DCA', *Art Monthly*, No. 243, February 2001.

Booth, Colin, 'Art: The Saatchi Collection', *The Face*, No. 60, April 1985.

Bradley, Will, 'Cathy Wilkes: Quiet Radical', *Untitled*, No. 25, Summer 2001.

Brighton, Andrew, 'Command Performance', *Guardian*, 12 April 1999.

Brook, Chris, ed., *K Foundation Burn a Million Quid*, London: Ellipsis, 1997.

Brown, Katrina, *Ross Sinclair: Real Life*, Glasgow: CCA.

Buchanan, Roderick, *Players*, exhibition catalogue, Dundee: Dundee Contemporary Arts, 25 November–4 February 1999/2000.

Bull, Malcolm, 'The Ecstasy Of Philistinism', *New Left Review*, No. 219, September/October 1996.

Burgess, John, and Coventry, Keith, *City Racing*, London: Black Dog, 2000.

Burrows, David, ed., *Who's Afraid of Red, White and Blue? Attitudes to Popular & Mass Culture, Celebrity, Alternative & Critical Practice & Identity Politics in Recent British Art*, Birmingham: Article Press, 1998.

—— 'Correspondences, Olympic Village, Waves in Particles Out, Beagles & Ramsay', *Art Monthly*, No. 213, February 1998.

—— and Smithard, Paula, 'Enjoy Your Alienation!', *Make*, No. 77, September–November 1997.

Button, Virginia, *The Turner Prize*, London: Tate Gallery Publications, 1997.

Calcutt, John, 'There + Then', in *Here + Now: Scottish Art 1990–2001*, exhibition catalogue, Dundee: Dundee Contemporary Arts, 2001.

Carol, Constance, 'Dear Make', *Make*, No. 90, December 2000/February 2001.

Carrier, David, 'The Origins of Museums: The Cabinet of Curiosities in Sixteenth- and Seventeenth-century Europe', *Leonardo*, Vol. 20, No. 1, 1987.

Cauty, Jimmy, and Drummond, Bill, *The Manual*, London: Ellipsis, 1988.

Charlesworth, J. J., 'Crash!: ICA; Urban Islands: Cubitt; Peter Kennard: Gimpel Fils; All London', *Art Monthly*, No. 233, February 2000.

Collings, Matthew, *Blimey! From Bohemia to Britpop: The London Art World from Francis Bacon to Damien Hirst*, Cambridge: 21 Publishing, 1997.

—— *Art Crazy Nation*, Cambridge: 21 Publishing, 2001.

Courtney, Cathy, 'Torah Torah', *Art Monthly*, No. 221, November 1998.

Davey, Kevin, *English Imaginaries: Six Studies in Anglo-British Modernity*, London: Lawrence & Wishart, 1999.

Ellis, Liz, 'A critique in three parts of the Britpack phenomenon and particularly the critical reception of Bank, Sarah Lucas and Sam Taylor-Wood', 1997, @ http://web.ukonline.co.uk/members/n.paradoxa/ellis.htm.

Ellis, Patricia, 'How Soon is Now', in *Die Young Stay Pretty*, exhibition catalogue, London: ICA, 13 November–10 January 1998/99.

Findlay, Judith, 'Roderick Buchanan, Tramway', *Flash Art*, No. 183, Summer 1995.

—— 'There's Not Much Art that's like a Good Story', *Art & Design*, Vol. 11, January/February 1996.

—— 'David Shrigley, Transmission, Glasgow', *Flash Art*, No. 186, January/February 1996.

—— 'Cityscape: Glaswegian Goods', *Flash Art*, No. 188, May/June 1996.

Ford, Simon, 'The Art of Legitimation', *Edinburgh Review*, No. 91, May 1994.

—— 'Clockwork Skinhead: The Systematic Extremism of Stewart Home', *Rapid Eye*, No. 3, 1994.

—— 'Myth Making', *Art Monthly*, No. 194, March 1996.

—— and Davies, Anthony, 'Art Capital', *Art Monthly*, No. 213, February 1998.

Gordon, Douglas, *Kidnapping*, exhibition catalogue, Amsterdam: Stadelijk van Abbemuseum, Eindhoven/Nai Publishers, 1998.

Gordon-Nesbitt, Rebecca, 'Urban Myths: A Tale of Two Cities', *Contemporary Visual Arts*, Issue 17, February 1998.

Hall, David, 'Artists' Thoughts on the 70s in Words and Pictures', *Studio International*, Vol. 195, No. 991/2, 1981.

Harding, David, ed., *Decadent: Public Art, Contentious Term and Contested Practice*, Glasgow: Foulis Press, 1997.

Hatton, Brian, 'Simulacra at the Riverside', *Artscribe*, No. 39, February 1983.

Hatton, Rita, and Walker, John A., *Supercollector: A Critique of Charles Saatchi*, London: Ellipsis, 2000.

Hayward Gallery, *Falls the Shadow*, exhibition catalogue, London: Hayward Gallery, 1986.

Heartney, Eleanor, 'The Hot New Cool Art: Simulationism', *Art News*, Vol. 86, January 1987.

Higgs, Matthew, and Godfrey, Tony, *British Art Show 5*, exhibition catalogue, London: Hayward Gallery, 2000.

Hirst, Damien, ed. Robert, Violette, *I Want to Spend the Rest of My Life Everywhere, with Everyone, One to One, Always, Forever, Now*, London: Monacelli Press, 1996.

Home, Stewart, 'The Art of Chauvinism in Britain and France', *Everything*, Issue 19, 1996.

—— 'Prostitution II: The Return of the "Male" "Gaze"', in *Multiple Choice*, exhibition catalogue, London: Cubitt Gallery, 7 March–6 April 1996.

—— 'From Arse to Arsehole: John Roberts and the Spectres of Philistinism', in his *Disputations on Art, Anarchy and Assholism*, London: Sabotage Editions, 1997.

Hutcheon, Linda, *Irony's Edge: The Theory and Politics of Irony*, London and New York: Routledge, 1995.

ICA, *City Racing 1988–1998: A Partial Account*, exhibition catalogue, London: Institute of Contemporary Arts, 25 January–11 March 2001.

Killam, Brad, 'David Shrigley, Hermetic Gallery, Milwaukee', *New Art Examiner*, Vol. 25, December 1997/January 1998.

Lawson, Thomas, 'Hello, It is Me', *Frieze*, No. 9, London, March/April 1993.

Lee, Rodney, 'Nostalgia and Nationalism/Two London Surveys', *C Magazine*, No. 70, Summer 2001.

Lillington, David, 'Comic Art', *Art Monthly*, No. 216, May 1998.

Lingwood, James, ed., *Rachael Whiteread: House*, Oxford: Phaidon, 1995.

Maloney, Martin, 'Douglas Gordon, Lisson Gallery', *Flash Art*, No. 182, May/June 1995.

—— 'In Conversation with Gemma de Cruz', in *Die Young Stay Pretty*, exhibition catalogue, London: ICA, 13 November–10 January 1998/99.

McCorquodale, Duncan, Siderfin, Naomi, and Stallabrass, Julian, eds, *Occupational Hazard: Critical Writing on Recent British Art*, London: Black Dog, 1998.

Miles, Malcolm, 'Fifth National Mural Conference: Edinburgh May 9th–11th 1986', *Alba*, No. 1, Summer 1986.

Musgrave, David, *Surfacing*, exhibition catalogue, London: ICA, 1998.

—— 'The Last Show: City Racing', *Art Monthly*, No. 222, December 1998/January 1999.

Nairne, Tom, *After Britain*, London: Granta Books, 2000.

Pagé, Suzanne, 'Preface', *Live/Life: La scène artistique au Royaume-Uni en 1996, de nouvelles aventures*, Paris: Musée d'Art Moderne de la Ville de Paris, 1997.

Phoca, Sophia, 'Protest and Survive', *Third Text*, No. 53, Winter 2000/2001.

Price, Dick, and Barnbrook, Jonathan, *Young British Art: The Saatchi Decade*, London: Booth-Clibborn Editions, 1999.

—— 'Don't Stop 'till You Get Enough', in *The New Neurotic Realism*, exhibition catalogue, London: Saatchi Gallery, 1999.

Renton, Andrew, 'Douglas Gordon, Tramway, Glasgow', *Flash Art*, No. 172, October 1993.

—— and Gillick, Liam, eds, *Technique Anglaise: Current Trends in British Art*, London: Thames & Hudson, 1991.

Roberts, John, 'Mad For It!', *Everything*, Issue 18, 1996.

—— 'Mad for It! Philistinism, the Everyday and the New British Art', *Third Text*, No. 35, Summer 1996.

—— 'Notes on 90's Art', *Art Monthly*, No. 200, October 1996.

—— 'Home Truths', *Everything*, Issue 20, 1997.

—— and Beech, Dave, 'Spectres Of The Aesthetic', *New Left Review*, No. 218, July/August 1996.

—— and Beech, Dave, 'Tolerating Impurities: On Ontology, Genealogy and Defence of Philistinism', *New Left Review*, No. 227, January/February 1998.

Rodney, Lee, 'Nostalgia and Nationalism/Two London Surveys', *C Magazine*, No. 70, Summer 2001.

Rugoff, Ralf, 'Yours Sincerely', *Frieze*, Issue 42, October 1998.

Saatchi Gallery, *Ant Noises at the Saatchi Gallery 2*, exhibition catalogue, London: Saatchi Gallery, 2001.

Sans, Jerome, 'Douglas Gordon, Centre Georges Pompidou', *Artforum*, Vol. 34, April 1996.

Savage, Jon, 'Vital Signs: Gillian Wearing's Talking Pictures', *Artforum*, Vol. 32, No. 7, March 1994.

Seymour, Benedict, 'Everything Must Go', *Mute*, Vol. 16, 2000.

Shrigley, David, *Merry Eczema*, Glasgow: Black Rose, 1992.

—— *ERR*, London: Bookworks, 1996.

—— *Why We Got the Sack from the Museum*, London: Redstone Press, 1998.

—— *The Beast is Near*, London: Redstone Press, 1999.

Sinclair, Ross, 'Capital of Culture/Culture of Capital: Representing Representation', *Alba*, 1990.

—— 'Bad Smells but No Sign of the Corpse', *Windfall* (Glasgow), 1991.

—— 'This is the Sound of the Suburbs: The Glasgow Model and the Cyclical Nature of Arts Communities', *Proceedings of the Global Culture & Arts Communities Symposium*, 13–17 October 1999, University of Alberta, Canada.

Stallabrass, Julian, 'Success and Failure of Peter Fuller', *New Left Review*, No. 207, September–October 1994.

—— 'In and Out of Love with Damien Hirst', *New Left Review*, No. 216, March/April 1996.

—— *High Art Lite*, London: Verso, 1999.

—— 'Art I Like', *Modern Painters*, Vol. 13, No. 2, Summer 2000.

Staple, Polly, 'Is Politics the New Black', *Make: The Magazine of Women's Art*, No. 87, March/May 2000.

Tatham, Joanne, O'Sullivan, Tom, and Bradley, Will, *The Glamour*, exhibition catalogue, Glasgow: Transmission Gallery, 2001.

Transmission Gallery, *Transmission*, London: Black Dog, 2001.

Tufnell, Rob, 'A Recent History of Artists' Initiatives in Scotland', in *Open Country:*

Contemporary Scottish Artists, exhibition catalogue, Lausanne, Switzerland: Musée cantonal des Beaux-Arts de Lausanne, 20 January–1 April 2001.

Wade, Gavin, ed., *Curating in the 21st Century*, Wolverhampton: The New Art Gallery Walsall/University of Wolverhampton, 2000.

Wakefield, Neville, *Brilliant!*, exhibition catalogue, at the Walker Art Center, Minneapolis, USA, October 22–January 7 1995/96.

Wallinger, Mark, and Warnock, Mary, eds, *Art For All? Their Policies and Our Culture*, London: Peer, 2000.

White, Nicola, ed., *Ross Sinclair: Real Life*, Glasgow: CCA, 1996.

Williams, Gilda, 'Heart and Soul', *Art Monthly*, No. 229, September 1999.

Williams, Richard J., 'Anything is Possible: The Annual Programme 1995–2000', *Life is Good in Manchester*, Manchester: Trice Publications, 2001.

Wilsher, Mark, 'David Shrigley: Stephen Friedman Gallery, London', *Art Monthly*, No. 246, May 2001.

Wilson, Andrew, 'Out of Control', *Art Monthly*, No. 177, June 1994.

Index